AA

KEYGUIDE

BARCELONA

184

CONTENTS

KEY TO SYMBOLS

- ✛ Map reference
- ✉ Address
- ☎ Telephone number
- ◉ Opening times
- ✋ Admission prices
- Ⓜ Underground station
- 🚌 Bus number
- 🚆 Train station
- ⛴ Ferry/boat
- 🚗 Driving directions
- ℹ Tourist office
- ◆ Tours
- 📖 Guidebook
- 🍴 Restaurant
- ☕ Café
- 🍸 Bar
- 🛍 Shop
- ① Number of rooms
- Ⓢ Air conditioning
- ≋ Swimming pool
- 🏋 Gym
- Ⓝ No smoking
- ❓ Other useful information
- ▷ Cross reference
- ★ Walk/drive start point

138

111

72

UNDERSTANDING BARCELONA

Understanding Barcelona is an introduction to the city, its geography, history and its people. Living Barcelona gets under the skin of Barcelona today, while The Story of Barcelona takes you through the city's past.

Barcelona, the chic Catalan capital, is a confident, prosperous, energetic, fun-loving city, with a passion for style and design and an obsession with its own image. It is a city of wide boulevards and striking modern architecture. The reinvention of Barcelona began in the late 1980s as it prepared to host the 1992 Olympic Games, but the rebuilding and the rebranding have been going on ever since. The Modernista architects have been rediscovered and the eccentric genius Antoni Gaudí (1852–1926) has become an icon for the city. The seafront has been revived as a busy urban entertainment area, with beaches and promenades taking the place of dilapidated warehouses and wharves. The warm climate, vibrant nightlife and designer shopping are drawing increasing numbers of visitors, and Barcelona has become one of the cultural hotspots of Europe.

LAYOUT OF THE CITY

The oldest parts of Barcelona are eminently walkable. Most visitors head straight for Las Ramblas (Les Rambles in Catalan), the avenue that runs down from Plaça de Catalunya to the port. To one side is the Barri Gòtic, a warren of dark, narrow, medieval streets clustered around the cathedral; to the other side is the up-and-coming, multicultural district of El Raval. Heading north from the monument to Columbus at the foot of Las Ramblas are the beaches and promenades of Port Vell, Barceloneta and the Port Olímpic. The commercial heart of modern Barcelona is found in L'Eixample, which heads inland from Plaça de Catalunya towards the outlying district of Gràcia and the mountain of Tibidabo. At the turn of the 20th century, L'Eixample became the outdoor studio of the Modernistas and a number of their creations can be seen on the main boulevard, Passeig de Gràcia. This street, which is virtually an extension of Las Ramblas, makes an easy walk but despite its rigid street plan L'Eixample is not conducive to strolling and for the more outlying attractions, such as Gaudí's La Sagrada Família (▷ 186–189), it is better to take the metro or bus.

PEOPLE AND LANGUAGE

Barcelona is usually classed as Spain's second city, after the capital Madrid, but this status is most definitely not the opinion of the locals. The majority of the population of around 1.65 million are Catalan, speak Catalan and are loyal first to their region. They do not consider themselves Spanish. But other residents, who are foreigners or immigrants from other regions of Spain, speak Spanish (also called Castilian), which has led to linguistic conflict. In recent years there has been a strong push towards making Catalan, and not Castilian, the language of government and education. This has resulted in all children now being taught principally in Catalan at school, yet many still speak Castilian at home. This bilingual attitude is also reflected in the media. The Catalan-language television channel, TV3, has the highest viewing figures, yet most people still read Spanish books and newspapers (▷ 246–247). But one thing that unites just about everyone in the city, Catalans and immigrants alike, is their love of the soccer team FC Barcelona and a desire to see them get one over their old adversary, Real Madrid, the capital's own soccer team.

CATALAN IN THIS BOOK

The use of Catalan in this book has been guided by what you will find in the region; where a Catalan name predominates, and it usually does, we have used it. Examples of this are Museu and Plaça (Catalan) not Museo and Plaza (Castilian).

ECONOMY AND SOCIETY

Barcelona was the driving force of Spain's 19th-century industrial revolution and Catalonia is the most economically active region in Spain. Although manufacturing is still important, traditional industries like shipbuilding, textiles, chemicals and cork are being replaced by service industries such as banking, finance, fashion, design and tourism. The number of visitors has doubled since the 1992 Olympics and now stands at more than 6.5 million per year, making Barcelona one of the most visited cities in Europe. Tourism is thought to provide at least one in 10 jobs, bringing financial benefits, but it has also created pressures as more and more people move into the city in search of jobs. As in any major European city unemployment, homelessness and crime are all problems. Despite the outward appearance of prosperity, there are still areas with low standards of living, especially in the outlying districts that few visitors see.

MODERNISME

Modernisme is the Catalan version of the art and design movement that swept through Europe at the turn of the 20th century, also known as art nouveau or Jugendstil. It was also part of the wider Catalan Renaixença (Renaissance) that celebrated all things Catalan. The designs of this movement emulated nature with soft, fluid forms, often using plants and flowers as the basis for an idea. The artists embraced new technology, which gave them the means to create these ideas. You won't want to miss the vast number of beautiful Modernista buildings in Barcelona, many of which still have a practical use.

AREAS AT A GLANCE

MONTJUÏC AND EL RAVAL

The green mountain of Montjuïc, overlooking the port, houses some of Barcelona's best museums and parks, plus the sports facilities built for the 1992 Olympics.

On the opposite side of Las Ramblas to the Barri Gòtic, the former red-light district of El Raval is becoming a chic place to be, thanks to the Museu d'Art Contemporani de Barcelona (MACBA).

BARRI GÒTIC AND LAS RAMBLAS

The medieval maze of the Barri Gòtic (Gothic Quarter) is the oldest part of the city and is a district of churches, intimate cafés and tapas bars, and quirky shops.

To the west of Barri Gòtic, the long, wide, tree-lined avenue of Las Ramblas is a focal point of the city. Filled with street entertainers and kiosks selling flowers, birds and small animals, the avenue stretches from L'Eixample down to Port Vell.

PORT VELL AND LA RIBERA

Port Vell, once a working port, is now a modern marina with eating and entertainment facilities. The former fishing village of Barceloneta lies at the start of a series of beautiful sandy beaches that stretch north to Port Olímpic and beyond.

La Ribera is also known as El Born after the main street, Passeig del Born. The medieval mercantile area to the east of the Barri Gòtic is now a hip hang-out of cool shops, and wine and tapas bars.

Diagonal Mar, a corner of working-class Poble Nou, has been transformed with shiny hotels, a shopping centre and even a new beach.

L'EIXAMPLE

Created in the 19th century, the grid system of L'Eixample is the business and commercial hub of the city and home to some of the best Modernista architecture and most upmarket shopping.

The former township of Gràcia, which sits beyond Avinguda Diagonal, retains a radical streak and a villagey, alternative feel.

Opposite *Gaudí's distinctive Modernista style is displayed perfectly on Casa Batlló in L'Eixample*
Below *The Rambla de Mar swing bridge is part of the Port Vell marina development and a seaward extension to Las Ramblas*

THE BEST OF BARCELONA

MONTJUÏC AND EL RAVAL

Boadas Cocktail Bar (▷ 83): A classic since it opened in 1933, Boadas still offers the most expertly mixed cocktails in town.

Dona i Ocell (▷ 76): Huge sculpture by Joan Miró, fashioned out of concrete and mosaic and completed shortly before his death.

Fundació Joan Miró (▷ 62–63): Playful paintings and sculptures in bright primary tones by an artist who sums up the spirit of Barcelona.

Inopia (▷ 86): Traditional tapas prepared with top-quality ingredients from Albert Adrià, brother of world-renowned chef Ferran Adrià.

Marsella (▷ 83): Drink absinthe at wrought-iron tables in this old El Raval bar, a hangover from the days when this was the city's red-light district.

Museu d'Art Contemporani de Barcelona (▷ 68–69): Stylish modern art museum at the heart of El Raval.

Museu Marítim (▷ 70–71): The beautiful old building of the royal shipyards almost outdoes the collection.

Museu Nacional d'Art de Catalunya (▷ 72–75): This collection of medieval art, modern art and Modernista furnishings is housed in a palace on Montjuïc.

BARRI GÒTIC AND LAS RAMBLAS

Agut (▷ 125): Catalan classics and serious steaks in the heart of the Barri Gòtic.

Café de l'Òpera (▷ 123): Mirrors, wooden panels and tables on the street at this coffee house on Las Ramblas.

El Corte Inglés (▷ 121): The huge department store on Plaça de Catalunya.

Deessa: Josep Clarà's nude goddess among the fountains of Plaça de Catalunya (▷ 110).

Formatgeria La Seu (▷ 121): A fabulous range of artisanal cheeses from across Catalonia and the rest of Spain make this shop a delight for foodies.

La Manual Alpargatera (▷ 121): An old-style Barri Gòtic workshop selling espadrilles.

Mercat de la Boqueria (▷ 120): The city's wonderful central market, just off Las Ramblas.

Quim (▷ 127): Stand-up bar in the Boqueria market serving no-nonsense classics like *callos* (tripe).

PORT VELL AND LA RIBERA

7 Portes (▷ 162): The oldest restaurant in Barcelona still serves the best paella in town.

Arola (▷ 163): Creative cuisine from the eponymous chef in a pop-art setting.

Barcelona Head (▷ 150): Vast sculpture by Roy Lichtenstein on the waterfront at Port Vell.

La Bombeta (▷ 163): Delicious seafood and generous tapas, ideal for those on a budget.

Can Majó (▷ 163): You won't get better or fresher seafood than at this Barceloneta beachfront restaurant.

Fish (▷ 150): Glistening golden fish sculpture by Frank Gehry and the symbol of Port Olímpic.

Above *The beautiful auditorium of Palau de la Música Catalana*

Homage to Barceloneta: Rebecca Horn's sculpture is a tribute to the *xiringuitos* (beach bars) on the beach (▷ 138).

Hotel Pullman Skipper (▷ 167): The ultimate in luxury in a skyscraper overlooking the waterfront at Barceloneta.

Hotel Vela (▷ 138): The city's most spectacular hotel, in a huge sail-shaped building surrounded on three sides by the sea, is Spain's first W Hotel, and was designed by Ricardo Bofill.

Kaiku (▷ 165): Superb paella is prepared with smoked rice and served on a terrace overlooking the sea.

Museu Picasso (▷ 142–143): A homage to one of the great Spanish artists, who spent his formative years in Barcelona.

Palau de la Música Catalana (▷ 144–147): This spectacular Modernista concert hall has a riot of vibrant mosaics and stained glass.

L'EIXAMPLE

Antonio Miró (▷ 194): The leading name among Barcelona's contemporary fashion designers, known for his casual but stylish men's suits.

Above *High-rise luxury hotels on the waterfront in Barceloneta*
Left *La Boquería market off Las Ramblas, famed for its fresh produce*

Casa Fuster (▷ 204): A sumptuous five-star hotel located in a Modernista landmark building whisks you back to early 20th-century style.

Casa Milà (▷ 176–177): Gaudí's wavy apartment block, popularly known as La Pedrera, meaning 'The Quarry', with a stunning roof terrace.

Colmado Múrria (▷ 195): A sumptuous array of food and wine behind a stunning Modernista shopfront.

Hotel Omm (▷ 205): The cream of Barcelona's contemporary design talent was employed to create this sleek and stylish winner.

Loewe (▷ 196): Classic leather goods in a Modernista mansion on Passeig de Gràcia.

Manzana de la Discordia (▷ 180–182): Three very different houses on Passeig de Gràcia by the holy trinity of Modernista architects.

Park Güell (▷ 184–185): Fairy-tale park overlooking the city, complete with a mosaic salamander, designed by Antoni Gaudí.

La Sagrada Família (▷ 186–189): Gaudí's masterpiece is the symbol of Barcelona.

Vinçon (▷ 198): An illustration of Barcelona's obsession with design, with views of Casa Milà (La Pedrera) from the terrace.

TOP EXPERIENCES

Wander down Las Ramblas enjoying the street entertainment and the flower stands at the heart of the city (▷ 114–115).

Dance the *sardana*, the Catalan national dance, in front of the cathedral on Sundays (▷ 124).

Join the locals for an afternoon on the beach at Barceloneta or Port Olímpic (▷ 138 and 150).

Hit the tapas trail in the bars of La Ribera, nibbling *pintxos* (Basque-style snacks) and drinking cava, a sparkling Catalan wine (▷ 260–261).

Move heaven and earth to get tickets to a concert at the Palau de la Música Catalana (▷ 144–147, 160).

Join the crowds to watch FC Barcelona play soccer or, at the very least, take a stadium tour (▷ 218).

Climb one of the towers at La Sagrada Família for close-up views of the intricate tile work (▷ 186–189).

Relax in the cool green corners of the Parc de la Ciutadella, with its boating lake, fountain and ornamental gardens (▷ 148).

Get lost in the romantic gardens of the Parc del Laberint and find Eros at the centre of the maze (▷ 219).

Take in a traditional Catalan festival, with its *dimonis* (devils), *correfoc* (fire-running) and *castells* (human towers; ▷ 254–255).

Go shopping, or window-shopping depending on your budget, along Passeig de Gràcia and spoil yourself in the luxury stores (▷ 194–197).

Take in the whole of the city at once from the peak of Tibidabo, which has views out over the sea and of Montjuïc (▷ 219).

Lose yourself in Barri Gòtic, the world's largest Gothic quarter, discovering the secret squares and narrow alleyways that have barely changed in more than 500 years (▷ 96–97).

Enjoy a lazy lunch at a beachfront restaurant, tucking into fresh seafood and crisp local wines, and watching the world go by from the terrace (▷ 162–166).

Taste the high life with a cocktail by the pool at one of the city's fashionable rooftop bars, found at some of the hippest hotels (▷ 88).

Below *When you need to cool off from a hot day's sightseeing, Parc de la Ciutadella has plenty of shady spots*

LIVING BARCELONA

BARCELONA: CAPITAL OF CATALONIA

Politically Catalonia has formed part of Spain for more than 500 years, but the firm belief that their land is a nation apart is still ingrained in many Catalans. Understanding this country-within-a-country mentality is essential to understanding Catalonia. The Generalitat, the region's autonomous government, has its own police, hospitals and schools, though it is ever fighting for more rights. The use of Catalan is a constant battle, with the Generalitat pushing for greater recognition in the European Union and for the right to use the language in more government documents. On the streets Catalan is thriving after being brutally outlawed during Franco's dictatorship (1939–75), as is a strong sense of national identity, a backlash against the repressions of those years. Catalan politics are dominated by constant bickering between the rival nationalist and socialist parties. Both parties support Catalan autonomy and are to the left of the Spanish political spectrum. Jordi Pujol ruled the nationalist Convergència i Unió (Convergence and Union) from 1980 to 2003. His hand-picked successor, Artur Mas, lost to socialist Pascual Maragall in 2003. José Montilla, president since 2006, is the only president in modern times to have been born outside Catalonia.

AN ECONOMIC CAPITAL
Catalans have always had a reputation for being thrifty and business-minded, a trait the rest of Spain loves to mock, as in the joke that wire was invented by two Catalans pulling on a coin. Yet the region is an important economic engine in Spain, responsible for more than a quarter of the country's exports and a fifth of its gross national product. Its per capita GDP, at €28,095 (2008), is similar to that of Germany, and higher than most other regions in Spain. The Catalan Institute of Statistics reports that Catalans earn more, spend more and save more than most Spaniards. And they also contribute more heavily to the rest of the country through the region's main industries of chemicals, energy and metals.

Clockwise from above *Venetian tower and Catalan flags in Plaça d'Espanya; sweet temptations—Catalan pastries; the Renaissance-style courtyard of the Generalitat in Barri Gòtic*

CASTING OFF FRANCO'S SHADOW

Franco seemed to make a special effort to punish Catalonia for opposing him throughout the Spanish Civil War (1936–39). He was brutal with dissenters here, taking thousands to work camps and executing others. In November 2002 the Spanish government officially condemned Franco's dictatorship for the first time ever and opened some previously undisclosed archives to the public. This move has encouraged people to talk more about the dictatorship and to come forward with information about that dark time. Until now, few details about the fates of Franco dissenters were known, but since November 2002, nine mass graves have been found in Catalonia alone. The graves hold the still-unidentified bodies of just some of the approximately 150,000 who died in the repressions.

THE WIDEST *PLAÇA*

At first glance, the Plaça de Sant Jaume is a simple sunny square, an open space between the Casa de la Ciutat (House of the City, or City Hall) and the Palau de la Generalitat (regional government headquarters). It's the perfect place for city celebrations and civic demonstrations. During the Festa de la Mercè, it hosts concerts and *correfocs* (fire runs). But there is more distance ideologically than there is physically between the two buildings staring each other down across the square. The town hall is traditionally socialist, focusing on projects of urban renewal and city improvement. The nationalist Generalitat is bent on gaining Catalan autonomy. Plaça de Sant Jaume is the barrier between these proud entities, creating an eternal stand-off and a constant reminder of the rivalry between the two.

GROWING PAINS

According to the city hall, growth is great, but it is making the city prohibitively expensive for residents, especially the younger ones. The average age at which a person moves out of the family house to get married is 29 (according to the Catalan Institute of Statistics). This is either a case of true family devotion or a reflection of the soaring housing prices that have rocketed by 87 per cent since 1997, calculated by the Municipal Housing Board, while salaries have risen by only 15 per cent. Even by the age of 29 many haven't saved enough to buy an apartment, so they either look outside Barcelona (the closest suburb, L'Hospitalet, is now Spain's seventh-largest city) or try to take advantage of one of the government-run housing schemes, which provide both financial aid to first-time buyers under the age of 35 and purpose-built, low-cost housing for young people to buy.

PARC DEL FÒRUM

Barcelona learned its lesson from the 1992 Olympics: a big-name international event does wonders for a city's image both at home and abroad. So these days the city is hard at work creating international events every year. A swathe of neglected coastline, north of the Olympic Village, was entirely redeveloped to host the 2004 Universal Forum of Cultures. Although the Forum attracted fewer visitors than hoped, and the striking new buildings lay empty for a few years, the development is finding its feet: the space now hosts outdoor bars and nightclubs during the summer, as well as several of Barcelona's most popular festivals (including the Feria de Abril, an Andalusian-style celebration with flamenco dancing and music). The Parc del Fòrum already has a marina, a swimming area, diving centre, and a new aventure park (the Bosc Urbà), and it is the future site of the city's Natural History Museum.

Boom periods in Barcelona's history have always been accompanied by spurts of architectural development. The region's 13th-century golden age saw the birth of Catalan Gothic, a simple and elegant version of the classic Gothic. The Catalan Renaixença (Renaissance) of the late 19th century brought Modernisme and all its glory, and post-Franco prosperity has ushered in a host of modern projects. But the best-known buildings are those of architect and designer Antoni Gaudí i Cornet (1852–1926). Gaudí took his inspiration from the natural world, creating ceiling beams shaped like tree branches, spiral staircases like snail shells, and tile mosaics that shimmer like water. Although Gaudí is often called a Modernista, his style defies classification. The real Modernistas were contemporaries like Josep Puig i Cadafalch and Lluís Domènech i Montaner, architects who, like Gaudí, were financed by the new Catalan bourgeoisie. Bold tones, lots of ornamentation and natural light were important elements of their style and were used to dizzying effect across the city. Barcelona's rich architectural legacy is still alive, and international architects like Richard Rogers and Jean Nouvel have given the city its newest emblematic structures.

SAINT GAUDÍ

Gaudí's buildings were radical and his work was hated as often as it was adored, but in May 2003, after three and a half years of research and testament gathering, the campaign for his beatification finally closed. A handful of priests, Gaudían scholars and architects believe that Gaudí's profound religious beliefs and all-engrossing dedication to La Sagrada Família (or 'catechism in stone') should be enough to propel him to the status of sainthood or 'God's architect'. Gaudí was so devoted to the project that he dedicated his final years to it, living like a hermit inside the unfinished shell and giving up all worldly pleasures. The Catholic Church is now investigating the evidence to see whether he should be made an example of holiness for Catholics worldwide.

Clockwise from above *The fantastic roof of Casa Batlló, designed by Antoni Gaudí; sculpture of St. George slaying the dragon on Casa Amatller; the ornate facade of Palau de la Música Catalana by Lluís Domènech i Montaner*

THE LEGENDARY MODERNISTAS

Pay attention to the ornate streetlights lining Passeig de Gràcia. Perched atop them are small iron bats with wings spread. The bats show up again on Gaudí's Palau Güell. What seems like a homage to Batman is really a reminder of Catalonia's medieval glory, when the bat was a symbol of powerful King Jaume I ($\triangleright$ 28). Jaume claimed that a bat once alerted him to an enemy presence, and he included it in his coat of arms. Other symbols of Catalan identity pop up in Modernista design. One of the most common is the dragon, which refers to the legend of Sant Jordi (St. George), who saved Catalonia by slaying a dragon, used at Casa Amatller and as a theme in Gaudí's Casa Batlló.

NEW KIDS ON THE BLOCK

On an endless quest for urban renewal, the city has a host of projects under way. The soaring bullet-shaped tower, known as La Torre Agbar was built by French architect Jean Nouvel, and now marks the Plaça de Glòries in northern Barcelona. The controversial Hotel Vela, a sail-shaped building designed by Ricardo Bofill, now dominates the skyline next to Port Vell. The luxury hotel has drawn equal amounts of praise and criticism from Barcelonans. Other soon-to-be landmarks are a dramatic structure by Frank Gehry near the Sagrera (the new high-speed railway station), and the bullring on Plaça d'Espanya, which is being converted into a shopping arcade by architect Richard Rogers.

THE EXTENSION THAT ALMOST WASN'T

If Barcelona city planners had had their way, the chequerboard grid of streets that makes up Barcelona's huge L'Eixample (Extension) district would never have existed. When in 1859 the town hall called for design proposals to expand the cramped city, they chose a plan consisting of a network of wide boulevards fanning out from the central Plaça de Catalunya. It was only after the last-minute intervention of Madrid bureaucrats that the job was given to Ildefons Cerdà, the engineer who thought up the utopian grid design that makes today's Barcelona so easy to navigate. His dream of wide streets and grassy squares, however, is a far cry from the dense urban space L'Eixample has become.

THE SLAVE-TRADE LEGACY

Gaudí's patron, Eusebi Güell, was one of many Catalan bourgeois who owed part of his fortune to trading with the New World. These businessmen-adventurers were dubbed *indianos* by Catalans as, after all, Columbus originally believed that he had discovered India when he found America. *Indianos* traded Spanish wine and textiles throughout the 19th century. Regrettably, from a modern perspective, the trade route often included a stop in Africa to pick up slaves to be sold in the Americas. This money funded large amounts of the Renaixença, paying for the Modernista creations as well as for railways and water pipes, forming the basis of the city you will see around you today.

Blame it on the inspirational Mediterranean Sea or the abundance of sunny days, but Barcelona is undeniably a hotspot for today's artists and designers. Areas like La Ribera and El Raval are full of studios, and a stroll through Barcelona's old quarter reveals an impressive number of shops selling locally designed jewellery, fashion and glassworks. Museums, galleries and exhibitions abound, and a great number of these are focused on contemporary art. One of the most important is Barcelona's modern art museum, the Museu d'Art Contemporani de Barcelona (MACBA, ▷ 68–69). The Fundació Antoni Tàpies (▷ 175), a foundation in the name of one of Catalonia's greatest living artists, and the Fundació Joan Miró (▷ 62–63) on Montjuïc are also important stops on Barcelona's museum route. Modern Catalan society has embraced art so strongly largely because of the lasting effects of the Modernista movement, whose heritage is everywhere and originally included painters and writers as well as architects. They helped to revive the city's artistic climate, paving the way for 20th-century artists like Picasso, Miró and Tàpies.

FOUR CATS

On Carrer de Montsió, hidden in a corner of the old town, is Els Quatre Gats (The Four Cats; ▷ 126). The main draw of this dark little tavern is its history. In 1897, the painters Ramon Casas, Santiago Rusiñol, Miquel Utrillo and Pere Romeu established an artistic society where they could promote and discuss their bohemian ideas about life and culture. Their meeting place, which soon turned into a friendly tavern with art on the walls, was set up in this building, designed by Puig i Cadafalch, and artists and free-thinkers streamed through its doors. Famously, it was here that a young unknown painter, Pablo Picasso, had his first-ever exhibition at the turn of the 20th century. Today the interior is filled with evocative paintings and photographs of the period.

Clockwise from above *Els Quatre Gats, a popular bohemian meeting place; Custo T-shirts are fashion essentials; Antonio Miró designs are simple but superbly tailored*

AN OUTDOOR MUSEUM

One of Franco's most visible legacies in Barcelona is the prison-style architecture he let sprout up in the 1950s and 60s. After the dictator's death in 1975, innovative urban planners, led by architect Oriol Bohigas, set out to create visual distractions from these brick eyesores. The result was a wave of outdoor art, making Barcelona one of the best open-air museums in the world. Joan Miró's *Dona i Ocell* (Woman and Bird), a bright piece with a bovine influence, is at the Parc de Joan Miró, and along the waterfront is the equally vibrant *Barcelona Head* by pop artist Roy Lichtenstein. Other world-famous artists brought in to liven up urban spaces, and paid only a fraction of their usual fees, were Antoni Tàpies, Josep Subirachs and Richard Serra. A catalogue can be found at www.bcn.cat/artpublic.

FASHION WARS

Watch out, Paris, Barcelona is on its way to becoming the latest thing in the world fashion scene. Barcelona has run the Pasarela Gaudí fashion show since 1985, and local designers like Antonio Miró, Lydia Delgado and Josep Font are finally becoming internationally known. Their success has convinced fashion promoters that the Pasarela Gaudí is destined for greatness. The industry agrees, as each year the fashion show draws more attention for the quality of its designers and their collections. The only fly in the ointment is the competition of Madrid's fashion industry. The two cities are historic rivals, fighting over soccer, the economy and now fashion. The most recent effort (in 2001) to combine the cities' runway shows failed—no one is giving up the fight for fashion glory.

CUSTO BARCELONA

Chances are you've seen and maybe even own a T-shirt by the fashion label Custo Barcelona. The brand was started here by two brothers (Custo and David Dalmau) but it's long gone global, and now their trademark tops hang in the closets of celebrities like Julia Roberts and Drew Barrymore. Custo designs even figured in the enormously popular TV show *Sex and the City*. The look is based on wild mixes of shades, fabric and texture. A typical Custo may be described as green knit sleeves with flapping cuffs hung off a cotton body with a big red swirl painted on the back and a close-up of a coy girl staring at you from the front. A Custo original can cost €180, but unscrupulous manufacturers have been creating fakes as fast as they can. Custo hasn't stopped at clothes and accessories: in 2009, the Spanish airline Vueling showcased their flamboyant designs on two aircraft.

GRAFFITI EARNS RESPECT

Graffiti is everywhere in the city and constant construction work ensures a ready supply of canvases. Experts on street art say the overall quality is the best in Europe and you need only to head down to the constantly changing mural on the roundabout in front of the port's ferry terminal to see what they mean. Some names, such as France's Miss Van, fetch big prices for their work at galleries like Iguapop. Iguapop's curator, Iñigo Martinez, says that it's a combination of great weather and overall tolerance that draws international grafiteros to the city. 'They tell me they never get hassled,' he adds. 'In fact, most people just stand back and admire their work.' The art of graffiti is celebrated during the annual Hipnotik festival, hosted by CCCB (▷ 59), one of the city's most influential contemporary arts institutions.

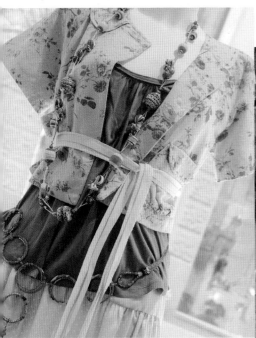

Barcelona is cosmopolitan and undeniably modern, yet it grips the reins of tradition as though its life depended on it. Much of Barcelona's charm is found in the combination of its old Roman ruins, Gothic buildings and sunny stone squares with its skyscrapers, international eateries and bold modern architecture. An important part of this mix is Barcelona's folklore, especially the traditional festivals still thriving here. Throughout the summer, Barcelona's districts (many of which were once independent towns) go all out for their respective *festes majors* (major festivals). Celebrations are held in the streets with parades of giant statues, fire-breathing dragons and monsters. The party can last for several days, with bands filling the nights with music and fireworks lighting up the sky. Barcelona is equally proud of religious celebrations, like Corpus Christi, when church fountains throughout the city are adorned with flowers and hollowed eggs are placed on them, left there to dance in the stream of water throughout the feast. These old traditions coexist with the customs Barcelona is creating today, like the annual film and music festivals and the car rallies that have almost become fiestas in their own right.

Clockwise from above Teams of castellers *build human towers during the festival of La Mercè;* la sardana *is performed every Sunday morning in front of Barcelona's cathedral;* gegants *(giants) regularly make their appearance at local* festas

THE ESSENCE OF A CATALAN

How can you explain a culture that claims to be both a serious economic power and the creative capital of Spain? The Catalans know the answer—*seny* and *rauxa*. These two concepts explain the two faces of the Catalan character and show up constantly in literature, folk phrases and everyday talk. *Seny* is a combination of common sense, self-control and practicality, and explains why Catalans are so frugal and logical. Its ideological opposite is *rauxa*, meaning emotion, passion and expression, seen in the lavishly decorated Modernista buildings and summer festivals. It's been said that *rauxa* and *seny* are like the opposite sides of the same coin: different but totally inseparable.

A SCATOLOGICAL MINDSET

If someone toasts you saying, 'Eat well and crap hard', don't be offended. It's just a sign of Catalonia's curious fascination with defecation. A symbol of the life cycle, it appears repeatedly in Catalan art and folk culture, such as in Joan Miró's *Man and Woman in Front of a Pile of Excrement* at the Fundació Joan Miró (▷ 62–63). Scatological traditions are most evident at Christmas. The *caganer*, a figurine of a red-capped peasant squatting with his pants down, is hidden in the manger scene. It may seem scandalous, but here it is considered harmless. The *caga tió*, another tradition that carries on the theme, is a log that children beat until it releases (or 'defecates') its gifts.

THE WORLD'S MOST DEMOCRATIC DANCE

Come to the square in front of Barcelona's cathedral any Sunday morning and the sight there may surprise you. The people holding hands in a circle aren't saying a prayer or having a seance. They're dancing that most revered dance, *la sardana*. It seems simple from afar—dancers bob up and down, moving now and then to the left or right—but the dance is actually a complicated set of precise steps. A band called the *cobla* provides the traditional music. The egalitarian circle is a symbol of social co-operation, and the dancers' positioning (an arm's length apart, with only the hands touching) is a visual symbol of Catalan restraint: a style that is far removed from the sensual flamenco dancing of southern Spain.

PLAYING WITH FIRE

If tossing firecrackers, running from fire-breathing dragons and getting sprayed with sparks sounds like fun, the festival of La Mercè in September is for you. Barcelona's biggest fiesta is, like many Catalan celebrations, filled with flames. The Catalans' love of fire is rooted in pagan festivals and can seem dangerous to outsiders, but few here seem to be worried about getting burned. The highlight of La Mercè is the fire run, or *correfoc*, when a parade of devils, monsters and dragons, who carry firecrackers in their mouths, makes its way through the Barri Gòtic, surrounded by people also carrying sparklers and firecrackers. Onlookers play a game of cat and mouse with the monsters, getting as close as they possibly can to the danger, then running quickly away.

THE BUSINESS OF EATING WELL

Jordi and Amèlia Artal, Canadian-born Catalans, returned to their roots in Barcelona to open their elegant restaurant Cinc Sentits ('five senses'; ▷ 201), in 2004, with Jordi, a largely self-taught chef, in the kitchen, and his sister Amèlia, an accomplished sommelier, in the dining room. Within months, the restaurant was garnering glowing reviews everywhere. International recognition was not long in coming and in 2008 Jordi earned his first Michelin star. Innovation, experimentation and the finest local produce remain at the core of the Artal philosophy. Unlike most restaurants, Cinc Sentits prides itself in being a 'tasting restaurant', and serves several small dishes, rather than the more traditional servings.

A DIVERSE COMMUNITY

Like the rest of Catalonia, Barcelona has been largely homogeneous for most of its existence. The first large waves of immigrants didn't arrive until the 20th century (first in the 1920s, later in the 1940s and 50s), when workers from southern Spain came searching for better jobs and a better life. Barcelona is still relatively ethnically homogeneous when compared to metropolises like New York, London or Paris, but newcomers from around the globe may be changing that, opening up the city to new influences. Since 1997, the number of resident foreigners in Barcelona has shot up almost tenfold, from 37,000 to over 300,800. Immigrants now make up more than 10 per cent of the city's total population. Nearly a quarter are from the European Union, and the others are largely from North Africa, South America and Asia. Barcelona is a popular destination for immigrants looking for work because it is accessible, with good transport links to and from other European countries, and is close to agricultural regions in need of workers. The city is also a magnet for European students because of the good climate and relatively low cost of living. Big business is changing too, with an influx of foreign companies, taking advantage of the new workforce.

EL RAVAL

According to studies by Barcelona's most prominent newspaper, *La Vanguardia*, the world's most ethnically and culturally diverse urban space is El Raval district, a corner of the city off Las Ramblas of little more than 1sq km (0.4sq miles). Some 40,000 people, half of them born outside Catalonia, live squashed together in this dense *barri* (district). The interaction this produces is an inspiration for free-thinkers and for artists, many of whom display their talent on the district's walls. Bars, second-hand clothes shops and art studios abound. On the not-so-positive side, it's a breeding ground for ethnic rivalries and gangs, which has created the first stirrings of racial tension in what has been, traditionally, a tolerant society.

Clockwise from above *People gather to watch the Font Mágica spectacular in Plaça d'Espanya; a friendly kickabout on Platja de la Nova Icària; sampling the laid-back atmosphere of the Gràcia district*

LATIN LOVERS

Figures from the Catalan Statistics Institute throw an interesting light on marriages between Catalans and foreigners. In recent years, the number of Catalan men marrying foreign women, particularly those from Colombia, Russia and Brazil, has doubled. This means that now more than 27 per cent of all weddings here have at least one fiancé saying 'I do' in a language other than their own. Some see this as a positive step towards cultural integration, but there is one curious factor about these statistics: The numbers of Catalan women marrying foreign men has remained pretty much stagnant.

Increasingly, Barcelona has become a popular wedding destination for people resident in other countries—particularly the Irish. Irish couples account for about 80 per cent of all the weddings performed for non-residents at Barcelona's city hall.

PUBLISHED IN ENGLISH

With more than 100,000 English-speaking nationals living in Catalonia, a niche market for news and media in English has opened up. *Barcelona Metropolitan* is a free monthly magazine with a good balance of reportage, restaurant and film reviews, and an extensive classified section. For news and features on the arts and sport there is *Catalonia Today*, a weekly 40-page broadsheet. Fashion and design victims arm themselves with *B-Guided*, the bilingual style bible profiling the best of the new wave of shops, eateries and galleries. Electronic media have not been ignored: *Le Cool* (www.lecool.com) is a free weekly e-zine offering a highly opinionated take on the week's hip, cool and ultramodern happenings, while www.bcnweek.com offers an alternative look at local news. (*BCN week* is also available as a free paper, distributed in bars and cafés.)

BIG BUSINESS

A survey of 500 European companies rated Barcelona as the best city in Europe in terms of employee quality of life. Companies like Renault, Volvo and Volkswagen, all of which have set up design workshops in Barcelona, are just a few of those enjoying the lifestyle here. Company directors say the sun, sea and creative vibe give their designers an edge. Other businesses, particularly chemical and pharmaceutical companies, have set up shop too, drawn as much by the climate as by the solid transportation system, infrastructure and economy. Today nearly 70 per cent of all new small businesses in the city are funded by foreigners: from humble corner stores to dot.coms and start-ups in the tourism sector.

THE *GUIRI* CULTURE

It's not much of a compliment to be called a *guiri*, or foreigner, but the European and North American immigrants who've adopted Barcelona out of love for its mild winters and active nightlife have accepted the nickname with a smile. *Guiri* probably has its root in the word *guirigay*, which means gibberish or language that is difficult to understand, and was meant as an insult by the resident Catalans. But the *guiris* have an extrememly large presence in the city. Many are students in the Erasmus scheme, which enables university students to spend time studying at another university, or they work as teachers, bartenders or translators, living in the old flats of the Barri Gòtic or La Ribera.

Until the 1980s, Barcelona was pretty indifferent to its waterfront. The city's port was shallow and not very interesting, and anyway, coastal areas were traditionally reserved for fishermen and industry. The heart of the city was (and is) well inland, completely ignoring the presence of the Mediterranean. All of that changed when Barcelona renovated its coast in preparation for the 1992 Olympics. Port Vell (Old Port) was transformed from a commercial eyesore into one of the city's liveliest nightspots, with clubs, restaurants and even an IMAX cinema. The utilitarian containers of the commercial port were moved south, out of sight behind the mountain of Montjuïc. The highway that had long separated Barcelona from the sea was redirected underground, new seaside walkways were put in and a whole new port, the Port Olímpic, was created. The process of improving the waterfront is continuing, with major urban renewal going on in the northern fringe of Barcelona, in districts like Poble Nou. According to visionaries, this is the Barcelona of tomorrow, and serious amounts of money are being invested. The well-groomed waterfront now extends from the base of Las Ramblas to the northern rim of the city.

Clockwise from above *Yachts fill the marina at Port Vell; hotel towers on the esplanade at Port Olímpic; strolling along Moll d'Espanya at Port Vell*

ROOMS WITH A VIEW
Until the area around the Port Olímpic was developed in the early 1990s, the only way to get a home with a view of the sea in Barcelona was to die. The New Cemetery, built in 1883, looks like a miniature city on the slope of Montjuïc and has a perfect view of the glistening Mediterranean. The fact that it, and not homes or other buildings, was put here reflects Barcelona's old indifference to the sea. The regular layout of the cemetery—coffins are neatly stacked one on top of the other like apartments in a block—imitates the order of L'Eixample, which was still new when this cemetery was founded. Local residents joke that they're condemned to live in flats in both life and death.

THE CITY THAT ATE THE SEA

Barcelona's shipyards, now the Museu Marítim (▷ 70–71), are one of the world's most splendid examples of medieval industrial architecture. How is it possible then, you may ask, that it is landlocked and not the least bit accessible from the sea? The answer is that Barcelona, blocked on two of its borders by the mountain of Montjuïc and hills of Collserola, has grown into the Mediterranean by the manual filling in of huge areas of sea with roads and buildings. The same thing happened along other parts of the coast. The Santa Maria del Mar church, in La Ribera, was once practically on the beach; now it's a good 10-minute walk from the water.

CRUISIN' RIGHT ALONG

Over 2 million cruise-ship visitors arrive in Barcelona each year, making the city the cruise capital of Europe and fifth largest world port. March and April (the Easter months) are cruise-ship high season, and on some days as many as seven *cruceros* will be docked at the port at the end of Las Ramblas, changing the city's skyline in a spectacular, if transient, fashion. To accommodate such a massive influx of tourists, the Port Authority is investing over €1.7 billion in its facilities. But the port's most illustrious visitor can't wait. In spring 2005 the *Queen Mary 2*, the largest and most luxurious cruise ship in the world, added Barcelona to its transatlantic route and the city continues to be a port of call in 2010.

SUPERSTITIOUS SAILORS

Traditionally, fishermen are a superstitious lot, and those working the waters off Barcelona's coast weren't much different. It was bad luck for women to set foot on board a fishing boat, but even worse if they urinated in the sea, which would surely bring a mighty storm. A woman exposing her private parts to the sea, however, calmed the waters. If that didn't work, each boat carried a wind rope, made by witches to control the breeze, and a manatee skin to keep lightning away. If a sailor drowned, bread blessed by a priest was thrown into the water and would supposedly float to his body. Today, pollution and marine traffic have greatly reduced the number of fishermen here, but until the mid-1800s many of these rituals continued to be closely observed.

THE NEW ICÀRIA?

You'll sometimes hear the Vila Olímpica, or Olympic Village, referred to as Nova Icària. It was the original name for the *barri* (district) and refers to Icària, a 19th-century French concept of a utopian, egalitarian city that was the inspiration for Cerdà's L'Eixample. A group of French and Catalan Icàrians set off from their homes in Europe in 1848 to found their ideal city in America, but the expedition failed only a year later with the suicide of one of the Catalan leaders. Exactly why Barcelona city planners decided to resurrect the name is unclear, but happily residents never did adopt it, insisting on calling the area Vila Olímpica. Interestingly, Avinguda d'Icària has managed to hold onto its name and is the avenue leading directly to the old cemetery.

When Barça fans declare that their team is more than a soccer club, there is some truth in their assertion. With over 130,000 paid-up members, FC Barcelona is the biggest soccer club in the world, yet it is its social dimension that makes Barça more than a sporting institution. The *socis* (members) regard membership as an essential sign of their Catalan identity, to be cherished and handed down through generations. From the newly born baby presented with a *carnet* (club card) days after baptism, to the grandparents who proudly sport the gold insignias given to those who surpass 50 years' membership, Barça's support base cuts across class, political allegiance, age and gender. As a focus for regional pride and identity, symbolism is an important issue. This is one of the reasons that since 2006 Barça have had the UNICEF logo on their kit rather than the name of a commercial sponsor—they pay UNICEF, rather than the other way round! The 2008–09 season was one of the most successful in Barça's history: among several titles, they won the UEFA Champions League and La Liga Española.

KNOW YOUR ENEMY

The rivalry between Real Madrid, the capital's team, and Barça stems from a number of complex factors—some of them political, some sporting—but is so intense that sometimes it is unclear whether Barça fans derive more pleasure from Madrid's failures or from their own team's successes. Supporters grow up on stories of injustices from Franco's time onwards, and so the capital's team is linked with the curse of central government. Matches between the two teams are seen as part of a historical struggle, so when Madrid come to town the Camp Nou stadium is packed with 115,000 screaming fans reminding the players that, in this match, they are playing for far more than just three league points.

Above *'More than a club', Camp Nou stadium*

THE WAR YEARS

The first soccer martyr was Josep Sunyol, president of the club at the outbreak of the Spanish Civil War (1936–39). Sunyol was paying a visit to the front line in his new car, when he inadvertently ended up driving down the wrong road and straight into fascist troops. When his captors executed him, they were well aware of the significance of the act and the effect it would have on the morale of a people who used their team as a focus for Catalan nationalism and opposition to the new regime. But despite Franco's best efforts, Barça survived thanks to the club secretary Rosendo Calvet, who spirited away the club's money to a Swiss bank account, and to Patrick O'Connell, the Irish coach who escaped to America with his best players, many of whom stayed in the US for the rest of the war.

THE STORY OF BARCELONA

Lovers of legends like to think Hercules founded Barcelona but the reality is more prosaic. Neolithic tribes lived around Montjuïc and it is possible that a Carthaginian village existed, named after their general Hamilcar Barca (died 228BC), but this has never been proved. The Romans established a base here after their invasion of Spain in 218BC and in 15BC named it Barcino, but it remained a minor port in the shadow of Tarraco (Tarragona), Rome's provincial capital. The fall of Rome opened the gates to a succession of invaders but greater turmoil washed over Spain with the arrival of the Moors in AD711. They swept all before them and by AD717 had subdued Barcelona. An invasion by the Franks (a western Germanic tribe) in the ninth century meant Louis the Pious, Charlemagne's son, conquered the city. The Franks established local nobles as their lieutenants, and of these, Guifré el Pelós (Wilfred the Hairy, AD840–97) rose to be Count of Barcelona and the most powerful Catalan lord. However, the vassalage of the Catalan lords evaporated in AD985 when the Franks failed to help defend the city in the face of a Moorish assault. The counts, now on their own, spent the 11th and 12th centuries reconquering Catalonia; the last outpost surrendered in 1153.

Clockwise from above Thr Roman aqueduct at Tarragona is 1km (0.5 miles) long; Santa Eulàlia is patron saint of sailors and of Barcelona; an illustration (possibly a self-portrait) from a manuscript of the Usatges de Barcelona by Pere Albert (1291–1327)

LIFE IN ROMAN BARCINO

By the time the final set of stout walls, still in evidence today, was raised around Barcino in the fourth century AD, the city had become prosperous. Citizens inevitably gathered in the central forum, roughly where Plaça de Sant Jaume is, and worshipped at the nearby Temple of Augustus (four columns of which remain, ▷ 117), on a small rise known as Mont Tàber. Just east of the temple was a busy commercial area, whose paved streets were lined with *tabernae* (shops), warehouses for storing *garum*—a pungent fish paste staple extremely popular around the Mediterranean in Roman times—and wine stores. Intact remains of Barcino are preserved beneath the Museu d'Història de Barcelona (▷ 106–107).

THE BLITZ AND BARCELONA'S REVENGE

Al-Mansur (the Victorious) was the vizier to the Caliph of Córdoba from AD978. He was virtual ruler of late 10th-century Moorish Spain and he tirelessly harried the Christian kingdoms in the north. In AD985 he fell upon Barcelona with a fury and ruled for three years, after which the Catalan Count Borrell II retook the city. The count's Frankish overlords had left him to face Al-Mansur alone, for which he repaid them by officially confirming his autonomy. Then he mounted a blitz on Córdoba, a spectacular operation by the day's standards, as no Christian ruler had yet attempted to strike so deeply into the Moorish heartland. No lasting damage was done but the propaganda value was considerable.

A MEDIEVAL CODE OF LAW

By the middle of the 12th century, Catalonia's judges were implementing new laws known as the *Usatges de Barcelona*. A complex mix of Roman and Visigothic law and local custom, the *Usatges* were designed to consolidate the rule of the Counts of Barcelona by depriving rival nobles of the right to take the law into their own hands. They also aimed to reduce lawlessness and give peasants and the newly emerging merchant class basic protection. The *Usatges* remained at the heart of Catalan jurisprudence until 1716 but some of its clauses were weakened over time: 'Let the rulers render justice as it seems fit…by cutting off hands and feet, putting out eyes, keeping men in prison for a long time.'

THE MARTYRDOM OF SANTA EULÀLIA

A splendid alabaster tomb in Barcelona's cathedral houses the remains of Santa Eulàlia, the city's co-patron saint and martyr. In the early fourth century the Roman emperor Diocletian launched a final and ultimately fruitless campaign to stamp out Christianity in the empire. The fearless virgin Eulàlia chose this rather inauspicious moment to publicly decry the wayward pagan lifestyle of Barcelona's townsfolk. For her trouble she was cruelly tortured with hot irons, pincers and other horrible instruments, and rolled down a hill in a barrel filled with nails. She was crucified and finally died at the stake in AD304. But some sceptics claim that Santa Eulàlia is a figment of medieval biographers' imagination.

GUIFRÉ AND THE BIRTH OF CATALONIA

Covered with hair in the most unlikely places, some say even on the soles of his feet, Guifré el Pelós (Wilfred the Hairy) is considered Catalonia's founder. From AD870 to 878 he conquered and cajoled his way around the north of the region that was not under Moorish rule and southern France, keeping his fellow nobles in check and consolidating the entity that would become Catalonia. Centuries later his chroniclers even attributed the creation of the Catalan flag to him. Louis the Pious, they say, walked into Wilfred's tent to find his gold shield bore no heraldry. So Louis dipped his fingers in Guifré's blood and traced four stripes down the shield. It's a nice story, except for one detail: Guifré was born the year Louis died.

MEDIEVAL BARCELONA 1153–1410

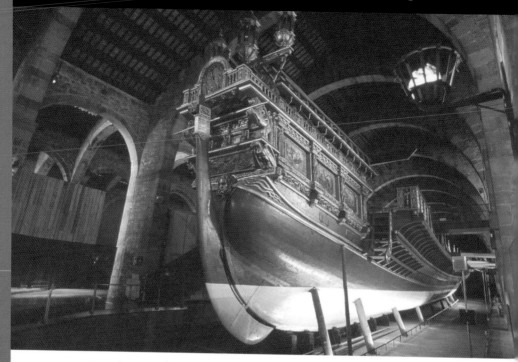

The Counts of Barcelona ruled most of Catalonia and swathes of southern France when Count Berenguer IV married the heiress to the throne of Aragon in 1137. The new rulers of this merged Crown of Aragon came to be known as *comtes-reis* (count-kings). But when the French defeated Pere I in 1213 at the Battle of Muret, Catalonia lost much of its French territory. Pere's successor, Jaume I, El Conqueridor (The Conqueror, 1208–76), in 1229 wrested Mallorca from the Moors and by 1245 occupied Valencia. When the last count-king, Martí I, died heirless in 1410, the Crown's territories also included Murcia in southern Spain, Roussillon and Montpellier in France, Sicily and Sardinia. Conquest brought boom to Barcelona and the city walls were expanded in the 13th and 14th centuries. This was the golden age of Gothic building, from the Drassanes Reials (royal shipyards, ▷ 70–71) to the powerful Basílica de Santa Maria del Mar (▷ 152). The importance of the business class led to the creation of the Corts Catalanes (parliament) and Consell de Cent (city council). It was also a very harsh time as plague, anti-Jewish pogroms and riots rocked the city.

Clockwise from above *The Gothic royal shipyards are preserved in the Museu Marítim; the Sardinian port of Alghero where old Catalan is still spoken; the banquet at which the conquest of the Balearic Islands was agreed in 1228*

BLOOD-RED ROBES

Jaume I formed a citizens' committee in 1249 as he recognized the need for a burgeoning Barcelona to have decent administration. By 1274 this had become the Consell de Cent (Council of One Hundred). The council of well-to-do citizens and a handful of tradesmen elected five of their number to run the city's day-to-day affairs. The five also nominated the following year's council members. They wore flowing tunics of red or purple, symbolizing their own blood which they would willingly shed in the service of their city, and took off their hats before no man, not even the count-king. Its successor, the Ajuntament (town council), still operates in the same building on Plaça de Sant Jaume.

THE QUESTS OF RAMON LLULL

Ramon Llull (1232–1316) was born in Mallorca three years after Jaume I conquered the island. He was the first notable writer to pen much of his opus in Catalan, with touches of Latin and Arabic. A rake in his youth, Llull changed path radically after claiming to see visions of Christ crucified. He then spent his life writing 250 religious and philosophical works, and visiting North Africa and Asia Minor to spread the faith. He constantly sought backing for missions at royal courts all around the Mediterranean, but was politely turned away on many occasions. His most lasting works were the *Ars* (Art of) series, a compendium of contemporary knowledge. He still carried out missionary work in Tunis as late as 1315, where it is thought he died.

BARCELONA'S WALL STREET

As Barcelona boomed, the hub of its commercial life shifted to La Ribera, also known as El Born, and especially the area around Passeig del Born. The scene of medieval pageants, jousts and executions, the Born was also the heart of Barcelona's medieval financial district. Side streets were the preserve of money-changers and banks, and in the late 14th century La Llotja (▷ 157), Spain's first stock exchange, opened. (In the 20th century, it became Barcelona's stock exchange once again, until 1994.) Carrer de Montcada, in the Born, became one of the wealthiest streets in town and it is still lined with the Gothic-era mansions built by the city's then leading entrepreneurs.

PLAGUE AND POGROM

In May 1348, plague-infested rats began to spread their bubonic payload around the city and almost half the population succumbed. Some thought this disease a divine punishment, while others sought terrestrial scapegoats, including Jews who were accused of poisoning water wells. Mostly crowded into Barcelona's ghetto, the Call, the Jewish community held an ambivalent but often privileged position. Many of the city's North African and Near Eastern trade was in Jewish hands and their finances were key to Catalonia's economic well-being. But bigotry was rife. In 1391 a mob rampaged through the Call in a horrendous pogrom. Ten years later the Call was abolished and its residents were allowed to live where they chose. Under Ferdinand and Isabella repression of the Jews became severe. In 1492, all Jews who refused to convert to Christianity were expelled from Spain.

SARDINIA'S LAST STAND

When Catalan and Aragonese troops disembarked at Sardinia in 1323, the island had known centuries of foreign interference. This latest conquest proved gruelling and the newcomers were none too polite. When the port town of Alghero rebelled in 1354, Pere III retook it and replaced its population with Catalans, whose descendants still speak old Catalan. This ethnic cleansing was tried less successfully in other towns. The western region of Arborea remained independent and its ruler, Eleonora, reopened hostilities in 1391. She defied the Crown of Aragon until her death in 1404 but five years later resistance collapsed and Arborea became a Catalan duchy. But Eleonora had one last act of defiance up her sleeve—her law code, the Carta de Logu, so impressed the occupiers that they adopted it throughout Sardinia.

Barcelona's fortunes nosedived in the 15th century. Trade declined and the Crown of Aragón passed from Catalan hands to Fernando of Antequera in 1412. Years of civil disorder ensued and Catalonia was sucked into Castile's orbit when the Catholic Monarchs, Ferdinand II and Isabella I, united Spain in 1479. They finished the Reconquista (the Reconquest, capturing lands for the Christian Crown), defeating Granada's Moors in 1492. In that same year the Jewish community was expelled from Spain and Christopher Columbus discovered the Americas for their majesties. Castile asserted its mastery in the 16th century, dominating South American gold and transatlantic trade. Shut out, Barcelona slipped into torpor and the increasingly impoverished Catalan countryside was devastated by uprisings like the Guerra dels Segadors (Reapers' War) in 1640–52. Charles II died in 1700 without an heir and this event unleashed the War of the Spanish Succession in 1702. Barcelona joined Austria and Britain against the French-backed Philip V but was left alone after the 1713 Treaty of Utrecht, when these two allies made separate peace deals with France. Philip kept his throne but lost all of Spain's European territories. And Barcelona fell to a vengeful Philip in 1714.

Clockwise from above The Surrender of Granada in 1492, *painting by Francisco Pradilla y Ortiz; the monument to Christopher Columbus at the port end of Las Ramblas; a representation of the Reapers' War in the Museu d'Història de Catalunya*

THE INQUISITION

Four years after uniting Spain, the Catholic Monarchs introduced the Spanish Inquisition to Barcelona. This feared institution had been set up in 1478 to keep an eye on Jews and *conversos* (Jews who had converted to Catholicism), and during this time thousands of Jews were burned at the stake. These executions were grand, ghoulish, public spectacles, torture was used and no defence was allowed. In 1492 the first Grand Inquisitor, Tomás de Torquemada (1420–98), himself a *converso*, persuaded the Catholic Monarchs to expel all Jews who refused baptism. This decision was incredibly shortsighted as well as bigoted, costing Barcelona (and Spain) its most dynamic business class at a stroke.

COLUMBUS'S CARIBBEAN CRUISE

In 1493 the Catholic Monarchs were in Barcelona when their daring Genoese navigator, Christopher Columbus, returned to report on his first voyage to what he thought was China and the Indies. Europeans hoped a direct sea route westwards might lead to the riches of India and the Far East, which were increasingly difficult to reach by land east of Europe. But Columbus refused to believe that he had found a new world. Whether he liked it or not, he had bumped into the Caribbean islands. At the Spanish royals' behest, he undertook three more voyages to the area and so Spain's South American adventure began. Within a few decades, Spain would control most of what is now Central and South America, presiding over what came to be one of the world's largest global empires.

DON JOHN AND A FAST-MOVING CHRIST

In 1571 Don Juan of Austria led a Christian armada against the Ottoman Turkish fleet off Lepanto in Greece. Don John's ornate galley, a reproduction of which is in the Museu Marítim (▷ 70–71), was one of the finest vessels to be built in Barcelona's royal shipyards. Prisoners and conscripts provided the muscle power. Chained to their oars, they ate, slept and relieved themselves where they sat—you could smell a fleet of galleys from some distance. As the fleets closed, Don John led his flagship into the fray and the figurehead of Christ is said to have miraculously dodged a Turkish cannonball. The curiously bending sculpture is now in Barcelona's cathedral (▷ 98–101). It was a good omen for the Christians, who went on to rout the Turks.

A GRIM REAPERS' WAR

Fighting losing wars on several fronts, Spain needed extra troops and cash from the regions. Barcelona refused. So Madrid decided to invade France from Catalonia in 1639, creating an excuse to base troops in the area and get a tighter grip on the still largely autonomous region. The rural populace, already pressed by poverty and taxes, rose up in 1640 and overwhelmed the soldiers. Reapers armed with scythes converged on Barcelona and assassinated the viceroy. So started the Guerra dels Segadors (Reapers' War). As Madrid sent more troops, Barcelona appealed for French aid. By 1641, Paris had unseated Madrid as master of Catalonia, but Madrid finally retook Barcelona in 1652. The war was concluded in 1659 with the Treaty of the Pyrenees.

THE SIEGE OF BARCELONA

By 1714, Barcelona stood hopelessly alone against Philip V as its allies in the War of the Spanish Succession had left the field. Armed with whatever came to hand, and assisted by a few thousand weary troops, the townspeople fought on doggedly. And in a moment of desperate inspiration, the city rulers declared the Virgin of La Mercè, the city's co-patron saint, commander-in-chief: After all, she had saved the city from plague the previous century. It was to no avail and on 11 September (now Catalonia's national day) the city fell. Philip stripped Catalonia of its privileges. He banned Catalan, closed the universities and built a huge fortress, the Ciutadella, in the park of the same name, to watch over his reluctant subjects.

Barcelona slowly pulled itself up by its bootstraps after being cowed by Philip V in 1714. In 1778 it was allowed trading access to Spain's American colonies, exporting brandy and textiles. The growth of the latter business spawned other industries and by the end of the 18th century Catalans were manufacturing everything from artillery to farm implements. Yet these industries suffered a setback as Spain became embroiled in Napoleon's maelstrom, first as a reluctant ally in 1800 and then, from 1808, as an occupied territory under Joseph Bonaparte. Insurgents joined Wellington's British army, who trounced the French in 1813. Barcelona's factories recovered from this violent interlude in the 1830s and more growth took place. In 1848 Spain's first railway, between Barcelona and Mataró, opened and industrialization gathered pace. Iron, cotton, shipbuilding, cork and wine production grew, but so did an abject underclass. A soaring population led to the removal of Barcelona's city walls in 1854 and, in 1869, an ambitious grid-plan enlargement began. The 1888 Universal Exhibition marked a high point, but glee turned to gloom when Spain lost Cuba, Puerto Rico and the Philippines in a clash with the US in 1898, a development that hit the city's economy hard.

URBAN RENEWAL

Years after thousands of people in La Ribera had lost their homes to make way for the huge Ciutadella fortress, Spanish military engineers cooked up a plan to rehouse them. Juan Martín Cermeño drew up diagrams for Barceloneta (Little Barcelona), a triangle of reclaimed land upon which tight rows of cheap, uniform housing along narrow, claustrophobic lanes were to be raised. Work began in 1753 and some of the original family houses can still be seen. Most, however, were later replaced or swallowed up by much taller, often squalid and always overcrowded buildings. Barceloneta became a congested, fetid workers' and fishermen's quarter that even today, despite creeping gentrification, retains a whiff of its lively waterfront past.

Clockwise from above *The esplanade at Barceloneta, once an overcrowded workers' quarter; detail of town houses along Las Ramblas; the broad, tree-lined boulevard of Las Ramblas*

THE BUILDING OF A BOULEVARD

In the Middle Ages Barcelona's most famous street, Las Ramblas, was little more than a stinking open-air sewer. By 1775, the rivulet had become a dusty, irregular roadway. That year, it was decided to tear down the long-irrelevant 13th-century walls built by Jaume I that lined the road, and a new-look, tree-lined avenue was laid out in the late 1770s. Jaume's defences had come to serve as a structural wall for slum hovels that were built against the side of it. These were all swept away with the walls and almost immediately the great and the good started to erect grand town houses along the revitalized boulevard, and many of these neoclassical caprices, like the Palau de la Virreina (▷ 104), still stand. Flower kiosks were opened in the mid-19th century, and the plane trees, which still shade the Ramblas, were introduced in 1859.

THE BURNING OF THE CHURCHES

On 26 July 1835 a bullfight ended in a riot as spectators burst on to the arena incensed by the poor quality of the bulls. In fact, the bulls simply acted as a catalyst in an already volatile situation. The mob spilled into central Barcelona, where soapbox orators urged an assault on churches and convents. The Catalans had long considered the clergy a reactionary ally of the Spanish ruling class and a wave of anticlerical violence had swept the region days earlier after the assassination of some Catalan liberals. An orgy of arson ensued. Some of Madrid's politicians shared these sentiments and in 1837 Spain's finance minister, Juan Álvarez Mendizábal, ordered the divestment of Church land to stimulate the economy. Around 80 per cent of Church property in Barcelona was sold at auction.

DIVE, DIVE, DIVE!

Driven by an obsessive curiosity with the depths of the oceans, Narcís Monturiol, a Barcelona socialist and editor, became a submarine inventor. In 1859 he launched his *Ictineo*, a fish-shaped contraption powered by human muscle. Monturiol made repeated short dives but could find no one to fund further research, so he plunged himself into debt to produce a better model. The 17m (56ft) *Ictineo II*, launched in 1864, had a revolutionary system for providing oxygen and a steam-driven motor. It was far more advanced than anything else thus far created, including submarines built by the Confederates during the American Civil War (1860–61). Monturiol could still find no backers and, crushed by debt, had to watch as his creation was scrapped in 1872.

THE FIASCO OF 1898

By the mid-19th century Spain's only remaining South American colonies were Cuba and Puerto Rico, but both provided Barcelona with a healthy living from cotton plantations and as export markets. In the 1890s, demands in the islands for self-government, and then outright independence, grew. Spain met the challenge with repression that triggered an insurgency and the US came to the rebels' aid. A hopelessly ill-equipped Spanish fleet despatched to challenge the Americans was sent to the bottom of the sea in 1898 and the islands passed to US control. Soon the main import on Barcelona's docks were half-starved returning Spanish soldiers. And all that remained were the nostalgic *havaneres* (sea shanties) sung by sailors on the Barcelona to Havana trade routes.

Even before the 20th century dawned, Barcelona revelled in its Renaixença (Renaissance), a sparking of renewed interest in all things Catalan. The language and its literature were revived and Catalan nationalism flourished. The greatest expression of this rebirth came in architecture. Modernisme (the Catalan version of art nouveau) began in the 1880s and reached its apogee in the early 1900s. Above all, Antoni Gaudí (1852–1926) dazzled with his unique buildings. Barcelona's population doubled to 1 million from 1900 to 1930 and worker unrest led to the rise of the radical Left. In 1931 a republic was proclaimed in Spain. Catalan nationalists reinstated the Generalitat (the regional government) and declared Catalonia an autonomous republic, drawing an artillery bombardment in 1934. In Madrid, the left-wing Popular Front's 1936 election victory enraged the Right and in July General Franco (1892–1975) launched the Spanish Civil War. In Barcelona, a coalition of anarchists and Trotskyists (supporters of social revolution) took control, later replaced by communists. In 1937 the national republican government moved here, then fled to France shortly before the city's fall to Franco on 25 January 1939. The war ended in March that year.

A SACRED PROJECT

An enormous, sinewy church is being built in Barcelona. They have been at it since 1882 and La Sagrada Família (▷ 186–189) may be finished in around 2026. Antoni Gaudí, king of eccentric architecture and the soul of Modernisme, dedicated much of his life to this incredible house of God. But Barcelona's well-to-do tired of it and funds became scarce. Gaudí, believing his cause sacred, gave it all he had and lived like a pauper on site. When he died in 1926, only one tower, portal and the apse were complete. But Barcelona has carried on, even after anarchists destroyed many of Gaudí's on-site plans and models in 1936. By 2010, two more facades, plus the nave and choir were largely complete. Work has also begun on the largest tower.

Clockwise from above *The sheer height of the spires of La Sagrada Família was intended to draw the eyes heavenwards; General Francisco Franco in 1936; FC Barcelona football scarves*

BARCELONA BLUES

In 1900 a precocious artist called Pablo Picasso (1881–1973) put on an exhibition in the Els Quatre Gats tavern, a bohemian haunt run by Barcelona's artistic avant-garde. Born in southern Spain, the fiery-eyed youth had been brought to Barcelona by his art teacher father in 1895. Picasso was already a fine academic painter in his teens but became bored with conventions and began experimenting. In his Blue Period, inspired by the death of a friend, all his works, whether portraits, cityscapes or snapshots of street life, were literally tinged with a forlorn, mournful blue. Many of his subjects inhabited El Raval, the city's poorest quarter. For Picasso, the end of this, one of many artistic phases to come, coincided with his move from Barcelona to Paris in 1904.

SOCCER COMES TO BARCELONA

In the dying years of the 19th century, northern European expatriates in Barcelona and elsewhere around Spain began forming teams to kick a ball around a field. In 1899 the FC Barcelona soccer team was established, mostly of English, German and Swiss players, along with several other squads that started playing in friendly competitions. Intrigued by this odd sport, locals joined in and by late 1900 there was a Catalan league of 12 teams. Two years later at the first national championships, FC Barcelona lost 2–1 to Biscaia. By 1910 the side was the strongest in Catalonia and its clashes with Real Madrid were already a national event, frequently rigged in favour of the capital's team reckon Barcelona fans even today.

THE CITY OF BOMBS

During the 1890s, the anarchist movement gained ground among discontented workers, and bomb attacks against the rich became a fact of city life. By 1907 the anarchists had switched to strikes and founded the powerful Confederación Nacional de Trabajo trade union. The bombs kept coming in the 1900s, mostly from agents provocateurs aiming to discredit independent-minded Catalans and anarchists. In this volatile atmosphere, Madrid called up Catalan troops to fight a miserable colonial war in Morocco in July 1909. As the conscripts departed, the city rose. A general strike was accompanied by an anticlerical rampage. Enraged citizens burned and looted 80 churches in what came to be known as the Setmana Tràgica (Tragic Week).

AN ENGLISHMAN ABROAD

In December 1936 George Orwell found himself in anarchist-ruled Barcelona, with a 'notion of writing newspaper articles'. Instead, he joined the Trotskyist POUM militia and was sent to the front line. His return to Barcelona coincided with the brief civil war that broke out on 1 May with a communist assault on the anarchist-held telephone exchange on Plaça de Catalunya. Trouble had been brewing for some time. The Soviet-backed communists wanted to eliminate potential opposition and the anarchists seemed more preoccupied with social revolution than defeating Franco. The communists won and disarmed the anarchists and the POUM, throwing many into jail. Orwell described the events in *Homage to Catalonia*, which was published in 1938.

After the war came repression. The castle on Montjuïc became the scene of torture and execution for many thousands of Franco's opponents. Lluís Companys, former president of the short-lived Generalitat, was handed over by the Gestapo and shot here. Franco banned Catalan and set about making the region much more Castilian. The 1940s and 50s were known as the Years of Hunger in Spain and massive migration from its poorer regions to Barcelona and other cities continued well into the 1960s. Up to 1.5 million converged on Barcelona, creating whole non-Catalan quarters for the first time. Anti-Franco activity continued in the form of protests and strikes but he clung to power until his death in 1975. The monarchy, under King Juan Carlos, and parliamentary democracy were restored. Under the new constitution, Catalonia and other regions were granted a generous degree of self-rule. In 1980, the pragmatic Catalan nationalist Jordi Pujol was elected president of the Generalitat, a post he retained until 2003. One of the most significant events of this era was the 1992 Olympics. The city's popular mayor, Pascual Maragall, launched an ambitious project in the late 1980s to regenerate the city and the waterfront for the Olympics. They were a hit and the impetus to clean up the city continued in their wake.

CATALONIA RECOVERS SELF-RULE

Few in Barcelona mourned the death of Franco in November 1975. In fact, it is said that the corks were popped from every bottle of cava in the city. The restoration of parliamentary democracy was good news for Catalonia, which awaited self-rule under the new constitution, and in 1979, King Juan Carlos gave the region's Autonomy Statute his approval. Josep Taradellas, head of the Catalan government-in-exile in Mexico, arrived in Barcelona in 1978 and declared simply: *Ja soc aquí* (loosely meaning 'I am back'). Taradellas was succeeded by Jordi Pujol, who had once been imprisoned for singing a banned Catalan anthem in front of Franco, as the head of the new Generalitat after regional elections in 1980.

Clockwise from above *Masts in Port Olímpic front the high-rises of the Diagonal Mar quarter; the facade of the restored Gran Teatre del Liceu; signs are primarily in Catalan in Barcelona*

PHOENIX FROM THE ASHES

In January 1994, flames and a thick pall of smoke filled the air above Las Ramblas as fire consumed the city's premier opera house, the Gran Teatre del Liceu. All that remained standing was the main vestibule—the same one left by a similarly destructive blaze in 1861. A foundation was quickly set up to organize funding for its reconstruction and plans were soon put in place. Architects decided to incorporate what had survived of the original opera house and to re-create faithfully the main auditorium. The latest techniques would be used to improve acoustics and comfort. They wasted no time and in September 1999, the new-look Liceu opened its doors to the delight of the city's opera-lovers.

ETA STRIKES IN BARCELONA

Barcelona was left in a state of shock when Socialist politician and historian Ernest Lluch was shot dead by ETA (the Basque separatist terror group) outside his home on 21 November 2000. Since breaking a ceasefire earlier in the year, ETA had mounted several attacks in Barcelona. But the assassination of Lluch struck a particular chord, as he had a long history of promoting dialogue and a peaceful solution to the Basque problem. The three assassins were caught and each condemned to 33 years in prison. Since 2000, ETA has assasinated more than 50 people in Spain and southern France, including one death in Catalonia: Santos Santamaría Avendaño, a Catalan policeman, killed in a car bomb explosion in Roses.

THE OLYMPICS COME TO TOWN

Awarded the 1992 Olympic Games over rivals ranging from Belgrade to Brisbane, Barcelona did not disappoint, much to the relief of Juan Samaranch, then president of the International Olympic Committee and local boy. The Olympics prompted a campaign to revitalize the city, notably the derelict Port Vell (Old Port) waterfront and Montjuïc, where most of the events were held. The city also got a new marina around the seaside Olympic village, whose flats were later sold off to locals. King Juan Carlos opened the Games on 25 July, and for the first time in 20 years all nations were present with more than 9,000 athletes. The former USSR romped home with 45 gold medals, ahead of the US with 37 and Germany with 33; Spain came in eighth with 13 golds.

SPEAKING IN TONGUES

In 1998 the Generalitat caused a storm with its latest law on linguistic normalization, the restoration of Catalan as the prime language of daily discourse. Catalan is the main language of public administration and education, and many primarily Spanish-speaking residents of Barcelona feel discriminated against. The 1998 law allowed the Generalitat to demand that up to half of dubbed and subtitled foreign films shown in Catalonia be in Catalan, and the Generalitat announced it would impose quotas to that effect. The cinema industry denounced the move as folly, saying the pointless extra cost (virtually all Catalans speak Spanish too) would mean that many films simply did not screen in Catalonia. In the end the Generalitat backed off.

Barcelona has entered the 21st century optimistic and forward-looking but also conscious that it is losing ground to its eternal rival Madrid. The port city remains in a building and renewal frenzy that began with the Olympics, and to many outsiders it appears inward-looking and too caught up in chip-on-shoulder questions of offended Catalan identity. Barcelona, with its reputation for business sense and hard work, and long the country's economic powerhouse, is watching with a sense of almost helpless dismay as the political capital, Madrid, scoots ahead as Spain's undisputed financial hub.

Above *The dramatic exterior of MACBA, the museum of contemporary art in Barcelona*

URBAN REVOLUTION

Ever anxious to bestride the world stage, Barcelona hosted the Universal Forum of Cultures in 2004. It wasn't quite the major success the organizers hoped for, but it did prompt a new bout of urban development. El Diagonal, one of the city's main arteries, was extended to the coast north of the city. This last remaining swathe of underdeveloped land has been transformed into a belt of luxury apartments, hotels and offices, and a dot.com epicentre. Another pocket of the city that is ringing loud with the sound of the jackhammer is Sant Andreu, where the old Sagrera train station is being transformed to accommodate the AVE, the new high-speed train linking Madrid to Barcelona, and eventually to Paris. When complete, it will be equipped to cope with an annual traffic of more than 100 million passengers.

THE CATALAN STATUTE OF AUTONOMY

In 2006, an extraordinary rumpus erupted in Catalonia. The furore was caused by the Catalan government's insistence that the region's Statute of Autonomy, which granted the government a certain extent of self rule, should be revised to recognize Catalonia's 'nationhood'. The spectre of Spain's fragmentation into numerous small nations was raised, and a bitter, hate campaign unfolded across the country. In some supermarkets, signs were posted urging people not to buy Catalan products such as cava. In another incident, a Spanish army officer threatened to invade Catalonia if necessary. Locals were shaken by the extent of anti-Catalan feeling, but, nonetheless, the amendments were made to the Catalan Statute with the approval of the Spanish parliament.

ON THE MOVE | BARCELONA

ON THE MOVE

On the Move gives you detailed advice and information about the various
options for travelling to Barcelona before explaining the best ways to get
around the city once you are there. Handy tips help you with everything from
buying tickets to renting a car.

ARRIVING BY AIR

The profusion of budget airlines and the resulting price war makes flying to Barcelona from some European countries, even for a short weekend break, a very real possibility. The advent of direct flights from the US to Barcelona with Iberia and Delta Airlines has also improved access, but most flights from North America involve a stopover in Madrid or another of the major European city airports such as Paris, London or Amsterdam.

Barcelona has one major airport, 13km (8 miles) southwest of the city at El Prat de Llobregat, with the airport code of BCN. There are two terminals: **T1** and **T2**. The new T1 building was inaugurated in 2009. T2 incorporates the old A, B and C terminals, now known as **T2A, T2B** and **T2C**. Terminals 1 and 2 are linked by a shuttle bus. Major airlines using T1 and T2 are listed below, but these may be subject to change and you should check with your airline before travel. There are tourist information offices (open Mon–Sat 9.30–8, Sun 9.30–3) in the arrivals halls of T2A and T2B, and there are helpful airport information points throughout both terminals. A hotel reservation desk is in arrivals at T2B (only a short walk from T2A). There is a good selection of shops in both main terminals, including newspaper shops and bookstores. Money-changing

facilities and ATMs are in the arrivals halls of T2A and T2B.

Some budget airlines, notably Ryanair, fly to two smaller airports in Catalunya: Girona and Reus. **Girona** (100km/62 miles north of Barcelona) is the larger of the two, and is linked by a coach service to Barcelona (for timetables see www.barcelonabus.com; €12 single/€21 return, journey time 1 hour 20 min). From **Reus** airport (about 100km/62 miles south of Barcelona), take the local bus from outside the arrivals hall to Reus train station (€2; journey time 20 min) and then take a train to Barcelona (€6.50–€14.50; journey time 1 hour 25 min to 1 hour 45 min). A taxi from Girona or Reus to Barcelona may cost about €125 (for up to four passengers, with luggage and tolls), but agree the price with the driver before boarding as there have been reports of scams.

TRANSFERS FROM BARCELONA AIRPORT TO THE CITY
By Train
The airport has its own train station, Aeroport del Prat-Barcelona, which is connected by a raised corridor with moving walkways to T2. The service operates from the airport to Estació de Sants and Estació de França stations every 30 minutes from 6.08am to 11.38pm. You must buy your ticket, costing around €2.80, before boarding but there are a number of integrated passes that you can use (▷ 43).

Estació de Sants station is on regional train line C2, (although this may change, depending on the progress of the high-speed AVE train; ▷ 51). It has an interchange with the metro, where the station's name is Sants. Other stopping points on the route include Passeig de Gràcia (journey time 25 min).

MAJOR ARRIVALS AND DEPARTURES					
T1				**T2**	
Aeroflot	American Airlines	Iberia	Spanair	Aer Lingus	Jet2.Com
Air Canada	Austrian Airlines	KLM	Swiss International	Air Berlin	Monarch
Air Europa	British Airways	LOT	Airlines	bmibaby	Thomas Cook Airlines
Air France	Brussels Airlines	Lufthansa	TAP	Clickair	Wizz Air
Air Nostrum	Continental Airlines	SAS	US Airways	easyJet	
Alitalia	Delta Airlines	Singapore Airlines	Vueling	German Wings	

By Bus

There are two Aerobús services: A1 and A2. The A1 goes directly to T1, while the A2 is for T2. Both depart from from Plaça de Catalunya and also pick up at Plaça d'Espanya; the journey takes 25 to 30 minutes. The bus has limited space for luggage so if you have lots of bags and find there is a long queue, you might prefer to catch the train or take a taxi. Aerobús A1 departs daily every 5 to 10 minutes. The fare is €5 for a single journey and €8.65 return. Aerobús A2 departs every 8 to 15 minutes daily, and costs €4.25 one way and €7.30 for a return trip.

If you arrive during the night, you can catch a night bus (N17), which departs from outside T2A, T2B and T2C and terminates at the Plaça de Catalunya. Tickets cost €1.35, and integrated passes are also valid.

A new 'hotel bus' service (www. barcelonahotelbus.es) links Barcelona with the airport. The hourly shuttle bus service runs daily from 8am to 8pm throughout the year, and picks up/drops off at eight central hotels. A one-way ticket costs €12, and pre-booking is essential.

By Car

Several of the major car rental companies have rental desks at the airport, but you are likely to get better deals if you book, and pay, before you arrive. Another way of getting a good deal is to use a Spanish firm who will be able to offer very competitive rates—ATESA is the main one (tel 93 298 34 33). Ask at the tourist information desks at the airport.

To rent a car in Barcelona you will need your driver's licence and a credit card to cover the deposit. Licences from major countries, such as Canada, the US, the UK and other EU countries, will be accepted. It is compulsory to carry your licence with you at all times. The minimum age required for car rental is 21, but this can often be higher, and you will need to have been driving for at least a year.

The road for Barcelona from the airport is the C-31, which connects with the C-32. The turn-off to the airport on your return is well signposted. The journey should take about 20 minutes, but will depend on traffic.

By Taxi

Taxis are available from directly outside the terminal buildings T2A and T2C; the rank outside T2B is to the right. Journey time to central Barcelona is 20 minutes, depending on traffic, and the fare should be €20 to €25. For more information about taxis, ▷ 49.

TIPS

» If you are getting the train from the airport and staying in the older part of town, you may find the connection at the Passeig de Gràcia more useful than getting off at Sants. It also provides greater access to the metro system.

» You can confirm arrivals and departures in real time at www.aena. es—just insert the flight number into the box provided.

USEFUL TELEPHONE NUMBERS
Airport reception: 902 404 704
Tourist information desks:
93 478 47 04 (terminal T2A)
or
93 478 05 65 (terminal T2B)
Lost and found: 93 259 64 40

MAJOR AIRLINES

American Airlines	www.aa.com
British Airways	www.britishairways.com
easyJet	www.easyjet.com
Iberia	www.iberia.com
KLM	www.klm.com
Lufthansa	www.lufthansa.com
Virgin	www.virgin.com

TRANSFERS

	TIME	PRICE	FREQUENCY
Train	25–30 min	€2.80	Every 30 min (approx)
Aerobús A1	25–30 min	€5	Every 5–10 min
Aerobús A2	25–30 min	€4.25	Every 8–15 min
Car	20 min	—	—
Taxi	20 min	€20–€25	—

CAR RENTAL COMPANIES

COMPANY	T2B	T2C	WEBSITE
Avis	93 298 36 00	93 298 36 00	www.avis.es
Budget	As Avis	As Avis	www.budget.es
Europcar	93 298 33 00	93 298 33 00	www.europcar.es
Hertz	93 298 36 37	93 298 36 37	www.hertz.es

rest of Spain's road network via the AP-2 and AP-7. The website www.autopistas.com has a good range of useful information, including current road toll charges.

Once in the city, signs for Port Vell will take you to the main exit for the old town.

An alternative to driving all the way across mainland Europe is to use the Autotrain. (The French Motorail system was suspended in 2010 at the time of writing). Cars are boarded on an overnight train from Paris to several destinations in France, including Narbonne (the closest to Barcelona, 250km/155 miles away). Passengers follow a day or two later to collect their cars. Prices are from €49 to €265 one way. Visit the website www.eurotunnel.com for more information on the Channel Tunnel, and for more detail on getting around by car ▷ 50.

ARRIVING BY TRAIN

The Spanish national railway company, RENFE, operates services throughout the country and some suburban lines. Estació de Sants is the terminal for most international and national train journeys and has its own tourist office, hotel booking office, banks and taxi stands. Estació de França, near Barceloneta, has train connections to some regional lines as well as the main international train to Perpignan and Montpellier. Other possible points of entry are Plaça de Catalunya, Plaça d'Espanya and Passeig de Gràcia, which are on the suburban and metro lines.

The international Talgo trains, which are faster and more luxurious than most, run a service connecting Paris, Zurich, Milan and Montpellier to Barcelona. If you want to travel overnight from Paris there is a direct service on the hotel trains, taking about 12 hours.

For information on RENFE's international routes call 902 24 34 02, for national routes call 902 24 02 02, or visit the website at www.renfe.es.

ARRIVING BY BUS

Long-distance bus services run from Portugal, France, the UK and other western European countries to Barcelona. These services provide comfortable conditions on modern buses and can be less expensive than other forms of international travel. But the journey times are long. For example, Paris to Barcelona is 15 hours and London to Barcelona is 25 hours.

Eurolines (www.eurolines.com) is one of the biggest bus operators, and their multi-day passes cover travel to up to 31 countries. Visitors from outside the UK can use this site or use the contact details in the panel below.

There are two main terminals. Estació del Nord (tel 902 26 06 06) is on the eastern side of the city. The nearest metro station to here is Arc de Triomf, five minutes' walk away, which is also served by local suburban trains. The Estació Autobusos de Sants (tel 93 490 40 00), to the west of the city, is just around the corner from the main rail station, which has connections to the metro.

ARRIVING BY CAR

The AP-7 is one of the country's main toll *autopistas* (motorways or expressways). It connects France to Barcelona, and you can access the

ARRIVING BY BOAT

Car ferry services from Britain to Spain are operated by Brittany Ferries (tel 08709 076 103), running from Portsmouth to Santander (three return sailings a week, journey time 24 hours) and Plymouth to Santander (one return sailing a week, journey time 20 to 24 hours depending on the ship used). There is a luxury car ferry between Genoa in Italy and Barcelona, run by Grandi Navi Veloci; journey time is 18 hours. Check the website www.gnv.it for details. Ferry services also operate to the Moll de Barcelona, from the Balearic Islands. The largest company is Trasmediterranea; book online at www.trasmediterranea.es (national 902 45 46 45; international 93 295 91 34/35; UK office 0870 499 1305).

EUROLINES SERVICES
General information
www.eurolines.com
France
892 89 90 91; www.eurolines.fr
Italy
055 512 84 19; www.eurolines.it
Germany
069 7903 501; www.touring.de

The best way to get a feel for any city is to walk its streets and Barcelona is no exception. Most of the southern areas, particularly around the pedestrianized Barri Gòtic, demand legwork. But some of the city's best sights are not in the main part of town, so you are likely to need the excellent local transport system.

Barcelona's urban transport system consists of buses, the metro (underground or subway), Ferrocarrils de la Generalitat de Catalunya (FGC) suburban trains and the Cercanías (Rodalies) trains. You are most likely to use the metro and the bus system.

The metro is an efficient system and very useful for covering longer distances than you may feel like walking. The bus network complements the metro with a huge array of routes, most of which pass through Plaça de Catalunya, Plaça d'Espanya or Universitat. The pedestrianized area around the Barri Gòtic makes it difficult to catch a bus across the city, so be prepared to walk for some of your journey, or use the metro.

The transport system is divided into zones, with Zone One being the most central. However, Zone Two and the outer zones start a long way out and cover smaller towns and the suburbs. As a visitor, you are very unlikely to need anything other than Zone One.

TMB

» Transports Metropolitans de Barcelona (TMB) runs both the metro and the main bus service.
» Pick up a network map from tourist information offices (▷ 245) or at one of the TMB information offices.
» TMB's website at www.tmb.net is a great interactive site in English, Spanish and Catalan. It is full of information on getting about the city and it will tell you what bus number or line you need to catch.
» For more details or if you wish to speak to someone about TBM and its services, you can call 010, which is the city council's information line. The advisors speak a number of languages. Or call the TMB information service (tel 93 318 70 74).

DISCOUNT PASSES

A single ticket can be bought for any journey, but buying these repeatedly is likely to become expensive. Passes are available in a number of combinations that provide different access to the metro, buses and the FGC. Buy them from ticket offices and automatic machines at all metro and train stations, kiosks and tobacconists. The most useful ones are:

» T-Dia provides unlimited 24-hour travel for one person.
» T-10 is valid for 10 journeys and can be shared, so it just needs to be validated for each person using it.
» T-50/30 is good for those staying in the city for a while, as it allows travel for 50 journeys over 30 days.
» Special visitor passes are available, valid for two, three, four and five days (costing €11.20, €15.90, €20.40, and €24.10 respectively). These allow unlimited use of public transport, but are only useful for visitors planning to do a lot of sightseeing.
» If you forget how many trips you have left on a transport pass, look on the back of your ticket. When you validate a journey (▷ 44 and 46), the machine prints the date and time of each journey here.

TRANSFERS

» You cannot transfer on a single ticket; you must travel on a pass.
» Once you have activated your pass on boarding a bus or entering a metro station, you have 75 minutes in which you can transfer to another method of transport: bus, metro, FGC or the Cercanías, before it is charged as a second journey.
» You cannot take the bus, get off, then get back on the same route, or leave the metro and get straight back on that line on a single trip.

BARCELONA CARD

This pass entitles you to free, unlimited travel on the metro and buses, and reductions on admission charges at many places of interest, some shops and restaurants, plus money off the Aerobús, the TombBus and the funicular (▷ 49).

One-, two- or five-day passes are available, costing between €26 and €42 for adults, with reductions for children between four and twelve years, and free for children under four. They are available at tourist information offices (▷ 245) and El Corte Inglés department store (▷ 121). Tickets are also available at www.barcelonacard.com, with a 5 per cent discount for purchases made online.

TIPS

» Smoking is not allowed anywhere on the metro (trains, platforms and stations) or on buses. If you are caught, there is a €30 fine.
» Children under four travel for free on both the buses and metro.
» Lost items found on a TMB metro or bus are sent to the Information Office at Universitat station (see panel below). Wait until the following day to contact them by calling 93 318 7074, and if your lost item is there you will need some form of ID. Items which are not claimed are sent to the City Hall Lost and Found Office (tel 010).

TMB OFFICES

Plaça de la Universitat
Mon–Fri 8–8

Sagrada Família
Mon–Fri 7am–9pm

Sagrera
Mon–Fri 8–8

Sants
Mon–Fri 7am–9pm, Sat 9–7, Sun 9–2

The city's metro is relatively small by other European city standards, with 85km (58 miles) of track and seven lines.

But it is a fast and frequent service that is used by 300 million people per year.

Metro stations are recognized by the white diamond and red M sign. All metro stops are within Zone One.

TICKETS AND TRAVEL

» Single tickets and passes can be bought from the ticket office or the ticket vending machines, which accept cash or credit cards.

» The T-10 pass (▷ 43) can be bought from tobacconists around the city.

» Some ticket machines use a touch-screen method.

» To enter the system, push your ticket through the slot on the turnstile. This activates your ticket.

» There are regular ticket checks.

» The fine for not producing a ticket is €40.

» On the platform there is a board showing the line and stops.

» Some trains have signs at the end of the carriages to show which side of the carriage the doors will open.

» Not all the doors on the train open automatically at each stop. If there is a lever on the door it must be pushed before the door will open.

» Exit signs in metro stations are grey and marked *Sortida*. The sign will also list the street name that you are about to exit onto.

» You don't need your ticket on the way out; just push through the gate.

TIPS

» Try to avoid the rush hours, around 7.30–9am and 6–8pm. The metro and buses are also busy at lunchtime.

» The metro runs Mon–Thu 5am–midnight, Fri–Sat all-night non-stop service, Sun 6am–midnight.

» After 10pm you may find that a station with several entrances has only one open.

» Avoid changing lines if possible, as most interchanges, particularly at the Passeig de Gràcia, have a long walk between lines.

» If you have any difficulties at the stations, an internal phone connects directly to the station manager.

UNDERSTANDING THE METRO MAP

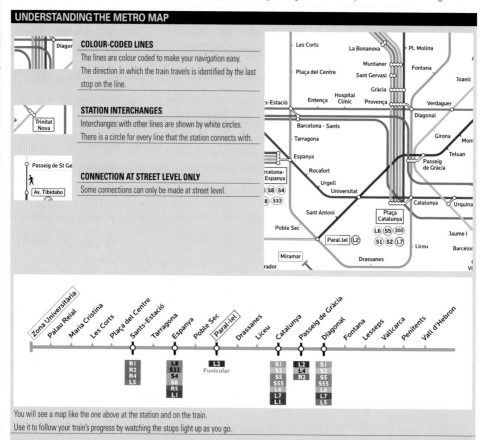

COLOUR-CODED LINES

The lines are colour coded to make your navigation easy. The direction in which the train travels is identified by the last stop on the line.

STATION INTERCHANGES

Interchanges with other lines are shown by white circles. There is a circle for every line that the station connects with.

CONNECTION AT STREET LEVEL ONLY

Some connections can only be made at street level.

You will see a map like the one above at the station and on the train.

Use it to follow your train's progress by watching the stops light up as you go.

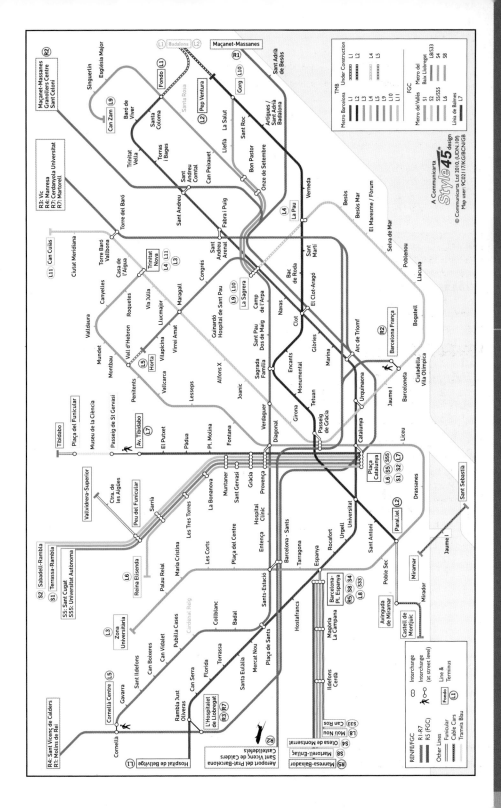

BUSES

Buses are the most practical way of reaching the sights that are farther away from the main part of town, for example Park Güell or Monestir de Pedralbes. They are air-conditioned single-deckers and give a comfortable ride, but traffic can slow your journey-time down.

USING THE BUSES

» Free maps showing all routes are available from tourist offices (▷ 245) and TMB offices (▷ 43).

» Once you have decided on your route, look for the arrow on the timetable at each bus stop to check that you are catching the bus in the right direction.

» Place names are displayed on the front of the bus. The top name shows where the bus has come from, the bottom name where it's going to.

» Board the bus through the front doors by the driver, who will sell you single tickets only, not passes.

» If you have a pass, remember that it will need to be validated. Place it vertically into the white on-board machines behind the driver (not the grey ones in front of the driver) for stamping.

» When you want to get off, press the button on the handrails, which will light up a sign to say the bus is stopping (parada solicitada). Exit via the back doors.

» If the bus is busy and you are standing nearer the front doors, you can get off this way.

BUS TURÍSTIC

» This is a hop-on, hop-off service (www.barcelonabusturistic.cat).

» Buses follow three interlinked circular routes (red, blue and green) that take in the city's main sights.

» The Green Route (summer months only) is the shortest, passing through the Port Olímpic and the northern beaches and finishing at Parc del Fòrum.

» You can get on and off as many times as you like on the one ticket, and each stop is announced in Catalan, Spanish, English, German and French.

» The guides will also provide small bits of commentary.

» Tickets cost €22 for one day, €29 for two consecutive days, with a reduction for children (€14 and €18 respectively) and free for those aged under four.

» Tickets can be bought at tourist offices or on the bus.

» Your ticket also comes with discounts on admission charges to a number of major sights around the city.

» The frequency of the service depends on the season.

» The wait for a bus ranges from six minutes up to 30 or 40 at very busy times, with long lines for the mid-morning buses from the Plaça de Catalunya.

» To make the most of this service, be realistic about what you can see in one day, as it would be impossible to fit in all the sights on the three routes.

» Buses only travel in one direction around the route, so it can be difficult to get back to somewhere, unless you are prepared to sit all the way around the loop.

» The red and blue loops (▷ opposite) take about 2 hours.

» The green route takes about 40 minutes.

» The two-day pass enables you to use the service as a city bus tour and orient yourself on the first day. Then on the second day you can pick out the sights you want to visit.

NIGHT BUSES

Once the TMB buses have finished for the day, special night buses (Nitbus) take over. They run regularly from 11pm to 4.30am on selected routes. Most routes start at the

BUS TURÍSTIC BLUE ROUTE

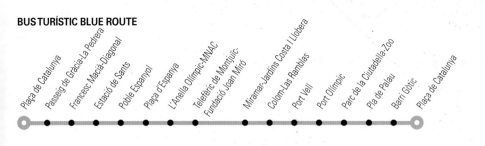

Plaça de Catalunya · Passeig de Gràcia-La Pedrera · Francesc Macià-Diagonal · Estació de Sants · Poble Espanyol · Plaça d'Espanya · L'Anella Olímpic-MNAC · Telefèric de Montjuïc-Fundació Joan Miró · Miramar-Jardins Costa i Llobera · Colom-Las Ramblas · Port Vell · Port Olímpic · Parc de la Ciutadella-Zoo · Pla de Palau · Barri Gòtic · Plaça de Catalunya

BUS TURÍSTIC RED ROUTE

Plaça de Catalunya · Passeig de Gràcia-La Pedrera · Sagrada Família · Park Güell · Monestir de Pedralbes · Tramvia Blau-Tibidabo · Palau Reial · Futbol Club Barcelona · Francesc Macià-Diagonal · MACBA-CCCB · Plaça de Catalunya

BUS NO. 14

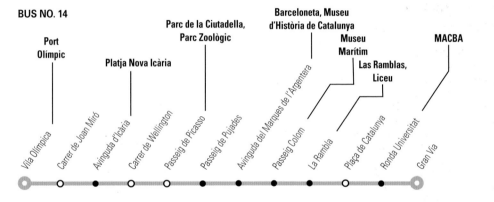

Port Olímpic · Platja Nova Icària · Parc de la Ciutadella, Parc Zoològic · Barceloneta, Museu d'Història de Catalunya · Museu Marítim · Las Ramblas, Liceu · MACBA

Via Olímpica · Carrer de Joan Miró · Avinguda d'Icària · Carrer de Wellington · Passeig de Picasso · Passeig de Pujades · Avinguda del Marques de l'Argentera · Passeig Colom · La Rambla · Plaça de Catalunya · Ronda Universitat · Gran Via

BUS NO. 17

Beaches, cable car tower to Montjuïc · Museu d'Història de Catalunya · Santa Maria del Mar · Barri Gòtic, Catedral, Plaça del Rei, Plaça de Sant Jaume · Palau de la Música Catalana · Plaça de Catalunya, Las Ramblas · Casa Milà (La Pedrera), L'Eixample, Manzana de la Discordia · Gràcia · Tramvia Blau for Tibidabo

Barceloneta · Passeig Joan de Borbó · Plaça de Palau · Via Laietana · Palau de la Música · Carrer de Jonqueres · Plaça Urquinaona · Ronda Sant Pere · Passeig de Gràcia · Avinguda Diagonal · Via Augusta · Plaça Molina · Carrer de Balmes · Passeig St. Gervasi · República Argentina

47

Plaça de Catalunya. Nitbus route numbers start with N.

TIPS

» Most buses run daily from 5am to 10pm, every 5 to 10 minutes; exact route times are listed at each stop.
» The bus system uses the symbol of a red circle with a white B. It is displayed at bus stops and places that carry bus information.
» A free bus Pocket Plan is available from TMB offices (▷ 43).
» Bus timetables list all the stops, which are not always the same in both directions, so check carefully.
» For more information check the TMB website at www.tmb.net.

BUS NO. 22

Casa Milà (La Pedrera), L'Eixample, Manzana de la Discordia

Las Ramblas

Gràcia

Tibidabo

Monestir de Pedralbes

Plaça de Catalunya · Passeig de Gràcia · Plaça Joan Carles I · Gran de Gràcia · Carrer Bolivar · Plaça Lesseps Park Güell · Avinguda de la Republica · Argentina · Passeig Sant Gervasi · Tramvia Blau · Plaça Sarrià · Passeig Reina Elisenda · Monestir Pedralbes

BUS NO. 50

Palau de la Música Catalana, Plaça de Catalunya, Las Ramblas

CaixaForum, MNAC, Parc de Joan Miró

Hospital Santa Creu i Sant Pau

Sagrada Família

Poble Espanyol

L'Anella Olímpica

Fundació Joan Miró

MACBA

Funicular

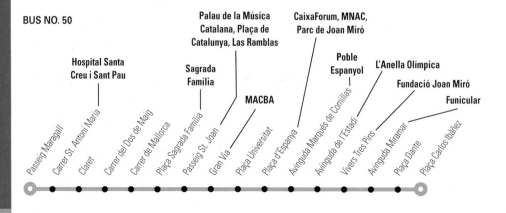

Passeig Maragall · Carrer St. Antoni Maria Claret · Carrer del Dos de Maig · Carrer de Mallorca · Plaça Sagrada Família · Passeig St. Joan · Gran Via · Plaça Universitat · Plaça d'Espanya · Avinguda Marqués de Comillas · Avinguda de l'Estadi · Vivers Tres Pins · Avinguda Miramar · Plaça Dante · Plaça Carlos Ibáñez

TRAIN

The metro is supplemented by the Ferrocarrils de la Generalitat de Catalunya (FGC), a local train service run by the Catalan government. It is integrated with the metro and will take you out into the suburbs. There is also a regional service run by RENFE, the national train operator, which is signposted as Rodalies (Cercanías in Spanish) RENFE. This covers the province of Barcelona and also takes you to the coast.

» The suburban and regional lines are colour-coded and numbered, but prefixed by a letter. For getting around the city it's unlikely you will make much use of these lines, but the FGC line from Plaça de Catalunya to Tibidabo (line L7) is a quick way to reach the foot of the mountain, and the airport station is on Rodalies line C2 (Nord).

» The same pricing and ticketing system as the metro applies, as long as you stay within Zone One. Check the zone maps that are on display at stations.

» Estació de Sants, Plaça de Catalunya and Plaça d'Espanya are main hubs for these local routes. You can get further rail information at www.renfe.es, or call 902 24 02 02 for national travel and 902 24 34 02 for international travel.

TAXIS

There are around 11,000 licensed black-and-yellow taxis in central Barcelona.

» Smoking is not allowed.

» Guide dogs are allowed but pets are at the driver's discretion.

» There is a schedule of approved fares for around the city, but fares are not expensive: Between 8am and 8pm there is a €2 minimum fare; when you order by phone there is a €3.40 minimum fare. The standard rate is €0.86 per km.

Surcharges:

Luggage: €1

Pets: €1

To/from airport:€3.10

To/from port: €2.10

» If the green light on top of the taxi is lit, then it's available.

» Except in radio taxis, make sure the meter is set to zero at the start of your journey.

» The meter still runs when the taxi is stationary (such as in traffic jams).

» For items lost in a taxi call 90 210 15 64.

» For more information contact Institut Metropolità del Taxi, www.taxibarcelona.cat (tel 93 223 51 51).

BICYCLES

» You can get information on bicycle routes from the tourist office (▷ 245), or the information line 010.

» Un Cotxe Menys rents out bicycles by the hour, day or week. Their offices can be found at Carrer de Esparteria 3 (tel 93 268 21 05; open Mon–Fri 10–2) or visit www.bicicletabarcelona.com.

» Biciclot (Passeig Marítim 33, tel 93 221 97 78; open Jul–end Sep daily 10–8; Oct Sat, Sun, hols 10–8; Apr–end Jun Mon–Thu 10–3, Fri–Sun, hols 10–8; Nov–end Mar Sat–Sun, hols 10–3) also rents out bikes; visit them at www.biciclot.net. Don't forget to take some ID with you.

» Subscribers to the Bicing scheme can use bicycles for a 30-minute period, picking them up and dropping them off at bike stations across the city. For more information see www.bicing.com.

OTHER SERVICES

» The **Tramvia Blau** tramway runs through the suburb of Tibidabo, from Avinguda Tibidabo to Plaça Doctor Andreu. It joins up with the funicular that takes you to the top of the mountain.

» The **funicular** to Montjuïc runs from the Paral.lel metro station to Avinguda de Miramar. It is probably the easiest way up onto Montjuïc but

Above *Transbordador Aeri cable cars arriving at Torre de Jaume I*

much of the two-minute ascent is inside the mountain, so there's little to see.

» Use the **PM bus** (daily) to visit the attractions on the summit of Montjuïc. Hop on at MNAC (Museu Nacional d'Art de Catalunya) near the Plaça Espanya.

» To visit Palau Reial de Pedralbes pick up the **tram** (Trambaix) from Plaça Francesc Macia or from the Maria Cristina metro stop (www.trambcn.com).

» **Horse-drawn carriages** can be rented at the bottom of Las Ramblas, near the Monument a Colom (▷ 139).

» **The Transbordador Aeri** cable car runs over Port Vell from San Sebastià in Barceloneta to Miramar at the foot of Montjuïc.

MOTORCYCLE RENTAL

There are a number of companies in the city to rent motorcycles from, and the same laws apply as for car rental (▷ 50).

	ADDRESS	TELEPHONE	FAX
Motisimo	Portbou 14–28	93 490 84 01	93 490 84 01
Over-Rent	Av. Josep Tarradellas 42	902 410 410	93 419 96 30
Piaggio	Brasil 19	93 330 95 00	93 330 96 97
Vanguard	Viladomat 297	93 439 38 80	93 410 82 71

If you are planning to stay within the city, then it really isn't worth driving as it's just too busy, but if you want to explore the surrounding country, a car may be useful.

THE LAW
» You will need to be at least 21 to rent a car and you must have with you the vehicle registration document, motor insurance and a valid driver's licence.
» Licences (with photograph) from major countries, such as the US, Canada, the UK and other EU countries will be recognized by authorities if you are a tourist.
» If it is your own vehicle, you will need valid insurance and all supporting documents.
» Wearing seat belts is compulsory for drivers and front seat passengers, and for rear passengers if the vehicle is fitted with them.
» It is illegal to carry children under the age of 12 in the front passenger seat unless they are big enough to use the standard fitted seat belts safely.
» The drink-driving limit is 0.5g per 1,000 cubic cm (0.3g for new drivers) and if you are stopped it is compulsory to comply with the alcohol tests.

PARKING
» Most of the central car parking in Barcelona is run by B:SM, which operates 45 underground parking areas in the city.
» To get into these, you need to drive down a ramp—they are signed with the international parking symbol, a white P on a blue square.
» Prices start at €2.66 an hour, or €30 for 24 hours.
» A new service for visitors allows 8 days' parking for €75 in the car park by the Estació del Nord. This is central and convenient for metro and bus links.
» Leaving your vehicle in a secure parking area during your stay in the city may well be the most convenient option.

ON-STREET PARKING
» On-street parking is extremely difficult to find in Barcelona.
» Visitors need to park in a blue zone (easily identified by the blue parking symbols painted on the road).
» Do not park in green zones, as these are only for local residents with a special pass.
» Parking in a blue zone costs around €2 per hour.
» You can buy tickets from the machines located near the parking zone.
» Note that the tickets emerge from a half-hidden slot located at the bottom of the machine—it's easy to confuse them with the credit card slot and assume that your ticket has not been issued.
» Tickets should be clearly displayed on the dashboard.

INFORMATION FOR ROAD USERS
It is compulsory for all drivers to carry the following equipment in their vehicle at all times. If you have rented a car, ensure that this equipment is provided and is functioning before you leave the rental office.

2 x self-standing warning triangles
1 x set of spare headlight and rear light bulbs
1 x set of spare fuses
1 x spare wheel
1 x reflective vest or jacket

SPEED LIMITS
Motorway (expressway): 120kph (75mph), 80kph (50mph) for vehicles with trailers
Roads with overtaking lanes: 100kph (62mph), 80kph (50mph) for vehicles with trailers
Other roads outside built-up areas: 90kph (60mph), 70kph (44mph) for vehicles with trailers
Towns/built-up areas: 50kph (31mph)

ROAD NAMES
Autopistes: motorways (expressways) prefixed by AP or E and followed by a route number
Autovies: non-toll dual carriageways (divided highways)
Peatje: toll roads
Carreteres Nacionals: main roads, prefixed by N or CN
Carreteres Comarcals: local roads, prefixed by C

SPANISH ROAD SIGNS

No parking (clearway)

Maximum speed

No overtaking

No half-turns

Minimum speed

Pedestrian lane

Road narrows

Two-way traffic

Motorway (expressway)

Two-lane highway

All vehicles prohibited

Parking

There are a host of places to visit, just two or three hours away from the city. A good network of connections will help you to enjoy the region.

TRAINS

» Estació de Sants is the main station to use for national travel. There are direct trains to Malaga, Granada, Seville, Valencia, Zaragoza, Madrid and most other main cities in Spain. Some international trains currently depart from Estació de França, while work is carried out on the high-speed train line that will eventually link Madrid and Barcelona with France. The new Sagrera station, currently under construction, will also be a major hub (with Sants) for the new high-speed international rail line linking France and Spain. This link is already in service between Barcelona and Madrid, and is expected to be extended to Figueres and Perpignan in 2012–13.

» Grandes Líneas, the umbrella term for trains that cover long distances, include the following trains: Euromed, Alaris, Tren Estrella, Diurno, Trenhotel, Talgo, Arco and Altaria.

» AVE are high-speed trains that travel up to 300kph (188mph) and operate between Tarragona–Zaragoza–Madrid and Barcelona. They are more expensive than the Grandes Líneas.

» Regional trains in Catalonia are the Catalunya Express or Delta.

» First- (preferente) and second- (turista) class travel is available on long-distance trains; first class costs about 40 per cent more.

» There is little to distinguish first from second class on day trains, but the difference is more obvious on the overnight trains. You can travel in asiento turista (a seat, not reclining), in cama turista (a berth for four or six people in the same compartment), or cama preferente (couchettes for one or two people) with a shower and washbasin (sink) and breakfast.

» Overnight trains go from Barcelona to Madrid and major cities in Andalucía, Galicia, the Basque Country, Cantabria and Asturias.

TICKETS

» It is best to book your tickets in advance, especially in July, August, Christmas, New Year and Easter.

» Contact RENFE on 902 320 320, or www.renfe.es to buy tickets online.

» Tickets can be also be bought from travel agencies and RENFE ticket

offices at Estació de França, Estació de Passeig de Gràcia and Estació de Sants.

DISCOUNTS ON TRAINS

» Children under four travel for free if they don't use a seat, and children aged four to thirteen are entitled to a 40 per cent discount.

» If you book a four-couchette berth in the same compartment you get a 10 per cent discount.

LONG-DISTANCE BUSES

The biggest national company is Alsa Enatcar, tel 902 42 22 42, www.alsa.es.

» They have two types of buses on many routes: Supra or Eurobus; the latter is more expensive but makes fewer stops and is more comfortable.

» Most buses leave from Estació del Nord. A few leave from outside Sants train station.

» For more destinations and companies the Estació del Nord has its own booking service: Estació del Nord, tel 902 26 06 06, open 7am–9pm, www.barcelonanord.com.

COMPARISONS

The table below outlines train and long-distance bus journey times and prices. The general rule is that the faster the service the more expensive the ticket price. However, the speed restrictions around Barcelona mean that the less expensive regional trains are just as fast as expensive long-distance trains.

TRAIN VERSUS BUS				
	TRAIN		**BUS**	
Figueres	€9.40–€22.40	1hr 45 min–2 hr	€15	2hr 20 min
Girona	€8.80–€19.40	1hr 5 min– 1hr 30 min	€9.40	1hr 20 min
Madrid	€42.80–€135	2hr 43 min–9hr	€28.20	7hr 30 min
Seville	€61.90–€137.90	5hr 37 min–12hr	€87–€94	11–15hr
Sitges	€3	29–40 min	—	—
Tarragona	€6.40–€19.80	52 min–1hr 20 min	€7.65–€9.30	1hr 15min
Valencia	€24.30–€43.10	3–5hr	€25.35–€30	4hr 30 min
Vilafranca del Penedès	€3.60	50 min	—	—
Zaragoza	€24.30–€63.70	1hr 51 min–5hr 25 min	€13.75–€24.70	3hr 30 min

VISITORS WITH A DISABILITY

ARRIVING

By Air

Barcelona airport, particularly the new terminal T1, is modern and is well equipped for those with disabilities: look for adapted toilets, reserved parking spaces, elevators and ramps.

» Distances from the gates to the main terminal buildings and between terminals are not very large.

» If you need particular assistance, you should let the airline know in advance, as they can arrange help.

» For more details call the information line at the airport (tel 902 404 704, www.aena.es).

» The Aerobús has not been adapted for those with disabilities.

» Trains are more useful for transfers, changing at Sants or Catalunya, which have elevators. Be careful, however, as there is a gap between the train and platform edge.

By Train

» The RENFE station Sants is a good station to arrive at, and use when you are in the city, as there are elevators to every platform and no stairs to access the building.

» Other accessible stations are: Plaça de Catalunya and Passeig de Gràcia. FGC stations include Catalunya, Provença, Bonanova, Tres Torres, Los Planos and Muntaner.

» RENFE has wheelchairs available for transfers at their main stations but they must be booked in advance.

GETTING AROUND

» The tourist office's accessibility guide (see panel) provides plenty of useful information.

» The newer museums, such as MACBA (▷ 68–69), have good access for those with a disability, but many places can still prove a problem. Many buildings date from either the Gothic or the Modernista period and do not have elevators.

» The narrow, cobbled streets of the Barri Gòtic are difficult to negotiate, especially when it is crowded, but at least it is pedestrianized.

» Finding a place to stay should be straightforward, as many hotels are easily accessible. Call ahead if you have specific requirements.

» The Taxi Amic service has minivans which can fit wheelchairs easily, but it is a very popular service and you will need to make a reservation at least 24 hours ahead (tel 93 420 80 88, www.taxi-amic-adaptat.com).

» All TMB buses have been adapted for wheelchair access using ramps.

» The metro lines 2 (purple) and 11 (lime) are the only complete lines to have been adapted. Other main metro stations include: Passeig de Gràcia, Paral.lel, Universitat, Sagrada Família and Fontana. Metro plans, available at all stations, show which stations have been adapted.

» Most metro stations have screens that indicate when the next train is arriving, and all have announcements.

USEFUL CONTACTS

WITHIN THE CITY

» ECOM, the federation of private organizations for the disabled at Avinguda Gran Via de les Corts Catalanes 562, 08011; tel 93 451 55 50; www.ecom.cat

» Municipal Institute of Disabled People in Barcelona (IMD); tel 93 413 27 75

» Accessible Barcelona can arrange and book accessible hotels, transfers from the airport, transport and guided tours. They also offer equipment hire, including wheelchairs, scooters (buggies) and hoists. The website also lists wheelchair-friendly sights and attractions.

» The Accessible Barcelona Guide can be downloaded from Barcelona's tourist website, www.barcelonaturisme.com. Available in several languages, it gives information on accessible transport and sights, as well as links to local businesses.

ABROAD

UK: RADAR, 12 City Forum, 250 City Road, London, EC1V 8AF; tel 020 7250 3222; www.radar.org.uk

US: SATH, 347 5th Avenue, Suite 610, New York City, NY 10016; tel 212/447-7284; www.sath.org

Australia: The Disability Information and Resource Centre Inc, 195 Gilles Street, Adelaide SA 5000; tel 08 8236 0555; www.dircsa.org.au

New Zealand: Disabled Persons Assembly (DPA), PO Box 27–524, Wellington 6035; tel 644 801 9100; www.dpa.org.nz

REGIONS

This chapter is divided into four regions of Barcelona (▷ 7). Region names are for the purposes of this book only and places of interest are listed alphabetically in each region.

Barcelona's Regions 54–207

MONTJUÏC AND EL RAVAL

Montjuïc and El Raval may be neighbours geographically speaking, but they couldn't be more different in spirit. Montjuïc is the city's green lung, a small mountain carpeted with lush gardens. El Raval, in contrast, is intensely urban, a tight little warren of narrow streets which hovers between arty modernity and downright seediness. Sandwiched between them is the long swoop of the Avinguda Paral.lel, one of Barcelona's main arteries, and, at the foot of Montjuïc, the humble but enticing little district of Poble Sec.

A few hundred years ago, things were very different. El Raval hadn't yet been enclosed by the city walls, and the only buildings were a handful of churches scattered amid fields and orchards. Once consumed by the city, however, it was gradually filled with factories and tenements, home to the poor and sick so searingly portrayed by Picasso during his Blue Period. The arrival of the glossy contemporary arts museum (MACBA) in 1995 galvanized the gentrification of El Raval, which is now home to many of Barcelona's most avant-garde galleries, boutiques, restaurants and bars, although the southern section still retains a few insalubrious corners.

Montjuïc, the green mountain which cuts off the city to the south, was superbly landscaped for the 1992 Olympic Games, and its breathtaking gardens are still wonderfully maintained. In spring, they are truly spectacular. The stadia and swimming pools, another Olympic legacy, remain a big draw, as does the lofty castle right at the summit of the hill. The splendid pavilions erected for the 1929 Universal Exhibition now house a slew of fine museums, particularly the outstanding Museu Nacional d'Art de Catalunya, where the highlights include Modernista furnishings and Romanesque frescoes. The engaging neighbourhood of Poble Sec, on the lower flanks of Montjuïc, is full of great bars, cafés and restaurants.

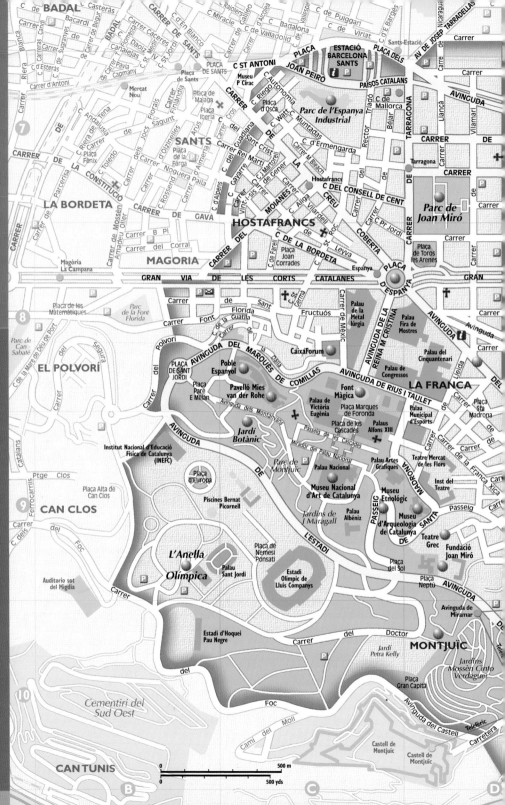

BADAL

CARRER DE SANTS

PLAÇA DE SANTS

ESTACIÓ BARCELONA SANTS

PLAÇA DELS PAÏSOS CATALANS

AV DE JOSEP TARRADELLAS

C ST ANTONI

PLAÇA JOAN PEIRO

Museu P Cirac

Parc de l'Espanya Industrial

AVINGUDA

TARRAGONA

SANTS

Hostafrancs

C DEL CONSELL DE CENT

Parc de Joan Miró

LA BORDETA

CARRER DE GAVA

HOSTAFRANCS

C DE LA BORDETA

CARRER DEL

CREU

COBERTA

Plaça de Toros les Arenes

MAGORIA

Magòria La Campana

Plaça Joan Corrades

Espanya

PLAÇA D'ESPANYA

GRAN VIA DE LES CORTS CATALANES

GRAN

Parc de la Font Florida

CaixaForum

Palau de la Metal·lúrgia

Palau Fira de Mostres

AVINGUDA DE LA REINA M CRISTINA

Palau del Cinquantenari

EL POLVORÍ

Parc de Can Sabaté

AVINGUDA DEL MARQUES DE COMILLAS

PLAÇA DE SANT JORDI

Poble Espanyol

Font Màgica

Palau de Congressos

AVINGUDA DE RIUS I TAULET

LA FRANCA

Plaça Pare E Millan

Pavelló Mies van der Rohe

Palau de Victòria Eugènia

Plaça Marques de Foronda

Palau Municipal d'Esports

Plaça Sta Madrona

Institut Nacional d'Educació Física de Catalunya (INEFC)

Jardí Botànic

Palaus Alfons XIII

Teatre Mercat de les Flors

Inst del Teatre

AVINGUDA DE

Mirador del Palau Nacional

Parc de Montjuïc

Palau Artes Gràfiques

Plaça d'Europa

Palau Nacional

Museu Etnològic

Museu d'Arqueologia de Catalunya

CAN CLOS

Piscines Bernat Picornell

Museu Nacional d'Art de Catalunya

Palau Albéniz

PASSEIG

Plaça Alta de Can Clos

Jardins de l Maragall

Teatre Grec

Fundació Joan Miró

L'Anella Olímpica

Plaça de Nèmesi Ponsati

L'ESTADI

Plaça del Sol

Auditorio sot del Migdia

Palau Sant Jordi

Estadi Olímpic de Lluís Companys

Plaça Neptú

AVINGUDA

Avinguda de Miramar

Estadi d'Hoquei Pau Negre

Jardí Petra Kelly

MONTJUÏC

Jardins Mossèn Cinto Verdaguer

Plaça Gran Capita

Cementiri del Sud Oest

Castell de Montjuic

Telefèric

Castell de Montjuïc

CAN TUNIS

0   500 m
0   500 yds

B   C   D

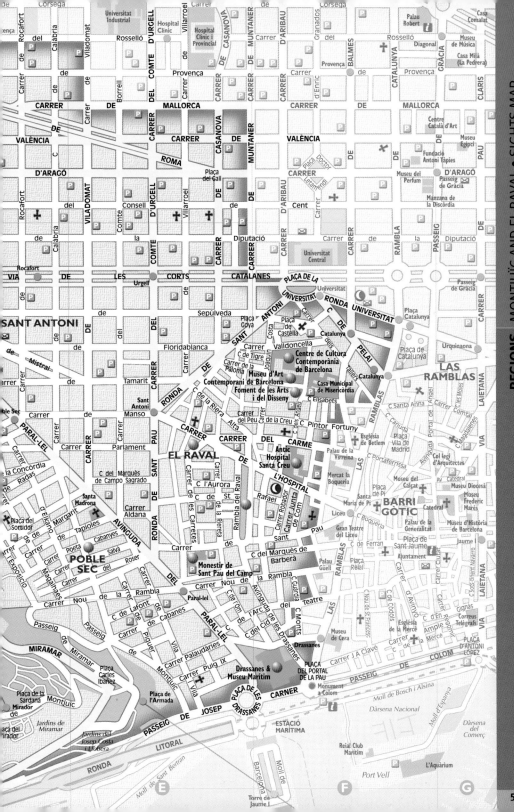

L'ANELLA OLÍMPICA

www.fundaciobarcelonaolimpica.es

The eyes of the world were on Spanish archer Antonio Rebollo when he shot his fiery arrow to ignite the Olympic torch at the opening ceremony of the 1992 Games. The focus of the athletic action was here at the Estadi Olímpic (Olympic Stadium), which forms part of L'Anella Olímpica—the Olympic Ring—on Montjuïc, along with the daring Palau Sant Jordi and the Picornell sports centre and outdoor swimming pools.

The stadium was originally designed in 1929 by the architect Pere Domènech i Roura to house the alternative to the Berlin Olympic Games, but these games were cancelled on the outbreak of the Spanish Civil War (1936–39). The original facade was retained for the 1992 Games and the stadium refitted to hold 77,000 people. You can also visit the Museu Olímpic i de l'Esport (www.museuolimpicbcn. com; Apr–end Sep Tue–Sat 10–8; Oct–end Mar Tue–Sat 10–6, Sun 10–2.30). The museum, situated just outside the Estadí Olimpíc, opened in 2007 and is principally dedicated to the Barcelona Games with photographs and memorabilia.

The Picornell swimming pools, designed by the world-renowned local architect Ricardo Bofill, are open to the public (▷ 84) and hold open-air cinema screenings in July and August. But the grandest legacy of the trio is the stunning Palau Sant Jordi, designed by Japanese architect Arata Isozaki. The domed roof was actually assembled on the ground then raised into position, and the surrounding portico gives the structure space and dynamism. The Palau is now the city's main venue for big-name music stars and large-scale meetings and conventions.

➕ 56 B9 ✉ Avinguda de L'Estadi
🚇 Espanya 🚌 50, 55

ANTIC HOSPITAL SANTA CREU

The Hospital of the Holy Cross was completed in 1417 and is one of the largest and most impressive surviving Gothic monuments in Barcelona. It remained in use as a hospital for more than five centuries: indeed, one of its very last patients was Antoni Gaudí, who was brought here after being knocked over by a tram in June 1926.

After the hospital was moved to the sumptuous new Modernista edifice designed by Domènech i Montaner (▷ 179), the original Gothic complex was bought by the city hall and now functions as the Catalan National Library. The stone halls with their soaring vaults are no longer accessible to the public (except on special occasions, such as Catalan National Day on 11 September), but the lovely courtyard, with its sculpted cloister and orange trees, remains open to all. A pretty outdoor café, El Jardí (▷ 83), has opened in one corner of the courtyard.

➕ 57 F9 ✉ Carrer de l'Hospital 56 , 08001
🚇 Liceu

AVINGUDA PARAL.LEL

The Avinguda Paral.lel, which was officially inaugurated in 1894, gets its name from the fact that it neatly follows latitude 41°22'34". A century or so ago, this broad street was Barcelona's answer to New York's Broadway, or London's West End, packed with theatres, cabarets, music halls and bars. Bomb damage during the Civil War and the resulting soulless redevelopment have almost entirely stripped the street of its former theatrical pizazz, but a few tiny pockets survive.

One of the best-known cabarets of the first decades of the 20th century was El Molino (The Windmill), which comes complete with sails like the Moulin Rouge in Paris and is currently being entirely revamped: locals hope this will be the first step in Paral.lel's eventual return to glory. A handful of other historic theatres have also survived along this street, but these now occupy modern premises: the only exception is the graceful, but long closed, little Teatre Arnau, built in 1894.

For now, Paral.lel functions merely as a busy throughfare, linking the Plaça d'Espanya with the port, and dividing the neighbourhoods of El Raval and Poble Sec.

➕ 56 D8 ✉ Avinguda Paral.lel
🚇 Diagonal

CAIXAFORUM

▷ 60.

CENTRE DE CULTURA CONTEMPORÀNIA DE BARCELONA (CCCB)

www.cccb.org

Stunning modern architecture is one of the highlights of a visit to the CCCB. This bustling arts centre behind the MACBA (▷ 68–69), and was transformed from a 19th-century workhouse, the Casa de la Caritat. The entrance is through an elegant courtyard and its key feature is the mural on the wall in front of you, which has a floral and harp motif that has survived from the original building. On the left the restructuring work of the CCCB takes shape in an impressive steel-and-glass structure topped by an exterior mirror that lets you see the cityscape behind.

CCCB stages a wide variety of cutting-edge shows and events and there is no permanent collection on display. The annual independent short film festival is held here, and the CCCB is taken over every June by thousands of fans of modern music for the international techno and multi-media festival Sónar (▷ 255). It also hosts the annual Hipnotik festival, celebrating the art of graffiti. Events range from conferences on 'culture jamming' to exhibitions on the Parisian Surrealist movement. Be prepared for anything.

➕ 57 F8 ✉ Carrer de Montalegre 5, 08001 ☎ 93 306 41 00 🕐 Tue–Wed, Fri–Sun 11–8, Thu 11–10 💷 Adult €4.50, child (under 16) free 🚇 Catalunya 🚌 16, 17, 24, 59 and all lines to Plaça de Catalunya 🖥 🏛

Opposite *The lovely cloister of the Gothic Antic Hospital Santa Creu*

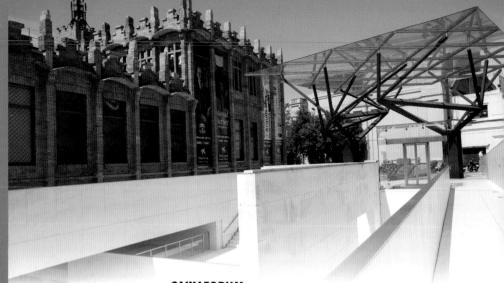

INFORMATION

www.fundacio.lacaixa.es

➕ 56 C8 ✉ Avinguda del Marquès de Comillas 6–8, 08038 ☎ 93 476 86 00 🕐 Tue–Fri, Sun 10–8, Sat 10–10 ✋ Free 🚇 Espanya 🚌 9, 27, 30, 56, 57, 65, 79 and all routes to Plaça d'Espanya 🍴 ♿

CAIXAFORUM

Opened in 2002, this is one of the city's most vibrant art spaces. The museum is funded by La Caixa, Catalonia's largest bank, and has been praised by both the art world and residents since it opened. A disused textile factory known as the Casaramona, one of the jewels of Spanish industrial architecture by the Modernista master Josep Puig i Cadafalch (1867–1957), was faithfully restored to hold the Forum's exhibition spaces, an auditorium and a research centre. Its patio and entrance were added by Japanese architect Arata Isozaki, who also designed the Palau Sant Jordi (▷ 59).

THE COLLECTION

Contemporary art in all its forms is the Forum's main agenda. The collection of 950 pieces was first started in 1985 and has grown into the most important of its type in Spain. The permanent collection is shown on a rotating basis, changing three times during the year.

The Forum also hosts other activities, ranging from concerts to puppet shows. A full programme is available at the entrance or you can check online (website in Catalan and Spanish only).

THE EXHIBITS

After crossing the patio embedded with lights, you are greeted at the entrance by a huge abstract mural in primary shades by Sol LeWitt. From here, elevators take you up to the three exhibition spaces; one for the permanent collection and two dedicated to works on loan. The rooms lead onto a sunny, central interior patio, the setting for music recitals.

The startling *Room of Pain* by the German conceptual artist Joseph Beuys is often hailed as the collection's most powerful work. But there are also pieces by artists of the calibre of Tàpies, Julian Schnabel, Susana Solano and other international and national names covering the full gamut of modern and contemporary art from the 1970s to the present day. Note that works are constantly being rotated, as well as being lent to other La Caixa cultural centres across the country, so phone ahead if there are specific pieces you want to see.

The quality of the temporary exhibitions held here has been equally high, with names like Picasso, Renoir and Matisse featuring prominently, while a homage to architect Mies van der Rohe (whose pavilion is across the road from the Forum, ▷ 76) has also won praise.

Above *The patio and entrance to the CaixaForum was designed by Arata Isozaki, who also designed the Palau Sant Jordi at L'Anella Olímpica*

FOMENT DE LES ARTS I DEL DISSENY

www.fad.cat

Barcelona is a reference point for professionals working in all fields of design. From a park bench to a paint can, many of the city's home-grown objects and products have received the *disseny* (design) touch. Foment de les Arts i del Disseny (FAD) is the body much credited with consolidating this tradition. Founded more than a hundred years ago, the headquarters is now in a renovated Gothic convent. The organization's aim is to bring the general public and design worlds closer together through a full calendar of exhibitions and events. These include MerkaFad, where young fashion designers are given space within the FAD to market their wares, and the enormously popular Tallers Oberts (Open Workshops), an annual week-long event where artists give free lessons in their crafts all over El Raval. Exhibitions act as a showcase for national and international designers in all fields, whether it be jewellery, textiles or graphic design, and are changed on a regular basis.

✚ 57 F8 ✉ Plaça dels Àngels 5–6, 08001 ☎ 93 443 75 20 🕐 Mon–Sat 11–9 (can vary according to exhibition) 🎟 Free 🚇 Catalunya or Liceu 🚌 14, 18, 38, 59 and all routes to Plaça de Catalunya 🍴

FONT MÀGICA

The northern slopes of Montjuïc were newly landscaped for the Universal Exhibition of 1929, which bequeathed a number of fine pavilions and gardens to the city. But perhaps the loveliest survivor of all is the Font Màgica, a truly magical fountain designed by Carles Buigas, which uses acrobatic water displays, music and colours to create one of the city's most enchanting spectacles. The original mechanism still functions after almost a century of use, although the music—which now usually includes the 1992 anthem 'Barcelona' by Freddie Mercury and Montserrat Caballé—has been updated. Traditionally, an enormous firework show takes place around the Font Màgica at the end of the Festa de la Mercè, Barcelona's biggest annual festival. It is one of the best free events in the city, and attracts around 250,000 people every year.

✚ 56 C8 ✉ Plaça d'Espanya, 08038 🚇 Espanya

FUNDACIÓ JOAN MIRÓ

▷ 62–63.

JARDÍ BOTÀNIC

www.jardibotanic.bcn.es

Opened to the public in 1999, the Jardí Botànic is a superb example of contemporary landscape gardening. Geometric paths and staircases run throughout the inclined terrain, creating a modern topography. The garden focuses on Mediterranean vegetation, with sections dedicated to particular countries with a Mediterranean climate. In the Australian section you can see indigenous species such as eucalyptus, while the California section is replete with various species of cacti. The Iberian species occupy the large perimeter of the garden and the other countries' flora are laid out within this. Try to visit in spring when the native flowers are in bloom. The garden has been praised by park and garden experts all over the world and sets the standard for future projects of this type.

✚ 56 C9 ✉ Doctor Font i Quer s/n, Parc de Montjuïc, 08038 ☎ 93 426 49 35 🕐 Jun–end Aug daily 10–8; Apr–end May, Sep daily 10–7; Feb–end Mar, Oct daily 10–6; Jan, Nov–end Dec 10–5 🎟 Adult €3.50, child (under 16) free, Sun afternoon free 🚇 Paral.lel (then funicular) 🚌 50, 55, PM 🍴

MONTJUÏC

▷ 64–66.

MUSEU D'ARQUEOLOGIA DE CATALUNYA

▷ 67.

MUSEU D'ART CONTEMPORANI DE BARCELONA

▷ 68–69.

MUSEU ETNOLÓGIC

www.museuetnologic.bcn.es

This fascinating museum offers a journey through the world of artefacts from ancient (and not-so-ancient) cultures, with more than 10,000 items from each of the continents. Highlights include wonderfully intricate robes from Euristan, and breathtaking jewellery made of beads and butterfly wings from the Amazon; even the crude clothing and tools from Pyrenean shepherd communities are intriguing. Spend time drawing parallels between different cultures, and ponder how little basic design has changed over time. The exhibits are well laid out and there are explanations in English. The vistas of the city skyline from the windows are marvellous.

✚ 56 C9 ✉ Passeig de Santa Madrona s/n, 08038 ☎ 93 424 68 07 🕐 Jun–24 Sep Tue–Sat 10–6, Sun 10–2, 3–8; 25 Sep–end May Tue, Thu, Sat 10–7, Wed and Fri 10–2, Sun 10–2, 3–8 🎟 Adult €3.50, child (under 16) free 🚇 Espanya 🚌 55

Below *Foment de les Arts i del Disseny*

INFORMATION

www.bcn.fjmiro.cat

✚ 56 D9 ✉ Parc de Montjuïc, 08038 ☎ 93 443 94 70 🕐 Jul–end Sep Tue–Sat 10–8, Sun 10–2.30 (also Thu 10–9.30); Oct–end Jun Tue–Sat 10–7 (also Thu 10–9.30), Sun 10–2.30 ✋ Adult €8.50, child (under 14) free. Temporary exhibitions only: adult €4, child (under 14) free 🚇 Paral.lel then Funicular de Montjuïc 🚌 50, 55, PM 🎧 Audiotour €4 in English, French, Catalan, Spanish, German, Japanese and Italian. Guided tours in Catalan and Spanish only, temporary exhibition Sat 11.30pm, permanent exhibition Sun 11.30pm, free 📖 Very good, pocket-size guidebook available in Spanish, Catalan, English, French and Japanese for €13 🍴 Stylish café-restaurant with summer terrace 🛍 Two shops, one with an excellent selection of books about Miró and his contemporaries and the other selling gifts and gadgets

Above *The Fundació Joan Miró is one of the world's best gallery spaces*

INTRODUCTION

The Fundació Joan Miró, housed in a gleaming white building on the hilltop of Montjuïc with panoramic views across the city, is the perfect setting in which to appreciate the work of this extraordinary Catalan artist. The simple white walls, terracotta flagstones and arched roofs neatly complement the vibrancy of Miró's work, symbolized by its childlike shapes and bold use of primary tones. Much of the collection of more than 14,000 pieces, with more than 200 paintings, by this most prolific and iconic of Catalan artists is displayed in 10 purpose-built galleries and bathed in natural light. You can wander around at will, but for a greater understanding of Miró's work you should take the audiotour, which helps to explain the motivation and political statements behind some of the paintings and sculptures.

Joan Miró (1893–1983) was born into a family of artisans. He moved to the town of Montroig in his early twenties, where he decided to take up painting. Miró was sometimes described as a visual poet, whose work could be enjoyed simply for its vivid tones and animated forms. Instantly recognizable and symbols of the city itself, Miró's trademark figures include birds, women, Catalan peasants (a metaphor for his deep-rooted sense of Catalan identity) and above all heavenly stars, all portrayed with sweeping brushstrokes in his famed palette of red, yellow, blue and green. The Fundació Joan Miró was established by Miró himself not just as a permanent setting for his works but also as a focus for modern art in Barcelona, with a library, bookshop and auditorium as well as gallery spaces. The building was designed for Miró in 1972 by his friend Josep Lluís Sert, a Catalan architect who had also designed Miró's studio on Mallorca. The extensive collection, much of it donated by Miró, covers a wide range of styles, allowing you to trace his development from youthful realism to later experiments with Surrealism and abstract art, all in his own uniquely Miróesque style.

WHAT TO SEE

FOUNDATION TAPESTRY
This monumental tapestry was designed especially for the Fundació Joan Miró in 1979. It was produced in collaboration with Josep Royo, who had worked with Miró on a series of textiles which also incorporated aspects of painting and collage. The tapestry is all reds, greens, blues and yellows, with a star and crescent moon in the background. For the best views, you need to look at it from the upstairs gallery.

PORTRAIT OF A YOUNG GIRL
This charming portrait, dating from 1919, is full of lyrical expression and clearly shows the influence of Van Gogh as well as the medieval masters. It is in the Sala Joan Prats, named after Miró's friend, patron and art dealer who donated many of these works. The room has several examples of Miró's early style.

MAN AND WOMAN IN FRONT OF A PILE OF EXCREMENT
Despite the playful nature of much of his work, Miró was deeply political and this work from 1935 is an expression both of his Catalan identity and his anguish and foreboding at the approaching Spanish Civil War (1936–39). The bright tones of this painting are set off by powerful imagery, with apocalyptic scenes of darkness and broken limbs. It is displayed in the Sala Pilar Juncosa, named after Miró's wife, which contains items she donated.

MORNING STAR
Several paintings in the Sala Pilar Juncosa reveal the familiar themes which were starting to characterize Miró's style by the 1940s, with repeated images of women, stars, the moon and birds. His fascination with the night sky is particularly evident in this painting from 1940, which forms one of a series known as *Constellations*.

THE ROOF TERRACE
The rooftop terrace makes a good place to unwind, with quirky sculptures and dreamy views over the city. Among the items on display is *Caress of a Bird* (1967), a bronze sculpture covered in red, blue, green and yellow.

GALLERY GUIDE
BASEMENT
Room 13: Espai 13, dedicated to young artists
Rooms 14–15: Homage a Miró, works lent by other artists
GROUND FLOOR
Rooms 1–10: Temporary exhibitions
Rooms 11–12: Tapestry Room and Sculptures Room
Room 16: Sala Joan Prats
FIRST FLOOR
Room 17: Sala Pilar Juncosa
Rooms 18–20: Mid-life development, 1960–1970s
Rooms 21–22: Works on long-term loan from Japanese collector Kazumasa Katsuta, who owns the world's largest private collection of works by Miró

Below *Paintings and sculpture by Joan Miró in one of the galleries*

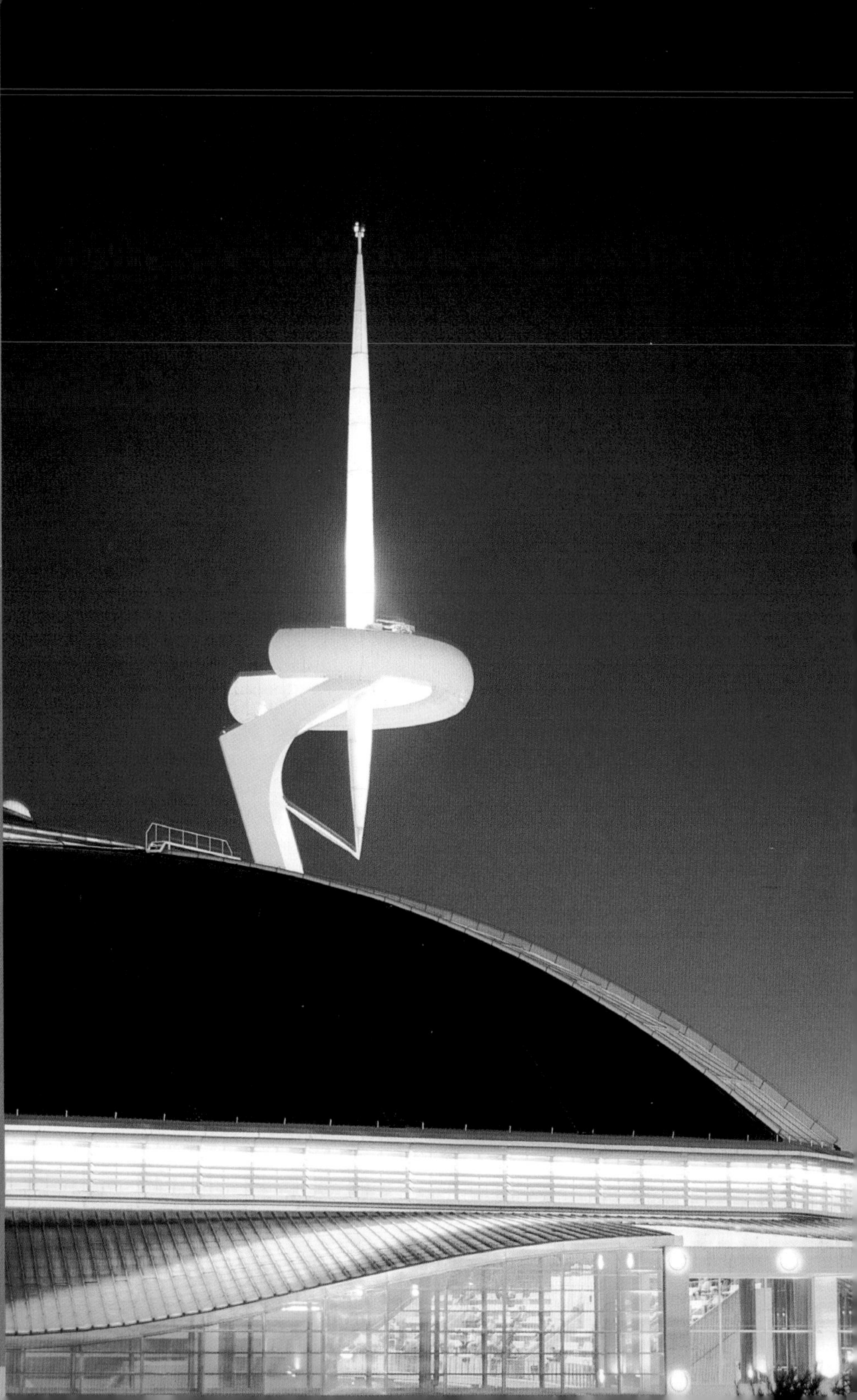

INTRODUCTION

The greenery of this mountain acts as the city's lungs and is the largest recreational area in Barcelona, with spectacular views across the city. Montjuïc is home to the stadium of the 1992 Olympic Games. The mountain juts out into the Mediterranean and is the first thing you notice if arriving by sea or air. A series of avenues winds through its woodland, drawing hundreds of joggers, cyclists and day trippers at weekends. Some of the city's top museums are here, such as the MNAC and the Fundació Joan Miró, as well as the Olympic Ring. Much of this is concentrated on the lower slopes, while the previously neglected higher sections are undergoing renewal. You can access the bottom of Montjuïc via the Plaça d'Espanya and Avinguda de la Reina Maria Cristina. Take the funicular from Paral.lel station to the higher slopes. A *telèferic* (cable car) whisks visitors from the funicular exit up to the Castell de Montjuïc at the top of the hill.

Although it was the first part of the city to be colonized by the Romans—a shrine to Jupiter was found on the site—Montjuïc's lack of any substantial water source meant that it was unsuitable for residential development. The site was ignored for a long period, but it did become the city's cemetery. In 1929 its lower slopes were chosen as the site of the Universal Exhibition. In 1992, the main events of the Olympic Games took place here and now the local government is sprucing up neglected pockets, turning Montjuïc into the city's own Central Park.

WHAT TO SEE

CASTELL DE MONTJUÏC

King Felipe V ordered the construction of the first fortification on this spot in 1640, in order to keep watch on the rebellious Catalans. Expanded and remodelled, it later functioned as a prison for political activists, who were imprisoned, tortured and executed. At the culmination of the Spanish Civil War (1936–39), hundreds of republican prisoners were rounded up and shot at the fortress walls, including the President of the Catalan government, Lluís

INFORMATION

Montjuïc Information Office

✠ 56 D10 ✉ Passeig Santa Madrona 28, 08004 🕐 Mon–Sun 10–2 🚇 Espanya then No. 50, 55 or PM bus; Paral.lel then Funicular de Montjuïc; a cable car from Barceloneta, then a 10-minute uphill walk

Tourist Information Office

www.barcelonaturisme.com
ℹ Plaça d'Espanya 🕐 Jul–end Sep daily 10–8; Oct–end Jun 10–4

Opposite *The Palau Sant Jordi stadium was built for the 1992 Olympics*
Above *La Sardana sculpture celebrates the traditional Catalan dance*

Companys. The castle remained a prison until 1960, when it was converted for use as a military museum. In 2008, it was finally ceded to the city of Barcelona and is being transformed into an international centre of peace.

✚ 56 C10 ✉ Parc de Montjuïc, 08004 ☎ 93 329 86 13 🕐 Nov to mid-Mar Tue–Sun 9.30–5; mid-Mar to end Oct Tue–Sun 9.30–7 🖐 Adult €3, child (under 14) free ▢ 🏛

THE HIGHER SLOPES

The five-star Hotel AC Miramar stands on the most sea-facing point of Montjuïc's summit. Up here you'll also find a couple of sculptures, *La Sardana*—a ring of young people performing Catalonia's traditional dance—being the most famous. The Jardins Cinto Verdaguer, behind the cable-car station to the top of the mountain, are full of perfect picnic spots, particularly next to the lily ponds. The nearby Jardins Joan Brossa are beautifully landscaped and full of activities—including musical instruments for children and a path crossing the park made of musical 'cushions' that emit sounds when they are trodden on.

THE LOWER SLOPES

This part of the mountain is much more accessible, reached via the ceremonial Avinguda de la Reina Maria Cristina that houses two huge trade-fair buildings on either side. At the end of the avenue, the MNAC (▷ 72–75), the Mies van der Rohe Pavilion (▷ 76) and the CaixaForum (▷ 60) are within easy reach, and the rest of the landscaped gardens and sights can be navigated via a series of escalators. The outdoor Teatre Grec (▷ 77), used only during the festival of the same name (▷ 255), its picturesque gardens and La Font del Gat (a restaurant and information centre) can be found slightly farther up the mountain. The latter, between the Teatre Grec and the Fundació Joan Miró (▷ 62–63), is a curious building. It is attributed to Puig i Cadafalch and has been returned to its original use as a fashionable outdoor restaurant (summer only). Only the baroque facade of the original remains but its charm is intact.

Below *Teatre Grec was built by Ramon Raventos in 1929*

MUSEU D'ARQUEOLOGIA DE CATALUNYA

The city's archaeological museum occupies a pink-and-cream Noucentista (an early 20th-century Catalan cultural movement opposed to Modernism) pavilion, originally built for the 1929 Universal Exhibition. The museum's fine collection of ancient finds is attractively laid out in modern, well-lit displays.

THE COLLECTION

Objects date from as far back as 40,000BC, and there are exhibits from the Bronze Age, plus finds relating to the Greeks, Phoenicians and Etruscans. Although most of the displays are of predominantly Catalan origin, there are some substantial finds from the Balearic Islands, which were under Catalan control during the Middle Ages. Look for the collection of Punic jewellery and terracotta goddesses found at a dig in Ibiza, and an exquisite display of Greek jewellery from Mallorca, with a particularly magnificent necklace formed of delicately wrought leaves and flowers.

FINDS FROM EMPÚRIES

The most spectacular and extensive discoveries come from Empúries, a Greek settlement founded in the sixth century BC (▷ 214). The Romans arrived in Catalonia in 218BC, using Empúries as an entry point, and the settlement grew into a wealthy little city as trade flourished: the port once supplied markets around the Mediterranean with olives, nuts, wine and wheat. Artefacts from Empurion form the core of the museum's outstanding Roman collection, with huge quantities of Roman glassware, kitchen utensils and other everyday items. Most dazzling of all are the extensive mosaics, which include a charming depiction of the Three Graces and the celebrated Mosaic de Belerofont i la Quimera, which shows the Greek warrior Bellerophon grappling the fire-breathing monster.

INFORMATION

www.mac.cat

✚ 56 D9 ✉ Passeig de Santa Madrona 39–41, Parc de Montjuïc, 08038 ☎ 93 423 21 49 🕐 Tue–Sat 9.30–7, Sun 10–2.30 🎫 Adult €3, child (under 16) free Ⓜ Espanya 🚌 55 🚌

Above *The archaeological museum occupies a pavilion originally built for the 1929 Universal Exhibition*

MACBA MUSEU D'ART CON...POR

INFORMATION

www.macba.cat

✚ 57 F8 ✉ Plaça dels Àngels 1, 08001
☎ 93 412 08 10 🕐 24 Jun–24 Sep
Mon, Wed, Fri 11–8, Thu 11am–12am,
Sat 10–8, Sun 10–3; 25 Sep–23 Jun
Mon, Wed–Fri 11–7.30, Sat 10–8, Sun
10–3 🖐 Adult €3, child (under 14)
free; temporary exhibitions: adult €6,
child (under 14) free; free the day after
a temporary exhibition is opened;
combined admission: adult €7.50, child
(under 14) free; Wed (except hols) €3.50
🚇 Catalunya 🚌 9, 14, 16, 17, 22, 24,
38, and all routes to Plaça de Catalunya
🚶 Guided tours of permanent collection
Mon 6pm (English); Wed and Thu 6pm,
also Sat 12pm and 6pm, Sun 12pm
(Catalan); Fri 6pm (Spanish); audiotour
included in admission price 📖 Large
format catalogue of the permanent
collection for €30 ☕ Café is shared with
the CCCB; there are a number to pick from
outside 🎁 Very good gift and bookshop
selling books about contemporary art,
catalogues from past exhibitions and
designer objects and accessories

Above *Swathes of white and glass greet
you at the facade of the museum*

INTRODUCTION

This dramatic structure, one of the most architecturally ambitious museums
in Spain, opened in 1995. This museum of contemporary art was established
considerably later than similiar institutions, and frankly admits that it was too
late to acquire pieces by groundbreaking artists such as Cézanne or Picasso,
or even Pollock, Johns or Warhol. As a result, the MACBA decided to focus on
emerging artists in a variety of contemporary media. What you see will depend
almost entirely on when you go. Although there is a permanent collection
focusing on modern art of the late 20th century to the present day, with works
by Catalan and Spanish artists including Antoni Tàpies, Miquel Barceló and
Eduardo Chillida, a system of rotation means that only a small amount is on
display at any one time. Much of the gallery space is given over to temporary
and frequently challenging exhibitions of contemporary and avant-garde
painting, sculpture, photography, video and conceptual art. The audioguide is an
extremely useful tool to help you understand what's there.

The MACBA was conceived as the focus of an ambitious project of urban
renewal encompassing the entire district of El Raval. Once a byword for
poverty and social decay, by the 1990s El Raval was in desperate need of
reform. Tenement blocks in cramped, narrow streets were torn down almost
overnight in an attempt to let in the light and create airy, open spaces. At the
same time, Barcelona was looking for a suitable spot for a first-class museum
of contemporary art. Richard Meier's stunning museum has succeeded on
both counts. Visitors and locals now flock to El Raval and the area around the
MACBA, with its new restaurants, cafés, galleries and boutiques.

WHAT TO SEE

THE BUILDING

The luminous white facade of Richard Meier's contemporary art museum
dominates Plaça dels Àngels, the large open square on which it stands in
the northern half of El Raval. Natural light floods into the building through

swathes of glass, designed to create a dialogue between the museum and its surroundings. Inside the museum, the overwhelming impression is of space and light, with gentle ramps connecting the different floors and creating a sense of fluid movement through the galleries.

DAU AL SET
This Catalan surrealist movement, whose name, Dau Al Set, means the seven-spotted dice, was founded in the late 1940s by Joan Brossa (1919–98), Barcelona's celebrated visual poet. Typical of Brossa's style is his *Poema-Objecte* (1956), a straw broom with a handle fashioned out of dominoes. The aim of such pieces was to provoke a reaction through the medium of everyday items, using a juxtaposition between two apparently unrelated items to set off a chain of associations in the mind of the onlooker.

HIA
The Spanish painter Antonio Saura was born in the small Pyrenean town of Huesca in 1930. In 1957 he helped to form the El Paso avant-garde movement, whose first exhibition in Barcelona brought him into contact with artist Antoni Tàpies and other members of Dau Al Set. *Hia* (1958) is one of Saura's most powerful works, a monochrome portrait of the female body which was heavily influenced by Goya and his black paintings series, which are on display at the Prado in Madrid.

CAPELLA MACBA
Opposite the MACBA, the former Convent dels Àngels, a handsomely renovated Gothic complex, is now the headquarters of FAD (Foment de les Arts i del Disseny; ▷ 61). This is Barcelona's main contemporary design body, and its exhibitions neatly complement those at the MACBA across the square. Part of the complex, a beautiful Renaissance chapel found just off the Plaça dels Àngels, is now permanently dedicated to MACBA exhibitions. The museum's exciting, newest space, the centuries-old stone vaults and thick walls of the Capella MACBA form a striking contrast with the contemporary artworks on display in the galleries within.

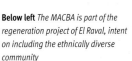

Below left *The MACBA is part of the regeneration project of El Raval, intent on including the ethnically diverse community*
Below *The light and airy interior*

MUSEU MARÍTIM

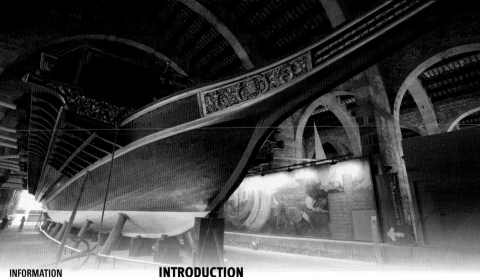

INFORMATION

www.museumaritimbarcelona.com
✚ 57 F10 ✉ Avinguda de les
Drassanes s/n, 08001 ☎ 93 342 99
20 ⓘ Mon–Sun 10–8 (last entry
at 7pm). *Santa Eulàlia*: May–end
Oct Tue–Fri 12–7.30, Sat–Sun 10–7;
Nov–end Apr Tue–Fri 12–5.30, Sat–Sun
10–5.30 🖐 Adult €2.50, child (7–16)
€1.25, child (under 7) free (this general
ticket includes admission to shipyards
and *Santa Eulàlia*); first Sat of every
month free to all after 3pm. Temporary
exhibitions: prices vary. Planetarium: €3
🚇 Drassanes 🚌 14, 18, 36, 38, 57,
59, 64, 91 🎧 Audiotours in Spanish,
Catalan, English, French, German, Italian
and Japanese included in admission price
📖 Pocket guidebook available in French,
Italian, Spanish, Catalan and English.
€7 ☕ Full café service available with a
terrace overlooking the gardens 🏛 Sells
nautical-related books and souvenirs,
good gifts for children

INTRODUCTION

The royal shipyards are the finest example of their kind in the world. Here you can learn about Barcelona's maritime history in one of the city's most impressive museums, in terms of both its setting and contents.

The soaring arches and columns of the former Drassanes Reials (royal shipyards) make an elegant and highly appropriate setting for a museum devoted to the city's long relationship with the sea. Beneath the Gothic naves of this secular cathedral is an impressive collection of fishing boats, yachts, seafaring memorabilia and a full-scale replica of a royal galley. The visit is made more enjoyable by an entertaining audiotour, referred to as The Great Sea Adventure, with everything from a simulated storm at sea to the conversations of emigrants leaving Barcelona by steamer for a new life in South America. The exhibits are arranged in a logical order and it's easy to follow the floor plan that you can pick up. The museum has recently been extended, providing space for temporary exhibitions. These often include big blockbuster international exhibitions, such as 'The Treasures of King Tutankhamun'.

The Drassanes Reials were built, and sections and strongholds added, between 1283 and 1612, replacing the smaller Arab-built shipyards that formerly occupied the same site. The royal shipyards provided warships for the Catalan Crown at a time when Catalonia was a major power in the Mediterranean, with conquests including the Balearic Islands, Sardinia, Sicily and Naples. Originally standing on the water's edge so that vessels could be pulled up for repair, the shipyards consisted of a series of long parallel aisles facing the sea. All the great European seafaring cities, such as Venice, had their own covered shipyards, but Barcelona is the only city to have conserved the original layout and these are the finest example of their kind in the world. The Drassanes Reials continued to be used for shipbuilding until the end of the 17th century.

WHAT TO SEE
FIGUREHEADS

Figureheads served a variety of functions. On warships they acted as a deterrent, using symbolism such as lions, warriors and sea monsters to strike fear into the hearts of the enemy and prey on man's deep fears of the sea. At other times they

Above La Galera Real, *a replica of the
1568 royal galley built in the shipyards*

served a religious or decorative purpose. The figureheads on display were mostly retrieved from Catalan sailing vessels of the 19th century. Among the most impressive is the Negre de la Riba, a figure of a Native American warrior.

LA GALERA REAL

The focal point of the museum is this spectacular replica of the royal galley built in these shipyards for Don John of Austria in 1568. This was the flagship of the squadron of the Holy League formed by Spain, Venice, Malta and the Papal States, which defeated the Turkish fleet at Lepanto in 1571 (▷ 31). It was this victory that ended Ottoman dominance throughout the Mediterranean. The replica was built in 1971 to celebrate the fourth centenary of the battle and its dimensions follow the original. It is 60m (197ft) in length and more than 6m (20ft) wide, with 59 oars rowed by 236 oarsmen, four to an oar, many of whom were chained to the benches as slaves.

The boat occupies the central aisle of the museum and you can walk right around its entire gilt and red lacquer hull, peeking into the hold and up onto the deck. It is worth taking a close-up look at the spectacular prow, with its lavish gilt carvings and figurehead of Neptune riding a dolphin.

SANTA EULÀLIA

The adventure does not end when you leave the magnificent shipyards. Across the road in the old port is the three-masted schooner *Santa Eulàlia*. Launched in 1918 as *Carmen Flores*, it has been used for a whole host of tasks, such as a trading ship and tourist boat. It was acquired by auction by the museum in 1997 and named after one of the city's patron saints. The masts and rigging have been rebuilt and restored to working order and the tall ship is once again fully seaworthy.

Left *Different eras of maritime history are brought to life*
Below *One of the items of seafaring memorabilia on display in the museum*

INFORMATION

www.mnac.es

✚ 56 C9 ✉ Palau Nacional, Parc
de Montjuïc, 08038 ☎ 93 622 03 75
🕐 Tue–Sat 10–7, Sun 10–2.30 ✋ Adult
€8.50, child (under 12) free. Temporary
shows: adult €3–5, child (under 12)
free. Free 1st Sun every month. Combined
ticket with Poble Espanyol: adult €12
🚇 Espanya 🚌 9, 13, 27, 30, 50,
55, and all routes to Plaça d'Espanya
☞ Free guided tour Sat and Sun at
12.30pm in Spanish, English, French,
German, Japanese; audioguides included
in admission price 📖 A range of
guidebooks focusing on different sections
of the collection: from €9 🍽 Restaurant
on second floor 🍵 Café on ground floor
at rear. Also summer-only café on terrace
by main entrance 🎁 Excellent gift shop
selling books on all the movements
covered in the museum plus assorted gifts

Above *The neo-baroque palace of the
MNAC houses art from Romanesque
to modern*

INTRODUCTION

The museum is housed in the Palau Nacional, the neo-baroque palace on
Montjuïc conceived by Josep Puig i Cadafalch (1876–1956) as the centrepiece
of the 1929 Universal Exhibition. This grandiose domed building is visible from
across the city and dominates the views of Montjuïc from Plaça d'Espanya
(▷ 76–77). The museum itself is divided into two main sections on the ground
floor, which are devoted to Romanesque and Gothic art, and two on the upper
level devoted to baroque and Renaissance and modern art. After passing
through the main entrance, you'll find the Romanesque galleries on the left
and the Gothic on the right, separated by a central hallway. The Romanesque
collection is divided into 21 rooms or ambits, with the frescoes displayed in
faithful reproductions of their original settings. Each of the ambits, in addition
to full-size works, displays explanatory photographs and scale models of the
churches that the frescoes came from. The Gothic gallery consists of 19 ambits,
and both galleries are broadly laid out in chronological order.

Romanesque art was the first great artistic movement to spread across
western Europe, between AD900–1200, reaching Catalonia through
pilgrims who crossed the Pyrenees on the medieval route to Santiago de
Compostela. It was designed for a community that was largely illiterate and
so is characterized by bright tones, vivid expressions and graphic imagery
to explain religious notions and biblical texts. However, until the late 19th
century, Romanesque art was largely ignored by art historians who considered
it unsophisticated in comparison with the richness of the Gothic and
Renaissance periods that followed. It was only in the early 20th century, when
collectors began to strip bare Catalonia's isolated Pyrenean churches, that the
nation woke up to the value of its Romanesque heritage. At the same time,
new techniques for stripping frescoes from walls were being developed in Italy,
allowing experts to remove the frescoes intact in order to protect them from

disintegration, vandalism and theft. In 1934 these treasures found a home in the Palau Nacional. The Italian architect Gae Aulenti was employed to restore the elegant arches and columns of the palace to create a suitable home for a comprehensive museum of Catalan art and it opened in its current form in 1995. In 2004, the museum underwent major refurbishment in order to house the city's collection of modern art, along with a small but wonderful collection of early photography and a fine numismatic collection. The museum now contains art spanning an entire millennium.

The MNAC is also home to the Cambó Collection, a bequest of Renaissance and baroque art from financier Francesc Cambó, including pieces by Rubens, Goya, Velázquez, Tintoretto and Gainsborough. The Thyssen-Bornemisza Collection, a selection of works by European artists, including the likes of Rubens and Huber, has joined the Cambó Collection. The Modern Art collection focuses on the glories of the Modernist movement, and has some outstanding decorative art pieces from the top architects and craftsmen of the period. Also here are the national Catalan collections of coins and photography, which are small but fascinating.

WHAT TO SEE
ROMANESQUE HIGHLIGHTS
Christ in Majesty

Christ in Majesty (room 5) was painstakingly removed from its original home in the remote Pyrenean church of Sant Climent de Taüll at the beginning of the 20th century. This magnificent fresco, painted c.1123, is from the apse of the church and is considered a masterpiece of Catalan Romanesque art. It depicts Christ with wide eyes and flowing hair, looking down upon humanity and holding up a book inscribed with the Latin words Ego Sum Lux Mundi (I am the light of the world). The portrait of Christ is set off by the intense blue pigment of a lapis lazuli background. The anonymous artist was influenced by French, Italian and Byzantine styles but managed to create a personal vision through his particular use of colour and geometric form, giving the work an unrealistic but striking feel.

Below Frescoes from the central apse of the church of Sant Climent de Taüll, depicting Christ in majesty, were sensitively remounted to show how they would originally have been seen

Batlló Majesty

This extraordinarily well-preserved wooden sculpture dating from the mid-12th century (on display in room 8) depicts Christ on the Cross in royal robes, triumphant at the moment of death. His expression transcends suffering, as he looks downwards impassively, already detached from the world of men. This extremely rare piece is noted for its delicate craftsmanship and for the fact that it still has most of its original colours. This styling also betrays a Syrian influence.

GOTHIC HIGHLIGHTS

Conquest of Mallorca

Works of art with a civil theme are also on display at the MNAC. The powerful merchant class of the Middle Ages used the Gothic form to celebrate their achievements and display their wealth. The fragments of this painting (*c.*1285–90), in room 22, formed part of an epic depiction of different episodes of the conquest of Mallorca by Jaume I in 1229. It once decorated the Palau Berenguer d'Aguilar, now part of the the Museu Picasso (▷ 142–143). Its vibrant dynamism and the artist's singular use of narrative give this work a comic-book feel.

Madonna of the Councillors

This painting by Luís Dalmau, in room 32, is rich in political symbolism and dates from the mid-1440s. It was commissioned by the Barcelona city council to show the power and sanctity of the city's rulers by cleverly blending secular and religious imagery. The picture shows the Madonna and Child sitting upon a throne resting on four lions surrounded by several portraits of prophets. The five councillors who commissioned the work are kneeling piously at her feet. The contract for the painting, which stipulates that a faithful and holy representation of the donors be made, still exists.

Altarpiece of St. Michael and St. Stephen

Among the many important Catalan Gothic artists represented in these galleries is Jaume Huguet, one of the most brilliant and innovative artists of the age. The central compartment of this grand altarpiece (*c.*1455–60) is in room

Above left *Retable of St. Barbara*
Above right *The museum entrance hall*

34, and was originally in the church of Santa Maria del Pí (▷ 111). It depicts St. Michael holding a cross in his right hand and a sword in his left hand, having slain the apocalyptic dragon. He daringly challenges the viewer by looking directly out of the painting.

THE THYSSEN-BORNEMISZA COLLECTION

In 1993, the extensive private collection belonging to the Austrian Baron Hans-Heinrich von Thyssen-Bornemisza was bought by the Spanish state. Although the majority of the work now resides in the huge museum named after the Baron in Madrid, a small selection was sent to Barcelona. The Thyssen-Bornemisza collection is a global view of European art from the 13th to 18th centuries and was amassed over two generations by the Baron's family.

The Madonna of Humility

The jewel of this collection strikes you upon entering the first hall (room 48): Giovanni da Fiesole's (or Fra Angelico, 1395/1400–1455) *Madonna of Humility* was executed in the 1430s and marks a great moment in Florentine painting. The wholeness of the compositional elements, such as the sumptuous curtain, the cherubs with their musical instruments and the delicate features of both the Virgin and the infant Jesus, is a conscious step by Fra Angelico and his contemporaries to lend religious art a more humanistic touch.

The Virgin and Child with St. John and St. Isabel

This outstanding work by Peter Paul Rubens (1577–1640), from which many versions were made, portrays the meeting between the Holy Family and St. John and St. Isabel, a popular subject for Florentine painters during the Renaissance. The painting was completed in 1618 and is a religious subject with heavy domestic overtones, making it a hugely popular work of the time.

MODERN ART HIGHLIGHTS

The term 'modern' will be misleading to some, as the collection is largely concentrated in the 19th century and finishes with the art deco movement. Although there are many paintings by the artists of the calibre of Casas, Fortuny and the Impressionist School of Olot, it is the decorative arts that make this collection truly outstanding. The Modernista furniture and fittings (including some outstanding pieces by Gaudí), even fireplaces and doorknobs, show the true richness of these dwellings and the life that went on inside them.

Above Christ on the Cross *by Francisco de Zurbaran (1598–1664)*
Below *The gardens surrounding the Palau Nacional are dotted with sculptures*

Ramon Casas and Pere Romeu on a Tandem

All of room 71 is dedicated to the work of Ramon Casas: painter, thinker, bohemian and one of the key figures of Barcelona's exuberant artistic movement, Modernisme. This emblematic painting originally hung in the restaurant Els Quatre Gats (▷ 126; a reproduction now hangs in the place of the original) and portrays the artists on a tandem bicycle with the waiter of Els Quatre Gats, Pere Romeu. It remains one of the most popular images of the time and a symbol of the movement.

FURNISHINGS FROM CASA LLEÓ MORERA

These pieces (room 73) originally resided in the home of Doctor Lleó Morera, a Modernista mansion in the famous Manzana de la Discordia (▷ 180–182) designed by Lluís Domènech i Montaner. The architect collaborated regularly with the Mallorcan-born master craftsman Gaspar Homar (1870–1955) and the magnificent furniture you see here is a superb example of his technique and genius. Homar employed an exotic mixture of woods and embellished his pieces with intricate inlaid motifs designed by popular artists of the period. In the next room you can see his creativity employed in a different medium: huge mosaic murals carried out with the help of artist Josep Pey (1875–1956).

PARC DE L'ESPANYA INDUSTRIAL

www.bcn.cat/parcijardins

In the run-up to the 1992 Olympic Games, Barcelona underwent a frenzied urban renewal that resulted in the building of new public places and squares. The Parc de l'Espanya Industrial, directly behind Sants station, is the largest and most ambitious of these very Catalan hard squares. You are first struck by the park's odd-shaped boating lake, complete with rowing boats for rent. It is flanked by an amphitheatre-type seating area and 10 futuristic, lighthouse-style watchtowers. The rest of the park is also dotted with public sculptures, predominantly of the post-modern school, and towards the southern end of the park there is a more urban woodland feel. The park underwent major renovation, completed at the end of 2009.

🕂 56 C7 ✉ Carrer de Watt 24, 08014 (access: Plaça dels Països Catalans and Carrer de Muntadas) 🕐 Daily 10–dusk 💲 Free 🚇 Estació de Sants or Hostafrancs 🚌 27, 30, 43, 44, 52, 53, 56, 57, 78, 109

PARC DE JOAN MIRÓ

www.bcn.cat/parcijardins

The Parc de L'Escorxador, more commonly known as the Parc de Joan Miró, was the first of a series of public parks to be laid out in locations made obsolete by their previous use, in this case the city's slaughterhouse or *escorxador*. The park looks decidedly barren on first approach. The towering sculpture *Dona i Ocell* (Woman and Bird) by Miró (1893–1983) is its focal point, and for many is the only thing worth closer inspection. But the main purpose of these areas is to provide light and space for a densely populated city. Palm trees are used to create avenues on the hard concrete surface, and pergolas, pines and evergreen oaks complete the landscape. Glimpses of the adjoining bullring, Las Arenas, through the vegetation lend the space a southern Mediterranean air. It's one of the few city parks where dog-walking is actively encouraged, and the absence of children's play areas make it very appealing to residents and workers in its immediate vicinity who are seeking out a tranquil spot. A massive refurbishment of the park was completed in 2008.

🕂 56 D7 ✉ Carrer d'Aragó 1, 08026 🕐 Daily 10–dusk 💲 Free 🚇 Espanya 🚌 9, 13, 27, 30, 38 and all routes to Plaça d'Espanya

PAVELLÓ MIES VAN DER ROHE

www.miesbcn.com

This pavilion was built by Ludwig Mies van der Rohe (1886–1969), one of the masters of modern architecture. While other architects were busy imitating Spanish baroque and Renaissance styles for the 1929 Universal Exhibition at Montjuïc, Mies van der Rohe built what was to become a classic of the international style. It is a key work in the development of functional architecture, with clean lines and austere interiors, using a diverse range of materials: travertine, marble, onyx, chrome and glass. Most critics consider it to be one of Mies van der Rohe's best works, remaining as a point of reference in 20th-century European architecture. He also designed a chair for his project, the Barcelona Chair, reproductions of which are sold in the city's top designer stores. The pavilion was dismantled after the exhibition and spent some time occupying a suburban plot. In the early 1980s, prominent architect and urban planner Oriol Bohigas started a campaign to have it moved back to its original site, which is where it now stands, exuding a tranquillity that brings relief from the exuberant Modernista buildings.

🕂 56 C8 ✉ Avinguda del Marquès de Comillas s/n, 08038 ☎ 93 423 40 16 🕐 Daily 10–8 💲 Adult €4.50, child (under 18) free 🎫 Wed and Fri in English, Catalan and Spanish; included in admission price 🚇 Espanya 🚌 13, 50, 55 and all routes to Plaça d'Espanya 🚇

PLAÇA D'ESPANYA

www.bcn.cat/fonts

Plaça d'Espanya is another of Barcelona's principal thoroughfares and landmarks. Originally designed to be the access point for the 1929 Universal Exhibition, the square is now a busy roundabout. The Plaça d'Espanya is the best way to approach Montjuïc, and many of its museums lie within a short walk. The two mock-Venetian bell towers mark the entrance of the two trade-show halls, the biggest and busiest in Spain. On the opposite side, the now-disused bullring Las Arenas, where the Beatles played in 1966, is currently being transformed into a shopping and entertainment centre due to be completed by end 2010. In the middle of the roundabout a classical Italianate fountain by Gaudí's protégé Josep Maria Jujol watches over the constant stream of traffic.

The main attraction in the immediate area itself is undoubtedly the Font Màgica (Magic Fountain): a sound, light and water spectacle. The spouting, illuminated water dances to a mixture of pop and opera classics, but almost always including the Olympic tune 'Barcelona', belted out by the late Freddie Mercury and the Catalan opera diva Montserrat Caballé. The Magic Fountain also co-stars with gigantic fireworks displays in

Below *The Venetian campaniles at the entrance to Plaça d'Espanya*

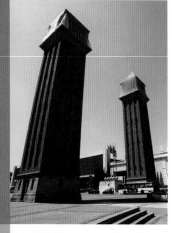

the city's festivals of *llum i aigua* (light and water) put on for grand occasions and events.

✚ 56 C8 ⊙ Magic Fountain displays: May–end Sep Thu–Sun every half-hour from 9.30pm—last show at 11pm; Oct–end Apr Fri–Sat every half-hour from 7pm—last show at 8.30pm 🖰 Free 🚇 Espanya 🚌 13, 50, 55 and all routes to Plaça d'Espanya

POBLE ESPANYOL
www.poble-espanyol.com

Where else would you get 115 examples of Spanish architecture in one place? The Poble Espanyol (Spanish Village) lying at the foot of Montjuïc was constructed for the 1929 Universal Exhibition and, curiously enough, its fake vintage buildings have now had enough time to look properly aged. The village also has its own community of artisans—both traditional and innovative—working away on textile painting, toy making, ceramics and other disciplines. Their goods are sold at the large, central craft market. The prestigious Massana design school also has its jewellery and engraving department inside the Poble Espanyol, further adding to its claim to be the City of Artisans.

Once you enter through the replica of the grand gateway to the walled city of Ávila and its huge Plaza Major, you'll find dozens of tiny streets laid out with architecture that includes whitewashed Andalusian homes and the high-Gothic style of Burgos. From the typical hanging balconies of Galicia to the mansions of Castile, all of the 17 regional Spanish vernaculars are crammed into its 23,000sq m (247,578sq ft). At night the place is buzzing with dozens of bars, a couple of cabaret-restaurants (including one of the best flamenco shows in the city) and some of Barcelona's top clubs. During the Barcelona Festival Grec, over the summer, the village's main square is used for outdoor concerts.

Despite being kitsch, the Poble Espanyol is a pleasant place to spend an afternoon in the city. It's also great for children, who like

to explore its wide spaces where they can let off steam.

✚ 56 C8 ✉ Avinguda del Marquès de Comillas 13, 08038 ☎ 93 508 63 00 ⊙ Tue–Thu 9am–2am, Fri–Sat 9am–4am, Sun 9am–12am, Mon 9–8 🖰 Adult €8, child (7–12) €5, child (under 7) free, free entry Sun 8pm–midnight. Combined ticket with MNAC €12 🚇 Espanya 🚌 9, 13, 38, 50, 55, 57, 91 🍴 🖰 🏧

POBLE SEC
The working-class neighbourhood of Poble Sec grew up on the lower flanks of Montjuïc in the 19th century, and gets its name (which means 'dry village') from the fact that it didn't receive its first public fountain until 1894. The fountain (which can still be found on Carrer Margarit) was the focus of a huge street party.

Even now, Poble Sec retains an old-fashioned, neighbourly feel, and celebrates numerous local festivals with considerable verve. It's become increasingly multicultural in recent years, and the old-fashioned taverns and grocery stores are being replaced with kebab shops and halal butchers. Although it was traditionally a humble, workers' neighbourhood, it is liberally smattered with modest Modernista mansions—not as grand as those found in the Eixample, but still charming. In recent years, it has become popular with a laid-back, bohemian crowd, and the streets and squares (particularly Carrer Blai and Plaça Surtidor) are now home to a slew of arty cafés and bars which come into their own after dusk.

✚ 57 E9 🚇 Poble Sec

RAMBLA DEL RAVAL
As part of the major regeneration of El Raval, a tangle of seedy, tenement-lined streets was bulldozed in 2000 to make way for the broad, palm-lined Rambla del Raval. It is lined with tall palm trees and benches, and a wide cross-section of the Raval's multi-ethnic community gathers on summer evenings to chat, play cricket, or kick a ball around. Cafés, restaurants and

bars are clustered around the edge, many with terraces, and there's an excellent fashion and crafts market here on summer weekends. Fernando Botero's huge bronze *Cat*, bought by the city in 1987 and shunted from park to park for years, has finally found a permanent home at the southern end of the Rambla, where local children ride its plump back and pull the sturdy whiskers. The latest addition to the boulevard is the dramatic Barceló Raval hotel (▷ 88), a neon-lit cone, endowed with a spectacular terrace bar (open to all) with 360-degree views.

✚ 57 E9 🚇 Sant Antoni

EL RAVAL
▷ 79.

SANT PAU DEL CAMP
▷ 78.

TEATRE GREC
The Teatre Grec, a large, open-air theatre built in the style of the Greek theatres of antiquity, was created in 1929 for Barcelona's Universal Exhibition. The theatre is the centrepiece of the city's main performing arts festival, the Barcelona Festival Grec (also known as the Barcelona Festival), and it provides a spectacular setting for theatre, ballet, contemporary dance and other events. The theatre is surrounded by ivy-covered stone walls, and its acoustics are considered excellent. The gardens, with their rose bowers and citrus groves, are entrancing, particularly in spring when the air is filled with the scent of orange blossom. During the Barcelona Grec Festival, an outdoor restaurant is installed in the gardens, which are romantically lit with candles and lanterns. The gardens were designed by the celebrated French landscape artist, Jean Claude Nicolas Forestier, who was responsible for most of the spectacular gardens created for the 1929 Universal Exhibition.

✚ 56 D9 ✉ Passeig Santa Madrona 36, 08004 ☎ 93 316 90 00 🚇 Poble Sec, Espanya 🚌 55, PM

INFORMATION
✚ 57 E9 ✉ Carrer de Sant Pau 99,
08001 ☎ 93 441 00 01 🕐 Mon–Fri
10–2, 6–7.45, Sat 10–2 ✋ Free; cloister
€3 🚇 Paral.lel 🚌 36, 57, 64, 91

SANT PAU DEL CAMP

This is Barcelona's oldest church, founded in the 10th century, and the finest surviving example of Romanesque architecture in the city. When it was built, it was surrounded by open fields and orchards, as recalled in its name, which means 'St. Paul of the Countryside'.

THE CHURCH

The church is thought to have been established by Guifré Borrell, son of the legendary founder of Catalonia, Guifré el Pilós (▷ 27), and replaced an earlier Visigothic church. A pair of columns from the older church, dating back to the seventh or eighth century, have been incorporated into the main portal. Romanesque sculptures, time-worn but still powerful, adorn the facade, including a hand of God above the main portal, flanked by a lamb, a lion, a winged man and an eagle—symbols of the apostles. There are also stubby ridges, the remnants of fortified walls, which serve as a reminder that the little church is all that survives of a larger Benedictine complex, destroyed twice by Moorish armies—in 985 and then in 1114.

Inside, a stone cupola floats above the small church, which is quiet, dimly lit and deeply atmospheric. The church was abandoned in 1835, and functioned briefly as an army barracks and then as a school. After the city-wide destruction of the Setmana Tràgica of 1909 (▷ 35), it was sensitively restored, the Gothic and baroque trappings stripped away to reveal the original thick stone walls and high slitted windows.

THE CLOISTER

A doorway leads to the real jewel of this complex: the exquisite, if miniature, cloister. Slender columns, each carved with a medieval menagerie of fabulous beasts, support delicate arches, clearly influenced by Mozarabic architecture. It's a peaceful space, and one of the loveliest and most unexpected corners in Barcelona. Just off the cloister, the tomb slab of Guifré Borrell, the church's founder and a leader of the nascent nation of Catalonia, bears the date 911.

Below *The Romanesque exterior of the church of Sant Pau del Camp*

EL RAVAL

The largest district of Barcelona's old town is El Raval (Catalan for 'the suburb'), and many say it's the true Barcelona. It is divided into two distinct areas. North of the Carrer de l'Hospital is the somewhat gentrified *barri* that contains the MACBA (▷ 68–69). South of here, in the direction of the port, lies the Barri Xino, a warren of tiny streets whose fame is of a less salubrious kind.

THE BARRI'S DEVELOPMENT

The 1920s writer Francesc Madrid dubbed the southern area El Chino, or Chinatown, because it reminded him of the ganglands of San Francisco. These days the local council is tearing down entire apartment blocks to widen its dank streets, most vividly around the Rambla del Raval for a new luxury hotel and new state-of-the-art cinema. The hotel, Barceló Raval, has opened (▷ 88), but the cinema is still under construction. But the district's reputation still lingers, so if you are exploring this part of El Raval, keep an eye on your wallet.

Farther north the ambitious town-planning projects for the area have borne fruit, particularly around the MACBA and the enormous Plaça dels Àngels. After its completion, it wasn't long before the surrounding streets started sprouting new bars, restaurants and galleries alongside the more traditional establishments selling *bacallà* (cod fish) and bed linen.

El Raval's major historic buildings include the Gothic Antic Hospital Santa Creu (▷ 59). The old chapel is now used as an occasional exhibition space, while the hospital itself houses the Catalan National Library. The latter is not open to the public, but the colonnaded cloister and garden (with pretty outdoor café) are accessible to all. To complete your tour of the *barri*, stop for a drink at the Plaça Martorell, a lively meeting place for locals.

INFORMATION

✚ 57 E9 🚹 Plaça de Catalunya 17, 08002 ☎ 93 285 38 34 🕓 Daily 9–9 Ⓜ Catalunya or Liceu 🚌 24, 120

Above *Skateboarding in El Raval*

EL RAVAL

This walk takes you through the heart of El Raval, past music halls and markets, art museums and monuments—both historic and contemporary. Amble down ancient streets and modern boulevards, window shopping in galleries and offbeat fashion boutiques, and pass a string of arty cafés and bars.

THE WALK

Distance: 2.5km (1.8 miles)
Time: 3 hours, including visits to museums
Start/end at: Paral.lel metro station

HOW TO GET THERE

Metro: Paral.lel station is on lines 2 and 3.
Bus: 36, 57, 64, 91 to Avinguda del Paral.lel.

★ Just outside the northern exit of the Paral.lel metro station is a small, triangular square overlooked by the historic facade of El Molino (The Windmill), complete with scarlet sails. If it reminds you of the famous Moulin Rouge in Paris, that's no coincidence: Paral.lel was once the heart of the city's theatre and cabaret district, and El Molino is one of very few pre-war survivors. Although the street is still

home to a handful of the city's top theatres, they now occupy bland, modern buildings. It's hoped that the renovation of El Molino will spearhead a movement to restore Paral.lel to its pre-war glory.

From Avinguda Paral.lel, turn right on Carrer de Sant Pau where you will soon see a little church set in a palm-filled garden on the right.

❶ The church of Sant Pau del Camp (▷ 78) was established in the 10th century and is the best preserved Romanesque monument in the city. When it was built, it was surrounded by fields *(camps)* and it remains a charming retreat from the city hubbub beyond its gates.

El Raval is the most ethnically mixed neighbourhood in Barcelona, home

to sizeable Pakistani, Moroccan, Philippino and South American communities. As you continue down Carrer de Sant Pau, you may notice that the sports centre on the right just beyond the church of Sant Pau doubles as a mosque. Turn left onto Rambla del Raval (▷ 77), a wide promenade lined with palm trees.

❷ A tangle of ancient streets were destroyed to make way for this modern Raval, which was created about a decade ago in an attempt to open up the neighbourhood. Now, it's home to a couple of modern hotels, including the distinctive and striking, conical Barceló Raval (▷ 88), which has a marvellous bar offering wonderful views, several arty cafés and bars, and a lively weekend market selling offbeat fashions during the summer.

Opposite *The beautiful cloister of the church of Sant Pau del Camp*

At the top of Rambla del Raval, turn right down Carrer de l'Hospital, named after the Antic Hospital Sant Creu (▷ 59), which you'll find hidden behind huge stone walls on the left.

❸ The Antic Hospital Sant Creu is now the Catalan National Library (not open to the public except on special occasions), but you can admire the stunning Gothic courtyard, with its tinkling fountains and fragrant orange trees. There's a wonderful outdoor café, El Jardí, tucked into one corner.

Take the northern exit from the courtyard and emerge on Carrer del Carme. A cluster of boho-chic cafés as well as a children's playground can be found on the corner with Carrer del Doctor Dou, which turns up to the left.

❹ This small street is a good example of the gentrifiation of the upper Raval, with its galleries and restaurants, shops selling organic produce and cool boutiques.

At the top of Carrer del Doctor Dou, you'll emerge onto the pretty, narrow street of Carrer d'Elisabets (which also has a handful of fashion shops). Turn left to reach Carrer dels Àngels, then right and then immediately left.

❺ Here you will find the dazzling, white Museu d'Art Contemporani de Barcelona (MACBA; ▷ 68–69), designed by Richard Meier and opened in 1995. This overlooks a vast square, hugely popular with the city's skateboarders, who skim up and down the ramps in front of the museum. The MACBA, along with the neighbouring CCCB (▷ 59), are the lynchpins of Barcelona's cutting-edge contemporary arts scene, with world-class exhibitions and a dynamic programme of cultural events. The neighbourhood

has become a hub for arty cafés and galleries, and the small shops along the Carrer Ferlandina, which leads east off the Plaça dels Àngels, is a good reflection of the Raval's alternative arts culture.

Continue walking straight ahead along Carrer Ferlandina until you reach the Ronda Sant Antoni, then turn left.

❻ You will be confronted by huge white tents, the temporary home (until 2013) of the Mercat de Sant Antoni. The original Modernista edifice, still visible, is being massively refurbished.

Continue down Ronda Sant Pau to return to the Paral.lel metro station, or consider picking up the purple line at Sant Antoni.

WHEN TO GO

Anytime is a good time to do this walk, although note that the MACBA is closed on Tuesdays, and the Mercat de Sant Antoni is closed on Sundays. Shops and cafés in this arty neighbourhood often won't open until 11am.

WHERE TO EAT

There are scores of great cafés in the area, including El Jardí in a Gothic cloister and another in the trendy CCCB (▷ 59).

EL JARDÍ

(▷ 83).

RESOLIS

The dark, atmospheric wood-panelled bar attracts a boho-chic crowd. It serves great tapas including plenty of vegetarian options.

✉ Carrer Riera Baixa 33, 08001 ☎ 93 441 29 48 ⏰ Mon–Sat 1pm–12am Ⓜ Liceu 🚌 14, 59, 91, 120

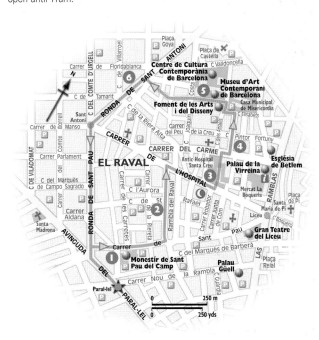

REGIONS **MONTJUÏC AND EL RAVAL** • WALK

SHOPPING

BUFFET I AMBIGU

www.catalogobuffet.com

Tucked down a passage behind the Boquería market, this small shop sells books for cooks, and many of them are in English. From Ferran Adría's collector's editions detailing his famous food experiments to collections of simple tapas recipes, there is something for all tastes.

☩ 91 F9 ✉ Passatge 1800 s/n, 08001 ☎ 93 243 01 78 ⊕ Mon–Fri 8.30–6 Ⓜ Liceu

CASTELLÓ DISCOS

www.discoscastello.com

The first Castelló Discos opened its doors in 1934 and the company now owns eight shops in the Raval area (based around Nou de la Rambla and Sant Pau). You'll find some rare and interesting imports among the CDs and discs.

☩ 91 F8 ✉ Carrer dels Tallers 3, 08001 ☎ 93 301 35 75 ⊕ Mon–Sat 10–2, 4.30–8.30 Ⓜ Catalunya

ESPAI RAS

www.rasbcn.com

This store is part bookseller and part exhibition space. The bookshop deals in national and international contemporary architecture and design publications. The exhibitions give young designers exposure, and recurring themes are urbanism and landscape design.

☩ 91 F9 ✉ Carrer del Doctor Dou 10, 08001 ☎ 93 412 71 99 ⊕ Tue–Sat 11–9 Ⓜ Catalunya

GIMENÉZ & ZUAZO

Gimenéz & Zuazo is one of the city's more prominent urban fashion labels for bold womenswear. The fabrics used are normally pure cotton or wool, which they jazz up with wild prints or appliqués. Look for their quirky hand-printed Boba T-shirt range.

☩ 91 F8 ✉ Carrer d'Elisabets 20, 08001 ☎ 93 412 33 81 ⊕ Mon–Sat 10.30–2.30, 5–8.30 Ⓜ Liceu

HERBOLARI

Established in 1927, this shop is dedicated to healing herbs from all over the world and its staff are experts with many years' experience. Follow their advice on the most suitable herbs for any complaint, and how best to prepare them, even if it's just a soothing drink. Credit cards are not accepted.

☩ 91 F9 ✉ Carrer d'en Xuclà 23, 08001 ☎ 93 301 14 44 ⊕ Sep–end Jul Mon–Sat 9–2, 4–8; Aug 9–2 Ⓜ Catalunya

LLIBRE D'OCASIÓ

Mercat del Llibre d'Ocasió attracts a diverse crowd outside the old Mercat de Sant Antoni every Sunday. The main theme here is books *(llibre)* and even if old books aren't your thing, it's pleasant to stroll around and there are numerous places to grab a bite to eat before lunch.

☩ 91 E8 ✉ Carrer del Comte d'Urgell 1, 08011 ☎ 93 423 42 87 ⊕ Sun 9–2 Ⓜ Sant Antoni

LORING ART

www.loring-art.com

This shop stocks more than 3,000 design and contemporary art titles, including classics and rare finds. In addition, enthusiasts will find a range of specialist magazines and books by independent publishers. Loring Art supports contemporary art festivals in Barcelona, which is often reflected in their creative window displays.

☩ 91 F8 ✉ Carrer de Gravina 8, 08001 ☎ 93 412 01 08 ⊕ Mon–Fri 10–8.30 Ⓜ Universitat

POBLE ESPANYOL

▷ 77.

Above *CaixaForum shop and lobby*

RIFT

www.riftshop.com

Right opposite the MACBA
(▷ 68–69), this shop-cum-exhibition space offers edgy street fashion for hip young men and women. To get the whole look, check out the range of shoes, bags and jewellery. Labels include Fly53, Junk de Luxe, Yes, No, Maybe, and Homecore, with footwear from Creative Recreation, Keds, Le Coq Sportif and more.
✚ 91 F8 ✉ Carrer de Ferlandina 31, 08001 ☎ 93 329 44 15 🕐 Tue–Sat 11–3.20, 4.30–8.30 🚇 Liceu

SANT ANTONI

This market's association with the best-quality food extends back into the 19th century. There's the food market inside, a fashion and general market (four days a week) outside and a second-hand book market in the street on Sunday mornings. The original Modernista buildings are currently being restored, and the temporary location is nearby on Ronda Sant Antoni.
✚ 91 E8 ✉ Carrer del Comte d'Urgell 1, 08011 ☎ 93 423 42 87 🕐 Food market: Mon–Thu, Sat 7–2.30, 5.30–8.30, Fri 7–8.30; clothes market: Mon, Wed, Fri–Sat 8–8 🚇 Sant Antoni

TWIGGY

Carrer d'Elisabets is one of the prettiest old streets of El Raval, with its high stone walls and clusters of leafy trees. There is a clutch of great boutiques here, including this chic little shoe store.
✚ 91 F8 ✉ Carrer d'Elisabets 20, 08001 ☎ 93 301 75 78 🕐 Mon–Sat 10.30–2.30, 4.30–8.30 🚇 Catalunya

ENTERTAINMENT AND NIGHTLIFE

BAR ALMIRALL

A long-established classic, the Almirall has a Modernista doorway and delicate stained glass. Inside, the white marble bar is also original. It is a relaxed, friendly local bar, with a faithful crowd of regulars mingling happily with the crowds of tourists who drop by to admire its original Modernista charms.

✚ 91 F8 ✉ Carrer de Joaquín Costa 33, 08001 ☎ 93 318 99 17 🕐 7pm–3am 🚇 Universitat

BCN ROUGE

Ring the doorbell to gain entry here. Its rooms are not vast, but have dark velvet walls bathed in candlelight. It's the perfect place for that romantic date, especially as the bar staff serve creative cocktails.
✚ 91 E10 ✉ Carrer del Poeta Cabanyes 21, 08004 ☎ 93 442 49 85 🕐 Thu 11pm–3am, Fri–Sat 11pm–4.30am 🚇 Paral.lel

BENIDORM

With its shrewd 1960s interior, Benidorm brings new life to the term kitsch, with retro gadgets placed throughout the bar. It is a light-hearted place for a drink to start the evening. Credit cards are not accepted.
✚ 91 F8 ✉ Carrer de Joaquín Costa 39, 08001 ☎ 93 317 80 52 🕐 Mon–Thu 7pm–2am, Fri–Sat 7pm–3am 🚇 Sant Antoni

BETTY FORD'S

The vibe is friendly and laid-back at this lively bar in El Raval, with a good mixture of arty young locals and ex-pats propping up the bar. They mix a mean cocktail here.
✚ 91 F8 ✉ Carrer de Joaquín Costa 56, 08001 🕐 Daily 5pm–2am 🚇 Universitat

BOADAS COCKTAIL BAR

Picasso and Hemingway were regulars here. The cocktails are among the best in town and it is a perfect place to stop for an aperitif. Credit cards are not accepted.
✚ 91 F8 ✉ Carrer dels Tallers 1, 08001 ☎ 93 318 88 26 🕐 Mon–Thu noon–2am, Fri–Sat noon–3am 🚇 Catalunya

CAFÉ TEATRE LLANTIOL

www.llantiol.com

This is a small, intimate theatre with a wide-ranging programme, spanning everything from clown or mime acts to dramatic monologues. It has become a popular venue for English-speaking comics—mostly from Britain or North America.

✚ 91 E9 ✉ Carrer de la Riereta 7, 08002 ☎ 93 329 90 09 ✋ From €3 🚇 Sant Antoni

CAIXAFORUM

www.fundacio.lacaixa.es

This arts centre opened in 2002 (▷ 60). It has art galleries, a good restaurant, a café and a shop. The large, modern auditorium plays host to a range of music events.
✚ 90 C8 ✉ Avinguda del Marquès de Comillas 6–8, 08038 ☎ 93 476 86 00 ✋ From €12 🚇 Espanya

GRANJA DE GAVÀ

This café serves juices, coffees and other drinks. The interior has plenty of candles, flowers and plants, and there are regular poetry readings, exhibitions and live music. Credit cards are not accepted.
✚ 91 F8 ✉ Carrer de Joaquín Costa 37, 08001 ☎ 93 317 58 83 🕐 Mon–Wed 8am–1am, Thu–Sat 8am–3am 🚇 Universitat

EL JARDÍ

Tucked away in a corner of the impressive Gothic courtyard of the Antic Hospital Sant Creu, this pleasant outdoor café is open year round for drinks, snacks and light meals. In the winter, heaters and blankets keep out the chill.
✚ 91 F9 ✉ Carrer de l'Hospital 56, 08001 🕐 Tue–Sun 10.30–10 🚇 Liceu

LONDON BAR

This art nouveau bar attracts a mix of locals and visitors, and there is sometimes live music and other acts ranging from trapeze to theatre. Credit cards are not accepted.
✚ 91 F9 ✉ Carrer Nou de la Rambla 34, 08001 ☎ 93 318 52 61 🕐 Daily 7pm–4am 🚇 Liceu

MARSELLA

Barcelona's oldest bar, dating back to 1820, Marsella is something of an institution. The dusty cabinets and marble-topped tables complement period mirrors on the walls and absinthe behind the bar.
✚ 91 F9 ✉ Carrer de Sant Pau 65, 08001 ☎ 93 442 72 63 🕐 Mon–Thu

10pm–2.30am, Fri–Sat 10pm–3.30am
🚇 Liceu

MOOG
www.masimas.com
Moog, although relatively small, stages some of the city's best DJ sets. The music varies from room to room. Credit cards are not accepted.
➕ 91 F9 ✉ Carrer de l'Arc del Teatre 3, 08002 ☎ 93 301 72 82 🕐 Daily 12am–5am 🖐 €10 🚇 Drassanes

TEATRE GOYA
www.teatregoya.cat
Teatre Goya opened in 1917 and its art nouveau auditorium has been well preserved. It stages a variety of theatre, ballet and musicals from a diverse range of companies.
➕ 91 F8 ✉ Carrer de Joaquín Costa 68, 08001 ☎ 93 343 53 23 🖐 From €23 🚇 Universitat

TEATRE ROMEA
www.teatreromea.com
This is one of Barcelona's most popular theatres. It has preserved its original structure and interior, including the magnificent entrance. All kinds of performance can be seen here, by well-known Spanish and international playwrights.
➕ 91 F9 ✉ Carrer de l'Hospital 51, 08001 ☎ 93 301 55 04 🖐 From €12 🚇 Liceu

TEATRE TANTARANTANA
www.tantarantana.com
This wonderful little theatre lies on the edge of Barcelona's historic theatre district (Avinguda Paral.lel). The auditorium is small (it seats just 145) but the theatre presents two excellent programmes: one for adults and another for children. The output is very varied, with everything from classic drama to dance for adults, and musicals and puppet shows for children.
➕ 91 E9 ✉ Les Flors 22, 08004 ☎ 93 441 70 42 🖐 From €7 🚇 Paral.lel

TEATRE VICTÒRIA
www.teatrevictoria.com
This area housed a proud cluster of theatres and concert halls in the early 20th century. Sadly, only a few remain as reminders of those glorious days: The Victoria is one of the original set, showing comedies, classical dance and flamenco.
➕ 91 E9 ✉ Avinguda del Paral.lel 67, 08004 ☎ 93 329 91 89 🖐 From €18 🚇 Paral.lel

LA TERRRAZZA
When the warm weather comes to the city, the party moves outside; at La Terrrazza you can dance under the stars in a stunning outdoor venue within the Poble Espanyol complex. The club attracts top international DJs. Come prepared to wait in line—this is one of the best summer clubs. There is a discount with the flyer, available from city-centre bars.
➕ 90 C8 ✉ Avinguda del Marquès de Comillas, 08004 ☎ 93 272 49 80 🕐 May–end Sep Fri–Sat midnight–6am 🖐 €15 🚇 Espanya

TINTA ROJA
It is worth making your way out to the unfashionable side of the town centre to experience this unusual nightspot, which mixes a New World Buenos Aires bohemian vibe with cabaret, tango acts and even a spot of trapeze to go with your drinks.
➕ 90 D9 ✉ Carrer Creu dels Molers 17, 08004 ☎ 93 443 32 43 🕐 Tue–Sat 9.30pm–2.30am 🚇 Poble Sec

SPORTS AND ACTIVITIES
BERNAT PICORNELL
www.picornell.cat
This swimming pool was renovated for the 1992 Olympic Games and as a result is one of the best in the city. There is a public gym with a complete range of sporting facilities. It is suitable for families. Credit cards are not accepted.
➕ 90 C9 ✉ Avinguda de l'Estadi 30–40, 08038 ☎ 93 423 40 41 🕐 Mon–Fri 7am–12am, Sat 7am–9pm, Sun 7.30am–8pm (until 4, Oct–end May) 🖐 Adult €9.65, child €5.95 🚇 Espanya

HEALTH AND BEAUTY
LA PELU
This hair salon is in the busy shopping area close to Carrer de Pelai. Not many hairdressers in Barcelona give you the opportunity to get online and surf the net while you wait. Booking is advisable.
➕ 91 F8 ✉ Carrer dels Tallers 35, 08001 ☎ 93 301 97 73 🕐 Mon–Sat 10.30–8 🖐 Women €35, men €20 🚇 Catalunya

MAILUNA
www.mailuna.net
This welcoming space offers a range of massages and therapies using all natural products. There is also a healthy restaurant. A number of courses and workshops are offered: check the website for details.
➕ 91 F8 ✉ Carrer de Valldonzella 48, 08001 ☎ 93 301 20 02 🕐 Daily 11–10 🖐 1hr facial from €58, 1hr massage €58, 30-min massage from €36 🚇 Universitat

FOR CHILDREN
CASTELL DE MONTJUÏC
Enjoy the view from the top of Montjuïc before visiting this castle, which has plenty to keep the kids entertained (▷ 65–66). Credit cards are not accepted.
➕ 90 C10 ✉ Passeig de Montjuïc 66, 08038 ☎ 93 329 86 13 🕐 Mid-Mar to end Oct Tue–Sun 9.30–8; Nov to mid-Mar Tue–Sun 9.30–5.30 🖐 Free 🚇 Para.lel, then funicular and Telefèric de Montjuïc

LA FONT MÀGICA
▷ 76–77.

FUNDACIÓ JOAN MIRÓ
▷ 62–63.

MUSEU MARÍTIM
▷ 70–71.

POBLE ESPANYOL
www.poble-espanyol.com
The Spanish Village holds workshops for families where you can try crafts like engraving. There are also demonstrations of traditional local customs such as folk dances and fiesta celebrations (▷ 77).
➕ 90 C8 ✉ Avinguda del Marquès de Comillas s/n, 08038 ☎ 93 325 78 66 🕐 Fri–Sat 9am–4am, Sun 9am–midnight, Mon 9–8, Tue–Thu 9am–2am 🖐 Adult €8, child €5, child (under 7) free. Family ticket €20 🚇 Espanya

PRICES AND SYMBOLS

The prices given are the average for a two-course lunch (L) and a three-course dinner (D) for one person, without drinks. The wine price is for the least expensive bottle.

For a key to the symbols, ▷ 2.

ÀNIMA

Ànima is a welcome addition to El Raval's legion of small trendy restaurants. The young staff are friendly and efficient, the dining room is decorated with avant-garde touches, but is still comfortable. The food bears all the hallmarks of fashionable cooking trends, such as balsamic ice cream, tuna in sesame crust and pea foam, and is incredibly tasty and satisfying. American Express is not accepted.

✚ 91 F9 ✉ Carrer dels Àngels 6, 08001 ☎ 93 342 49 12 🕐 Mon–Sat 1–4, 9–12. Closed lunchtimes Aug 🖐 L €20, D €25, Wine €12 🚇 Liceu

BAR RA

Bar Ra, behind La Boquería, is so popular that an extension has been added. It is great for a late breakfast or a health-conscious lunch or dinner, including Thai and West Indian fare. In summer, sit outside on the sunny terrace; in winter, a candlelit dining area is cosier. Credit cards are not accepted.

✚ 91 F9 ✉ Plaça de la Gardunya 3, 08001 ☎ 93 301 41 63 🕐 Daily 10am–12.30am. Breakfast 10–12.30, lunch 1–4 (until 4.30 Sat and Sun), dinner 9–12 (summer), 8.30–12.15 (winter) 🖐 L €15, D €30, Wine €9 🚇 Liceu

BIBLIOTECA

www.bibliotecarestaurant.cat
Biblioteca is a restaurant, even if its name means library, but it does come complete with its own collection of cookbooks for guests to scrutinize. The chef, who purchases all his ingredients fresh at the La Boquería market (▷ 120), constantly updates the menu. The different choices will encourage you to explore a range of new tastes. The eclectic dishes include oysters with dark beer, marinated tomatoes with basil and cod with clams.

✚ 91 F9 ✉ Carrer de la Junta de Comerç 28, 08001 ☎ 93 412 62 21 🕐 Mon–Sat 8–11.30 🖐 D €30, Wine €10 🚇 Liceu

BIOCENTER

www.restaurantebiocenter.es
Biocenter was one of the first vegetarian restaurants to appear in this part of town, and the scope of the menu has increased with demand. You will give the dishes top marks for imaginative presentation that makes good use of colour and texture, along with high-quality ingredients; for example the extensive salad bar displays a plethora of different leaves and vegetables. Other staple dishes are curries, couscous and pizza. Credit cards are not accepted.

✚ 91 F9 ✉ Carrer del Pintor Fortuny 25, 08001 ☎ 93 301 45 83 🕐 Mon–Sat 1–5, 8–11.15, Sun 1–5 🖐 L €12, Wine €10 🚫 Section 🚇 Catalunya

CA L´ISIDRE

www.calisidre.com
Over the last 25 years, this family-owned restaurant has perfected a

Above *Biblioteca restaurant*

dynamic, varied menu. Delicacies fall into two main groups: market cuisine and confectionery. The menu can change on a daily basis according to seasonal availability of some ingredients; for example, duck liver might be served with plums, chestnuts, puréed grapes or Chinese mandarins. Montse, Isidre's daughter, is the driving force behind the desserts, such as chocolate soufflé with coconut ice cream and apricot tart topped with toasted cumin seeds.

♥ 91 E9 ⊠ Carrer de les Flors 120, 08002 ☎ 93 441 11 39 🕐 Mon–Sat 1.30–4, 8.30–11. Closed public holidays, Easter week and 2 weeks in Aug 🖐 L €70, D €80, Wine €22 🚇 Paral.lel

CASA LEOPOLDO

This is a relatively unknown, yet outstanding restaurant in the old town. A mixture of Andalusian tavern, French bistro and Italian trattoria, it opened in 1929 and is well known in Barcelona for serving traditional Catalan dishes, such as fried fresh fish and oxtail stew, with some dishes varying according to season.

♥ 91 F9 ⊠ Carrer de Sant Rafael 24, 08001 ☎ 93 441 30 14 🕐 Mon–Sat 1–3.30, 8–11. Closed Easter and Aug 🖐 Lunch menu €40, set menus €49–€74.90, Wine €20 🚇 Liceu

FRAGILE

If you're at the MACBA (▷ 68–69), Fragile is a convenient place to stop for a bite to eat as it's just across the square. The kitchen serves both Mediterranean and Asian food, and weather permitting, guests can sit outside in the shade of the museum, facing a tile mural by the Basque artist Eduardo Chillida.

♥ 91 F8 ⊠ Carrer de Ferlandina 27, 08001 ☎ 93 442 18 47 🕐 Mon–Sat 10–2 🖐 L €15, Wine €8 🚇 Sant Antoni

HELLO SUSHI

www.hello-sushi.com

Hello Sushi is a rather hectic place known for its Japanese fast food. Enjoy a seaweed salad and the mixed tempura, or make use of the barbecue, upon which guests can grill food to their own tastes. Sushi and sashimi are also on the menu. To round off your meal, order one of the chef's sake cocktails. From time to time there are circus-style performances or poetry readings.

♥ 91 F9 ⊠ Carrer de la Junta de Comerç 14, 08001 ☎ 93 412 08 30 🕐 Tue–Sat 12.30–4.30, 8–1, Sun 8pm–1am 🖐 L €10, D €20, Wine €7 🚫 Section 🚇 Liceu

INOPIA

Albert Adrià, brother of legendary chef Ferran Adrià, owns this bright, modern tapas bar. His concept is simple: Choose the most traditional and best-loved Spanish tapas and prepare them with the finest ingredients. The results are outstanding. A simple salad of tuna and tomato melts divinely in the mouth when prepared with succulent Montserrat tomatoes, or try a marinated artichoke wrapped around an anchovy. It's a neighbourhood favourite, well off the beaten track, and not to be missed.

♥ 91 D8 ⊠ Carrer de Tamarit 104, 08015 ☎ 93 424 52 31 🕐 Tue–Fri 7–11, Sat 1–3.30, 7–11 🖐 L and D €30, Wine €12 🚇 Poble Sec

MAMA CAFÉ

The relaxing Mama Café was designed according to the principles of feng shui, and calm prevails even when it's packed. It is spacious, with the central kitchen painted in bright shades of red, blue, yellow and orange. The salads are delicious, and the vegetable soups, turkey with mustard, and old-fashioned hamburgers are all particularly good. It is also open as a café in the afternoon.

♥ 91 F9 ⊠ Carrer del Doctor Dou 10, 08001 ☎ 93 301 29 40 🕐 Mon–Sat 1–1 🖐 L €10, D €27, Wine €9 🚇 Catalunya

MAUR

www.restaurantmaur.com

This rustically themed restaurant errs a little on the cheesy side with its dried corn cobs and heavy furniture, but the baskets of tomatoes and garlic (for making your own *pa amb tomàquet*) are a nice touch. The thin, crispy pizzas, baked in a wood-fired oven are great, as are the spears of chargrilled meat, sausage, steak and hunks of chicken. There are two other branches—at Carrer de Floridablanca 119 and Carrer Urgell 121.

♥ 91 E8 ⊠ Carrer Comte d'Urgell 9, 08011 ☎ 93 423 98 29 🕐 Daily 1.30–4, 8–midnight 🖐 L €9.50, D €25, Jug of wine €7 🚇 Urgell/Sant Antoni

MESÓN DAVID

www.mesondavid.com

This is a riotous restaurant that is popular with large groups with events to celebrate. Mesón David dishes out hearty meals from all regions of Spain such as Galician steamed octopus, grilled trout stuffed with *jamón serrano* (cured ham) from Navarra or Castilian roast suckling pig. Spontaneous singing, visiting acts and jovial waiters provide the entertainment.

♥ 91 E9 ⊠ Carrer de les Carretes 63, 08001 ☎ 93 441 59 34 🕐 Tue–Sun 1–4, 8.30–11.30. Closed Aug 🖐 L and D €20, Wine €12 🚇 Paral.lel

ORGANIC

www.antoniaorganickitchen.com

This old warehouse, in the heart of El Raval, has been transformed into a relaxed vegetarian shop and restaurant. All the organic goods sold or served here come with a quality guarantee label. Credit cards are not accepted.

♥ 91 F9 ⊠ Carrer de la Junta de Comerç 11, 08001 ☎ 93 301 09 02 🕐 Daily 12.30pm–midnight 🖐 L and D €20, Wine €8 🚫 🚇 Liceu

ORXATERIA SIRVENT

This is well known as the city's finest producer of *orxata*, a delicious creamy drink made from crushed tiger nuts. It's perfect on hot summer's days. Sirvent also produce outstanding ice creams, which you can eat at the counter, in the café or take away. In the run-up to Christmas, Sirvent makes the nougat-like *turrón*, for which Catalonia is famous.

91 E9 ✉ Carrer del Parlament 56, 08015 ☎ 93 441 27 20 🕐 Summer daily 9am–midnight; winter Sat–Sun 9–9 ✋ Orxata from €1.70, ice cream from €2 🚇 Sant Antoni

PLA DELS ÀNGELS

Opposite the MACBA (▷ 68–69), this colourful restaurant offers great value salads, pasta, grilled meat and fish dishes. The home-made desserts, especially the wickedly rich chocolate cake, are deservedly popular. The interior is surprisingly spacious, with a curious rock pool taking centre stage in the main dining room, but it's the sunny terrace that draws the crowds.
✚ 91 F8 ✉ Carrer de Ferlandina 23, 08001 ☎ 93 329 40 47 🕐 1.30–4, 9–11.30 ✋ L €12, D €20, Wine €9 🚇 Universitat

QUIMET, QUIMET

This is undoubtedly the best place to go for an early bite to eat in Poble Sec. There are just three high, chairless tables, so customers stand while drinking a glass of wine. Tapas are prepared in full view at the bar, and include beans with cod, tuna with pepper, and anchovies with sun-dried tomatoes.
✚ 91 E9 ✉ Carrer del Poeta Cabanyes 25, 08004 ☎ 93 442 31 42 🕐 Mon–Fri 12–4, 7–10.30, Sat 12–4. Closed Aug ✋ Tapas €2–€12, Wine €9 🚇 Paral.lel

RÍAS DE GALICIA

www.riasdegalicia.com
This Galician restaurant is the place to come to for excellent shrimp, giant prawns and lobster brought straight from Galicia. The chef, Argelio Díaz, is an expert in perfectly cooked fish, and counts mouth-watering hake among his many specials. Live piano music is played while you eat.
✚ 90 D8 ✉ Carrer de Lleida 7, 08004 ☎ 93 424 81 52 🕐 Daily 1.30–4, 8.30–12 ✋ L and D €80, Wine €25 🚇 Espanya

RITA BLUE

This is a restaurant, bar and club rolled into one but split over two spacious, diverse floors. Rita Blue is a trendy and bustling place. The restaurant serves Mediterranean, Mexican, Greek, Moroccan and Lebanese cuisine, from fried fish to couscous. There's an outdoor terrace in summer.
✚ 91 F9 ✉ Plaça de Sant Agustí 3, 08001 ☎ 93 412 40 86 🕐 Mon–Wed 7pm–2am, Thu–Sat 7pm–3am ✋ D €20, Wine €9 🚇 Liceu

SAN TELMO

San Telmo is considered one of the city's best Argentinian restaurants, specializing in grilled and roast meats. The products are all of the finest quality and are imported directly from Argentina. You'll also find of fish, salads and desserts, all presented with creativity. There's a solid wine list and attentive service.
✚ 91 E9 ✉ Carrer de Vilá i Vilá 53, 08004 ☎ 93 441 30 78 🕐 Mon–Sat 1–4, 8–11 ✋ L and D €40, Wine €12 🚇 Paral.lel

SILENUS

Silenus' modern style reflects its location near to the modern art museum, the MACBA (▷ 68–69), and it has become a meeting place for young artists. The time is projected onto an interior wall. The food is creative and elaborate; for example, rabbit rice with mushrooms and rosemary, and ravioli with chocolate and banana chutney. The exhibitions of paintings and photos change monthly.
✚ 91 F9 ✉ Carrer dels Àngels 8, 08001 ☎ 93 302 26 80 🕐 Mon–Sat 1.30–4, 8.30–11.30 ✋ L €12, D €35, Wine €12 🚇 Liceu

TAPIOLES 53

www.tapioles53.com
Not a restaurant as such but a 'gastronomic club' (you'll be asked to sign up when you arrive— membership free), Tapioles 53 is run by ex-pat Australian Sarah Stothart. Choose from either the three- or a five-course set menu of delightful Mediterranean cuisine. Starters may include mascarpone cheese and porcini mushroom tart or a selection of antipasti, followed by spinach gnocchi or beef bourguignonne. Desserts include Australian pavlova or marinated figs. Reservations are essential as seating is restricted.
✚ 91 D9 ✉ Carrer de Tapioles 53, 08004 ☎ 93 329 22 38 🕐 Tue–Sat, kitchen open from 9pm– 10.30pm. Closed Aug ✋ Set menus €34 (three courses), €54 (five courses), wine included in price 🚇 Paral.lel

LA TOMAQUERA

A long-established classic in the Poble Sec neighbourhood, La Tomaquera is famously eccentric. For a start, the only drinks available are house wine, available by the glass, half litre or litre, water or fruit juices. Despite this—or perhaps because of it—there are always people waiting outside the door, and the restaurant buzzes with a lively young crowd. It is a great place to try classic Catalan dishes such as snails, hearty casseroles and barbecued meats.
✚ 91 D9 ✉ Carrer de Margarit 58, 08004 🕐 Tue–Sat 1.30–3.30, 8.30–10.30, Sun 1.30–3.30 ✋ L €12, D €20, Wine €7 🚇 Poble Sec

PRICES AND SYMBOLS

Prices are the lowest and highest for a double room for one night. Breakfast is included unless noted otherwise. All the hotels listed accept credit cards unless otherwise stated. Note that rates can vary widely throughout the year.

For a key to the symbols, ▷ 2.

BARCELÓ RAVAL

www.barceloraval.com

The conical Barceló Raval is an ultra-modern testament to the Rambla del Raval's ongoing transformation. (The area remains a little edgy, and not everyone will feel comfortable here after dark.) The hotel rooms are spacious, and the rooftop bar (open to all) offers 360-degree views.

✚ 91 E9 ✉ Rambla del Raval 17–21, 08001 ☎ 93 320 14 90 💷 €120–€160

① 186 ⬛ ⬛ ⬛ Outdoor
Ⓜ Liceu

CASA CAMPER

www.casacamper.es

Located in the heart of El Raval, this hip hotel has a 24-hour snack bar (all snacks included in price). The rooms have sleek sleeping areas in bold combinations of red and black and a private lounge across the hall with free WiFi, a TV/music system plus a sofa. All rooms and public areas are non-smoking.

✚ 91 F8 ✉ Carrer d'Elisabets 11, 08001 ☎ 93 342 62 80 💷 €225–€265, excluding breakfast **①** 25 ⬛ ⬛ **Ⓜ** Liceu

CATALONIA DUCS DE BERGARA

www.hoteles-catalonia.es

Built in 1898, this hotel features the original marble staircase, moulded ceiling and dome, and comes with a restaurant, coffee bar, garden, solarium and business facilities. There's a small rooftop plunge pool, and access to the wellness area and spa in their partner hotel.

✚ 91 F8 ✉ Carrer de Bergara 11, 08002 ☎ 93 301 51 51 💷 €99–€209, excluding breakfast **①** 149 ⬛ ⬛ Outdoor **Ⓜ** Catalunya

CATALONIA ROMA

www.hoteles-catalonia.com

The interior of this modern, modest hotel near Sants makes full use of wood, creams and whites; the rooms have a minibar and satellite TV. There is also a restaurant, meeting rooms and parking.

Above *There is a good choice of accommodation in this region*

🔲 90 D7 ✉ Avinguda de Roma 31, 08029 ☎ 93 410 66 33 🖐 €55–€129, excluding breakfast 🕐 49 🔲 🚇 Estació de Sants or Entença

CENTER RAMBLAS
www.center-ramblas.com
This youth hostel is open 24 hours a day. Facilities include internet access, a bar, lounge with satellite TV, kitchen, laundry, dining room, vending machines, sheet and towel rental, safety deposit lockers, board games and a travel library.
🔲 91 F9 ✉ Carrer de l'Hospital 63, 08001 ☎ 93 412 40 69 🖐 Over 26 years €20.85–€25.55; under 26 years €17–€21.50 🕐 33 rooms, 201 beds 🔲 🚇 Liceu

GAT RAVAL
www.gatrooms.es
Look for the striking green and black cat (gat) logo if you're trying to find inexpensive accommodation. The Gat Raval is ideal for budget travellers who want a clean, yet stylish, room, with TV and bathroom, at an affordable price.
🔲 91 F8 ✉ Carrer de Joaquín Costa 44, 08001 ☎ 93 481 66 70 🖐 €45–€74, excluding breakfast 🕐 24 🚇 Universitat

HOSTERIA GRAU
www.hostalgrau.com
Book well in advance to find a room at one of the city's best-loved hostals. Family run and welcoming, it's an old-fashioned spot, but it charms visitors with its original ceramic tiles and ironwork Rooms are attractively priced and come with or without private bathrooms; there are also a number of self-catering apartments available.
🔲 91 F8 ✉ Carrer Ramelleres 27, 08001 ☎ 93 301 81 35 🖐 €60–€110 🕐 19 🚇 Catalunya

HOTEL CIUTAT VELLA
www.hotelciutatvella.com
This hotel in the heart of the old city is a good choice for style-conscious travellers with a limited budget. The striking black, white and scarlet decoration extends to the lobby, where there's an internet café.

There are cafés close by for a good, inexpenisve breakfast, so you may prefer to give the pricey hotel buffet a miss.
🔲 91 F8 ✉ Carrer dels Tallers 66, 08001 ☎ 93 481 37 99 🖐 €60–€140, excluding breakfast 🕐 40 🔲 🚇 Universitat

HOTEL JAZZ
www.hoteljazz.com
This may look like a bland chain hotel on the outside, but the Hotel Jazz offers all kinds of unexpected extras which set it apart from many central choices. The rooms are spacious, decorated in fashionable monochromatic tones, and there's a fabulous little rooftop pool with sun deck. Look on the website to find some amazing deals.
🔲 91 F8 ✉ Carrer de Pelai 3, 08001 ☎ 93 552 96 96 🖐 €100–€300 🕐 108 🔲 🏊 Outdoor 🚇 Catalunya

LLEÓ
www.hotel-lleo.com
Lleó, a smart, functional hotel, is next to Plaça de la Universitat. All rooms have a bathroom, satellite TV, minibar and safe. Other services include a buffet breakfast, cafeteria, and non-smoking dining hall.
🔲 91 F8 ✉ Carrer de Pelai 22–24, 08001 ☎ 93 318 13 12 🖐 €70–€140, excluding breakfast 🕐 89 🔲 🚇 Catalunya

MARKET HOTEL
www.markethotel.com.es
This smart little hotel is part of a popular chain. The rooms are decorated in black and white, with splashes of red to add warmth. Set in a traditional neighbourhood, the Market Hotel is close to the Mercat de Sant Antoni (▷ 83), so early morning noise can be a problem. It is a great bargain so make reservations well in advance.
🔲 91 E8 ✉ Passatge Sant Antoni Abad 10 (Carrer de Comte Borrell 6), 08015 ☎ 93 325 12 05 🖐 €75–€97 🕐 30 🔲 🚇 Sant Antoni

PENINSULAR
The Peninsular is a little oasis away from bustling El Raval. It was built at the end of the 19th century and has

retained the original features of an art nouveau house. Rooms are basic but spacious and clean; each has a bathroom, telephone and safety deposit box, and most overlook family apartments. Walls are thin, however, and light sleepers should consider earplugs. An additional benefit is the beautiful tiled inner courtyard, surrounded by lush hanging plants.
🔲 91 F9 ✉ Carrer de Sant Pau 34, 08001 ☎ 93 302 31 38 🖐 €75 🕐 80 🔲 🚇 Liceu

SILKEN RAMBLAS
www.hoteles-silken.com
Also known as the Ambassador, this hotel is set in a contemporary building close to Plaça de Catalunya, with a grey facade and modern metal balconies. The public areas and the guest rooms are decorated with purple and blue furnishings. But probably the best thing about the hotel is the rooftop, where you can take in great views of the city and in the summer freshen up in the swimming pool. The Carmen restaurant serves local and international cuisine.
🔲 91 F9 ✉ Carrer del Pintor Fortuny 13, 08001 ☎ 93 342 61 80 🖐 €124–€241, excluding breakfast 🕐 125 (50 non–smoking) 🔲 🏊 Outdoor 📺 🚇 Catalunya

TORRE CATALUNYA
www.expogrupo.com
The Torre Catalunya's modern skyscraper accommodation is one of the few quality hotel options in the vicinity of Estació de Sants, the city's main train station. All rooms are generously sized; they have marble bathrooms which feature walk-in showers and deep bathtubs. Head to the hotel's acclaimed restaurant on the 23rd floor for a bird's-eye view of the skyline. There's free parking, and a state-of-the-art spa, making the Torre Catalunya very good value.
🔲 90 D7 ✉ Avinguda de Roma 2–4, 08014 ☎ 93 325 81 00 🖐 €140–€188, excluding breakfast 🕐 129 🔲 📺 🚇 Sants

BADAL

C Casteras

CARRER DE SANTS

PLAÇA
ESTACIÓ
BARCELONA
SANTS

PLAÇA DELS
PAÏSOS CATALANS

Catalonia
Roma

AVINGUDA

Torre
Catalunya

PLAÇA
JOAN PEIRÓ

Museu
P Clirac

C ST ANTONI

PLAÇA
DE SANTS

Mercat
Nou

Plaça
de Sants

Plaça
de Malaga

Plaça
Iberia

Parc de l'Espanya
Industrial

TARRAGONA

CARRER DE

Tarragona

CARRER

SANTS

PLAÇA
Finlàndia

Plaça
de la
Farga

Hostafrancs

C DEL CONSELL DE CENT

Parc de
Joan Miró

LA BORDETA

CARRER DE LA CONSTITUCIÓ

CARRER DE GAVÀ

HOSTAFRANCS

Plaça
de Toros
les Arenes

MAGORIA

CARRER DEL

Plaça
Joan
Corrades

PLAÇA
D'ESPANYA

GRAN VIA DE LES CORTS CATALANES

GRAN

Plaça de les
Matemàtiques

Parc
de la Font
Florida

Carrer

Fructuós

Palau de la
Metal·lúrgia

Palau
Fira de
Mostres

Avinguda

Parc de Can
Sabaté

EL POLVORÍ

CaixaForum

Palau del
Cinquantenari

AVINGUDA DEL MARQUÈS DE COMILLAS

Ríos de
Galicia

LA FRANCA

AVINGUDA DE RIUS I TAULET

Plaça
Sta
Madrona

PLAÇA
DE SANT
JORDI

Poble
Espanyol

Font
Màgica

Plaça
Parè
E Millàn

Pavelló Mies
van der Rohe

Palau de
Victòria
Eugènia

Plaça Marquès
de Foronda

Palau Alfons XIII

Palau
Municipal
d'Esports

AVINGUDA

Jardí
Botànic

Plaça de les
Cascades

Teatre Mercat
de les Flors

CAN CLOS

Institut Nacional d'Educació
Física de Catalunya
(INEFC)

Plaça
d'Europa

Mirador del Palau Nacional

Palau Artes
Gràfiques

Inst del
Teatre

Plaça Alta de
Can Clos

Palau
Nacional

Museu
Etnològic

Piscines Bernat
Picornell

Parc de
Montjuïc

Museu Nacional
d'Art de Catalunya

Museu
d'Arqueologia
de Catalunya

Jardins de
J Maragall

Palau
Albèniz

PASSEIG

L'Anella
Olímpica

Plaça de
Nemesi
Ponsati

Teatre
Grec

Fundació
Joan Miró

Auditorio sot
del Migdia

Palau
Sant Jordi

Estadi
Olímpic de
Lluís Companys

L'ESTADI

Plaça
del Sol

Plaça
Neptú

AVINGUDA

Estadi d'Hoquei
Pau Negre

MONTJUÏC

Avinguda de
Miramar

Jardi
Petra Kelly

Jardins
Mossèn Cinto
Verdaguer

Cementiri del
Sud Oest

Plaça
Gran Capità

Castell de
Montjuïc

Telefèric

Carretera

CAN TUNIS

0   500 m
0   500 yds

B   C   D

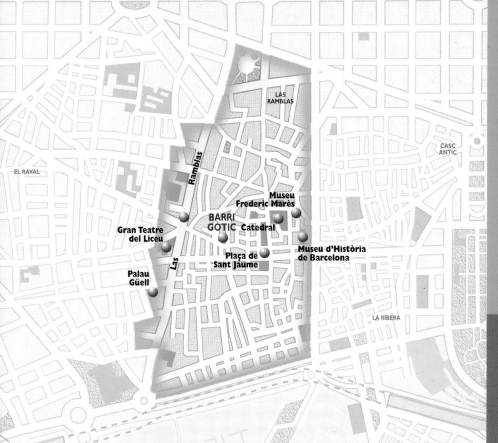

BARRI GÒTIC AND LAS RAMBLAS

The most iconic street in Barcelona, Las Ramblas is a long, tree-shaded avenue which cuts a swathe from the city centre all the way down to the port. Crowds flow past the mime artists and street performers, flamenco dancers and football players, enjoying the colourful spectacle which unfolds all day long. Kiosks sell everything from flowers to canaries, just as they have for the last century or so. Although tacky fast-food restaurants and souvenir shops have sprung up in recent years, Las Ramblas is still home to some of the city's best-loved institutions, including the glorious Boquería market, one of the largest and most diverse in Europe, and the elegant Liceu opera house. Although the terrace cafés are the most expensive in the city, they afford wonderful views of the fascinating human theatre.

Las Ramblas forms the southern boundary of the Barri Gòtic (Gothic Quarter), an enticing stone maze of passages and squares still partly encircled by medieval walls. It grew up over Roman Barcino, and surprising vestiges of the 2,000-year-old Roman colony—including the gigantic columns of a long-gone temple—are hidden away in secret courtyards and alleys. The neighbourhood is dominated by the enormous Gothic cathedral, covered in leering gargoyles and topped with a soaring spire. Nearby is a string of superb Gothic palaces, including one containing the Saló del Tinell, the magnificent medieval throne room where King Ferdinand and Queen Isabella received Christopher Columbus before his great voyage of discovery. Many of these palaces have been converted into museums, including the Museu d'Història de Barcelona which reveals a spectacularly intact example of Roman Barcino in its subterranean chambers. Yet, for all its stunning historic architecture, the Barri Gòtic is not stuck in the past: it remains a lively commercial and entertainment district, full of shops and cafés, bars and restaurants.

GRAN VIA DE LES CORTS CATALANES

Plaça de la
Universitat

Universitat

RONDA

UNIVERSITAT

Plaça
Catalunya

Carrer de Sepulveda

Catalunya

C Bergara

Plaça de
Catalunya

Carrer de Floridablanca

8

Catalunya

C de Tamarit

Plaça
Goya

Plaça de
Castella

Carrer

Valldoncella

Centre de Cultura
Contemporania
de Barcelona

C Santa Anna

Museu d'Art
Contemporani
de Barcelona

Casa Municipal
de Misericòrdia

RAMBLAS

Plaça
Vila de
Madrid

C Canuda

Foment de les
Arts Decoratives

C Elisabets

C Portaferrissa

Col·le
d'Arquitect

C de la Riera Alta

Carrer del Peu de la Creu

Carrer Pintor Fortuny

Església
de Betlem

LAS

Plaça de
Felip Neri

CARRER DEL CARME

EL RAVAL

CARRER

DE

L'HOSPITAL

Antic
Hospital
Santa Creu

Palau de la
Virreina

Mercat La
Boqueria

Plaça
de Pi

BARRI
GÒTIC

Museu del
Calçat

C l'Aurora

C de St Rafael

Santa
Maria de Pi

Liceu

Centro de
Interpretacion
del Call

Palau de
Generali

9

Carrer Junta de Com

C de Boqueria

Plaça de
Sant Jaume

Gran Teatre
del Liceu

C de Ferran

Carrer

de

Monestír de
Sant Pau del Camp

Pau

C del Marquès de Barberà

Plaça
Reial

Ajuntamen

AVINGUDA

Carrer Nou de la Rambla

LAS RAMBLAS

Nou de la Rambla

Palau
Güell

C Nou de St Francesc

C de Codols

Paral-lel

DEL

PARAL-LEL

C de Cabanes

Teatre

Arts
Santa Mònica

Museu
de Cera

Església
de la Mercè

10

Drassanes

Carrer J A Clavé

Carrer de Palaudàries

Drassanes &
Museu Maritim

Plaça
del Portal
de la Pau

PASSEIG DE COLOM

PLAÇA DE LES
DRASSANES

Monument
a Colom

Moll de Bosch i Alsina

Dàrsena Nacional

PASSEIG DE JOSEP CARNER

E

F

GRAN VIA DE LES CORTS CATALANES

Passeig de Gràcia

Plaça de Tetuan

Tetuan

Carrer

Casp

Carrer

de

Casp

CARRER DE CLARIS

CARRER DE PAU

CARRER DE LLÚRIA

CARRER DE ROGER

BRUC

CARRER DEL

Girona

de

CARRER DE

BAILÈN

CARRER JOAN

CARRER DE SANT

de

PASSEIG DE

CARRER DE ROGER

FLOR

Napols

Casa Calvet

d'Ausiàs

Marc

RONDA

Urquinaona

DE SANT PERE

Plaça Urquinaona

Carrer

d'Ausiàs

Carrer

Marc

Carrer

d'Alí

Bei

LAS RAMBLAS

VIA LAIETANA

Carrer de Ribes

ANTIGA ESTACIÓ DEL NORD

CARRER DE

TRAFALGAR

Arc de Triomf

Carrer

Comtal

C Magdalenes

C les Moles

Palau de la Música Catalana

Carrer Sant Pere més Alt

SANT PERE

Carrer Sant Pere Mitjà

Carrer Sant Pere més Baix

Plaça St Pere

CASC ANTIC

Arc del Triomf

CARRER DE FLOR

Napols

CARRER DELS ALMOGÀVERS

PASSEIG LLUIS COMPANYS

CARRER DE ROGER

de

CARRER DE BUENAVENTURA MUÑOZ

A F Cambó

C J Giralt

C Metges

C Cortinas

C Portal Nou

CARRER

Catedral

Museu Diocesà

Museu Frederic Marès

Catedral

Plaça del Rei

Museu d'Història de Barcelona

Mercat Santa Caterina

Carders

Carrer

Museu de la Xocolata

PASSEIG DE PUJADES

Museu de Zoologia

Jaume I

CARRER DE LA PRINCESA

C Comerç

PASSEIG DE PICASSO

Museu de Geologia

Parc de la Ciutadella

Plaça de Sant Just

DHUB Montcada

Museu Barbier-Mueller d'Art Precolombi

C Montcada

Museu Picasso

C del Rec

C del

Antic Mercat del Born

Carrer de Comercial

VIA LAIETANA

C sots-tinent Navarro

Santa Maria del Mar

Passeig del Born

C Ribera

LA RIBERA

Parlament de Catalunya

C Regomir

Gignàs

Correus Telègrafs

Fossar de les Moreres

C Consolat de Mar

AVINGUDA MARQUES DE L'ARGENTERA

Parc Zoològic

PLAÇA D'ANTONI LOPEZ

La Llotja

PG ISABEL II

Plaça del Palau

PASSEIG DE JOAN DE BORBÓ

ESTACIÓ BARCELONA DE FRANÇA

PASSEIG DE CIRCUMVAL.LACIÓ

Palau de Mar

Plaça de Pau Vila

CARRER DEL DR AIGUADER

Barceloneta

RONDA

Dàrsena del Comerç

Museu d'Història de Catalunya

CARRER

DEL

DR

AIGUADER

Carrer

Balboa

LITORAL

G

H

0   250 m
0   250 yds

BARRI GÒTIC

The Barri Gòtic (Gothic Quarter) is the most complete Gothic quarter in Europe. After Modernisme, the Gothic period is Barcelona's other great contribution to the world of architecture. Despite the famine, plague and social unrest that dogged the epoch, the city grew rapidly during medieval times, so much so that its expansion could no longer be contained within the old Roman walls. Not much is left of these walls, but the ensemble of 13th- to 15th-century buildings and narrow lanes of the Barri Gòtic should be on every visitor's itinerary.

GUILDS AND GHETTO

Guilds (or *gremis* in Catalan) were the backbone of Barcelona's medieval life and economic activity, and a forerunner of trade unions. Many of their shields can be seen on buildings dotted around the Barri Gòtic, denoting the headquarters of each particular trade. The tiny workshops were also here and many streets still bear the name of the activity that went on there for centuries, such as Escudellers (shield makers) or Brocaters (brocade makers).

El Call, the original Jewish ghetto, is also in the Barri Gòtic. A tiny area around the Carrer del Call and l'Arc de Sant Ramon del Call was the scene of the sacking of the Jews by Christian mobs in the late 1300s (▷ 29). Little visual evidence remains of medieval Jewish culture, but there is a plaque from 1314 at Carrer de Marlet with a passage in Hebrew commemorating past inhabitants. At the corner of the same street, the remains of Barcelona's main medieval synagogue have been discovered (www.calldebarcelona.org; Mon–Sat 11–7, Sun 11–3).

SECLUDED SQUARES

One of the prettiest and least visited squares in the Barri Gòtic is Plaça de Sant Felip Neri (▷ 111), tucked away to the right of the cathedral (▷ 98–101). The Plaça del Pí, on which the magnificent Gothic church of Santa Maria del Pí (▷ 111) stands, is another good place to take a break on your wanderings. It is filled with cafés and musicians and holds two regular markets. Carrer de Petritxol, just off the Plaça del Pí, had its foundations laid in 1465 and now houses some of the most celebrated *granjas* (▷ 257) in Barcelona.

The tranquil square of Sant Just has impressive fountainheads and the fine Gothic church of the same name.

INFORMATION

www.barcelonaturisme.com

✚ 94 F9 🛈 Plaça de Sant Jaume, Carrer de la Ciutat 2 (in the town hall), 08002 ☎ 93 285 38 34 🕔 Mon–Fri 9–8, Sat 10–8, Sun and holidays 10–2 🚇 Jaume I or Liceu

Opposite *The baroque church of Sant Felip Neri sits on a pretty square*
Below *A tranquil café outside the church of Sants Just i Pastor*

INTRODUCTION

The cathedral is the religious heart of the old town. With spectacular views over the Barri Gòtic from its high roof, it is one of the finest examples of Catalan Gothic architecture in the region. This site has always been important to the city because of its prime position on a hill. A Roman temple and a Moorish mosque were both here, as was an earlier cathedral from the sixth century. The plans for the interior of the present cathedral were laid down in 1298. The bishops ordered a single nave, 28 side chapels and an apse with an ambulatory behind a high altar. For the next 150 years four different architects worked on the edifice and produced beautiful Catalan Gothic cloisters and chapels.

You are likely to find the cathedral easily if you spend any time in the Barri Gòtic, as many of the area's narrow lanes seem to channel you in this direction. The main entrance to the cathedral is at Plaça de la Seu, and you are free to roam around the building. There is also a side entrance along Carrer del Bisbe that brings you into the cloister.

INFORMATION
www.catedralbcn.org

➕ 95 G9 ✉ Plaça de la Seu 3, 08002
☎ 93 342 82 60 ⏰ Main church, choir, roof: Mon–Fri 8–12.45, 5.15–7, Sat–Sun 8–12.45, 5.15–6. Cloister: Daily 9–12.30, 5–7. Museum: Daily 10–12.30, 5.15–7 💶 Museum: €2; elevator: €2.50; choir: €2.20 🚇 Liceu 🚌 16, 17, 19, 45 ➡ Guided visits available Fri and Sat by prior arrangement 📖 Various available from €5 to €10 🏪 Two kiosks on site selling guidebooks, postcards, key rings and other souvenirs

WHAT TO SEE

THE FACADE

The money for the building project ran out before the facade could be completed, and the front-facing facade and spires were only finished in 1913. The design was based on the plain brick and stone front that had been in place since the 15th century, and was paid for by wealthy local businessman Manuel Girona. Don't let this architectural sleight of hand put you off. Entering the cathedral from the main steps is a grand experience whatever its age. Flanked by two towering spires and embellished with hundreds of carvings of angels, saints and other religious imagery, as well as some fine stained-glass windows, its detail is almost as dizzying as its dimensions. The structure measures 93m (305ft) long, 40m (131ft) wide and 28m (92ft) high. The cathedral's bell towers are 53m (174ft) high, while the main tower is 70m (230ft).

CAPELLA DEL SANTÍSSIM SAGRAMENT

This is the first of the chapels to your right as you come through the main entrance. It was designed and built while Arnau Bargués was in charge of construction, the third of the four architects to be so, having just completed the original facade of the Ajuntament (town hall) on Plaça de Sant Jaume. The chapel's vaulted roof soars to more than 20m (66ft) and its treasure is the 16th-century figurine of the Christ of Lepanto. This life-size icon is believed to have been on board the flagship of Don John of Austria, who led a Christian fleet against the Turks in the Gulf of Lepanto in 1571 (▷ 31). The figure of Christ on the crucifix is curiously bent: According to a famous legend, it miraculously swerved to avoid a Turkish cannonball during battle.

THE CRYPT

The crypt is one of the cathedral's more intimate corners. The alabaster tomb of Santa Eulàlia is set into the wall at the back and dates from the 14th century. Eulàlia was martyred at 13 under gruesome circumstances by the Romans, and is now the patron saint of Barcelona. Many local children are named Eulàlia after the young martyr. It is thought her remains were brought here in 1339 from Santa Maria del Mar in La Ribera (▷ 152). The front face of the sarcophagus depicts the solemn act of transferring her relics to their present resting place. The crypt often has a handful of people kneeling in devotion in front of it. Put a euro coin in the machine to illuminate the crypt and see the designs on the sarcophagus in detail.

Opposite *Soaring pillars are a typical feature of Catalan Gothic architecture*

TIP

» If you want to see the cathedral without the crowds, visit during the special lunchtime session. There is a small fee, which goes towards the current restoration project, but the peace and tranquillity that you experience merit the outlay.

THE CHOIR

The central choir has beautifully carved 14th-century stalls. The coats of arms represent members of the chapter of the Order of the Golden Fleece, a meeting of which was organized by the Holy Roman Emperor Charles V in 1519 and attended by a host of European monarchs. Peek under the *misericordias* (stone seats) to see the sculptures of hunting scenes and games.

THE CLOISTER

A few minutes spent among the cloister's orange and medlar trees, shady palms and tranquil pond, is an effective battery charger. This cool oasis has close ties to the area's medieval working life as key members of the various guilds (▷ 97) are buried underneath its stone slabs. Its mossy, central fountain once provided fresh water for the clergy. During Corpus Christi in early June, an empty eggshell is placed on top of the fountain's jet and left to bob away for an entire week. Known as *L'ou com balla* (how the egg dances), the tradition is not found elsewhere in Spain and its origins have been lost in time. The surrounding pond is home to a gaggle of white geese who are said to represent the purity of Santa Eulàlia, Barcelona's patron saint. The Chapel of Santa Llúcia leads off the cloister and it provides a quiet place for worship.

THE VIEW

The elevator on the opposite side to the cloister takes you to the roof, from where magnificent panoramic views of the city and the cathedral's spires can be enjoyed from a platform placed over the central nave. The statue you see perched on top of the highest, central spire is of St. Helen, and the two bell towers are also named after saints: Eulàlia and Honorata. There is a riot of sculptural detail on both, depicting saints, crucifixes and animal life.

Below *The eastern facade of the cathedral was constructed in the 14th century*

THE ORGAN

The enormous organ, built for the cathedral in the 16th century and protected by its original Renaissance case, still functions and is regularly used in services. Beneath the organ, a carved head with movable eyes and jaw operated by the organist, used to spew sweets for children on feast days.

THE ROYAL TOMBS

Numerous important Catalan monarchs and aristocrats are buried in the cathedral. The most notable are Roman Berenguer I, Count of Barcelona, and his wife, Almodis de la Marca, whose surprisingly small sarcophagi are suspended on an elaborately painted wall near the Sacristy.

PORTAL DE SAN IVO

Saint Ivo's Gateway is the oldest section of the cathedral, completed at the end of the 13th century. Before the neo-Gothic facade was added in the 1890s, it functioned as the main entrance for more than 500 years. It is surrounded by some superb early Gothic reliefs, including one depicting a soldier wrestling with a griffon and another of Samson spearing the lion.

CAPELLA DE SANTA LLÚCIA

The late Romanesque chapel of Saint Lucy, which sits just off the cloister, was constructed before the cathedral but later incorporated into the complex. Inside are a pair of fine Gothic tombs, belonging respectively to a bishop and canon of the cathedral. On the exterior wall near the entrance, you can still see vestiges of an inscription which reads 'A 2 Canas La Pou': these refer to medieval measuring units, etched into the wall so that anyone who suspected they had been swindled by a shopkeeper could come here to check.

Above *Angels watch over you and serenade you as you step inside*

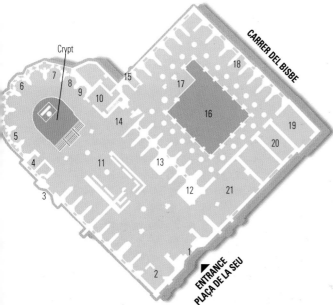

KEY TO FLOOR PLAN

1 Main entrance
2 Baptistery
3 Doorway of Sant Iu
4 Capella (chapel) de les Sants Innocents
5 Capella de la Mare de Déu de la Mercè
6 Capella de Sant Gabriel i Santa Helena
7 Capella de la Transfiguració del Senyor
8 Capella de la Visitació de la Mare de Déu
9 Capella de Sant Antoni Abat
10 Sacristy
11 Choirstalls
12 Capella de Sant Antoni de Pàdua
13 Capella de Sant Raymund de Penyafort
14 Doorway of Sant Serveri
15 Doorway of Mercy
16 Cloister
17 St. George's Well
18 Doorway of Santa Eulàlia
19 Capella de Santa Llúcia
20 Chapter House
21 Capella del Santíssim Sagrament

ARTS SANTA MÒNICA

www.artssantamonica.net

At the bottom of Las Ramblas, the sparse remnants of an 18th-century convent have been incorporated into a striking contemporary arts centre, including fragments of the baroque cloister which now forms part of the gallery space. Unusually, the art centre does not have its own permanent collection: instead, it hosts a varied and dynamic programme of exhibitions, talks and performances. The mission of Arts Santa Mònica is to provide a forum for all the expressive arts—including cinema, architecture, music and dance. The exhibitions are often bold and challenging: one of the most original recent events included an 'intinerant musical action' in which a musician played a piano, topped by two declaiming actors, which was slowly pulled down the entire length of Las Ramblas.

✚ 94 F10 ✉ La Rambla 7, 08002
☎ 93 316 28 10 🕐 Tue–Sun 11–9
✋ Free 🚇 Drassanes 🚌 13, 14, 36, 57, 59, 64, 157

BARRI GÒTIC

▷ 96–97.

CATEDRAL DE LA SEU

▷ 98–101.

Below left Baroque Església de la Mercè
Below right Església de Betlem

COL.LEGI D'ARQUITECTES

www.coac.net

This is the hub of Barcelona's architectural world, with regular workshops and exhibitions about architecture and urban planning. A modern structure in the old part of town, its most outstanding feature is its exterior mural, a simple line drawing of a Nativity scene. It was designed by Picasso in the 1950s but carried out by Carl Nesjar, at a time when Picasso was in self-exile from Spain for his political beliefs. There is a bookshop in the basement, as well as a restaurant, and an extensive library in the building opposite. The Col.legi d'Arquitectes organizes half- and full-day tours of aspects of the city's architecture, from Modernisme to town planning. They are directed at professionals in the field, but interested parties are welcome. Information can be obtained from the Col.legi during the mornings.

✚ 94 G9 ✉ Plaça Nova 5, 08002
☎ 93 301 50 00 🕐 Mon–Fri 10–9, Sat 10–2. Closed Aug ✋ Free 🚇 Liceu 🚌 16, 17, 19, 45

ESGLÉSIA DE BETLEM

This vast, imposing church looms up over Las Ramblas like a behemoth. The church dates from the late 17th century and was an addition to a Jesuit compound that was built in 1553. A rose window tops its lofty entrance but this, as with many of its features, was added after the interior of the church was destroyed during the Spanish Civil War in 1936. The interior never regained its richness, but is still an excellent example of baroque architecture. Every December, in the basement, there is an exhibition of *pessebres*—Christmas Nativity dioramas. It's also home to the *caganer* (▷ 19).

✚ 94 F9 ✉ Carrer del Carme 2, 08027
☎ 93 318 38 23 🕐 Mid-Jun to mid-Sep daily 7.30–2, 5.30–9.30; mid-Sep to mid-Jun 7.30–2, 4.30–8 ✋ Free 🚇 Liceu 🚌 14, 38, 59

ESGLÉSIA DE LA MERCÈ

A visit to this church is important for what it represents. According to legend, La Mercè, Our Lady of Mercy, appeared in the dreams of Jaume I (1208–76), instructing him to start a monastic order that would protect Barcelona from North African pirates. The first church of the Order of Mercy was built here in 1267. The saint is said to have freed the city from a plague of locusts in 1637 and was subsequently named the patron of Barcelona by a grateful city council. The church is topped by an elegant sculpture of the saint. Barcelona's main fiesta is also dedicated to La Mercè.

✚ 94 F10 ✉ Plaça de la Mercè 1, 08002
☎ 93 310 50 51 🕐 Daily 10–1, 6–8
✋ Free 🚇 Drassanes 🚌 14, 20, 36, 38, 57, 59, 64

GRAN TEATRE DEL LICEU

The city's residents mourned when a fire swept through their beloved opera house in 1994, but after six years of careful renovation it was returned to its former glory. Now its lush interior and superb acoustics make it one of the best in Europe.

A trip to the Liceu represented social prestige for the city's bourgeoisie during the mid-1800s. From its inauguration in 1847, the institution became a metaphor for good taste and social display. But then El Liceu was never intended to be a people's theatre. The original funding for the project did not come from the government of the time but from private donations. At the time the Liceu was being built, a craze for the German composer Robert Wagner (1813–83) was sweeping across Europe. This heavily influenced the architectural style, which was bold and grandiose.

RENOVATION AND INNOVATION

After the fire little of the original structure remained and a complete change of direction was needed to attract the funds to resurrect the building. After private and corporate donors were found, a new wing was built to house rehearsal and administration rooms and the interior was meticulously restored. The new building also ushered in a new musical direction with the staging of works by more avant-garde and lesser-known composers.

INFORMATION

www.liceubarcelona.com

🕇 94 F9 ✉ La Rambla 51–59, 08001
☎ 93 485 99 00 🎧 Guided tours (1hr 10 min): Daily 10am. Adult €8.70, child (under 10) free. Unguided tours (20 min): Daily 11.30am, 12pm, 12.30pm and 1pm. Adult €4, child (under 10) free. Stage and backstage tours: Daily 9.30am. Adult €10, child (under 10) free. Reservations in advance necessary, tel 93 485 99 14
📷 €10 🚇 Liceu 🚌 14, 18, 38, 59

Above *The grandiose facade of the internationally acclaimed Liceu opera house on Las Ramblas*

MUSEU DEL CALÇAT

This small shoe museum has a fascinating history. It is the fruit of the Catalan order of the Cofraria de Sant Marc, a religious fraternity dedicated to the patron saint of cobblers (St. Mark) and the oldest *cofraria* in Europe. The building itself, set on the oval-shaped square of Sant Felip Neri, dates back to 1565 and was the original headquarters of the *cofraria*. The examples of Roman sandals and medieval footwear are reproductions, but still remarkable. These oversized slippers hung outside the cobblers' workshops in the Barri Gòtic, announcing their trade during a time when their customers could not read nor write. The rest of the collection is based around the 18th to 20th centuries, from the dainty satin boots of the 1700s to the 1930s boots of Catalan musician Pau (Pablo) Casals (1876–1973). The collection also has a dozen or so pairs of sports shoes from the 1970s, which are now highly covetable items.

✚ 94 F9 ✉ Plaça de Sant Felip Neri 5, 08002 ☎ 93 301 45 33 ⏱ Tue–Sun 11–2 ✋ Adult €2.50, child (under 12) free 🚇 Jaume I 🚌 14, 17, 19, 40, 45

MUSEU DE CERA

www.museoceracbcn.com

Barcelona's waxworks museum may not rank alongside London's Madame Tussaud's, but the mannequins—who at times look amusingly unlike their models—give an insight into who is considered famous in Catalonia and Spain. This ranges from political figures such as Jordi Pujol (▷ 36), General Franco, Bill Clinton and Yasser Arafat to Gaudí, Bonnie and Clyde, and Dracula. The curators have added some cunning special-effect lighting and music that enhance many of the exhibits. The setting for the Museu de Cera is a late 19th-century building, with a winding staircase, period rooms and frescoed ceilings that are attractions in themselves.

El Bosc de les Fades (▷ 123), the café outside in the adjoining lane, is embellished with running brooks and magic mirrors.

✚ 94 F10 ✉ Passatge de la Banca 7, 08002 ☎ 93 317 26 49 ⏱ Jul–end Sep daily 10–10; Oct–end Jun Mon–Fri 10–1.30, 4–7.30, Sat–Sun 11–2, 4.30– 8.30 ✋ Adult €12, child (5–11) €7, child (under 5) free; audioguide €3.50 🚇 Drassanes 🚌 14, 18, 36, 38, 57, 59, 64, 91 📷 🏛

MUSEU DIOCESÀ

www.argbon.org

The museum, inaugurated in 1982, houses a small but excellent collection of religious art in a restored early-Gothic building. Sections of the rear wall are actually part of the original Roman wall. The collection starts on the ground floor with pieces of Roman funerary art found at Montjuïc, but quickly passes into the world of Catalan religious objects on the first and second floors. On the second floor, the series of triptychs, altarpieces and panels portraying saints and martyrs is the most interesting. The 15th-century altarpiece of Sant Quinze and Santa Julita is particularly gruesome, showing how the unfortunate duo had their throats cut by court guards before being dismembered.

✚ 95 G9 ✉ Avinguda de la Catedral 4, 08002 ☎ 93 315 22 13 ⏱ Jun–end Sep daily 10–8; Oct–end May Tue–Sat 10–2, 5–8, Sun 11–2 ✋ Adult €6, child (under 7) free 🚇 Jaume I 🚌 17, 19, 40, 45 🏛

MUSEU FREDERIC MARÈS
▷ 105.

MUSEU D'HISTÒRIA DE BARCELONA
▷ 106–107.

PALAU DE LA VIRREINA

The Palau de la Virreina was built in the 1770s for Manuel d'Amat, a viceroy returning from a long stint in Peru. It is now a good place to find out what's going on in the city. On the ground floor is the office that issues information and tickets to the city's main events such as the Grec summer festival (▷ 255). There are also frequent free exhibitions, ranging from contemporary art and photography to profiles of local personalities. The *gegants* (giants; ▷ 254) Jaume and Violant are usually in the main entrance and make appearances at carnival and other city fiestas.

✚ 94 F9 ✉ La Rambla 99, 08001 ☎ 93 316 10 00 ⏱ Tue–Sat 11–2, 4–8, Sun 11–3 ✋ Exhibition Room 1: Free; Exhibition Room 2: Adult €4.10, child (under 16) free 🚇 Liceu or Catalunya 🚌 14, 18, 39, 59 and all routes to Plaça de Catalunya

PALAU GÜELL
▷ 108–109.

Left *A detail of the sumptuous interior at Palau de la Virreina, where there are also two gallery spaces*

MUSEU FREDERIC MARÈS

Sculptor and teacher Frederic Marès i Deuloval (1893–1991) was a prolific collector, who was deeply interested in Catalan history and spent his time visiting ancient ruins, abandoned villages, flea markets and junk shops in order to amass his wonderfully eccentric collection. The museum that bears his name now displays a vast array of objects, displayed over several floors.

THE COLLECTION

Among the earliest pieces are hundreds of tiny Iberian ex-voto figurines, as well as carved Roman sarcophagi and masks. However, the main focus of Marès' interest was Romanesque and Gothic sculpture. There are scores of 12th- and 13th-century crucifixes and polychrome Madonnas, stylized yet still strangely powerful. Marès also gathered a superb collection of architectural fragments from the same period, including delicately sculpted church portals and columns with carved capitals. The highlight of the entire collection is undoubtedly the superb relief *Appearance of Jesus to His Disciples at Sea,* created by an artist known only as the Master of Cabestany, who was active in the latter half of the 12th century across northern Spain, southern France and Tuscany. The relief was created for the western portal of the monastery of St. Pere de Rodes near Cadaquès. Among the paintings is a portion of an exquisite gilded altarpiece by Jaume Huguet, one of the most prolific and gifted Gothic artists.

The second part, called the Collector's Cabinet, is the fruit of determined flea-market searching, with such items as snuff boxes, cigarette papers and perfume bottles. There are thousands of objects: wrought-iron door handles, keys, fans, toys, even a whole room full of memorabilia relating to Montserrat. It is curiously absorbing, and offers an intriguing snapshot of the hothouse life of bourgois Barcelona at the end of the 19th century.

The museum occupies a huge palace next to the cathedral, and the entrance is probably the prettiest in Barcelona. The Verger, the garden of the building that was once the Royal Palace of the Counts of Barcelona, has a central fountain and is dotted with orange trees and benches, providing a cooling city oasis. The museum is currently undergoing restoration, scheduled to be completed in mid-2011. In the meantime, huge screens out in the courtyard show highlights from the museum's collection. There is a wonderful outdoor café in summer.

INFORMATION

www.museumares.bcn.es
✚ 95 G9 ✉ Plaça de Sant lu 5–6, 08002 ☎ 93 310 58 00 Ⓒ Closed for refurbishment until summer 2011
Ⓜ Liceu or Jaume I 🚌 17, 19, 40, 45

Above *Some of the fascinating items on display in the museum*

MUSEU D'HISTÒRIA DE BARCELONA

The relics of two millennia of Barcelona's history are on vibrant display at this museum (usually referred to as MUHBA). The entrance is through the 15th-century Casa Pedellas, which was moved here stone by stone in the 1930s. It was during this move that the Roman remains were found. The visit consists of two parts. First, you descend to the building's foundations to visit the vestiges of the Roman city, which at 4,000sq m (43,000sq ft) are the most extensive remains found underground in Europe. Once you have explored this Roman world, you are brought back upstairs to Gothic Barcelona and the palace complex of the Plaça del Rei (▷ 110).

ROMAN BARCELONA

After seeing a small collection of Iberian and Roman objects found at Montjuïc, such as sandstone columns and busts, you are ushered to an elevator, which pronounces that you are about to be whisked back 2,000 years. The beautifully preserved Roman streets and alleys contain houses, *bodegas* (wineries), shops, dye works, laundries, *garum* (fish sauce) vats, a chapel and pretty much everything else you would expect to find in a functioning town of the era. Worth seeking out are the fish-preserving tanks from one of the best-preserved sections of the site. Cleverly lit, this Roman section is viewed from an intricate series of walkways perched above the remains, and explanatory leaflets take you through the workings of a Roman home. There are a couple of stunning mosaics that were once the floors of the *triclinium* (dining room) of a wealthy Roman home.

GOTHIC BARCELONA

The museum continues above ground. The Saló del Tinell (throne room) is a key architectural work of the era. Its six semicircular arches are the largest stone arches ever to be erected in Europe. It was used for parliament meetings in the late 14th century and in 1493 Ferdinand and Isabella are said to have received Christopher Columbus here after his return from the New World. This grand hall is often used for classical music recitals. The graceful Gothic Capella de Santa Agata, begun in 1302, is dedicated to the martyr Saint Agatha. It contains a superb altarpiece by Jaume Huguet depicting the Epiphany. Once outside again, don't forget to admire the Mirador del Rei Martí, or watchtower of King Martin, the last of the Barcelona Count-Kings.

INFORMATION

www.museuhistoria.bcn.es

✚ 95 G9 ✉ Plaça del Rei s/n, 08002 ☎ 93 256 21 22 🕐 Jun–end Sep Tue–Sun 10–8; Oct–end May Tue–Sat 10–2, 4–7, Sun 10–8 💶 Adult €6, child (under 16) free; first Sat of every month free after 4pm; Sun free after 3pm; admission allows free entry to the seven sites run by MUHBA, including Casa-Museu Verdaguer, Monestir de Pedralbes and the Centre d'Interpretació del Park Güell 🚇 Jaume I 🚌 17, 19, 40, 45 🎫 In Catalan or Spanish: Jul–end Aug Wed 6pm; Sep–end Jun Sun 11.30; adult €5, child (under 7) free; tours in English by appointment 📖 Large format, beautifully produced guidebook available in Spanish, Catalan and English for €24 at the ticket office and gift shop 🎁 Very good gift shop on the corner of Carrer Llibreteria sells books and objects related to Barcelona, including an interesting selection of books and toys for children, all with a Barcelona theme

Above *The courtyard of the museum*
Opposite *A 16th-century skyscraper contains five floors of galleries, towering over little Plaça del Rei*

INFORMATION

www.palauguell.cat

✚ 94 F9 ✉ Carrer Nou de la
Rambla 3–5, 08002 ☎ 93 317 39 74
🌀 Currently scheduled to reopen after
major refurbishment 23 April (St. Jordí's
Day) 2011 ✋ Free 🚇 Liceu 🗓

INTRODUCTION

The magnificent Palau Güell, built between 1886 and 1890, is one of the earliest major works by Antoni Gaudí, whose unique vision would transform Barcelona's cityscape so dramatically around the turn of the 20th century. The mansion was constructed for the wealthy industrialist Eusebi Güell, who was Gaudí's most prominent patron throughout his life. The palace is undergoing a complete restoration and is scheduled to reopen in late spring 2011.

In 1886, all of Barcelona was abuzz with preparations for the upcoming Universal Exhibition of 1888, and Eusebi Güell suggested that Gaudí create an extravagant new mansion as part of the celebrations. The young architect had already completed several commissions for his friend and patron, including extensive works in the Güell estate in Pedralbes. A site on Carrer Nou de la Rambla was chosen because of its proximity to an older family mansion around the corner on Las Ramblas, and the two properties were eventually linked with a passage (which still exists). The street was narrow and the site was cramped, but Gaudí made ingenious use of the limited light and space in extraordinary and entirely original ways. It would be Gaudí's most important commission to date, and he had what every architect dreams of: a patron who told him to spare no expense. The palace, when complete, glistened with the most lustrous materials that money could buy.

WHAT TO SEE

If you've seen any of Gaudí's later buildings, such as the Casa Batlló or La Pedrera (Casa Milà), the Palau Güell might look surprisingly austere, particularly the facade. Covered with a mesh of whiplash ironwork and emblazoned with an enormous Catalan coat of arms, it looks distinctly forbidding. There are two gates, so that carriages could sweep in through one gate and exit via the other. Within, a ramp leads down to the stables, where Gaudí made use of his characteristic exposed brick arches.

A flight of stairs with a stained-glass window bearing the Catalan standard (both Güell and Gaudí were ardent Catalan nationalists) leads to the splendid reception rooms. Light filters in through a long gallery with graceful arches supported by slender marble columns and sumptuous coffered ceilings which reflect Gaudí's fascination with Mudéjar architecture. At the end of the gallery

Above *Intricate wrought-iron detail on the facade of Palau Güell*

is a visitor's room, with a particularly elaborate ceiling: look closely, and you might spot the tiny spyholes, where the Güells could listen in on their guests' conversation.

Two spectacular marquetry doors lead into the heart of the house, the magnificent central hall. The lofty room is dominated by an enormous dome, with curved stained-glass windows and shafts of light entering through tiny windows scattered like a constellation across the ceiling. Güell, like Gaudí, was deeply religious, and the hall was designed to be used in several ways, including a chapel-oratory. An ingenious cupboard made of tropical hardwood, built into the southern wall, unfolds into a magnificent private chapel. Although stripped of its original fittings during the Civil War (1936–39), it is still inlaid with rare tortoiseshell. The hall, which boasts perfect acoustics, was also used for concerts, and musicians would play from a gallery enclosed with more whirling wrought iron which overlooks the salon. Behind the salon are the family's private dining room and sitting room, less impressive, but still lavishly embellished, with a huge marble chimney and a curving window seat. A small terrace allows visitors to admire the rear facade, with its coloured tile designs in shades of ochre and cobalt.

The family's private apartments are on the second floor, set around the gallery overlooking the main hall. Many of the stunning original details have been preserved, including beautiful fireplaces and more gilded, coffered ceilings. In the main bedroom, the initials 'E' and 'I' (for Eusebi and Isabel) are entwined romantically throughout the room. The bathroom and toilets have also survived intact, and are tiled with ceramics made specially for the palace. The servants' rooms are in the attic, from where a staircase leads up to the rooftop. As in so many of his later buildings, Gaudí let his imagination run wild on the roof terrace, as playful and colourful as the interior is dark and foreboding. The dome rises up to a lofty central spire, covered with pale pebbles, and is surrounded with swirling chimneys covered with multicoloured *trencadí* (tile fragments).

Below *Amazing detail characterizes Gaudí's design on the palace exterior*

Above *A classical statue stands in front of the fountain in Plaça de Catalunya*

of the city's line of Count-Kings. The mid-16th-century Mirador del Rei Martí on the left was used as a watchtower, and Palau de Lloctinent in front of it was the official home of the viceroy after Catalonia lost its independence in the 16th century.

The Basque sculptor Eduardo Chillida's (1924–2002) 1986 work *Topo* is the square's only reference to modernity. The severe half-cube in metal, with arches protruding from one side, somehow manages to blend in beautifully with the rich stone of the surrounding palaces.

The paved square once rang with the comings and goings of official visitors as well as buyers and sellers of flour and hay. It is now frequently used as an open-air stage for concerts during the Grec and La Mercè festivals, and there is no better place in the city to enjoy a drink al fresco.

✚ 95 G9 🚇 Jaume I 🚌 17, 19, 45

PLAÇA DE CATALUNYA
This is the hub of the city, the low-key equivalent of London's Piccadilly Circus or New York's Times Square. Even if you don't plan on going there, chances are you'll cross its paved surface at some point, possibly to have a drink at its celebrated Café Zurich. In addition to holding the largest of the El Corte Inglés department stores in Barcelona, the shopping complex El Triangle, and the largest tourist office, it is also the principal transport stop-off. You can catch a bus or train connection to anywhere in town, and the airport, from here.

Architecturally the square has lost a lot over the years through alterations to accommodate traffic and public transport. Built in 1927 by architect Francesc Nabot, its original 50,000sq m (538,000sq ft) have been somewhat reduced and are now populated by balloon and pigeon-seed sellers, students relaxing on its tiny lawns in front of the fountain and shoppers taking a breather on one of its many benches. The statue on the Las Ramblas side is a homage to Francesc Macià, the first president of Catalonia's autonomous government, the Generalitat.
✚ 94 F8 🚇 Catalunya

PLAÇA DEL REI
Flanked by the Palau Reial (Royal Palace), which houses the fascinating Museu d'Història de Barcelona (▷ 106–107), this is one of the most architecturally complete of Barcelona's medieval squares, and has one of the most interesting histories. The 14th- to 16th-century buildings, with the palace and magnificent Saló del Tinell (throne room), were once the residence

PLAÇA REIAL
The bars that line the large Plaça Reial are a magnet for both locals and visitors on balmy nights during the summer months. During the day, however, the square has a slower pace, which means its architecture can be more easily appreciated. A Capuchin convent was demolished to make way for the square that was designed in the 1840s by Daniel Molina, who was also responsible for the city's market La Boquería. It was one of the larger projects in Barcelona's urban renewal project of the 1880s and it is still the only one in Barcelona that was designed as a complete unit, including the housing, the porticoes and the fountain, inspired by the Three Graces, and the Gaudí-designed lampposts. The overall feel is one of tranquillity and elegance. Because of concerns about petty crime, pickpockets in particular, it is best to have your wits about you when visiting the square.
✚ 94 F9 🚇 Liceu or Drassanes 🚌 14, 17, 19, 38, 40, 45, 59, 91

Opposite *The Three Graces fountain (left) and cafés (right) on imposing Plaça Reial*

PLAÇA DE SANT FELIP NERI

One of the most enchanting corners of the Gothic Quarter, Plaça de Sant Felip Neri is a storybook vision of a medieval square, complete with tinkling stone fountain and pretty church. Yet, despite appearances, Plaça de Sant Felip Neri was only created in the 1950s, when historic buildings threatened by modern developments elsewhere in the old city were painstakingly rebuilt here. The area was formerly occupied by an ancient cemetery, but it was badly bombed during the Civil War: the damage is evident on the church facade, which is still pockmarked with shrapnel. These elegant buildings have been neighbours for only a few decades, yet they fit together so harmoniously that the stone ensemble seems to have stood here for centuries and exudes a timeless appeal. The Casa del Gremi dels Sabaters, the shoemaker's guildhouse, was built in 1565, and is now home to the delightful little shoe museum, the Museu del Calçat (▷ 104).

➕ 94 F9 🚇 Liceu, Jaume I 🚌 14, 59, 91, 120, 45, 40, 19, 17

PLAÇA DE SANT JAUME
▷ 112–113.

PLAÇA DE SANT JUST

Plaça de Sant Just is a magical little square, which rarely features on tourist itineraries and yet contains some of the old city's most charming monuments. A flight of steps leads to the church of Sants Just i Pastor, dedicated to a pair of now obscure child martyrs, whose cult was important in the city in the fourth century AD. It's believed that this church was one of the first to be consecrated in Barcelona, and the present 14th-century Gothic edifice was built over the ruins of a much older church. On the other side of the square, the Palau Moxó is exquisitely decorated with *esgrafiado* (decorative plaster work), depicting garlands and cherubs. The interiors are equally extravagant, and can even be visited if your pockets are deep enough to rent out the splendid salons. A neighbouring Gothic palace now houses the Reial Acadèmia de Bones Lletres, the entity which regulates the Catalan language. It is not open to the public, but the Gothic courtyard, with its graceful stone staircase, can be visited freely. A couple of bars and cafés have tables out on the little square, which is romantically candlelit on summer evenings.

➕ 95 G9 🚇 Jaume I 🚌 45, 40, 19, 17

LAS RAMBLAS
▷ 114–115.

SANTA MARIA DEL PÍ

The squat and imposing Santa Maria del Pí is a fine example of the single-nave church, typical of the austere Catalan Gothic style from around the 1300s. The nave spans roughly one third of its entire length and, like other churches of the period, there are no aisles, rather one giant space. There are 14 chapels in all, set between the buttresses, but even these do not detract from the dominating spatial clarity. A rose window sits over the entrance to the church, filling it with light, and an ingenious stone arch spanning the church's entire width has supported its choir stalls for centuries. The square on which the church sits is the perfect place to while away a lazy hour or so people-watching, as it is in one of the most picturesque pockets of the Barri Gòtic (▷ 97).

➕ 94 F9 ✉ Plaça del Pí 7, 08002 ☎ 93 318 47 43 🕐 Daily 9–1, 4–9 ✋ Free 🚇 Liceu 🚌 14, 18, 38, 59

INFORMATION

www.barcelonaturisme.com

✚ 94 F9 🛈 Carrer de la Ciutat 2 (inside the town hall), 08002 ☎ 93 285 38 34
🕐 Mon–Fri 9–8, Sat 10–8, Sun 10–2
🚇 Jaume I 🚌 16, 17, 19, 45

INTRODUCTION

A grand square in the heart of the city, Plaça de Sant Jaume is used for social and political gatherings. It is the political hub of Barcelona, where all major decisions about the running of the city and Catalonia are made. This generously proportioned square, halfway between Las Ramblas and Via Laietana, is flanked by the Casa de la Ciutat (the city's town hall, or Ajuntament) and the Palau de la Generalitat (the seat of the autonomous government). Public entry to both is restricted, but the expanse of flagstones between the two is a major stage for many public events. The Barça soccer team greets ecstatic crowds from the Casa de la Ciutat's balcony after a major win, and two great Catalan folk traditions—*castellers* (human towers) and the *sardana* (a group dance)—are played out here at weekends and public holidays. Whenever there is a demonstration, people generally start off or finish at the Plaça de Sant Jaume to make their voices heard by the politicians who can make a difference to their cause.

WHAT TO SEE

PALAU DE LA GENERALITAT

www.gencat.net

The Generalitat is both the name of Catalonia's autonomous government and the building from which it governs. One hundred and fifteen presidents of Catalonia have so far ruled from its beautiful Gothic interior, making it one of the few medieval buildings in Europe that have been continually used for the same purpose for which they were built. Its rather austere facade hides a wealth of interior lushness, only a minor part of which is accessible to the public, but visit if you can. When the president of the Generalitat is in town, he stays at the Casa dels Canonges, a set of 14th-century canons' houses next door to the Palau. The hanging enclosed walkway, which joins the two buildings, was modelled on Venice's Bridge of Sighs, but dates from the 1920s.

The main highlight comes as soon as you enter: the spectacular Pati de Tarongers (Courtyard of the Oranges), a luscious interior stone courtyard dotted

Above *The plain facade of the Palau de la Generalitat hides a fine Gothic interior*

with orange trees, with a central sculpture of St. George (or Jordi in Catalan), the region's patron saint and a recurring image throughout the Generalitat. The pink marble columns are topped with gargoyles, each of them with special significance to the history of Catalonia: The Turk's head is a reminder of the scourge of pirates that once roamed the Mediterranean, and the Macer was in charge of keeping the peace during rowdy parliamentary sessions.

The flamboyant Capella de Sant Jordi, a private chapel with a mainly red interior and embellished with 15th-century Gothic details, follows on from the courtyard. It has a giant stained-glass window and a silver embossed altar both showing St. George and his fearful dragon. The magnificent Flemish tapestries were woven in the mid-17th century and tell the story of Noah and the Ark. The splendid Saló de Sant Jordi, glimpses of which are possible from the Generalitat's main entrance, has a sumptuous domed ceiling. It has three naves separated by giant pillars, and the walls are covered in modern murals of key historical events. A huge chandelier crowns the room, giving this rather solemn civic space a touch of grandeur.

☎ 93 402 46 17 🕐 10.30–1, second and fourth Sat and Sun of each month, and 25 Apr, 11 and 24 Sep 🖐 Free, bring your passport

CASA DE LA CIUTAT

Across the road, the Ajuntament (meaning both town hall and local council) also has its roots in the Middle Ages. The institution started out as the Consell de Cent, a representative council of 100 guild leaders and ordinary citizens that was one of the first truly democratic political bodies in the world. Although not as spectacular as the Generalitat, the classic early-1900s facade hides a Gothic interior with recent additions. The highlight is the Saló de les Croniques with murals by painter Josep Maria Sert, carried out in 1928. Sert went on to decorate New York's Rockefeller Center.

☎ 93 402 00 00 🕐 Sun 10–3.30; tours every 30 min (at 11am in English) 🖐 Free

Below *The inner courtyard of the Generalitat is filled with orange trees*

LAS RAMBLAS

INFORMATION
www.barcelonaturisme.com
✚ 94 F9 ℹ Plaça de Catalunya 17,
08002 ☎ 93 285 38 34 (daily 9–8)
🕐 Daily 9–9 🚇 Catalunya, Liceu or
Drassanes

INTRODUCTION

No trip to Barcelona is complete without seeing Las Ramblas, considered to be the city's very heart. The avenue, 1km (0.5 mile) long, is ideal for people-watching—a giant stage for anyone with a story to tell or a song to sing.

The word *rambla* itself comes from the Arabic term *raml*, which means riverbed, and that is where the origins of Las Ramblas lie. A filthy gully that ran along the medieval city walls was filled in at the end of the 1700s, and cash-rich Catalans soon started to build their mansions along the city's newest and most fashionable address (▷ 33). Since 1994, people have been able to continue their stroll across the sea. The wooden walkway, the Rambla de Mar, starts from the Passeig de Colom and continues across the water to the Maremagnum entertainment complex. It is dotted with benches from where you can admire the port, and it's the ideal way to finish a visit to the city's most famous street.

Las Ramblas was once described by the writer W. Somerset Maugham (1874–1965) as the most beautiful street in the world, and despite the souvenir shops and fast-food joints that have begun appearing at a worrying rate, this tree-lined promenade remains popular among the city's residents. Las Ramblas is actually five streets in one, hence the plural vernacular, from Rambla de Canaletes at the Plaça de Catalunya end to Rambla de Santa Mònica, ending at the port, at the other.

WHAT TO SEE
LA RAMBLA DE CANALETES

Diehard Barça soccer fans gather here after a big win and sometimes there are thousands of flag-waving, hymn-singing supporters. Canaletes is the 19th-century fountain here and legend has it that anyone who drinks from this water source will return to the city. There are a few public chairs to sit on at this part of Las Ramblas, where shoe-shiners still do their rounds. Living statues are also seen along this stretch and are a good photo opportunity, as long as you remember to tip them.

Above *Las Ramblas is a great place to people-watch*

LA RAMBLA DELS ESTUDIS

This section is named after the university that once stood here. It is also commonly known as the Rambla dels Ocells (of the birds) because of the myriad birds and other animals that are locked in cages and sold from stalls here. The Teatro Poliorama at No. 115, once the home of Catalonia's National Theatre Company, was the place where writer George Orwell (1903–50) took refuge from gunfire during the Civil War while he was in the service of the International Brigade.

LA RAMBLA DE LES FLORS

This is the prettiest part of the avenue, with dozens of flower sellers and their blazing displays. This is its colloquial name, as it is officially the Rambla de Sant Josep, named after the 16th-century convent that once stood here. The convent was torn down to make room for the Boquería (▷ 120), still the city's principal fresh produce market. Opposite the Boquería is the bizarre Casa dels Paraigües (House of Umbrellas), constructed on the site of an old umbrella shop, and with a distinctive umbrella-decorated facade. A gigantic mosaic mural laid on the street in 1976 by Joan Miró marks the Plaça de la Boquería, the halfway point of Las Ramblas.

LA RAMBLA DELS CAPUTXINS

This is home to the city's opera house, the Liceu (▷ 103). Opposite here is the Café de l'Òpera (▷ 123), one of the oldest cafés in the city, which still serves the post-performance opera crowd during the season with their wonderful hot *xocolata* (chocolate).

LA RAMBLA DE SANTA MÒNICA

The next stretch is the threshold of Barcelona's port. There are dozens of portrait artists, advertising their talents through pictures pinned around their stands. Arts Santa Mònica (www.artssantamonica.cat) is an important public contemporary art gallery in a converted convent. The Teatre Principal, on the right, is the oldest theatre in the city—it started out in 1603 as a modest wooden building for the theatrical arts.

TIPS

» Watch your wallet and other belongings on Las Ramblas, as it is prime pickpocketing territory, and avoid the scams pulled on tourists with balls under a cup and card tricks.

» Don't even try to drive down Las Ramblas in your car (the road runs either side of the pedestrianized walkway), as the traffic during the day is horrendous.

» There are plenty of places to eat on the central avenue, but they are aimed at tourists and it is likely to be more expensive to take a table outside rather than eating inside the establishment—check prices beforehand. Cafés and restaurants on the streets leading off Las Ramblas will be less expensive.

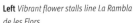

Left *Vibrant flower stalls line La Rambla de les Flors*
Below *Living statues and mime artists perform along Las Ramblas*

BARRI GÒTIC

Bars and restaurants have replaced many of the workshops that once dotted the narrow streets of Barcelona's medieval hub, but an afternoon spent here is richly rewarding, and essential to understanding Barcelona's Gothic architecture.

THE WALK

Distance: 1.5km (1 mile)
Time: 1–1.5 hours
Start/end at: Plaça de l'Àngel

HOW TO GET THERE

Metro: The closest station to the Plaça de l'Àngel is Jaume I on the yellow line 4.

★ Start the walk once you have exited the metro station onto the Plaça de l'Àngel. With your back to the large thoroughfare, Via Laietana, look for the road to your right, Baixada de la Llibreteria, and start walking along it.

❶ The Cereria Subira, at Baixada de la Llibreteria 7, is notable for being the oldest continuously trading shop in the city. Note the pair of elegant statues at the base of its staircase. The premises dates from 1761 and started life by selling ladies' apparel

long before the handmade candles you see on display today.

Continue walking up Baixada de la Llibreteria to the intersection with Carrer de Veguer and turn right, walking right to the end.

❷ This will bring you to Plaça del Rei (▷ 110), the very heart of the Barri Gòtic and home of the Museu d'Història de Barcelona (▷ 106–107). The 14th- to 16th-century complex was once used to rule Catalonia and it is said that Ferdinand and Isabella received Columbus here after his voyage to the New World.

With your back to the Plaça, take the right-hand exit onto Baixada de Santa Clara. You will then come to the rear of the city's cathedral (▷ 98–101). Turn right along Carrer dels Comtes, with the cathedral running parallel to your left.

Immediately to your right is the baroque Palau del Lloctinent, which forms part of the medieval palace-complex of the Plaça del Rei. It was built as the home of the Viceroy of Catalonia. You can enter the pretty courtyard and admire the fountain.

Continuing along the same street you also pass the Museu Frederic Marès (▷ 105) and its courtyard, with a fountain and citrus trees. Walk to the end of Carrer dels Comtes to the Plaça de la Seu. Turn left onto Carrer de Santa Llúcia.

❸ The Casa de l'Ardiaca is just after this intersection, on the right. It dates from the 16th century and was once the residence of the city's archdeacon. Today it stores the city's archives, but its exquisite patio, with a century-old palm tree, is open to the public.

Above *Casa de l'Ardiaca's patio*

Turn left onto Carrer del Bisbe and then turn hard right onto the winding Montjuïc del Bisbe.

4 This leads to one of the most charming squares in the *barri*: Sant Felip Neri. Apart from its 17th-century church, central fountain and the Museu del Calçat (Shoe Museum, ▷ 104), this tranquil spot is testimony to a dark past. The holes on the church's facade were caused by a bombardment by fascist troops during the Civil War (1936–39) during which 20 children, pupils from the school next door, were killed.

Take the farthest exit out of the square onto Carrer de Sant Felip Neri and then left onto Carrer de Sant Domènec del Call. You are now in the heart of El Call, the city's old Jewish ghetto. Turn left onto Carrer del Call and continue to the immense Plaça de Sant Jaume (▷ 112–113). Flanked on either side by the seats of Catalonia's regional governments, spend some time taking a tour of the facades of the Generalitat and Casa de la Ciutat.

For a short detour, take Carrer del Paradís, to your right as you look at the Generalitat. This brings you to the four Corinthian columns that are the remains of the Roman Temple d'Augustus. (They are tucked away in a Gothic courtyard belonging to the Catalan Excursionists.)

Once back in the Plaça de Sant Jaume, take Carrer de la Ciutat, the road to your left as you face the Casa de la Ciutat. After a minute or so of walking, the street changes its name to Carrer del Regomir and contains vestiges of Roman Barcelona.

5 The Pati Llimona, on the left at No. 3, is used for lively community events and has part of the old Roman water and sewerage systems, which are visible from street level. Next door is a tiny chapel dedicated to St. Christopher, dating from the 16th century.

Continue down Carrer del Regomir and then turn left onto Carrer del

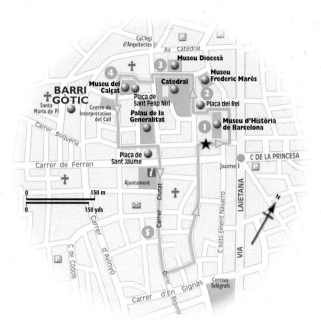

Correu Vell, named after the old post office in its immediate vicinity, and left again up the steep incline, Baixada Viladecols. Immediately on your right is the most complete section of the city's original Roman walls. After a few steps the street changes its name to Carrer de Lledó and will bring you to the Plaça de Sant Just (▷ 111), another pretty square with a Gothic church and the oldest water source in the city. A market selling artisan foodstuffs is set up here on the first Thursday of every month.

If you exit the Plaça the same way you entered, onto Carrer de Lledó, the entrance to a tiny lane, Bisbe Caçador, is opposite. Here you will see the threshold of the Acadèmia de Bones Lletres, one of the best-conserved historic palaces in the vicinity, which is not open to the public.

Back on Carrer de Lledó, turn right, where the road name changes to Carrer de la Dagueria. At the intersection with Carrer de Jaume I, turn right, and Plaça de l'Àngel, where you started, is on the left. The metro station, Jaume I, is also here.

WHEN TO GO
After lunch is the best time to avoid the tour groups.

WHERE TO EAT
The outdoor café at the Museu Frederic Marès (open Easter–Oct) has great vistas of the rear of the Roman walls.

PLACES TO VISIT
CASA DE L'ARDIACA
✉ Carrer de Santa Llùcia s/n, 08002 ☎ 93 318 11 95 🕒 Mon–Fri 8am–8.30pm, Sat 9–1 💺 Free

TEMPLE D'AUGUSTUS
✉ Carrer del Paradís 10, 08002 ☎ 93 315 11 11 🕒 Jun–end Sep Tue–Sat 10–8, Sun 10–2; Oct–end May Tue–Sat 10–2, 4–8, Sun 10–2 💺 Free

LAS RAMBLAS

No trip to the city is complete without a stroll along Las Ramblas. It is the sum of five different *ramblas* (pedestrian avenues), which together form one of the best-known images of the Catalan capital.

THE WALK

Distance: 2km (1 mile)
Time: 1 hour
Start at: Catalunya metro station, Las Ramblas entrance
End at: Plaça Portal de la Pau

HOW TO GET THERE

Metro: Catalunya station is on the red line 1 and green line 3.
Bus: A large number of buses run to or through the Plaça de Catalunya, including 14, 16, 17, 22, 24, 28, 39, 41, 45, 47 and 58.

★ Start your walk at the northern end of Las Ramblas, outside the main entrance of the Catalunya metro station, with your back to Plaça de Catalunya. This first section is known as Rambla de Canaletes, after the wrought-iron drinking fountain you see as soon as you hit the street. On the right, at No. 10, is the Farmàcia Nadal, an example of the elegant Noucentista style that followed Modernisme. Turn left onto Carrer de la Canuda.

❶ The Ateneu Barcelonès is on the right at Carrer de la Canuda 6, where the street meets Plaça Vila de

Madrid. It is the Modernista home of the city's elite literary and cultural association. It has a charming indoor patio and garden that is not strictly open to the public, but nobody seems to mind if you have a discreet look around. After a few paces you reach Plaça Vila de Madrid itself, which has remains of the necropolis of Roman Barcelona.

Return along Carrer de la Canuda to Las Ramblas. Turn left and continue for a minute or so until you reach the pedestrianized Carrer de Portaferrissa, also on your left. Turn down this road.

❷ This is one of the main shopping streets and is marked by a pretty ceramic drinking fountain at its entrance. Carrer de Petritxol, the second street along on your right, is known for its *granjas*, cafés serving cakes and cream-laden hot chocolate. If you continue to the end of Carrer de Petritxol, you reach Plaça del Pí, one of the Barri Gòtic's most attractive squares.

Retrace your steps along Carrer de Petritxol and Portaferrissa to Las

Ramblas and turn left. You are now in La Rambla de les Flors, named after the numerous flower-sellers who trade here.

❸ On your right, at No. 91, is La Boqueria (▷ 120), Barcelona's food market. It is famous for its masterful Modernista wrought-iron entrance, but it's worth taking a look at the quality of the local produce inside, even if you don't plan to buy anything. The noise and the energy of the place are exhilarating.

Continue along the same side of Las Ramblas for a short while to the corner of the tiny Carrer de Petxina on your right.

❹ The Antigua Casa Figueres is a glittering example of a Modernista ceramic facade. The shop is owned by the most celebrated family of pastry-makers in the city and is a haven for lovers of chocolates and confectionery.

Return to Las Ramblas, turn right and continue along the same side to the next intersection with Carrer de l'Hospital. You are now outside

Opposite *The seaward end of Las Ramblas is marked by the Monument a Colom*

Gran Teatre del Liceu (▷ 103), Barcelona's celebrated opera house. Directly opposite is the Café de l'Òpera, a city institution, and a few doors down, at No. 45 on the opera-house side, is the Hotel Oriente, where many famous opera stars have stayed while performing at the opera house. With your back to the hotel, turn right and continue along Las Ramblas until you are just past the junction with Carrer de Ferran.

⑤ The large square you see to the left is the Plaça Reial (▷ 110). With lamp posts designed by Gaudí and a central fountain, it is a popular place to hang out during the day and to have a drink at night. There are a few porticoed streets and small shops that flank its edges.

Return to Las Ramblas and turn left, continuing towards the port. The Arts Santa Mònica, the modern building on the right at No. 7, puts on mainly free exhibitions of contemporary artists from Spain and abroad. Just a few steps farther along Las Ramblas bring you to the tiny Passatge de la Banca, on the left. This is a pretty walkway that leads to the Museu de Cera (▷ 104). El Bosc de les Fades (The Fairy Forest) next door is the museum's café (▷ 123), which also has some whimsical installations, including magic mirrors and a running brook.

Return to Las Ramblas, turn left and walk toward the vast Monument a Colom (▷ 139). This marks the official end of Las Ramblas, but if you have the energy you can walk across the suspended bridge, La Rambla de Mar, directly in front, to cross to the shopping and entertainment complex of Maremagnum (▷ 159).

WHEN TO GO

Any time, but be aware of your personal belongings in crowded parts of Las Ramblas and at night in the streets around Plaça Reial.

WHERE TO EAT
CAFÉ DE L'ÒPERA
▷ 123.

LA GRANJA DULCINEA
Stop off at this wonderful old-fashioned café for *xocolata amb xurros* (hot chocolate and *churros*). ✉ Carrer de Petritxol 2, 08002 ☎ 93 302 68 24 🕐 Daily 10–9

PLACES TO VISIT
ANTIGUA CASA FIGUERES (PASTELERÍA ESCRIBÁ)
✉ Rambla de les Flors 83, 08002 ☎ 93 301 60 27 🕐 Mon–Sun 8.30am–9pm

ARTS SANTA MÒNICA
✉ Rambla de Santa Mònica 7, 08002 ☎ 93 316 28 10 🕐 Tue–Sun 11–9 💲 Free

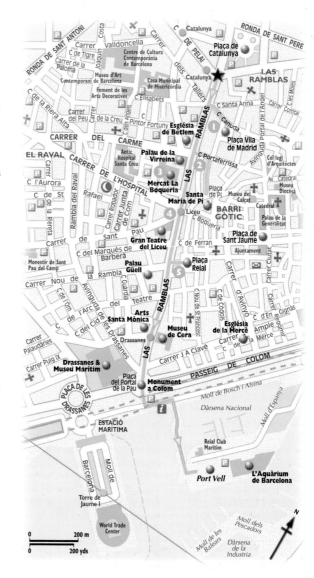

WHAT TO DO

SHOPPING

ANGEL BATLLE

In this street of many antiques shops, fitting for one of the oldest parts of town that also formed El Call, the Jewish ghetto, of the Middle Ages, Angel Batlle stocks beautiful old engravings, maps, fashion plates and prints as well as intriguing old texts in Spanish and Catalan. Credit cards are not accepted.

✚ 130 F9 ✉ Carrer de la Palla 23, 08002 ☎ 93 301 58 84 ◷ Mon–Fri 9–1.30, 4–7.30 Ⓜ Liceu

ANTIQUITATS HERITAGE

Step back in time the moment you enter this charmingly old-fashioned shop. It's packed to the rafters with costumes, feathers, beads, jewellery, gowns, shawls and much more. The earliest pieces date back to the 18th century. The prices may leave you reeling, however.

✚ 130 F9 ✉ Carrer dels Banys Nous 14, 08001 ☎ 93 317 85 15 ◷ Mon–Sat 10.30–2, 5–8 Ⓜ Liceu

LA BOQUERÍA

www.boqueria.info

Barcelona is not short of markets, but La Boqueria (also called Mercat de Sant Josep) is the most popular. Right at the heart of Las Ramblas, this covered market is an eruption of noise, colour and aroma, and is a great place to buy fresh produce. Once you've finished your shopping, stop at one of the bars to rest your feet.

✚ 130 F9 ✉ La Rambla 91–101, 08002 ☎ 93 318 25 84 ◷ Mon–Sat 8–8 (some stalls close at 3pm) Ⓜ Liceu

LE BOUDOIR

www.leboudoir.net

Naughty but very, very nice, Le Boudoir stocks luxurious lingerie and sleepwear, some sleek and sexy, and some downright kinky. Decked out like a 19th-century brothel, the shop sells accessories such as furry handcuffs and music for 'getting you in the mood'. It has a beautiful range of swimwear in the summer.

✚ 130 F9 ✉ Carrer de la Canuda 21, 08002 ☎ 93 302 52 81 ◷ Sep–end Jul Mon–Sat 10–8.30; Aug Mon–Sat 10–2, 5–8.30 Ⓜ Catalunya

LA CAIXA DE FANG

Marcelí Garreta has been in business since 1977 and sells wooden and clay kitchen utensils

Above Espardenyes *come in many hues*

from this shop. Although he insists that all items serve a practical purpose, most of his customers buy his wares (of which many are pots and spoons) for decoration. You'll also find pieces from all over Spain. Particularly popular are the flat-bottomed glasses that locals use for wine (the long-stemmed kind are usually reserved for chic restaurants and fine wines).

🚇 131 G9 ✉ Carrer de Frenería 1, 08002 ☎ 93 315 17 04 🕐 Mon–Sat 10–8 🚇 Jaume I

CALPA
www.bossesdepellcalpa.com
Creative and increasingly exclusive, Calpa is a friendly, busy store that can overwhelm customers with its jumble of bags, belts and other leather accessories. All shapes, styles and sizes are piled high in every available space. Prices are reasonable and you can find some very distinct and unusual designs here as many of the bags are made by young local designers.

🚇 130 F9 ✉ Carrer de Ferran 53, 08002 ☎ 93 318 40 30 🕐 Mon–Fri 9.30–2, 4.30–8, Sat 10–2, 5–8.30 🚇 Liceu

CASAS
www.casasclub.com
This is probably the most comprehensive of the city's shoe shops, where you'll find all the most prominent labels under one roof. Dr. Martens and Caterpillar for the young (or young at heart) and Début, Pura López, Mare, Rodolfo Zengarini and Robert Clergerie for the seriously trend-conscious. The house collection, Camilla Casas, will suit more conventional shoppers.

🚇 130 F8 ✉ Avinguda del Portal de l'Àngel 40, 08002 ☎ 93 302 11 32 🕐 Mon–Sat 10–9 🚇 Catalunya

CÓMPLICES
www.libreriacomplices.com
This bookshop, near the town hall in the heart of the Barri Gòtic, focuses on gay and lesbian literature. Art and photography titles, novels, poetry, essays and videos are available here. The bookshop is a good meeting point and source of information if you want to find out more about the gay scene in Barcelona.

🚇 130 F9 ✉ Carrer de Cervantes 4, 08002 ☎ 93 412 72 83 🕐 Mon–Fri 10.30–8, Sat 12–8 🚇 Jaume I

EL CORTE INGLÉS
www.elcorteingles.es
This is Spain's most popular department store. With branches all over the country, El Corte Inglés sells clothes, food, shoes, electrical appliances, sports gear and more. It is the perfect place to go if you are short on time and aren't able to trawl separate specialist shops. The top-floor café is a handy place to stop for a coffee or a light lunch, with great views over the city.

🚇 130 F8 ✉ Plaça de Catalunya 14, 08002 ☎ 93 306 38 00 🕐 Mon–Sat 10–10 🚇 Catalunya

FNAC
www.fnac.es
FNAC has three branches in Barcelona, all within shopping centres. This one is in El Triangle, and the other two are at L'Illa and Diagonal Mar. These stores sell so much more than CDs and there will be plenty to keep you amused: music, books, hi-fi systems, video and photographic supplies and an IT department covering everything from hardware to mouse mats and printer paper. Everything has a lowest price guarantee, so if you find something less expensive somewhere else, FNAC will refund the difference.

🚇 130 F8 ✉ Plaça de Catalunya 4, 08002 ☎ 93 344 18 00 🕐 Mon–Sat 10–10 🚇 Catalunya

FORMATGERIA LA SEU
www.formatgerialaseu.com
Scotswoman Catherine McLaughlin spent years scouring Spain for the best farmhouse cheeses and the result is this charming shop set in an old granja (dairy produce supplier) in the Barri Gòtic. From León to Llerida, and the mildest cheese to the downright smelliest, Catherine will introduce you to the fascinating world of Iberian artisan cheeses via her tasting sessions, cheese-making classes and wonderful array of cheeses for sale.

🚇 131 G91 ✉ Carrer Dagueria 16, 08002 ☎ 93 412 65 48 🕐 Tue–Thu 10–2, 5–8, Fri–Sat 10–3.30, 5–8. Closed Aug 🚇 Jaume I

GEMMA POVO
This cosily cluttered shop resembles a farmhouse kitchen, so it's the perfect place to shop if you want to re-create that Catalan masia (country house) look in your own home. Gemma Povo sells original ironwork lamps and furniture made in its own workshop, along with antique Spanish furniture and local crafts.

🚇 130 F9 ✉ Carrer dels Banys Nous 5–7, 08002 ☎ 93 301 37 76 🕐 Tue–Fri 9.30–2.30, 5–8, Sat 10–2, Mon 9.30–2.30. Closed Aug 🚇 Liceu

GOTHAM
www.gotham-bcn.com
This small shop in the Barrí Gòtic was the first to catch on to the collectibility of retro objects, and it stocks wares from the mid-20th century plus re-editions of design classics. From plastic chairs to wall fittings and 1950s tea sets, there's always something interesting, although the prices are more top-end than bargain-basement.

🚇 130 F9 ✉ Carrer de Cervantes 7, 08002 ☎ 93 412 46 47 🕐 Mon–Sat 10.30–2, 5–8.30 🚇 Jaume I, Liceu

LA MANUAL ALPARGATERA
www.lamanual.net
You'll find this shop, selling handmade espardenyes (espadrilles) and sandals, in the Barri Gòtic, where the open workshop enables customers to view the skilled craftswomen making the shoes. In addition to footwear, there's also a good collection of walking sticks and hats. The company has been trading in Barcelona since 1910, and the late Pope John Paul II was purportedly a one-time client.

🚇 130 F9 ✉ Carrer d'Avinyó 7, 08002 ☎ 93 301 01 72 🕐 Mon–Sat 9.30–1.30, 4.30–8 🚇 Jaume I

MIL BARRETS I GORRES

This hat shop has been a supplier of headgear to a discerning, wealthy clientele since 1850. It stocks a fine collection of traditional hats, a handful of modern, urban labels such as Kangol, and even a few Stetsons from the USA.

131 G8 ✉ Carrer de Fontanella 20, 08010 ☎ 93 301 84 91 ⊕ Mon–Fri 9.30–1.30, 4.15–8, Sat 10–2, 4.30–8 Ⓜ Urquinaona

PAPIRUM

www.papirum-bcn.com

Lovers of elegant stationery won't be able to resist the Barri Gòtic's Papirum, a tiny shop dealing in exquisite hand-printed paper, marbled blank books and writing implements. Desk accessories such as pencil cases are also stocked, some of which are even made out of paper. Credit cards are not accepted.

131 G9 ✉ Baixada de la Llibreteria 2, 08002 ☎ 93 310 52 42 ⊕ Mon–Fri 10–8.30, Sat 10–2, 5–8.30 Ⓜ Jaume I

PLAÇA DEL PÍ

The regular outdoor market held in Plaça del Pí sells artwork and marvellous home-made cheeses, honey, chocolate and other produce from rural Catalonia.

130 F9 ✉ Plaça del Pí, 08002 ⊕ First and third Fri, Sat and Sun of the month 11–2, 5–9 Ⓜ Liceu

PLAÇA REIAL

Anything and everything can be bought or exchanged here. Old coins and stamps from all over the world are traded at Plaça Reial on a Sunday morning. This street market also has some miscellaneous stalls brimming with objects of interest such as telephone cards and antique pins.

130 F9 ✉ Plaça Reial, 08002 ⊕ Sun 9–2 Ⓜ Liceu

PLAÇA DE LA SEU

If you find yourself in the Barri Gòtic on a Thursday, take some time to check out the antiques fair on Plaça de la Seu; the crowds mean you can't miss it. Wares include furniture, novels and comics, second-hand clothes, clocks and general bric-à-brac. Don't be shy in donning your bargaining hat to make sure that you get the price you want.

131 G9 ✉ Plaça Nova, 08002 ⊕ Thu 10–10. Closed Aug Ⓜ Jaume I

RAFA

This small, smart boutique sits at the heart of the shopping zone in the old town. In the chic and sleek shop, you can find an interesting range of bags from top makers such as Furla and Mandarina Duck.

130 F9 ✉ Avinguda del Portal de l'Àngel 3–5, 08002 ☎ 93 318 33 45 ⊕ Mon–Sat 10–8.30 Ⓜ Liceu

SANT JOSEP ORIOL

This picture market, said to be the equivalent of Paris's Montmartre art market, is a great place to browse on a weekend, where you can enjoy the pretty setting.

130 F9 ✉ Plaça de Sant Josep Oriol, 08002 ⊕ Sat–Sun 10–2 Ⓜ Liceu

SANTA LLÚCIA

This art and craft market is held every year around Christmas, usually from the beginning of December. All the items sold here are handmade, and you can choose from a range of Christmas tree decorations and imaginative jewellery.

131 G9 ✉ Plaça Nova, 08002 ⊕ 8–23 Dec daily 10–10 Ⓜ Jaume I

ZARA HOME

www.zara.es

The popular fashion chain Zara has its own line of home furnishings, which, like the fashion, are stylish and moderately priced. They sell everything from bedlinen and kitchenware, to photograph frames and vases. The range for kids is particularly appealing, with bright colours and fun prints.

131 F9 ✉ Avinguda del Portal de l'Àngel 24, 08002 ☎ 93 317 65 86 ⊕ Mon–Sat 10–9.30 Ⓜ Catalunya

ZSU ZSA

This small shop sells selected stock, but what is here is retro and trendy. Zsu Zsa has its own label—floaty and feminine, yet with unusual shapes and details—presented alongside the designs of Norma Álvarez, Bad Habits, Andrea B, Ricardo Ramos and Ixio. Choose your accessories from collections by Guilty, Pequeño Poder, Opa Loka and Locking Shocking.

130 F9 ✉ Carrer Calders 11, 08003 ☎ 93 295 66 59 ⊕ Tue–Sat 11–2.30, 5–8.30, Mon 5–8.30. Closed Jul–Aug Sat 5–8.30 Ⓜ Drassanes

ENTERTAINMENT AND NIGHTLIFE

L'ASCENSOR

This bar has been created using parts of other, older bars. L'Ascensor certainly has character. The major feature is an old elevator from which the bar gains its name. Latin-American cocktails set the mood and it's invariably busy at weekends. Credit cards are not accepted.

131 G9 ✉ Carrer de Bellafila 3, 08002 ☎ 93 318 53 47 ⊕ Daily 6.30pm–2am Ⓜ Jaume I

BAR DEL PÍ

www.bardelpi.com

One of the oldest bars in town, where the drinking space is split over three levels. The clientele love a good discussion of the political, cultural or intellectual kind. If you don't want to talk, there's a stunning view over the church Santa Maria del Pí and the Barri Gòtic, and you'll find basic tapas on the menu. Credit cards are not accepted.

130 F9 ✉ Plaça de Sant Josep Oriol 1, 08002 ☎ 93 302 21 23 ⊕ Mon–Fri 9am–11pm, Sat 9.30am–10.30pm Ⓜ Liceu

BLISS CAFÉ

Bliss Café has a comfortable lounge area, where you can sink into a mismatched armchair or leopard-skin print sofa, leaf through the international papers and magazines, drink coffee and tuck into home-made cakes. They also serve delicious light meals, including salads and quiches. In summer, there's a terrace out on the lovely Gothic square of Sant Just—the perfect place on a summer night.

Above *Schilling café in Barri Gòtic is gay friendly and popular with locals and visitors*

➕ 131 G9 ✉ Plaça Sants Just i Pastor s/n, 08002 ☎ 93 268 10 22 🕐 Mon–Fri 10am–11.30pm, Sat 10am–12am 🚇 Jaume I

EL BOSC DE LES FADES

www.museocerabcn.com
This bar is reminiscent of a fairy tale, complete with an enchanted forest, fairies and waterfalls. It takes you back to your childhood and is positively dreamlike. Storytellers perform here and it's also a venue for live music.

➕ 130 F10 ✉ Passatge de la Banca 7, 08002 ☎ 93 317 26 49 🕐 Mon–Thu, Sun 10am–1am, Fri–Sat 10am–2am 🚇 Drassanes

CAFÉ DE L'ÒPERA

This fin-de-siècle café is as popular with opera enthusiasts as the Gran Teatre del Liceu (▷ 103) is just across the road. Chocolate with typical Spanish *churros* is a must. The terrace looks out over the lively Rambla.

➕ 130 F9 ✉ La Rambla 74, 08002 ☎ 93 317 75 85 🕐 Daily 8.30am–2.30am 🚇 Liceu

CINE AMBIGÚ

www.cineambigu.com
Cine Ambigú hosts weekly screenings of alternative cinema. Focusing on European independent productions, Ambigú is the place to go to see good films that don't make it to mainstream screens (all films shown in original language with subtitles in Spanish). Screenings on Tuesdays but check schedules in advance (available online).

➕ 130 F9 ✉ Verdi Park, Carrer de Torrijos 49, 08012 ☎ 93 238 79 90 ✋ €6.50 🚇 Fontana

CLUB CAPITOL

www.grupbalana.com
You'll find comedy, recitals and cabaret, as well as other dramatic works at this modern theatre, at the top of Las Ramblas. There is a bar.

➕ 130 F8 ✉ La Rambla de Canaletes 138, 08002 ☎ 93 412 20 38 ✋ From €12 🚇 Catalunya

GINGER

This cocktail bar hits the spot with a relaxed atmosphere, even more relaxing comfy chairs and a wide range of drinks served from either of the bars, which are situated at different ends of the room. It also has an excellent selection of local wines and mouth-watering modern takes on tapas.

✚ 131 G9 ✉ Carrer Palma Sant Just 1, 08002 ☎ 93 310 53 09 🕐 Tue–Sat 7pm–2.30am 🚇 Jaume I

GLACIAR

Thanks to its most impressive selection of beers, Glaciar has become popular with visitors. It has a fantastic terrace on which to contemplate the comings and goings in Plaça Reial. Credit cards are not accepted.

✚ 130 F9 ✉ Plaça Reial 3, 08002 ☎ 93 302 11 63 🕐 Daily 12pm–2.30am 🚇 Liceu

GRAN TEATRE DEL LICEU

www.liceubarcelona.cat

One of the most prestigious opera houses in Europe, the Liceu underwent a full restoration following a fire in 1992 (▷ 103). The opera is first class; classical music concerts and top-class ballet productions are also held here. There is a bar on the premises.

✚ 130 F9 ✉ La Rambla 51–59, 08002 ☎ 93 485 99 00 💶 €10–€150 🚇 Liceu

HARLEM JAZZ CLUB

This was Barcelona's first commercial jazz club. Live music is a way of life for the owners. Regulars come for the tango, flamenco, Celtic music, bossa nova and, of course, the jazz. Credit cards are not accepted.

✚ 130 F9 ✉ Carrer de la Comtessa de Sobradiel 8, 08002 ☎ 93 310 07 55 🕐 Tue–Thu 8pm–4am, Fri–Sat 8pm–5am 🚇 Drassanes, Jaume I

JAMBOREE

Jamboree is one of the busiest jazz clubs in town. In a central location, just off Las Ramblas, it is popular with visitors. Live jazz and blues are played here and the later the hour, the funkier the music. Credit cards are not accepted.

✚ 130 F9 ✉ Plaça Reial 17, 08002 ☎ 93 301 75 64 💶 From €10 🚇 Liceu

PILÉ 43

Pilé 43's bar serves a wide range of beers, cocktails and teas. It is dotted with furniture and ornaments from the 1950s, 60s and 70s, all of which are for sale.

✚ 130 F9 ✉ Carrer d'Aglà 4, 08002 ☎ 93 317 39 02 🕐 Mon–Thu 10pm–2am, Fri–Sat 10pm–3am 🚇 Liceu

SCHILLING

Schilling, in the Barri Gòtic, is well known as one of the most gay-friendly cafés in the city centre and, therefore, attracts a mixed crowd of locals and visitors. Breakfast is served in the morning, coffee and delicious cakes in the afternoon and alcoholic drinks and a range of cocktails in the evening. The window tables, which offer a great view of the passing crowds, are particularly sought after.

✚ 130 F9 ✉ Carrer de Ferran 23, 08002 ☎ 93 317 67 87 🕐 Mon–Sat 10am–2.30am, Sun 12pm–2am (open from 6.30pm in Aug) 🚇 Liceu

SIDECAR FACTORY CLUB

www.sidecarfactoryclub.com

This club in the heart of the busy Plaça Reial has been offering live music to Barcelona's unwashed Indie kids for the last two decades. Despite a recent refit upstairs, Sidecar's basement still offers a suitably seedy location to hear local and international bands playing any kind of music involving loud guitars and shaggy haircuts. Most gigs kick off at 10pm and it opens late into the night.

✚ 130 F9 ✉ Plaça Reial 7, 08002 ☎ 93 302 15 86 💶 From €5 🚇 Liceu

LOS TARANTOS

www.masimas.com/tarantos

Other Spanish cities are more closely associated with flamenco, especially in the south of the country, but you'll find many a fan among the region's Andalusian residents. Los Tarantos gives you a taste of Seville in the heart of the

Barri Gòtic. You'll also find yourself dancing to tango, salsa and other Latin rhythms.

✚ 130 F9 ✉ Plaça Reial 17, 08002 ☎ 93 319 17 89 💶 From €5 🚇 Liceu

TEATRE POLIORAMA

www.teatrepoliorama.com

This is one of the oldest theatres in Catalonia, where writer George Orwell sheltered from snipers on the other side of Las Ramblas during the Civil War. It's in the former building of the Academy of Sciences and Arts, nestling behind an art nouveau facade. It is the headquarters of the Catalan troupe Dagoll Dagom and you'll find mainly comedies and musicals here (usually in Catalan).

✚ 130 F9 ✉ La Rambla 115, 08002 ☎ 93 317 75 99 💶 From €16 🚇 Catalunya

SPORTS AND ACTIVITIES

LA SARDANA

www.fed.sardanista.com

If you've ever wanted to try the *sardana*, the Catalan national dance, you can, outside the cathedral on Sunday afternoon or in Plaça de Sant Jaume on weekend evenings. These gatherings, organized by the Federació Sardanista, allow groups of varying abilities from beginners to the more advanced to dance in a circle.

✚ 131 G9 or 130 F9 ✉ Plaça de la Seu or Plaça de Sant Jaume, 08002 ☎ 93 319 76 37 🕐 Cathedral: Sun 12–2; Plaça de Sant Jaume: Sat 6.30pm–8.30pm, Sun 6pm–8pm 🚇 Liceu, Jaume I

HEALTH AND BEAUTY

A.K.A. PERRUQUERS

www.akaperruquers.com

A.K.A. Perruquers is in trendy Carrer d'Avinyó, famous for its alternative shopping. This hairdresser follows new styles, revives great classics or develops one to reflect your character; a formula that keeps the clients coming back. Appointments are advisable.

✚ 130 F9 ✉ Carrer d'Avinyó 34, 08002 ☎ 93 301 45 13 🕐 Tue–Sat 9.30–7 💶 Women €40, men €20 🚇 Liceu

EATING

PRICES AND SYMBOLS
The prices given are the average for a two-course lunch (L) and a three-course dinner (D) for one person, without drinks. The wine price is for the least expensive bottle.

For a key to the symbols, ▷ 2.

AGUT
This quiet, welcoming place was founded at the beginning of the 19th century and builds its menu on Catalan food. The Agut family, which has owned and managed the restaurant for the last three generations, has a menu reflecting seasonal availability as well as dishes that are popular all year round, such as *olla barrejada* (a typical Catalan stew with vegetables and meat) and *fideuà* (fish noodles), cod with red peppers and garlic mayonnaise.
✚ 131 G10 ✉ Carrer d'en Gignàs 16, 08002 ☎ 93 315 17 09 🕐 Tue–Sat 1.30–4, 8.30–11, Sun 1–4. Closed Aug ✋ L €15, D €35, Wine €9 🚇 Jaume I

ARC CAFÉ
www.arccafe.com
This bar-restaurant serves international cuisine that should cover everyone's tastes. The menu is not extensive but the dishes

are substantial and vary from month to month. Arc Café s Thai curries, which are faithfully made to traditional recipes and prepared with coconut milk, are particularly good, and a testament to the many influences upon this hardworking kitchen. After you have finished your dinner, stay for a cocktail and to listen to some music. They always have a vegetarian option, and there is free WiFi.
✚ 130 F10 ✉ Carrer d'en Carabassa 19, 08002 ☎ 93 302 52 04 🕐 Mon–Thu 1pm–12am, Fri–Sun 1pm–2am ✋ L €10, D €25, Wine €7.50 🚇 Drassanes

BRISA DEL MAR
On the rooftop of the fashionable Duquesa de Cardona hotel (▷ 129), this stylish outdoor café-bar offers heartstopping views over Port Vell, and out to sea. Unusual and sophisticated tapas, such as toast topped with Port-soaked pears and blue cheese, as well as light meals are served from Wednesday to Sunday nights, but cocktails are available every night. Come at dusk, and watch the lights twinkle on the yachts. There is a live jazz duo on Saturday nights in summer.
✚ 130 F10 ✉ Passeig de Colom 12, 08002 ☎ 93 268 90 90 🕐 Daily 7.30pm–1am,

tapas served Wed–Sun ✋ Tapas from €4, cocktails from €12 🚇 Drassanes

BUENAS MIGAS
www.buenasmigas.com
Buenas Migas is the perfect place if you don't have the time to linger or are on a budget. If you seek value, try one of the huge salads or a vegetable tart. The most popular dish is *focaccia*, a distant relative of the pizza, the portions of which are reasonable and there's a sizeable list of toppings. Make sure that you leave space for dessert—try *la bomba* (a chocolate cake) or an apple and cinnamon tart. There are several branches around town.
✚ 130 F8 ✉ Plaça del Bonsuccés 6, 08001 ☎ 93 481 51 38 🕐 Daily 9am–midnight ✋ L and D €7, Wine €5 🚇 Catalunya

CAFÈ DE L'ACADÈMIA
The lovely Plaça de Sant Just, one of the best preserved Gothic squares in the city, is the setting for this romantic restaurant. On the menu, you'll find expertly prepared Catalan cuisine with a contemporary twist. Try *bacallà* (salt cod) with tomato confit and garlic mousse, and don't

Above *Can Culleretes, an old favourite*

125

miss out on the wonderful desserts. In summer, a candlelit terrace opens on the square itself.

➕ 131 G9 ✉ Carrer de Lledó 1, 08002 ☎ 93 319 82 53 🕐 Daily 8.30–12. Closed 3 weeks in Aug ✋ D €30, Wine €11 🚇 Jaume I

CAFÉ DE L'ÒPERA

▷ 123.

CAN CULLERETES

www.culleretes.com

Founded in 1786, this is one of the city's oldest restaurants. There is a menu of Catalan dishes such as *suquet* (a stew of fish, potatoes and saffron) or chicken with the classic *samfaina*, a rich vegetable and tomato sauce. Desserts include a great *crema catalana*, the local version of crème brûlée.

➕ 130 F9 ✉ Carrer d'en Quintana 5, 08002 ☎ 93 317 30 22 🕐 Tue–Sat 1.30–4, 9–11, Sun 1.30–3.30. Closed Jul ✋ L and D €30, Wine €12 🚇 Liceu

GINGER

Ginger is a cocktail/tapas bar that became an immediate hit with the local ex-pat community, particularly because it is run by an English chef, whose tapas includes smoked salmon tartar, salad with grilled goat's cheese and foie gras. The cocktails are also excellent; it's one of only a few places in the city to get a genuine Pimms, which is served with ginger, the bar's namesake.

➕ 131 G9 ✉ Carrer de la Palma de Sant Just 1, 08002 ☎ 93 310 53 09 🕐 Tue–Sat 7pm–3am ✋ Tapas €4–6, Wine €19 🚇 Jaume I

JULIVERT MEU

This tavern-style Catalan restaurant can get a bit noisy in the evenings. That said, it does select the best elements of traditional Catalan cuisine: bread rubbed with garlic, tomatoes and olive oil; sausage with white beans; and selections of cold meats, hams and cheeses.

➕ 130 F8 ✉ Carrer del Bonsuccés 7, 08001 ☎ 93 318 03 43 🕐 Sep–end Jul daily 1–1; Aug Mon–Sat 1–4, 8pm–1am ✋ L €20, D €30, Wine €9 🚇 Catalunya

LIMBO

www.limborestaurante.com

This restaurant has a sleek, designer interior and a menu that successfully combines a number of cuisines. Among the most popular dishes are the hot grilled prawns and the tuna *tataki* with goat's cheese, lime and figs. However, look for new dishes as the chef works tirelessly at renewing and revitalizing the menu.

➕ 130 F10 ✉ Carrer de la Mercè 13, 08002 ☎ 93 310 76 99 🕐 Daily 9pm–12am ✋ D €35, Wine €7 🚇 Jaume I

LIVING

This discreet restaurant is in one of the Barri Gòtic's smaller streets. Unusually for Barcelona, Living has inexpensive, creative vegetarian dishes such as leek pancake and a range of salads; meat-eaters should try duck with honey, green beans and sesame seeds. Portions are generous and jazz and house music are played in the background.

➕ 131 G9 ✉ Carrer dels Capellans 9, 08002 ☎ 93 412 13 70 🕐 Mon–Thu, Sat 12.30–4.30, 8–12; café-bar Mon–Thu 9am–1am, Fri–Sat 9am–2am ✋ L €10, D €25, Wine €9 🚇 Urquinaona

IL MERCANTE DI VENEZIA

Soft classical music, candlelight and luxurious curtains evoke Renaissance Venice, yet prices here remain fairly reasonable. Fillet steak flavoured with lemon, a range of seasonal carpaccio and fresh pasta form the highlights of the menu. Also try the delicious pesto sauce and the unmissable tiramisù.

➕ 130 F10 ✉ Carrer de Josep Anselm Clavé 11, 08002 ☎ 93 317 18 28 🕐 Tue–Sun 1.30–4, 8.30–12 ✋ L €15, D €25, Wine €12 🚇 Drassanes

PITARRA

www.restaurantpitarra.com

Pitarra, a traditional Catalan restaurant, has no shortage of character. It was named after Serafí Pitarra, a famous Catalan actor and former resident, and the rooms are decorated with personal effects such as books and clocks. The cuisine is excellent, particularly the cannelloni

and the seasonal highlights, notably the mushroom-based dishes. The service is attentive.

➕ 130 F10 ✉ Carrer d'Avinyó 56, 08002 ☎ 93 301 16 47 🕐 Mon–Sat 1–4, 8.30–11. Closed Aug ✋ L and D €35, Wine €10 🚇 Drassanes

PLA

Pla is within walking distance of Plaça de Sant Jaume. The chef, Jaume Pla, draws on the influences of Mediterranean, vegetarian and international cooking, and creates seasonal specials. There's a wide selection of carpaccio: fish with prawns, beef with pineapple vinaigrette, and veal with liver. The house special is tuna *tataki* with lime leaves in a citrus and coconut sauce, on a banana leaf.

➕ 131 G9 ✉ Carrer de Bellafila 5, 08002 ☎ 93 412 65 52 🕐 Sun–Thu 9pm–12am, Fri–Sat 9pm–1am ✋ D €40, Wine €12 🚇 Jaume I

POLENTA

Bernardo and Patricio, two talented chefs and old friends, have combined their experience to serve a careful mix of local, South American and Japanese food. Let the chefs advise you and you won't be disappointed. The kitchen has glass walls so that diners can watch them in action.

➕ 131 G101 ✉ Carrer Ample 51, 08002 ☎ 93 268 14 29 🕐 Mon–Fri 1–4, 8.30–12, Sat 8pm–12am ✋ L €10, D €20, Wine €10 🚇 Jaume I

ELS QUATRE GATS

It's not just the food that draws people to this restaurant, although it is known for good Catalan fare. It was here that avant-garde artists of the early 20th century, such as Pablo Picasso and his contemporaries, used to meet. When you've finished absorbing the historical significance, tuck into some *botifarra i mongetes* (grilled black sausage with white beans) and *esqueixada* (salt cod salad with onion and peppers).

➕ 131 G9 ✉ Carrer de Montsió 3 bis, 08002 ☎ 93 302 41 40 🕐 Daily 1–1 ✋ L €18, D €50, Wine €14 🚇 Catalunya

QUIM

This is one of many stands in La Boquería market. Even though it has a tiny space in which to operate, the tapas are excellent. The cook, Quim, prepares the best *callos* (tripe) in the market, and his cod with garlic, rice dishes and stews also pull in the clientele. The lengthy wait is an accolade, but that makes it tricky to secure one of the 17 high stools. Credit cards are not accepted.

✚ 130 F9 ✉ Mercat de la Boquería 585–606, 08001 ☎ 93 301 98 10 🕐 Tue–Thu 7–4, Fri–Sat 7–5 ✋ L €12, Wine €5 🚇 Liceu

QUO VADIS

This restaurant dates back to the 1950s. The choice of dishes is wide, among them examples of Spanish and French cuisine with a modern slant. The frogs' legs and roasted pork with apple purée are both fabulous. They also serve good seasonal fare, especially mushroom-based dishes.

✚ 130 F9 ✉ Carrer del Carme 7, 08001 ☎ 93 302 40 72 🕐 Mon–Sat 1.15–4, 8.30–11.30. Closed Aug ✋ L €35, D €70, Wine €20 🚇 Liceu

EL SALÓN

The dining room is grand baroque with a bar tucked at one end, while the food here is sophisticated. Enjoy such taste-bud treats as goulash with clams and satay chicken with coconut spiked rice, followed by one of the delicious desserts.

✚ 131 G10 ✉ Carrer Hostal d'en Sol 6–8, 08002 ☎ 93 315 21 59 🕐 Mon–Sat 8.30–12. Bar open until 2am weekends ✋ D €30, Wine €12 🚇 Jaume I

SHUNKA

Shunka stands in one of the city's narrow medieval streets and attracts a loyal, almost entirely Japanese, customer base. The limited space has been put to good use, but if you prefer a bit more elbow room, eat at the bar. Try the salmon caviar, eel with rice, or the tuna, served in a variety of styles. The rice dishes and sake truffles are in a league of their own.

✚ 131 G9 ✉ Carrer de Sagristans 5, 08002 ☎ 93 412 49 91 🕐 Tue–Sat 1–3.30, 8.30–11.30. Closed 2 weeks in Aug ✋ L and D €40, Wine €12 🚫 Section 🚇 Urquinaona

SUKUR

With its gauzy drapes, flickering candlelight, and silk cushions, Sukur brings a little eastern exoticism to central Barcelona. The menu takes a tour around the eastern end of the Mediterranean, with Turkish, Greek and Lebanese dishes. Aromatic tagines, a chunky moussaka and tasty Lebanese dips including *baba ghanoush* are staple offerings, with honey-filled pastries and delectable sweets to finish up.

✚ 130 F10 ✉ Carrer d'Avinyó 42, 08002 ☎ 93 301 01 02 🕐 Mon–Fri 1–4, 8–12, Sat–Sun 8–12 ✋ L and D €15, Wine €10 🚇 Liceu

TALLER DE TAPAS

www.tallerdetapas.com

This 'tapas workshop' takes the mystery out of ordering tapas—sit down and study the multilingual menu. The dishes fly out of the open kitchen fast and furiously; chorizo cooked in cider, *patatas bravas*, pan-fried peppers, all the favourites are there plus some daily specials. Avoid peak times when possible: both food and service tend to suffer under pressure.

✚ 130 F9 ✉ Plaça de Sant Josep Oriol 9, 08001 ☎ 93 301 80 20 🕐 Sun–Thu 12–12, Fri–Sat 12pm–1am ✋ Tapas €3–€10, Wine €12 🚇 Liceu

TAXIDERMISTA

Taxidermista is resident in the old taxidermist's workshop, overlooking the city's liveliest square. The interior is bright and rather Parisian in style, and it has become a meeting spot for an international crowd. The menu features fresh and imaginative Mediterranean cuisine, such as a rocket (arugula) and pear salad with smoked Idiazábal cheese, or grilled turbot with a lemon and lime vinaigrette.

✚ 130 F9 ✉ Plaça Reial 8, 08002 ☎ 93 412 45 36 🕐 Restaurant daily 1.30–4, 8.30–12.30; café (snacks and tapas) daily 1–1; bar (coffee and cocktails) daily 12pm–2.30am ✋ L €11, D €35, Wine €12 🚇 Liceu

VENUS DELICATESSEN

Venus is affordable, has a great-value fixed-price lunch menu and is a good choice if you're looking for more varied dishes than the usual fare. Choices range from Greek moussaka and Arabic couscous to Mexican chilli con carne. Venus is in Carrer d'Avinyó, a street in the Barri Gòtic full of designer shops. Credit cards are not accepted.

✚ 130 F9 ✉ Carrer d'Avinyó 25, 08002 ☎ 93 301 15 85 🕐 Mon–Sat 12–12 ✋ L €9, D €12, Wine €9 🚇 Liceu

VINATERÍA DEL CALL

You'll find one of Barcelona's most charming wine bars amid the atmospheric Gothic streets of the old Jewish quarter. The food is simple but exquisite, and the tapas excel in both size and quality. The range of cheese and ham is served with typical Catalan bread rubbed with tomato, salt and olive oil. The wine list is impressive and includes Rioja, Penedès and a good Somontano. Owing to its popularity, there are two seatings at weekends, when you will need to make reservations in advance.

✚ 130 F9 ✉ Carrer de Sant Domènec del Call 9, 08002 ☎ 93 302 60 92 🕐 Mon–Sat 7pm–1am ✋ L €15, D €23, Wine €8 🚇 Liceu

ZOO

Zoo attracts a youthful crowd keen on the good music; after 1am, it's a bar playing ambient, funky and ethnic sounds. Inside, bright tones, flowers and miniature animals are set off by interesting recycled furniture, created by local design students. The dishes span Mexican enchiladas, Japanese noodles and Arabic stews.

✚ 130 F9 ✉ Carrer d'Escudellers 33, 08002 ☎ 93 302 77 28 🕐 Sun–Thu 6pm–2am, Fri–Sat 6pm–2.30am (kitchen closes at 1am) ✋ D €15, Wine €7 🚇 Drassanes

PRICES AND SYMBOLS

Prices are the lowest and highest for a double room for one night. Breakfast is included unless noted otherwise. All the hotels listed accept credit cards unless otherwise stated. Note that rates vary widely throughout the year.

For a key to the symbols, ▷ 2.

1898

www.hotel1898.com

The splendid late 19th-century building that once housed the Philippines Tobacco Company has been converted into a luxury hotel. Its location, on Rambla de Canaletes, is unbeatable. Inside classic elegance combines with contemporary style. The suites and bedrooms are decorated in a modern interpretation of colonial style, and equipped with plasma TVs and all the latest amenities. There is a rooftop terrace with plunge pool, and a stylish restaurant and bar.

➕ 130 F9 ✉ La Rambla de Canaletes 109, 08002 ☎ 93 552 95 52 💵 €180–€490, excluding breakfast ① 169 🚻 🏊 Indoor and outdoor 🍽 🚇 Catalunya

Above *Mid-range and luxury hotels abound in this part of the city*

CATALONIA ALBIONI

www.hoteles-catalonia.es

This boutique-type hotel is in a former 17th-century mansion in the heart of the city's major shopping strip. Vestiges of its former glory can be seen in the rear courtyard (where breakfast is served) and the grand marble staircase. Rooms vary, but all are comfortable and the location couldn't be better for major transport and service hubs. They also have a small spa area, and attractive garden restaurant, El Jardí de l'Angel (set menu €19, for three courses).

➕ 130 F8 ✉ Avinguda Portal de l'Angel 17, 08002 ☎ 93 318 41 41 💵 €129–€241, excluding breakfast ① 74 🚻 🚇 Catalunya

COLÓN

www.hotelcolon.es

This hotel's enviable position, facing the cathedral, has drawn a number of illustrious visitors over the years, including Miró, Hemingway, Tennessee Williams and Francis Ford Coppola. The furnishings are in neutral and red tones; guest rooms are equipped with TV, safe and minibar, and some have balconies overlooking the cathedral. There is a restaurant, La Catedral, and piano bar, plus parking is available.

➕ 131 G9 ✉ Avinguda de la Catedral 7, 08002 ☎ 93 301 14 04 💵 €107–€287, excluding breakfast ① 141 🚇 Jaume I

CONTINENTAL

www.hotelcontinental.com

If you want to be at the heart of things, then stay here. This 100-year-old, three-star hotel, where the novelist George Orwell once stayed, is at the Plaça de Catalunya end of Las Ramblas. The rooms are tidy and furnished in floral patterns; all have satellite TV, telephone, fridge, minibar and fan. There is also room and laundry service, internet access and a bar. Its more luxurious sister hotel is the Continental Palacete.

➕ 130 F8 ✉ La Rambla 138, 08002 ☎ 93 301 25 70 💵 €97–€137 ① 35 🚻 🚇 Catalunya

CORTÉS

www.hotelcortes.com

Like many hotels in the heart of the city, the Cortés was completely refurbished before the 1992 Olympic Games. It is now a modern, functional two-star hotel, with half the rooms overlooking a quiet courtyard. All are bright, clean and spacious, with a TV. There is also a restaurant and a bar. It's worth looking on the internet for deals; room rates can drop by half.

➕ 130 F8 ✉ Carrer de Santa Anna 25, 08002 ☎ 93 317 91 12 ✋ €74–€180, excluding breakfast ℹ 44 ♿ 🚇 Catalunya

DE L'ARC

www.hotelarclarambla.com

This renovated family hotel, at the port end of Las Ramblas has clean, unpretentious accommodation. The rooms, some of which have balconies looking onto the street, are reasonably spacious with cable TV, telephone and hairdryer. Meeting rooms, a bar and laundry service are also available. De l'Arc is a good choice if you don't want to spend a great deal on your accommodation, and it is close to the restaurants along the waterfront. There is free WiFi internet access.

➕ 130 F10 ✉ La Rambla 19, 08002 ☎ 93 301 97 98 ✋ €60–€125, excluding breakfast ℹ 98 ♿ 🚇 Drassanes

DUQUESA DE CARDONA

www.hduquesadecardona.com

A quiet, tasteful oasis in the heart of the Barri Gòtic, the Duquesa de Cardona hotel occupies an elegant 17th-century palace, rebuilt in the 19th century. The hotel prides itself on the quality of its service, and has a special concierge service, called 'Ask Me', to assist guests during their stay. The rooftop terrace has a small plunge pool and an outdoor café-bar, and offers spectacular views over the yachts bobbing in the port below.

➕ 130 F10 ✉ Passeig de Colom 12, 08002 ☎ 93 268 90 90 ✋ €160–€300, excluding breakfast ℹ 40 ♿ 🏊 Outdoor 🚇 Drassanes

HOSTAL ÍTACA

www.itacahostel.com

This youth hostel has a great location close to the cathedral. Dormitories sleeping five, six or eight, and one double room, are available. Facilities include internet access, a cafeteria with great murals, kitchen, lockers, parking and a book exchange service. The hostal,

which also offers self-catering apartments, is non-smoking.

➕ 131 G9 ✉ Carrer de Ripoll 21, 08001 ☎ 93 301 97 51 ✋ Dormitories €14–€26 per person, doubles €55–€65, breakfast €2 ℹ 4 rooms, 24 beds ♿ 🚇 Urquinaona

HOSTAL NÍLO

www.hotel-nilo.com

Strategically placed at the heart of the Barri Gòtic, this hostal is in an area full of bars and restaurants. It is perfect for visitors on a low budget, as it is clean but has a slightly faded edge about it. Credit cards are not accepted.

➕ 130 F10 ✉ Carrer de Josep Anselm Clavé 17, 08002 ☎ 93 317 90 44 ✋ €44–€54 ℹ 56 🚇 Drassanes

HOTEL NERI

www.hotelneri.com

This boutique hotel has fast become a favourite for visiting celebs. It's housed in a medieval palace in one of the prettiest squares in the neighbourhood and romance oozes from every pore. Bedrooms are plush, with a high volume of rugs, throws and little extras such as incense and candles. The rooftop garden is scented with jasmine and is candlelit at night. The in-house restaurant is overpriced.

➕ 130 F9 ✉ Carrer Sant Sever 5, 08002 ☎ 93 304 06 55 ✋ €275–€360, excluding breakfast ℹ 22 (10 non-smoking) ♿ 🚇 Jaume I, Liceu

HUSA ORIENTE

www.husa.es

Built in 1842, this is the city's original grand hotel. It's in a great spot right on Las Ramblas, just around the corner from the Gran Teatre del Liceu. You can marvel at the amazing glass dome in the dining room as you eat your breakfast. The comfortable, if plain, rooms have TV, direct-dial telephone and safety deposit boxes, and many have views of Las Ramblas. Meeting rooms and parking facilities are available.

➕ 130 F9 ✉ Las Ramblas 45–47, 08002 ☎ 93 302 25 58 ✋ €113–€187, excluding breakfast ℹ 142 ♿ 🚇 Drassanes

LE MÉRIDIEN BARCELONA

www.meridienbarcelona.com

Walk through the hotel's beautiful entrance and you may find yourself thinking you're in early 20th-century France. Despite revamps, including a complete refurbishment in 2007, the hotel has retained its fin-de-siècle look. Rooms have every conceivable comfort (including iPhones programmed with guides to the city) and this top-level luxury attracts celebrity guests. Try to get a room overlooking Las Ramblas—the double-glazing filters out a lot of the noise—or enjoy the view while having breakfast on the roof terrace. The hotel has its own parking.

➕ 130 F9 ✉ La Rambla 111, 08002 ☎ 93 318 62 00 ✋ €430–€465, excluding breakfast ℹ 233 (8 floors of non-smoking rooms) ♿ 📺 🚇 Catalunya

PENSIÓN SEGRE

www.pension45.com

This discreet *pensión* is often overlooked, despite being a few minutes' walk from the port, beach and the galleries of La Ribera. Only about half the rooms have private bathrooms, but all rooms are spacious and have the benefit of balconies facing a quiet street. Furniture and fittings are far more functional than flash, but the Segre is a good option for budget accommodation in the old city. Credit cards are not accepted.

➕ 130 F10 ✉ Carrer de Simó Oller 1, 08002 ☎ 93 315 07 09 ✋ €55–€70, excluding breakfast ℹ 24 🚇 Drassanes

REGENCIA COLÓN

www.hotelregenciacolon.com

This hotel exudes a pleasant and relaxing atmosphere, perfect after a hard day's sightseeing. The rooms are spacious and well kept, and there's a range of facilities such as TV, room service and minibar. A bar and two lounges are available, and you are free to use the restaurant at the nearby Colón hotel (▷ 128).

➕ 131 G9 ✉ Carrer de Sagristans 13–17, 08002 ☎ 93 318 98 58 ✋ €70–€160, excluding breakfast ℹ 55 ♿ 🚇 Jaume I, Urquinaona

GRAN VIA DE LES CORTS CATALANES

Plaça de la Universitat

Universitat

RONDA

UNIVERSITAT

Plaça Catalunya

Carrer de Sepulveda

Villarroel

Casanova

CARRER D'ARIBAU

Plaça Goya

Plaça de Castella

C. Bergara

Catalunya

C. DE PELAI

Carrer de Floridablanca

ANTONI

Carrer de Tigre

Carrer de la Paloma

Costa

Valldoncella

Centre de Cultura Contemporania de Barcelona

dels

Tallers

Catalunya

Plaça de Catalunya

Catalonia Albioni

C de Tamarit

SANT

DE

Joaquim

Museu d'Art Contemporani de Barcelona

Casa Municipal de Misericòrdia

dels Àngels

Continental

Cortés

C. Santa Anna

RONDA

C de la Riera Alta

Carrer

Foment de les Arts Decoratives

C Elisabets

Buenas Migas

Julivert Meu

C Santa Anna

C Canuda

Carrer del Peu de la Creu

Carrer Pintor Fortuny

Le Méridien Barcelona

LAS RAMBLAS

Plaça vila de Madrid

CARRER DEL CARME

1898

Església de Betlem

Quo Vadis

Carrer Portaferrissa

Col. d'Arquite

EL RAVAL

CARRER DE L'HOSPITAL

C l'Aurora

Antic Hospital Santa Creu

Palau de la Virreina

Mercat La Boqueria

Quim

Plaça de Pi

BARRI GÒTIC

Plaça de Felip Neri

Museu Calça

C de St Rafael

Carrer Robador

Carrer Junta de Com

les

Riereta

Rambla del Raval

Santa Maria de Pi

Centre de Interpretacion del Call

Hotel Neri

Palau General

Carretes

Pau

Sant

C del Marquès de Barberà

Liceu

LAS RAMBLAS

C Boqueria

Taller de Tapas

Vinateria del Call

Plaça de Sant Jaume

Gran Teatre del Liceu

Can Culleretes

C de Ferran

Carrer

Ajuntament

Monestir de Sant Pau del Camp

Avinguda

Rambla

Nou de la

Husa Oriente

Plaça Reial

Taxidermista

Carrer Nou de la Rambla

LAS RAMBLAS

Zoo

Venus Delicatessen

Paral-lel

C de l'Om

C de Cabanes

C de l'Arc del Teatre

C Guardia

Palau Güell

C de Cotols

Sukur

AVINGUDA

PARAL·LEL

C del Cid

C Monts

De l'Arc

Arts Santa Mònica

Drassanes

C Nou de St Francesc

Arc Café

Pitarra

Lir

Pensión Segre

Carrer

Palaudaries

Museu de Cera

Hostal Nilo

Església de la Mercé

Merc

Brisa del Mar

Duqu de Carde

Passeig de Vila

Puig

IX

Drassanes & Museu Marítim

Il Mercante di Venezia

Carrer J A Clave

PASSEIG DE COLOM

Passeig de Montjuïc

Plaça del Portal de la Pau

Monument a Colom

Moll de Bosch i Alsina

PLAÇA DE LES DRASSANES

PASSEIG DE JOSEP CARNER

E

F

Dàrsena Nacional

GRAN VIA DE LES CORTS CATALANES

Passeig
de Gràcia

Plaça
de Tetuan

Tetuan

Napóls

CLARIS

PAU

DE

LLÚRIA

BRUC

Girona

BAILÉN

JOAN

SANT

DE

FLOR

Casp

Carrer

de

Casp

Casa
Calvet

Marc

RONDA

Urquinaona

DE

CARRER DE ROGER

CARRER

DEL

DE

Carrer

d'Ausiàs

DE

Carrer

DE

PASSEIG

Carrer

Plaça
Urquinaona

SANT

PERE

CARRER

CARRER

Carrer

d'Alí

Bel

Carrer de Ribes

ANTIGA
ESTACIÓ
DEL NORD

LAS
AMBLAS

C les Moles

Comtal

s Quatre
ats

er

LAIETANA

VIA

CARRER

DE

TRAFALGAR

Arc de
Triomf

FLOR

DE

ROGER

Nápols

Magdalenes

Palau de la
Música Catalana

Carrer Sant Pere més Alt

Plaça
St Pere

Arc del
Triomf

X

ving

Shunka

SANT PERE

CASC
ANTIC

CARRER DELS ALMOGÀVERS

Regència Colón

Carrer Sant Pere Mitjà

Carrer Sant Pere més Baix

PASSEIG

COMPANYS

al Ítaca

ón

A F Cambó

C J Giralt

C Metges

C Cortinas

C Portal Nou

CARRER DE BUENAVENTURA MUÑOZ

Museu Diocesà

CARRER

LLUÍS

CARRER

Carrer

Museu
Frederic Marès

Mercat Santa
Caterina

Carders

edral

Plaça del Rei

Carrer

Museu
de la Xocolata

PASSEIG

DE

PUJADES

Museu d'Història
de Barcelona

Museu de
Zoologia

Jaume I

CARRER

DE

LA

PRINCESA

Comerç

Parc de la
Ciutadella

Plaça de
Sant Just

DHUB Montcada

Museu
Picasso

PICASSO

Museu de
Geologia

Ginger

Museu Barbier-Mueller
d'Art Precolombí

C Montcada

C del Rec

DE

Café de
l'Acadèmia

Antic Mercat
del Born

PASSEIG

El Salon

Santa Maria
del Mar

Passeig del Born

C

Carrer de
Comercial

Parlament
de Catalunya

Gignàs

Fossar de les
Moreres

LA RIBERA

C Ribera

Polenta

Correus
Telègrafs

C Consolat de Mar

AVINGUDA MARQUÈS
DE L'ARGENTERA

Parc Zoològic

VIA

LAIETANA

La Llotja

Plaça
del
Palau

PLAÇA
D'ANTONI
LÓPEZ

PG ISABEL II

PASSEIG DE JOAN DE BORBÓ

ESTACIÓ
BARCELONA
DE FRANÇA

PASSEIG

DE

CIRCUMVAL·LACIÓ

CARRER DEL DR AIGUADER

Palau
de Mar

Plaça
de Pau
Vila

Barceloneta

RONDA

Dàrsena
del
Comerç

Museu d'Història
de Catalunya

G

Carrer

Carrer de Ginebra

Balboa

DEL

DR

AIGUADER

LITORAL

H

0   250 m

0   250 yds

REGIONS

BARRI GÒTIC AND LAS RAMBLAS •
EATING AND STAYING MAP

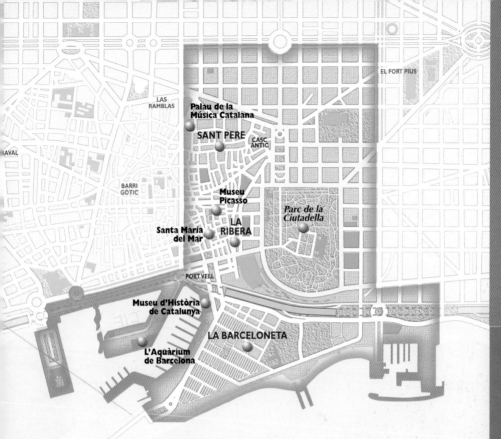

LAS
RAMBLAS

Palau de la
Música Catalana

SANT PERE

CASC
ANTIC

EL FORT PIUS

BARRI
GÒTIC

Museu
Picasso

Santa María
del Mar

LA
RIBERA

Parc de la
Ciutadella

PORT VELL

Museu d'Història
de Catalunya

LA BARCELONETA

L'Aquàrium
de Barcelona

PORT VELL AND LA RIBERA

Barcelona's entire seafront, which had become badly run-down and neglected, was dramatically and expensively remodelled in the run-up to the 1992 Olympics. A couple of fishing boats are the only reminders that Port Vell was once a working port: now it's a glamorous marina, packed with glossy yachts and pleasure craft. Wide, palm-shaded boulevards offer breezy views over the port, and old-fashioned Golondrinas ('swallow boats') cruise around the bay. A couple of old warehouses have been handsomely restored to contain stylish restaurants and the Museu d'Història de Catalunya. Across the undulating Rambla de Mar pedestrian bridge, is the Maremagnum, a glassy modern entertainment and shopping complex, and the aquarium.

La Ribera has become one of the city's most fashionable neighbourhoods, its narrow streets lined with chic boutiques and trendy bars. It also contains some of the finest surviving Gothic mansions in Barcelona, particularly along the Carrer de Montcada, once the grandest address in the city. Several have been converted into museums, including the enormously popular Picasso museum, which occupies five sumptuous palaces. Across the street, another sensitively restored palace contains the lesser-known but equally fascinating Museu Barbier-Mueller d'Art Precolombi with an outstanding collection of artefacts from South America. The Passeig del Born, once the scene of medieval tournaments, is now the hub of the area's lively nightlife, with countless bars and terrace cafés. This area is also home to Parc de la Ciutadella, Barcelona's best inner-city park, a green oasis complete with boating lake and fountains. At the southern end is the old-fashioned zoo, still a popular attraction.

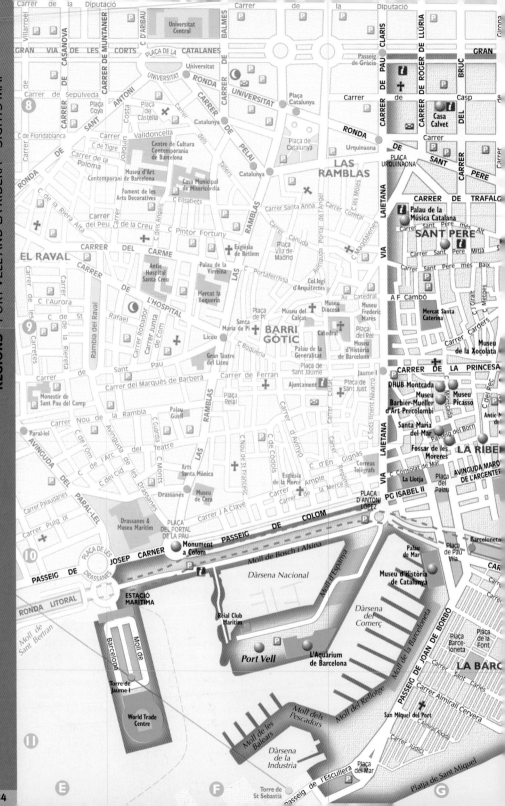

Carrer de la Diputació

Villarroel

GRAN VIA CASANOVA DE LES CORTS MUNTANER

Carrer de Sepúlveda

C de Floridablanca

⑧

Plaça Goya

Plaça de Castella

SANT ANTONI

Costa

Valldoncella

C de Tigre

Carrer de la Paloma

Museu d'Art Contemporani de Barcelona

Foment de les Arts Decoratives

C de la Riera Alta

Carrer del Peu

EL RAVAL

C de la Creu

CARRER DEL CARME

Centre de Cultura Contemporània de Barcelona

Casa Municipal de Misericòrdia

C Elisabets

C dels Àngels

C Pintor Fortuny

Església de Betlem

Antic Hospital Santa Creu

DE L'HOSPITAL

Palau de la Virreïna

Mercat la Boqueria

⑨

C de St Rafael

C l'Aurora

Carrer Robador

Carrer Junta de Com

Liceu

Santa Maria de Pi

Gran Teatre del Liceu

BARRI GÒTIC

Carrer de la Riereta

Sant

Pau

Carrer del Marquès de Barberà

C Boqueria

C de Ferran

Monestir de Sant Pau del Camp

C Nou de la Rambla

Palau Güell

C Guàrdia

C Monts

Plaça Reial

C d'En Gignàs

Paral·lel

AVINGUDA DEL PARAL·LEL

C de l'Om

C de l'Arc del Teatre

Arts Santa Mònica

Drassanes

Museu de Cera

C d'Avinyó

Església de la Mercè

Ample

Carrer J A Clavé

Carrer Palaudàries

Carrer Puig IX

PLAÇA DE LES DRASSANES

PASSEIG DE JOSEP CARNER

Monument a Colom

PASSEIG DE COLOM

Moll de Bosch i Alsina

Dàrsena Nacional

PLAÇA DEL PORTAL DE LA PAU

Drassanes & Museu Marítim

RONDA LITORAL

ESTACIÓ MARÍTIMA

Moll de Sant Bertran

Torre de Jaume I

World Trade Centre

⑩

PASSEIG DE DRASSANES

Moll de Barcelona

Moll de

Réial Club Marítim

Port Vell

Moll de les Balears

Moll dels Pescadors

Dàrsena de la Industria

Torre de St Sebastià

Passeig de l'Escullera

L'Aquàrium de Barcelona

Dàrsena del Comerç

Moll del Rellotge

San Miquel del Port

Plaça del Mar

Platja de Sant Miquel

⑪

Universitat Central

PLAÇA DE LA CATALANES

UNIVERSITAT

RONDA

CARRER DE PELAI

CARRER DE UNIVERSITAT

Plaça Catalunya

Plaça de Catalunya

Catalunya

LAS RAMBLAS

Carrer Santa Anna

Carrer Comtal

C Les Moles

Plaça Vila de Madrid

Portaferrissa

Canuda

Plaça del Pi

Museu del Calçat

Museu Diocesà

Museu Frederic Marès

Catedral

Museu del Rei

Museu d'Història de Barcelona

Palau de la Generalitat

Plaça de Sant Jaume

Ajuntament

Plaça de Sant Just

Correus Telègrafs

Carrer d'Ampurdà

PLAÇA D'ANTONI LÓPEZ

PG ISABEL II

Carrer de

CLARIS

Passeig de Gràcia

Carrer

CARRER DE PAU

CARRER DE ROGER DE LLÚRIA

BRUC

GRAN

Casp

Casa Calvet

Carrer

RONDA

PLAÇA URQUINAONA

Urquinaona

LAS RAMBLAS

VIA LAIETANA

CARRER DE TRAFALG

Palau de la Música Catalana

SANT PERE

Carrer Sant Pere més Alt

Carrer Sant Pere Mitjà

Carrer Sant Pere més Baix

A F Cambó

Mercat Santa Caterina

Museu de la Xocolata

CARRER DE LA PRINCESA

DHUB Montcada

Museu Barbier-Mueller d'Art Precolombí

Museu Picasso

Santa Maria del Mar

Fossar de les Moreres

LA RIBE

Antic

La Llotja

Consolat de Mar

AVINGUDA MARO DE L'ARGENTER

Plaça del Palau

Barceloneta

Palau de Mar

Plaça de Pau Vila

Museu d'Història de Catalunya

CAR

PASSEIG DE JOAN DE BORBÓ

Carrer Almirall Cervera

LA BARC

Plaça Barceloneta

Plaça de la Font

Carrer Sant Carles

E

F

G

Carrer   de   la   Diputació
JOAN   FLOR   Plaça Braus   El Monumental   AVINGUDA DIAGONAL
BAILÈN   Monumental   Monumental   PLAÇA DE LES
PLAÇA DE   Tetuan   LES   CORTS   MARINA   CATALANES   Glòries   GLÒRIES CATALANES
VIA   TETUAN   DE   Carrer de Nàpols   Sicilia   Monumental   Parc del Bosquet dels Encants
SANT   ROGER   Carrer   de   Casp   Lepant   Teatre Nacional de Catalunya
CARRER   DE   Marc   EL FORT PIUS   Ribes   l'Auditori y Museu de la Música   Carrer   d'Àvila   Bolívia
DE   PASSEIG   DE   Carrer d'Alí   Bel   Sardenya   MERIDIANA   Carrer   d'Àlaba   de   Tànger   Badajoz
Arc de Triomf   de   ANTIGA ESTACIÓ DEL NORD   Carrer   Sancho   Avila
CASC ANTIC   Arc del Triomf   Parc de l'Estació del Nord   Marina   ALMOGÀVERS   d'Àustria   Zamora   Pamplona
CARRER   DELS   CARRER   DE   PALLARS   Pujades
LLUIS COMPANYS   CARRER DE BUENAVENTURA MUÑOZ   AVINGUDA   Carrer   de   Bogatell   D'ÀLABA   BADAJOZ
PASSEIG   PASSEIG DE PUJADES   Carrer   Llull   D'ÀVILA   Turró   Trueta
PICASSO   Museu de Zoologia   WELLINGTON   Carrer   MARINA   Ramon   CARRER   DE
PASSEIG   Museu de Geologia   Parc de la Ciutadella   Carrer   de   de   del   Doctor   Trueta
Parlament de Catalunya   Universitat Pompeu Fabra   LA   Sensat   Bogatell   CARRER
ESTACIÓ BARCELONA FRANÇA   Parc Zoològic   Fargas   DE   R   l'Arquitecte Sert
CARRER   de   del   AVINGUDA   D'ICÀRIA
CARRER DEL DR AIGUADER   Trias   Carrer   Vila   Olimpica
DR AIGUADER   LITORAL   Ciutadella Vila Olimpica   Ramon   Plaça Voluntaris Olímpics   Parc del Port Olimpic   Plaça dels Campions   RONDA   LITORAL
Plaça Dr Pont i F   PG MARÍTIM DEL NOVA ICÀRIA   PASSEIG MARÍTIM DEL BOGATELL
Parc de la Barceloneta   Torre Mapfre   Platja   Nova   Icària
NETA   Poliesportiu Marítim   Marítim   Moll de Mestral   Moll de Gregal
Andrea Doria   Port Olímpic   Moll de Xaloc
Platja   de   la   Barceloneta

0   500 m
0   500 yds

H   J

135

L'AQUÀRIUM DE BARCELONA

Barcelona's state-of-the-art aquarium, one of the finest in Europe, is set in
Port Vell. There are 21 tanks in all, with creatures ranging from poisonous and
tropical fish to everyday varieties whose names you will recognize from local
restaurant menus. Interactive displays keep the children happily occupied.

THE DEEP BLUE SEA

The first section focuses on the Mediterranean. Here you will find communities
of cave and crevice dwellers from the rocky coasts, as well as eels and
octopuses. The next section, featuring creatures found in tropical waters and
the Red Sea, is much brighter. Reef sharks, vivid yellow butterfly fish and the
luminous marine life of the Caribbean, Hawaii and Australia are all found among
their natural vegetation, which has fully developed since the aquarium opened in
the mid-1990s.

The biggest crowd-pleaser is the close encounter with the sharks and
stingrays in the huge Oceanarium. A wide glass tunnel lets you see these sleek
creatures from all angles while being moved along by a conveyor belt. Grey
sharks, marble rays and guitar fish are just some of the majestic creatures in
this incredible show. The terrapin tank on your way out is also impressive, with
dozens of caimans, turtles and other amphibians.

Upstairs the Explora! section lets children become familiar with three
different Mediterranean seascapes: the marshland of the Ebro Delta, the
underwater caves of the Medes Islands and the Costa Brava. With more than
50 interactive games and activities, there is plenty to keep them happy while
adults can take in the spectacular views of the sea and the surrounding port
from the glass-enclosed terrace.

PLANETA AQUA

The Planeta Aqua section, also upstairs, illustrates the different ways in which
marine creatures adapt to watery conditions. In the Arctic and Antarctic
section, a colony of playful penguins is the biggest draw, but the tropical
piranhas come a close second. There is also a specially designed tank of rays,
with little passages and windows for children to clamber around in order to see
them swoop and glide at close quarters.

INFORMATION

www.aquariumbcn.com
✚ 134 F10 ✉ Moll d'Espanya s/n,
08039 ☎ 93 221 74 74 🕐 Jun, Sep
Mon–Fri 9.30–9, Sat–Sun 9.30–9.30;
Jul, Aug Mon–Fri 9.30–9, Sat–Sun
9.30–11; Oct–end May daily 9.30–9
✋ Adult €17.50, child (4–12) €12.50
🚇 Drassanes 🚌 14, 17, 19, 36, 38, 40,
45, 57, 59, 64 🍴

Above *Sharks are a major draw in the
Oceanarium*
Opposite *The walk-through glass tunnel*

INFORMATION

www.barcelonaturisme.com

⊞ 134 G10 ⓜ Barceloneta ℹ Plaça de Sant Jaume, Carrer Ciutat 2 (in the town hall), 08002 ☎ 93 285 38 34 ⓒ Mon–Fri 9–8, Sat 10–8, Sun and holidays 10–2

TIP

» *Biblioplatges* are beachfront cabins containing a selection of books and magazines in several languages, made available by the Barcelona public library system (summer only).

BARCELONETA

Barceloneta (Little Barcelona) is the city's best-loved playground. Even before the area was spruced up for the 1992 Olympics, it was always packed at weekends. Post-Olympics, the beach is cleaner and the restaurants are more chic, but the same people who always came make their way down here in droves on a sunny Sunday.

Barceloneta was the city's first stab at contemporary urban planning. Originally it was meant to house the displaced residents of La Ribera in the 1750s after the Ciutadella was constructed—the fortress was built in the park of the same name and was loathed by Catalans as a symbol of central government oppression. The original idea was to make the inexpensive housing low-rise, but this was ignored and attics and other extensions were added, giving the area its congested feel. A new landmark, the huge, sail-shaped Hotel Vela, Spain's first W hotel, dominates the seafront. It is reached by a new, palm-lined waterfront promenade. Rebecca Horn's sculpture commemorating the community *Homage to Barceloneta* (1992) stands on the beach.

FIESTAS

The local fiestas, Festes de la Barceloneta, are the most lively and least touristy in the city. The Diadeta, held in mid-September, is when members of local clubs or *penyas* dress up in traditional costume and celebrate the area's maritime history. The Festa Major (Big Festival), from late September to early October, is a week-long riot of local pride when dancing, outdoor feasts and other forms of revelry take place in its brightly decorated streets. Much of this activity is based around the Plaça de la Barceloneta, a picturesque square in the heart of Barceloneta with a fountain, a couple of cafés and the Església de Sant Miquel del Port, built in 1755. Its facade is its most interesting element, but it is also home to a giant figure of St. Michael himself.

The main boulevard of Barceloneta is the Passeig Joan de Borbó, stretching from the Plaça Palau all the way down to the sea. Rows of warehouses were torn down to make way for the marina and the concrete pedestrian area that runs its entire length. With its dozens of seafood restaurants and hawkers, it's easy to dismiss the street as a tourist trap until you realize that there are more locals than foreigners eating here. A paella amid the sea air of Barceloneta on Sunday is as traditional as *monas* (a type of cake) at Easter, and one to add to your list of culinary experiences.

Below *Street musicians entertain on Moll de la Barceloneta in Port Vell*

CASA CALVET

www.rutadelmodernisme.com

The Casa Calvet was designed and built by Antoni Gaudí (1852–1926) as a house, but has now been converted into apartments. The interior and the rear facade are not open to the public, but the building is worth admiring from the outside.

It was built for the textile manufacturer Pere Calvet at the turn of the 20th century and the monochrome facade is probably Gaudí's most restrained work. Its undulating, three-tiered crown is reminiscent of rococo churches, but the main interest lies in the symbolism of the decorative elements. Gaudí placed a flamboyant C, the owner's initial, over the door and there are mushroom reliefs on the main exterior, a reference to Calvet's interest in the study of mushrooms and fungi. The three heads of the crown represent St. Peter the Martyr, whom Calvet was named after, St. Genesius of Arles and St. Genesius of Rome, patrons of Vilassar, the family's home town.

The balustrades of the balconies and the *trencadís* work (surfaces covered with pieces of broken ceramics; ▷ 185) of the rear facade can be seen only in photographs. The many pieces of furniture Gaudí designed for the residence are more accessible, being on display at Casa-Museu Gaudí at Park Güell (▷ 1185). But the best way to get a taste of Casa Calvet is to eat at the restaurant on the ground floor. It has one of the original, fluid wooden benches and some of the stained glass of the rear facade, and has retained many Gaudían touches.

✚ 134 G8 ✉ Carrer de Casp 48, 08010 ☎ Restaurant: 93 412 40 12 🚇 Urquinaona 🚌 17, 19, 39, 41, 45, 47, 55, 62

DHUB MONTCADA

www.museutextil.bcn.es

Textiles were Catalonia's principal industry during the Industrial Revolution and the DHUB Montcada, previously called the Museu Tèxtil i d'Indumentària, is a satisfying collection of period costumes and accessories. Spread over two floors, it starts with the Gothic period and then moves through the Renaissance, baroque and Elizabethan periods and on to Regency. Also present in this section are ladies' gloves that would only fit a present-day 10-year-old and some wonderfully ornate fans and opera glasses. The second floor deals with 20th-century attire, and Spain's most celebrated couturier, the Basque-born Cristóbal Balenciaga, is well represented with more than 100 items he designed between 1934 and 1972. The chain-mail mini dress by Paco Rabanne would still stop traffic on any street in the world. The collection of Catalan lacework on the ground floor includes some beautiful *mantillas* (scarves). The museum's shop stocks a range of clothing, gifts and accessories, and the pretty café is in the Gothic courtyard.

✚ 134 G9 ✉ Carrer de Montcada 12, 08003 ☎ 93 319 76 03 🕐 Tue–Sat 10–6, Sun 10–3 ✋ Adult €3.50, child (under 16) free 🚇 Jaume I 🚌 14, 17, 39, 45 🛍 🏧

FOSSAR DE LES MORERES

This expansive square next to the Basílica de Santa Maria del Mar holds a very poignant place in the affections of Catalans. A tall, modern sculpture topped with an everlasting flame and inscribed with a patriotic poem remembers the thousands who died fighting against the Bourbon armies in 1714. Many of the fallen were buried here, and, although the cemetery was paved over a century or so later, a few mulberry trees *(moreres)* are still planted in their memory. Although the Catalans were defeated, their heroic resistance is still proudly recalled every year on 11 September, when locals gather at the monument. In recent years, the event has taken on increasingly political tones, and the speeches often urge Catalan independence from the Spanish state.

The square was unattractively remodelled in 1989, but it is still overlooked by a fine collection of historic buildings, with pretty wrought-iron balconies and stone arches.

✚ 134 G9 🚇 Jaume I

MONUMENT A COLOM

A statue of Christopher Columbus (1451–1506) is at the port end of Las Ramblas, perched on top of a column more than 60m (197ft) high. He supposedly points at the Americas, but because of the uneven coastline of Barcelona, he actually has his eyes firmly fixed on North Africa. The four imposing lions around the elaborate base are a homage to Catalonia's role in the colonization of the Americas and its subsequent economic independence from the region of Castile. The monument contains a tiny elevator, from which visitors ascend to the *mirador*, a glass-enclosed lookout tower. With a 360-degree view, the *mirador* gives new arrivals the opportunity to take in the layout of the city. But be warned, the windows are relatively small and it is not for those who suffer from claustrophobia.

✚ 134 F10 ✉ Plaça del Portal de la Pau s/n, 08001 ☎ 93 302 52 24 🕐 Jun–end Sep daily 9–8.30; Oct–end May 10–6.30 ✋ *Mirador*: adult €3, child (4–12) €1.70 child (under 4) free 🚇 Drassanes 🚌 14, 36, 38, 57, 59, 64

Below *Its sheer size makes the Monument a Colom a good meeting point*

INFORMATION

www.mhcat.net

✚ 134 G10 ✉ Palau de Mar, Plaça de Pau Vila 3, 08003 ☎ 93 225 47 00 🕐 Tue–Sat 10–7 (also Wed 7–8pm), Sun 10–2.30 ✋ Adult €4, child (7–18) €3, child (under 7) free; first Sun of every month free to all 🚻 Guided visits (Catalan) at 12pm on second floor, and at 1pm on third floor 🚇 Barceloneta 🚌 14, 17, 39, 40, 45, 57, 59, 64 🍴 Lunchtime snacks and à la carte in the evenings, on the fourth floor with sweeping views over Port Vell 🏪 Sells gifts made by local designers, and stocks a good range of books on a number of subjects, including Catalan history

Above *A restored brick warehouse houses Catalonia's history museum*

MUSEU D'HISTÒRIA DE CATALUNYA

The Museu d'Història de Catalunya's slogan is a 'stroll through history', and that pretty much sums up what it is. The huge museum is in a restored brick warehouse in Port Vell, often referred to as the Palau de Mar, and spans over four floors. The ground and first floors are dedicated to temporary shows; a moving photographic portrait of the Mauthausen concentration camp and a homage to Josep Tarradellas, the first president of the Generalitat, are two examples. The second and third floors are where the main exhibition is held. Because of the sheer expanse of it, you would be wise to follow the exhibition numerically as it takes you through the different periods and key events in Catalonia's history, such as the peasants' revolt, the Civil War and the first autonomous government of the modern age.

THE DISPLAYS

Starting with the Iberians, the exhibits consist of re-created scenes, reproduction maps and documents, historical sound recordings and footage, and interactive gadgets. Some of these are ingenious. The re-created medieval chapel complete with chanting monks is likely to make the hairs on the back of your neck stand up, and there is a suit of armour for children to try on. Some exhibits rely on verbal communication and as the majority of the text is in Catalan you may need to refer to the English handbook you will have been given at the entrance.

THE THIRD FLOOR

This section, starting with the Industrial Revolution, is a lot easier to digest, mainly because of the photographic and cinematic material available. The re-created cinema showing a propaganda film of Franco and his family is fabulous, as is the 1950s bar interior next door, which celebrates the coming of television and Catalan mass media.

MUSEU BARBIER-MUELLER D'ART PRECOLOMBI

www.barbier-mueller.ch

The magnificent medieval mansion of the Palau Nadal houses this outstanding collection of pieces from the indigenous cultures of Mexico, Central America, the Andes and the lower Amazon. It is a smaller version of the museum of the same name in Geneva, Switzerland, widely recognized to be one of the finest collections of anthropological art in the world. The collection in Barcelona starts with a room of gold adornments of the various deities of northern Peru from 1000BC. From there, three more rooms display Mayan pottery figures and Aztec sculptures, the focal point of which are some highly naïve but seductive statues of squat figures used in death rituals in pre-Christian Mexico. Two austere, 3000BC stone owls from Ecuador can be found at the far end of the exhibition. The darkened rooms add to the lost treasure feel of the museum, and—unusually for Barcelona—the exhibits are explained in French and English as well as Spanish.

🔲 134 G9 ✉ Carrer de Montcada 12–14, 08003 ☎ 93 310 45 16 🕐 Tue–Fri 11–7, Sat–Sun 10–8 ✋ Adult €3.50, child (under 16) free; free Sun afternoons 🚇 Jaume I 🚌 14, 17, 19, 39, 40, 45, 51 🎁 Great gift shop ☕ Café

MUSEU DE CIÈNCIES NATURALS

www.bcn.cat/museuciencies
www.museuzoologia.bcn.es

Set in the lovely Parc de la Ciutadella (▷ 148), this is one of the city's older museums. The Museu de Zoologia together with the Museu de Geologia are combined as the Museu de Ciències Naturals de la Ciutadella (City Natural History Museum).

One of the main reasons to visit is to see the fairy-tale mock fortress in which the Zoology Museum is housed. The Castell dels Tres Dracs (Castle of Three Dragons) was designed as a café-restaurant by Lluís Domènech i Montaner (1850–1923) for the 1888 Universal Exhibition. The ceramic plates

depicting flora and fauna under the building's battlements are a particularly relevant detail, reflecting the content of the museum itself. The theory of the bigger the better dominates some of the displays, as shown by the 5m (16ft) Nile crocodile and the gigantic Japanese crab. The museum also holds temporary exhibitions every three months on related subjects. Apart from anything else, the Zoology Museum gives you the feeling that you are stepping back into a Victorian-era research laboratory.

The Geology Museum is next to the greenhouse in the Parc de la Ciutadella, occupying a late 19th-century building. Designed as part of the Universal Exhibition of 1888, it was the city's first museum. This is the largest geological collection in Spain with more than 100,000 exhibits, only a tiny proportion of which is on show. Divided into two wings, there are displays of granites, quartzes, naturally radioactive rocks from around the world, and a fascinating fossil collection.

🔲 135 H9 ✉ Passeig de Picasso s/n, Parc de la Ciutadella, 08003 ☎ Museu de Zoologia: 93 319 69 12; Museu de Geologia: 93 319 68 95 🕐 Tue–Sat 10–6.30, Sun 10–2.30 ✋ Adult €3.50, child (under 16) free; free Sun afternoons; includes entry to both museums 🚇 Arc de Triomf 🚌 14, 39, 40, 41, 42, 51, 141

MUSEU D'HISTÒRIA DE CATALUNYA

▷ 140.

MUSEU PICASSO

▷ 142–143.

MUSEU DE LA XOCOLATA

www.museudelaxocolata.cat

Wandering through the clever, well-laid-out exhibits (a loose term, as the museum is structured as a giant textbook as opposed to a series of objects), you learn that it was the Spanish who brought cocoa from the New World to Europe and that the first industrialized chocolate-making machine was invented in Barcelona in 1780. The first section relates many other anecdotes, such as Native Americans using cocoa as a primitive form of money. The second half of the exhibition is dedicated to the thoroughly Catalan invention, the *mona*. Originally a humble, egg-laden yeast cake, *monas* have evolved into extravagant chocolate sculptures that appear in cake-shop windows at Easter. This is a particularly good time to visit the museum as it hosts the annual *mona* competition.

🔲 134 G9 ✉ Carrer del Comerç 36, 08003 ☎ 93 268 78 78 🕐 Mon, Wed–Sat 10–7, Sun 10–3 ✋ Adult €3.90, child (under 7) free 🚇 Arc de Triomf 🚌 14, 16, 17, 19, 36, 39, 40, 45, 51, 57 ☕ 🎁

Below *Tempting souvenirs on sale at the Museu de la Xocolata*

INFORMATION

www.museupicasso.bcn.es

✠ 134 G9 ✉ Carrer de Montcada 15–23, 08003 ☎ 93 256 30 00
🕐 Tue–Sun 10–8 ✋ Adult €9 (includes permanent and temporary exhibitions), child (under 16) free; free Sun afternoons; temporary exhibitions adult €5.80, child (under 16) free
🚇 Jaume I 🚌 14, 17, 39, 40, 45, 51, 59 🎧 Sat and Sun 12pm (Catalan), Tue and Thu 6pm (Spanish), Tue and Thu 4pm (English), included in admission price. Advance reservations necessary, tel 93 256 30 22, email museupicasso@bcn. cat 📖 Comprehensive, well-laid-out guidebook available in all major European languages and Japanese for €13.50
☕ Attractive café with big sofas and chandeliers, and an outdoor terrace in summer 🎁 Two gift shops on site, selling postcards, a good selection of catalogues from both past and present exhibitions, and assorted Picasso paraphernalia; both can get very busy

Above *One of the spacious galleries in the Museu Picasso*

INTRODUCTION

The Museu Picasso is in five separate medieval mansions along Carrer de Montcada, the beautiful street at the heart of La Ribera district. After years of restoration work the palaces have been carefully joined together, but you can still see traces of their original majesty in the Italianate courtyards, baroque salons and painted ceilings. The main entrance is through the 15th-century Gothic Palau Berenguer d'Aguilar. Arrows guide you around the permanent collection and you must follow this route, spread out over the first and second floors. Inevitably there is a focus on Picasso's early work, reflecting the time that he spent in Barcelona, which included his famous Blue Period (1901–04).

Pablo Picasso was born in Málaga in 1881. His family moved to Barcelona in 1895 and it was here that he spent his formative years as an artist. He moved to Paris in 1904 and settled permanently in France. The first donation to the collection was made by the artist himself. He gave *The Harlequin* to the local council in 1919, and a further 22 paintings donated by a private collector enabled the museum to open its doors in 1934. The Museu Picasso, in its current form, was founded in 1963 by Jaume Sabartés, Picasso's lifelong friend and secretary, who is featured in a number of portraits on display. In 1968, Sabartés died, leaving his entire private collection to the museum, a move which required expansion from the original Palau Berenguer d'Aguilar into the adjoining mansion. As a tribute to his friend, Picasso took an interest in the museum, bequeathing his entire *Las Meninas* series and many other works. Following Picasso's death in 1973, the museum acquired a significant body of his graphic work as well as a collection of ceramics that was donated by his widow, Jacqueline.

The museum is currently undergoing a massive refurbishment, which will include the construction of a new extension. Works may interrupt visits.

WHAT TO SEE

MAN WITH HAT (1895)

The small-scale oil paintings that line the walls of the opening galleries were the product of Picasso's childhood in Málaga and his adolescence in La Coruña and Barcelona, where his father taught at their schools of fine art. This portrait marks perhaps the first time that the young Picasso moved from straightforward realism towards something more expressive.

BEACH AT LA BARCELONETA (1896)
This painting comes from the same period as *Man with Hat* and its subject matter makes it a popular choice within the city. It is a splendid exercise in perspective, and the free brushwork continues the move towards a more abstract way of depicting the world.

CARRER DE LA RIERA DE SANT JOAN (1900)
At the end of the 19th century, Picasso was living in Barcelona and making friends with the Catalan artists Ramón Casas and Santiago Rusinyol. There are several paintings from this time, a number using Els Quatre Gats tavern (▷ 126) as a subject. One of the best is this view from his studio window, revealing his first hint of abstraction.

THE MADMAN (1904)
Picasso spent much of his Blue Period in Barcelona, producing haunting studies of poverty and despair. This classic of the period skilfully conveys the depth of human suffering.

THE HARLEQUIN (1917)
Picasso was fascinated by the world of the theatre, with dancers and pantomime characters a recurring theme in his work. This painting was produced on one of his visits to Barcelona with Diaghilev's Ballet Russe. The model for the portrait was the Russian dancer Léonide Massine. Picasso donated this work to the city of Barcelona in 1919 and it appeared as part of the Museu Picasso's collection on its opening.

LAS MENINAS (1957)
The high point of the collection is this series of 58 paintings hung together in the Great Hall. During the 1950s, Picasso began looking to the great artists for inspiration and in particular to Diego Velázquez (1599–1660). The result was a series of canvases on the theme of the Velázquez masterpiece *Las Meninas (The Maids of Honour)*, depicting the women of the Spanish court, and executed in a hermitic period in his studio in 1957. Picasso's Cubist reinterpretations of the original painting reveal this work by Velázquez in a completely new light.

TIPS
» Late afternoon is the best time to go to avoid the crowds. Even if it's busy you shouldn't have to wait for long as crowds are moved through the ticket office surprisingly quickly.
» Some may be disappointed by the absence of one of Picasso's most celebrated works, *Guernica* (1937), which is on display in Madrid.
» There is now a special 'carnet' available, which costs €10 (or €15 for family carnet). It allows admission for one year, but is of interest to visitors as it only costs €1 more than the general ticket—but entirely avoids the queues.

GALLERY GUIDE
Rooms 1–3: Works done in Malaga
Rooms 4–10: Works done in Barcelona
Room 9: *The Embrace*
Rooms 11–14: The Blue Period
Rooms 15–17: *Las Meninas* series
Rooms 18–19: Late years and ceramics

Below *A medieval Italianate courtyard is evidence of the original division of the mansions that comprise today's museum*

INTRODUCTION

Lluís Domènech i Montaner (1850–1923) was one of the best Modernista architects, and this outrageously over-the-top concert hall is perhaps the most emblematic Modernista building of all. It is in the narrow streets of the Sant Pere district, which means that it is difficult to get an overall view of the outside without craning your neck from the street. If at all possible, you should come to a concert here, as this is much the best way to appreciate the building—the music and the architecture were designed to be enjoyed together. Otherwise, you will have to take one of the regular guided tours to gain access to the building.

The Palau de la Música Catalana was built between 1905 and 1908 as a headquarters for the Orfeó Català. This choral society, founded in 1891, had played a leading role in La Renaixença, the revival of Catalan art, language and political thought which had a direct influence on the Modernista architectural movement. The choice of Domènech i Montaner was significant—he had a background as a Catalan nationalist politician and as the chairman of the Jocs Florals, the literary arm of La Renaixença. All of the main themes of Modernisme were employed in the design, from the extravagant use of floral decoration and themes from nature to the *trencadís* (mosaics of broken tiles) and the repeated use of Catalan nationalist symbols including the shield of St. George. The finest craftsmen and artists of the age were commissioned to work on the building, including sculptors Eusebi Arnau and Pau Gargallo, and mosaicist Lluís Brú. The Palau was completed in 1908, and opened to huge acclaim. The city authorities deemed it the finest building of the year, and awarded it a special prize.

By the 1920s, however, Modernisme had fallen completely out of fashion, and locals began to call the building 'the Palace of Catalan Junk'. Fortunately, it survived the threat of demolition and was handsomely restored and renovated in the 1980s. In 1960 it was the setting for a patriotic protest when Catalan nationalists sang their unofficial anthem during a concert for the dictator General Franco. Declared a UNESCO World Heritage Site in 1997, the Palau has been extended by contemporary architect Òscar Tusquets onto the site of an already demolished church. The extension provides an additional underground concert hall as well as an outdoor plaza for summer recitals.

WHAT TO SEE

THE FACADE

Before you go inside, it is worth spending some time admiring the facade. The first thing you will notice is the forest of bright floral mosaic columns, each one different, surrounding the main entrance. On the corner of Carrer d'Amadeu Vives and Carrer de Sant Pere Més Alt, beneath the shield of the Palau, is an extravagant sculptural ensemble which is entitled *La cançó popular catalana*. It has numerous references to popular Catalan folk song and culture, and includes the figures of St. George, Catalonia's patron saint, and a beautiful maiden bursting out of the stone. Higher up are the busts of some of the great composers—Bach, Beethoven, Palestrina and Wagner—a deliberate statement by architect Domènech i Montaner that Catalan folk art could sit comfortably with the classics.

At the summit of the facade, beneath a mosaic dome, is a fine allegorical mosaic of the Orfeó Català (Catalan Choral Society). Although this is very difficult to see from street level, the mosaic is rich in symbolism, from the jagged peaks of the mountain of Montserrat to the use of yellow and red from the Catalan flag and the shield of St. George.

INFORMATION

www.palaumusica.org

134 G9 Carrer de Sant Francesc de Paula 2, 08003 902 47 54 85 Daily 10–3.30 Adult €9, child (under 12) free Urquinaona 16, 17, 19, 45 and all routes to Plaça d'Urquinaona Guided tours every half-hour daily 10–3.30; 10–6 in Aug and at Easter. Cost €12, held alternately in Catalan, Spanish and English; tours may be cancelled at short notice because of rehearsals Small pocket guidebooks for €9, larger coffee-table book about the Palau with CD-ROM €28 (both available at the shop) The attractive, wood-panelled café is open to the public *Les Muses del Palau* gift shop sells tour tickets, books and other gifts with the Palau's motif, and assorted objects such as pottery

Opposite *Detail of the stunning facade designed by Domènech i Montaner*

TIPS

Below *The grand staircase sweeps upwards from the foyer*

THE FOYER

The recent remodelling of the Palau de la Música Catalana means that visitors no longer enter through the original entrance, but via a glassy new foyer set to one side. However, the original entrance foyer is an altogether more spectacular affair, formed by a series of elaborate arches and columns extravagantly decorated to resemble an enchanted forest. Domènech i Montaner conceived this building as a garden of music, open to the outside world, and the predominant material is glass in order to let in the light. This theme is furthered by a deliberate lack of clear division between the interior and the exterior, for example by the use of street lamps within the foyer. Even the vaulted ceilings between the columns are entirely encrusted with floral motifs, created by the outstanding Modernista mosaic artist, Lluís Brú. Pre-performance drinks are still served at the original bar, which is surrounded by swirls of dark wood.

From the foyer, a magnificent staircase swoops grandly to the upper levels, with extraordinary balustrades made of amber-coloured glass and studded with yet more ceramic flowers.

THE CONCERT HALL

The main concert hall is quite simply breathtaking. It is huge, with around 2,000 seats in the stalls (orchestra seats) and two circles on the upper levels, but the initial impact comes not from its size, but from the rainbow-coloured light pouring in through the stained-glass windows. There are arched windows on all three levels, but the pièce de resistance is the vast ceiling, a symbolic representation of a cloudless summer sky designed by Antoni Rigalt i Blanch. An expanse of glass in pale blues and violets culminates in a huge, inverted sphere in fiery tones of gold and red, a sensuous evocation of the sun. Around this stunning central skylight floats a heavenly choir composed of 40 beautiful

Above *A corner of the facade, dripping with Modernista detail*
Left *The fabulous central skylight in the main concert hall*

female heads. The theme of an enchanted garden is continued throughout the auditorium, and the entire ceiling is studded with more ceramic blooms, and delicate golden mosaics in the form of peacock tails fan between the exterior columns.

THE STAGE

The apse-shaped stage is seen through an arch set with dramatic sculptures created by Didac Masana and completed by the young Pau Gargallo. Josep Anselm Clavé (1824–75), a key figure in the revival of Catalan folk music and one of the founders of the Orfeó Català, sits beneath a tree of life representing the song 'Les Flors de Maig' (The Flowers of May). On the right, a bust of Beethoven peers through the winged horses from Wagner's 'Ride of the Valkyries' from *The Valkyrie*. This pair of sculptures is clearly designed to reinforce the message that the Palau was a temple to all kinds of music, from Catalan folk song to more traditional European works.

At the back of the stage, a mosaic panel with the Catalan shield is flanked by 18 female figures, their upper bodies sculpted in terracotta and their costumes fashioned out of mosaics by artist Lluís Brú. These are Les Muses de Palau, a group of muses each holding a different musical instrument in her hands, apart from one who is singing to represent the human voice. The muses, their flowing costumes linked by garlands of flowers, form a backdrop to the performers on the stage.

SALA LLUÍS MILLET

An elegant, high-ceilinged salon on the second floor of the Palau is named after Lluís Millet, one of the founders of the Orfeó Català who commissioned the construction of the building. A bust of Millet is one of several busts of celebrated musicans and artists connected with the Palau which have been gathered together here, including Pau Casals, the famous cellist and conductor. The salon is beautifully illuminated by another stained-glass window, also the work of Antoni Rigalt i Blanch, and flanked by a pair of gilded columns covered in intricate floral mosaics.

THE GUIDED TOUR

The 50-minute tour begins in the foyer and continues in the rehearsal room with a 20-minute film about the history of the building. Next, a double staircase with white marble handrails leads to the first floor and the entrance to the grand concert hall. You are taken into the upper circle for a closer look before ending in the Sala Lluís Millet. This hall fills the entire area behind the main facade of the Palau, and from its stained-glass windows there are close-up views of the mosaic-covered columns that you will have seen outside. The rest of the hall is subdued when compared to the richness of the auditorium, though there are sculptures and paintings of various figures associated with the history of the Palau.

INFORMATION

www.bcn.cat/parcsijardins
➕ 135 H9 ✉ Passeig de Picasso 15, 08003 🕐 Daily 10–dusk ✋ Free
🚇 Arc de Triomf 🚌 14, 17, 36, 39, 51, 57, 59, 64 💬

TIPS

» There are a number of play areas for children, a fish-filled boating lake and bicycles for rent.

» The park is a great place to visit on Sunday afternoons and people-watch.

» In summer, *The Cascade* makes a splendid backdrop for the weekly concerts held in a pretty wrought-iron bandstand nearby.

PARC DE LA CIUTADELLA

This is the largest and greenest park in the city centre, and at one time it was the only park in Barcelona. It was created when the fortress was demolished (▷ 32) and was used as the setting for the Universal Exhibition of 1888, which bequeathed a slew of Modernista architecture including the lavish, red-brick Arc de Triomf at the northern end of the park, which served as the main entry point for the Exhibition. The park's formal, leafy avenues, central boating lake and shady, hidden corners are very enticing, and it is home to various museums and the city zoo (▷ 149).

The over-the-top fountain-sculpture *The Cascade* is the combined effort of seven sculptors and emulates Rome's Trevi Fountain. Among the classical myths depicted is the Birth of Venus, and resplendant griffons guard the pools below the huge triumphal arch which forms the centrepiece. It is believed that the young Gaudí, then an unknown architecture student, worked on the project, and was responsible for some minor decorative details. The monument has been restored recently, and the rearing golden horses pulling Apollo's chariot atop the triumphal arch now gleam anew.

ARCHITECTURAL DIVERSITY

The Castell dels Tres Dragons, in the southeastern corner of the park, is one of the earliest Modernista works and was designed by celebrated architect Domènech i Montaner. Although the design evokes a Gothic castle, complete with crenellations, it incorporates some daring new engineering techniques, including the use of a metal frame beneath the brickwork. The building, along with the nearby neoclassical edifice, now contains the city's Natural History Museum (▷ 141). Nearby, the Umbracle (the Shade House) and the Hivernacle (Winter Garden) were both designed by Josep Fontseré, the park's original architect, and should be not be missed.

The grand pink-and-cream baroque building at the centre of the park was originally constructed as the arsenal for the now-destroyed Ciutadella fortress, but now serves as the seat of the Catalan parliament. A pale sculpture of a weeping woman, *El Desconsol,* by the renowned Noucentista artist Josep Llimona, sits amid a glassy pond in front of the parliament buildings.

Above *Griffons guard the pools of the ornate* Cascade

PARC DE L'ESTACIÓ DEL NORD

www.bcn.cat/parcsijardins

The Parc de l'Estació del Nord, completed in 1999, is one of Barcelona's greenest parks. It is a very busy place not just because of this, but also because it is situated next to the Estació del Nord, the city's principal terminal for national and international bus services. The entire park is covered in lawn, which is unusual for Barcelona. Various undulating levels give the space a fluid air, heightened by two works by the US-born sculptor Beverly Pepper. The ceramic works *Fallen Sky* and *Wooded Spiral* have been placed into the lawns, forming an integral part of the landscape. The only other vegetation is a small group of trees, and this restraint, seen in all the park's elements, has made this one of the most delicate public spaces in the city.

✚ 135 H9 ✉ Carrer de Nàpols 70, 08018 🕐 Daily 10–dusk 💲 Free 🚇 Arc de Triomf or Marina 🚌 6, 10, 19, 39, 40, 41, 42, 51, 54, 55, 141

PARC ZOOLÒGIC

www.zoobarcelona.com

The Parc Zoològic is set over 13ha (32 acres) of parkland on the eastern side of Parc de la Ciutadella. More than 400 species live at the zoo, but without a doubt its reputation lies in the primates section. Most of the primates here are in danger of extinction, most notably the Bornean orangutans and the mangabeys, the world's smallest monkey. Other fast-disappearing forms of animal life found at the zoo include the Iberian wolf and various big cats like the magnificent snow leopard from Central Asia. The Doñana Aviary is helping to repopulate Spain's diminishing bird life by breeding night herons, spoonbills and ducks from the southern marshlands of the same name.

The animal enclosures are currently very small, but conditions will improve when the zoo has expanded; the Zoo Marí (Marina Zoo) is scheduled to open in a new beachside location by the Fòrum in 2014–15. With the removal of the marine creatures to their new home, the animals remaining in the Parc de la Ciutadella location will enjoy considerably more space.

✚ 135 H10 ✉ Parc de la Ciutadella s/n, 08003 ☎ 93 225 67 80 🕐 Jun–end Sep daily 10–7; Oct 10–6; Nov–end Feb 10–5; Mar–end May 10–6 💲 Adult €16, child (3–12) €9.60, child (under 3) free 🚇 Arc de Triomf or Barceloneta 🚌 14, 39, 41, 42 🍴🎁

Below *More than 400 species live in the zoo's Parc de la Ciutadella site*

PORT OLÍMPIC

The Port Olímpic and Vila Olímpica (Olympic Port and Village) are the most visitor-friendly parts of the heritage of the 1992 Games. The area also has one of the city's best beaches at Nova Icària. Dozens of old factories and warehouses were bulldozed to make way for the apartments used as athletes' accommodation during the Games, and before 1992 neither the marina nor the esplanade—nor even the sand on the beach itself—existed. The Olympic area now serves both as a chic residential district and a lively entertainment place. The port is the biggest attraction here, and the esplanade heading past the luxurious Hotel Arts complex is buzzing with seafood restaurants, bars and cafés. The development is popular with residents and is largely credited with reversing the city's old reputation for ignoring the sea.

Don't miss the stunning metallic *Fish* by Frank Gehry, the architect responsible for Bilbao's Guggenheim Museum, in front of the Hotel Arts.
135 J10 Ciutadella-Vila Olímpica
6, 14, 36, 41, 92, 141

PORT VELL

Port Vell is the perfect place for a stroll or to while away a couple of hours. A cross between a pleasure playground and a port, all sorts of indoor pursuits are available at Maremagnum (▷ 159), the nearby entertainment complex.

Port Vell is the second of Barcelona's two Olympic ports and perhaps no other single project changed the face of the city so dramatically. Officially, it is the marina that sweeps along the length of the Passeig Joan de Borbó from the end of Via Laietana all the way down to Barceloneta beach. It's here you will see the expensive boats and yachts moored. Colloquially, the name also encompasses the vast pedestrianized Molls (wharves) d'Espanya and de Barcelona. The wooden swing bridge Rambla de Mar, an extension of Las Ramblas, leads to Maremagnum with its IMAX cinema and conglomeration of bars, eateries and shops, and the adjacent city aquarium (▷ 136–137). To the right of this is the World Trade Center, or the 'wedding cake' as it is locally known because of its huge white, round shape, and the terminal for the Balearic Ferries.

All these facilities mean that the place is constantly busy. Especially at the weekends, Port Vell is a hive of activity with people riding their bikes, and dog-walkers and families going for a stroll. On Sundays there is a craft market on the northern side of Palau de Mar, a restored series of brick warehouses that now accommodates the Museu d'Història de Catalunya (▷ 140). The area is also known for two of the city's most famous pieces of public art. The first is the unmissable *Barcelona Head*, created by US artist Roy Lichtenstein (1923–97), standing at the entrance of the marina. The second is the full-scale replica of the world's first steam-powered submarine invented by Catalan Narcís Monturiol (▷ 33), on the Maremagnum side of the port.
134 F10 Barceloneta or Drassanes
14, 17, 19, 20, 36, 39, 40, 45, 51, 57, 59, 64

Below *Frank Gehry's shimmering* Fish *sculpture (left) and the towering Hotel Arts are landmarks in Port Olímpic*

LA RIBERA

One of the city's most fashionable areas, La Ribera is more commonly known as El Born, which most believe is a reference to the jousts that used to take place on the neighbourhood's boulevard (borneo means 'joust' in Catalan). It is a small district between Via Laietana and Parc de la Ciutadella and it has changed dramatically in the past few years. La Ribera has been home to some of the larger museums, such as the Museu Picasso, for years, but fashion and design boutiques are springing up on an almost daily basis and it has a good number of the city's best private art galleries. Window shopping or having coffee at one of the many cafés has become the new Sunday pastime of the city's gens bonic (beautiful people).

A MERCANTILE PAST

Catalonia's trading history can be seen in a stroll around El Born. This was the city's trading area thanks to the old steel-and-glass Mercat del Born, which was inspired by the former market at Les Halles in Paris. It was on the main thoroughfare, the Passeig del Born, and was the wholesale market until 1971. You will find that the street names around it proclaim the commercial activity that once went on there: Argenteria (silver) was lined with silversmiths, Flassaders (blanket) was where you popped in to get a woven-to-order blanket and Vidrieria (glassworks) was once lit up with glass-blowers' torches and ovens. Near the Plaça de Palau and La Llotja (the stock exchange), Canvis Vells would have once rung with the sound of nimble fingers weighing foreign coins on scales. The market is still the area's landmark, and the Passeig del Born connects it with the Gothic church of Santa Maria del Mar (▷ 152).

The Estació de França near the Parc de la Ciutadella was built in 1848 to accommodate the first train line in Spain, to the outlying town of Mataró. With the trains now mostly using Sants station, the beautiful wrought-iron and marble structure has become something of a showpiece, although airport trains still terminate here. But the area's charm lies in finding its small, hidden architectural gems. Its series of squares and streets, and the smell of freshly ground coffee and spices from the few wholesale outlets that remain here, are the true jewels of this area.

INFORMATION

www.barcelonaturisme.com
✚ 134 G9 ℹ Plaça de Sant Jaume, Carrer Ciutat 2 (inside the town hall), 08002 ☎ 93 285 38 34 🕓 Mon–Fri 9–8, Sat 10–8, Sun 10–2 Ⓜ Jaume I or Barceloneta

Above Plaça Santa Maria makes a great place for a drink

INFORMATION

✛ 134 G9 ✉ Passeig del Born
🕐 Daily 9–1.30, 4.30–8 🖐 Free
🚇 Jaume I 🚌 14, 17, 19, 39, 40, 45,
51, 59 🍴 None, but a handful of cafés
and restaurants outside the church

TIPS

» Santa Maria del Mar is a functioning place of worship and it's not uncommon for the clergy to reprimand visitors whom they think are talking too loudly or showing disrespect. Silence is required, especially during Mass.

» The best days to move freely around the church are Monday to Thursday, when there are fewer ceremonies.

Above *The elegant central nave of Santa Maria del Mar*

SANTA MARIA DEL MAR

The most beautiful church in Barcelona, Santa Maria del Mar is the most complete example of Catalan Gothic architecture in the city. The Basílica de Santa Maria del Mar, to give it its full name, is in the heart of La Ribera. The funding for the building work came from the rich merchants of the area, collected in order to celebrate Catalonia's conquest of Sardinia, and the site was chosen as it was believed that Santa Eulàlia (the patron saint of Barcelona) was originally buried there. It is said that most of the able-bodied male workers in Barcelona were employed on the building work at one time or another over its 54-year construction period. The church was attacked during the Spanish Civil War (1936–39) and it was relieved of the adornments added over the years. Ironically, this act of vandalism has only added to the purity of style.

THE INTERIOR

The entrance remains the most highly embellished part of the church, but still in keeping within the formal aesthetic of the Catalan Gothic style, characterized by austerity, as well as sheer size. Inside, the central nave is 26m (85ft), the widest in Europe, and is flanked on either side by two aisles and the building's supporting columns. These soar up to a series of fan vaults—typical of the period—with a further set of eight at the far end of the church in a semicircle to define the presbytery. One decorative element that survived the attacks on the church during the war are the glorious stained-glass windows from the 15th to 19th centuries, which are placed on either side of its main walls, and in particular the enormous, opaque 15th-century rose window above the entrance to the church.

The church's acoustics make it perfect for concerts and recitals, mainly of classical and religious music, which are held here during the year—ask at the tourist office for details. Santa Maria del Mar is also a popular place in Barcelona in which to get married. Pull up a chair in the square outside and watch the stream of petal-throwing wedding parties on Saturdays.

SANT PERE

INFORMATION
✚ 134 G9 🚇 Jaume I, Urquinaona, Arc de Triomf 🚌 17, 19, 39, 40, 45, 51, 55, 141

Until recently, the little *barri* of Sant Pere offered a window into the old Barcelona—the Barcelona which existed before the town planners transformed the skyline in the 1980s and 1990s, and before the city became a hotspot for fashion-conscious urbanites. The neighbourhood's three main streets—Sant Pere Més Baix, Sant Pere Més Alt and Sant Pere Mitjà—offer a cheerful if decidedly unglamorous hotchpotch of grocery stores, butchers, and shops selling housecoats and long underwear. Among them, perhaps surprisingly, are some delightful little Modernista pharmacies, including the Farmàcia Padrell, at Carrer Sant Pere Més Baix 52. Despite its stained glass and swirling woodwork—part of a Modernista refit from around 1890—it dates back to 1561, which makes it the oldest recorded pharmacy in the city. Recently, offbeat fashion boutiques, record shops and hip little bars and restaurants have sprung up, and Sant Pere is becoming increasingly popular for the laid-back nightlife on offer. Its attractive squares, particularly the vaulted arches of the Plaça de Sant Agustí Vell, and the broad expanse of the Carrer d'Allada-Vermell, are filled with terrace cafés on balmy summer evenings.

The medieval neighbourhood of Sant Pere grew up around the fortified monastery of Sant Pere de les Puel.les, part of which still overlooks a pretty square with the same name. It was a rural district when the monastery was established in the 10th century, but gradually the fields filled up with textile factories. Textiles were the backbone of local industry for centuries, and the historic trades plied here are recalled in the street names: wool was traded on the Plaça de la Llana (Wool Square) and ropes *(cordes)* were made and bought on the Carrer dels Corders. It is fitting that the workers of this humble neighbourhood were behind its greatest monument: the Palau de la Música Catalana (▷ 144–147).

MERCAT SANTA CATERINA

The spectacular reconstruction of the Mercat Santa Caterina (▷ 159) has played a crucial role in bringing this former time-capsule of a neighbourhood to the attention of visitors. The square was once occupied by a convent, destroyed in the early 19th century and replaced with a neoclassical covered market. This was completely remodelled in 2005 by Enric Miralles and Benedetta Tagliabue, who added the glorious cap of multicoloured tiles, clearly influenced by the organic forms and vivid hues beloved by Gaudí. This extraordinary roof has become one of the old city's most evocative symbols.

Below *Santa Caterina market has a wonderful mosaic roof*

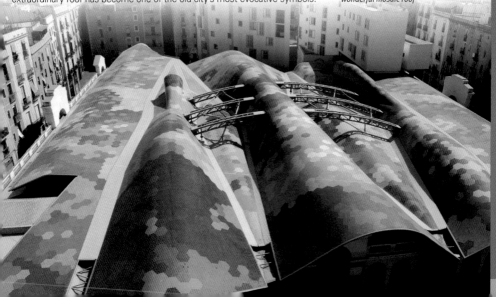

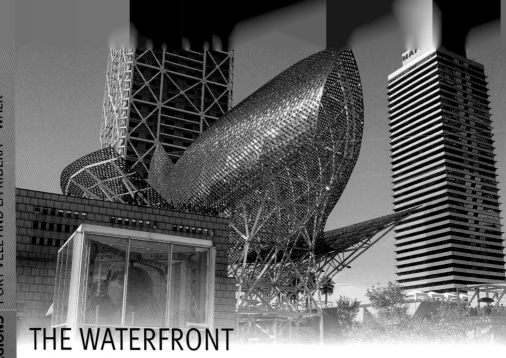

THE WATERFRONT

Before the 1992 Olympics, the coastline north of Barceloneta consisted of mud pools backing onto industrial estates. Now you can't keep people away from the shore, whether for a ramble along the boardwalks or to relax on the sandy beaches.

THE WALK
Distance: 3km (1.8 miles)
Time: 2 hours
Start at: Monument a Colom
End at: Ciutadella-Vila Olímpica metro station

HOW TO GET THERE
Metro: Drassanes station is on the green line 3.
Bus: Any of the following take you to Monument a Colom: 14, 36, 38, 57, 59, 64.

★ Start your walk outside the towering Monument a Colom (Columbus Monument, ▷ 139), which is at the port end of Las Ramblas, a few steps from the Drassanes metro. Cross over to the port, and with your back to the monument, turn left.

❶ This stretch of wide, well-paved walkway is known as the Moll de la Fusta (Wooden Quay). From here you get a splendid view of the Maremagnum entertainment complex (▷ 159) and the aquarium (▷ 136–137), both of which are accessible from the Rambla de Mar, the bridge to your right. Outside the aquarium there are vast stretches of grass to laze on and a full-scale replica of the world's first steam-powered submarine invented by Catalan Narcís Monturiol.

Continue to the end of the Moll de la Fusta, where it intersects with the Moll d'Espanya. Directly to your left is the eye-catching *Barcelona Head* by pop artist Roy Lichtenstein (1923–97). To the right, a small craft market takes place on weekends. Walk to your right along the Moll del Dipòsit, following the water's edge.
   The large building you see on your left is the Palau de Mar, an old warehouse that is now home to the Museu d'Història de Catalunya (▷ 140). Outside, there is a cluster of cafés and restaurants, a great place to soak up the sun. Continue walking with the water's edge to your right—you are now on the Moll de Barceloneta.

❷ On your right-hand side is Port Vell (▷ 150), the city's most exclusive marina where millionaires in their yachts drop anchor on a regular basis. On your left, Passeig Joan de Borbó is flanked by outdoor seafood restaurants, a traditional place for a Sunday paella.

Now turn left, so that you cross over the Moll onto Passeig Joan de Borbó, and continue walking right. On the corner of Carrer de l'Almirall Cervera stands a stunning example of early 1950s Catalan architecture, La Casa de la Marina, built as public housing. Walk to the end of Passeig Joan de Borbó. To your left is the large open space of the Plaça del Mar. Face the beach and turn left.

Opposite *Frank Gehry's giant bronze* Fish *fronts the city's tallest skyscrapers*

Follow the shoreline via the ample wooden boardwalk laid out in front of you.

After about 2km (1.5 miles) you will see the crown of a water tower on your left. Dating from the late 1800s, it was the first in Spain and now resides in the Parc de la Barceloneta. Continue along the boardwalk, which then changes its name to become the Passeig Marítim de la Barceloneta.

❸ As you reach the end of the Passeig, on your left-hand side you will pass the unmistakable form of Frank Gehry's celebrated *Fish* sculpture, a symbol of the city since it was installed in 1992. The twin skyscrapers behind it are the tallest in the city—the one on the left is the Hotel Arts, the city's most exclusive hotel. The multi-level gardens are open to the public.

At the end of the Passeig, turn right, then left and left again, walking around the Moll de la Marina to the marina on the opposite side.

❹ The glitzy Port Olímpic (▷ 150) is on your right, with more millionaires' boats and dozens of outdoor bars and restaurants lined up along the Passeig Marítim del Port Olímpic. This is the road that stretches away to your left as you look at the

marina. It is also one of the city's hottest spots after dark.

Continue walking away from the sea. To your left, the Plaça dels Voluntaris, with its huge central fountain, was named after the thousands of volunteers who helped out during the 1992 Olympic Games.

A few paces more will bring you to the corner of Carrer de Salvador Espriu and the heart of the former Olympic Village, housing that was built especially for the visiting athletes. On the left, in the Jardins d'Atlanta, is the quirky *Tallavents* (Windbreaker) sculpture by Francesc Fornells-Pla (1921–99). Walk to the next intersection with Avinguda

d'Icaria, turn left and walk for two blocks to the Ciutadella-Vila Olímpica metro station.

WHEN TO GO
A bright sunny day is best, but if you can't organize that, take a jacket: it gets windy along Barcelona's coast.

PLACE TO VISIT
PARC DE LES CASCADES
✉ Salvador Espriu s/n ☎ 24 hours

WHERE TO EAT
KAIKU
▷ 165.

Above *Yachts bob in the water of the marina at Port Olímpic*

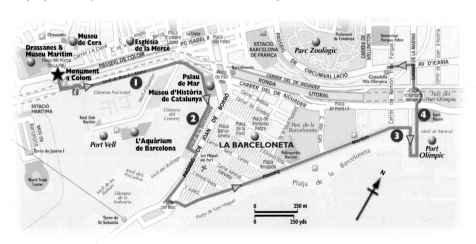

LA RIBERA

The tiny La Ribera district is a living testament to the fact that Catalans were noted as a nation of shopkeepers, and the Mercat del Born was once the city's wholesale market. These days the area is undergoing a new retail renaissance, as cutting-edge fashion and design shops take over traditional food shop premises

THE WALK
Distance: 1.5km (1 mile)
Time: 45 minutes to 1 hour
Start/end at: Plaça de Santa Maria del Mar

HOW TO GET THERE
Metro: Line 4 goes to Jaume I.

★ Leave the station, cross Via Laietana, then walk down Carrer de l'Argenteria, following the sign for Basílica de Santa Maria del Mar.

❶ The square in front of the Gothic Basílica de Santa Maria del Mar (▷ 152) is a good starting point for a walk around La Ribera. Take advantage of the abundant outdoor cafés from which you can admire its grand entrance and magnificent rose window. Don't miss the quaint Font de Santa Maria, one of the oldest water sources in the city, at the beginning of Carrer de l'Argenteria directly opposite the church.

Walk to the right of the church and continue onto Carrer de Santa Maria.

❷ A few steps up the road on the right is a plain, solemn-looking square that has a modern, arched column topped by an eternal flame. This is Fossar de les Moreres (Mulberry Graveyard, ▷ 139), a deeply significant place in the hearts of the Catalan people. It was the site of a massacre in the 1714 War of Succession.

Continue to the end of Carrer de Santa Maria, which brings you to the back of the Santa Maria del Mar basilica, and turn left, crossing over the Placeta de Montcada and into the Carrer de Montcada. This was where the city's noblemen once resided in their imposing mansions. Immediately to your right is the gated Carrer de les Mosques, a lane said to be the narrowest street in

Barcelona and now closed off to the public.

Continue along Carrer de Montcada, looking out for the baroque courtyard of the Palau Dalmases, on the left at No. 20. At the end of Carrer de Montcada turn right onto Carrer de la Princesa. Of the old wholesale outlets selling olives, dried cod and other foodstuffs, only one remains—the enticing spice emporium Àngel Jobal, at No. 38 on your right. Continue to the end of Carrer de la Princesa to the threshold of the Parc de la Ciutadella (▷ 148) and the fanciful Castell dels Tres Dracs, which houses the Museu de Zoologia (▷ 141). Turn right onto Passeig de Picasso and follow the perimeter of the park.

❸ You will walk under the elegant Porxes de Fontseré, a series of arches named after the architect

Opposite *Fossar de les Moreres, site of a massacre in 1714*

Right *Street performers entertain in pretty Plaça de les Olles*

responsible for the Parc de la Ciutadella, Josep Fontseré. On the opposite side of the Passeig de Picasso, near the intersection with Carrer de la Fusina, is the conceptual glass-and-water structure *Homenatge a Picasso* by Antoni Tàpies (born 1923).

Turn right onto Carrer de la Fusina and then left onto Carrer del Comerç.

❹ Here you walk around the facade of the former Mercat del Born. Its vast amount of ironwork looks like a homage to the industrial age. In 2001 excavation work revealed the amazingly complete remains from the 18th century. After much debate—the authorities originally planned to turn it into a library—the market is now destined to be a museum and community centre, displaying the subterranean ruins through glass floors.

With your back to the market, keep left, following Carrer del Comerç to the intersection with Avinguda del Marquès de l'Argentera. Directly in front of you is the beautifully restored Estació de França, from where the first train in Spain made its inaugural trip in 1848. Turn right onto the Avinguda and then right again onto Carrer de Pescateria—so named after the fishmongers that once lined the street.

Turn left onto Carrer del Bonaire, which brings you to charming Plaça de les Olles, a small square with outdoor cafés and apartment blocks with pretty facades. Carry on along Carrer del Bonaire, which farther on changes its name to Carrer del Consolat de Mar. Stop when you reach the intersection with Carrer dels Canvis Vells on your right.

❺ This will bring you face to face with the imposing Llotja, formerly

the city's stock exchange. Although its facade dates from 1802, it was originally built in the late 14th century and glimpses of the Gothic interior courtyard are possible from street level. The building has had a varied life. For most of the 19th century, its upper floors housed the art school where Picasso senior taught his young son, Pablo, for a time in the mid-1890s.

Turn right onto Carrer dels Canvis Vells, named after the money-changers who worked their nimble fingers in streets around La Llotja. Here you will see more examples of the district's picturesque arcades. At the end of the road is the Plaça de Santa Maria del Mar.

WHEN TO GO
During shop hours (remember to avoid the lunch closing hours 1–4pm). Many eccentric and esoteric shops are to be found in the streets around La Ribera.

WHERE TO EAT
DRAC CAFÉ
This charming outdoor café is next to the Modernista Castell dels Tres Dracs in the Parc de la Ciutadella. A tempting selection of cakes,

sandwiches and light meals are served.
✉ Passeig de Picasso s/n ☎ 93 310 76 06 🕒 Tue–Sun 9–9

PLACE TO VISIT
ÀNGEL JOBAL
✉ Carrer de la Princesa 38 🕒 Daily 10–2, 4–7.30

TIP
» Take care with your belongings around the Carrer de Montcada and the entrance of the Museu Picasso as pick-pocketing is rife.

SHOPPING

24 KILATES
www.24-kts.com

This is where fans of skate and graffiti culture head to peruse the great range of cult clothing, shoes, books, comics, music and other collectables. There is an exhibition space downstairs that plays host to shows on themes from art to anima. An interesting collection of Japanese toys and artefacts lines the walls on the top floor.

✚ 168 G10 ✉ Carrer del Comerç 29, 08003 ☎ 93 268 92 63 ⏱ Tue–Sat 11–2, 4–9 🚇 Barceloneta

LA BARCELONETA
One of the city's oldest indoor markets, Mercat de la Barceloneta has been spectacularly refurbished and is now encased in a striking, contemporary shell. Its proximity to the water lends it a maritime atmosphere, and the products you can buy here range from fresh fish, meat and vegetables to cold meat, beans and tinned foods. It is home to fine restauants, including Lluçanès (▷ 165).

✚ 168 G10 ✉ Plaça del Poeta Boscà s/n, 08003 ☎ 93 221 64 71 ⏱ Tue–Thu, Fri 7am–8.30pm, Sat 7–3, 5–8.30, Mon 7–3 🚇 Barceloneta

LA COMMERCIAL HOME
An ultra-stylish store in the fashionable Born neighbourhood, this sells original objects for the home, such as gilded bookends and contemporary porcelain dishes. From sumptuous throws to elegant vases, there's something to suit all tastes and pockets.

✚ 168 G9 ✉ Carrer del Bonaire 4, 08003 ☎ 93 295 46 30 ⏱ Mon–Sat 11–9 🚇 Jaume I, Barceloneta 🚌 14, 40, 41, 42, 141

COMO AGUA DE MAYO
This tiny boutique is filled with divine fashion and accessories for women, including a fabulous range of shoes. Labels include Masscob, Otto et Moi and Chie Mihara.

✚ 168 G9 ✉ Carrer de l'Argenteria, 08003 ☎ 93 310 64 41 ⏱ Mon–Sat 10–8.30 🚇 Jaume I

CUSTO
www.custo-barcelona.com

The clothes at Custo stand out for their funky mix of fabrics and prints. When a new batch of T-shirts arrives at their flagship store in La Ribera they fly out of the door. Although now pirated and copied by other designers, their look remains distinctly Barcelonese.

✚ 168 G9 ✉ Plaça de les Olles 6, 08003 ☎ 93 268 78 93 ⏱ Mon–Sat 10–9, Sun 11–8 🚇 Jaume I

CZAR
Choose sports shoes for men and women by the likes of Merrell, Asics, Converse, Adidas and Diesel. If you want something dressier try Paul Smith, Sessura, Fly London and W&LT. Watch and bag labels include Diesel, Le Coq Sportif and Levi's; for costume jewellery try Takeshi. They also sell mini Vans for babies.

✚ 168 G9 ✉ Passeig del Born 20, 08003 ☎ 93 310 72 22 ⏱ Mon–Sat 12–2, 5–9 🚇 Barceloneta

D BARCELONA
D Barcelona offers unusual, trendy design pieces for the home, as well as a range of imaginatively designed fashion accessories and playful gifts. It stocks (among other brands) Storm watches, Mathmos lava lamps, household utensils by Koziol and Pylones, inflatable armchairs and painted cows by Cow Parade.

✚ 168 G9 ✉ Carrer del Rec 61, 08003 ☎ 93 315 07 70 ⏱ Mon–Thu 10–10, Fri–Sat 11–11 🚇 Barceloneta

Above *Custo sells its own distinctive line in must-have T-shirts*

ETXART & PANNO

www.etxartpanno.com

Gorgeous, grown-up fashion for women is the hallmark of Etxart & Panno, whose clothes range from sharp trouser suits to the boardroom to floaty dresses in the filmiest of fabrics for hot summer nights. Stylish and contemporary, but with a timeless appeal, this is fashion to keep. They also produce accessories, including highly desirable shoes.

✚ 168 G9 ✉ Passeig del Born 14, 08007 ☎ 92 310 37 24 🕐 Mon–Sat 11–4, 5–8.30 🚇 Barceloneta

GLAMOOR

This optician brings a touch of glamour to La Ribera. It stocks exclusive designs and limited-edition glasses, sunglasses and accessories, and even has a minibar at which to deliberate your purchases. This is definitely a shop to consider if you are looking for innovative designs.

✚ 168 G9 ✉ Carrer de Calders 10, 08003 ☎ 93 310 39 92 🕐 Mon–Sat 10–2, 5–8.30 🚇 Barceloneta

KITSCH

This shop is an outrageous and vibrant display of what can be done with some paper, paste, paint and a bit of dexterity. Kitsch isn't actually all that kitsch but it is certainly curious. One of its most impressive lines is the papier mâché figurines. You can't miss the particularly startling flamenco figure in the doorway, to be found near the Santa Maria del Mar church.

✚ 168 G9 ✉ Placeta de Montcada 10, 08003 ☎ 93 319 57 68 🕐 Mon–Sat 11.30–8, Sun 11.30–3.30 🚇 Jaume I

MAREMAGNUM

www.maremagnum.es

The shops in this complex mostly sell gifts, accessories, casual clothes and souvenirs, though since a recent refurbishment fashion names like H&M, Desigual and Mango have moved in. There's a typical mall-style food court, plus bars and clubs open in the evenings. It's approached

across the wooden footbridge from Las Ramblas, with a good view of the harbour—though you may have to wait for up to 15 minutes if it's raised for boats to go through.

✚ 168 F11 ✉ Moll d'Espanya, 08039 ☎ 93 225 81 00 🕐 Daily 11–10 🚇 Drassanes

PORT VELL

If you stroll along Las Ramblas on a Sunday morning you'll encounter a host of antiques stands. This market is full of books, watches, bright tin boxes, unusual and dated electrical appliances, glass ornaments, small items of furniture and plenty of fascinating bric-à-brac. It is the place where you can hunt for bargains to your heart's content.

✚ 168 F10 ✉ Plaça de les Drassanes s/n, 08002 🕐 Sat–Sun 10–8 🚇 Drassanes

RECDI8

www.recdi8.com

A tiny shop stuffed with fascinating things, recdi8 has all kinds of unusual design objects for the home. The range leans towards the kitsch, fun, bold and colourful: The families of plastic Babapapas, for example, have proved big sellers. They also stock bags, T-shirts and jewellery.

✚ 168 G9 ✉ Carrer d'Espaseria 7, 08003 ☎ 93 268 02 56 🕐 Mon–Thu 11.30–2.30, 5–8.30, Fri 11.30–2.30, 5–9, Sat 12–2.30, 5–9 🚇 Barceloneta

SANTA CATERINA

Established in 1848, this food market's namesake is the convent that once stood on the site. The original building has been renovated by the Enric Miralles Benedetta Tagliablue architecture studio. You can't miss the spectacular, undulating roof decorated with multicoloured tiles.

✚ 169 H9 ✉ Avinguda Francesc Cambó, 08003 ☎ 93 319 21 35 🕐 Tue–Wed 7.30–3.30, Thu–Fri 7.30am–8.30pm, Sat 7.30–3.30, Mon 7.30–2 🚇 Arc de Triomf

SPECIAL EVENTS

Shopaholics will drool over the fabulous selection of women's

shoes, bags and jewellery from top international designers that are beautifully displayed in this sleek, white boutique. Among the brands on offer are cult French label Costume Nacional, Icebert, Exte, BOB-Best Of Barcelona, Christian Lacroix and Duffer of St. George. Just up the street at No.11, a second boutique offers an equally dazzling selection for men.

✚ 168 G9 ✉ Carrer dels Vigatans 6, 08003 ☎ 93 268 86 16 🕐 Tue–Fri 10.30–2, 5–9, Sat 11–9, Mon 5–9 🚇 Jaume I

VITRA

www.vitra.com

This spectacular, double-storey furniture showroom is the Barcelona outlet of the famed Swiss design retailers. On tempting display are re-editions and series of signature pieces by the likes of Phillipe Starck, Charles and Ray Eames and Frank Gehry. There's not much that will fit into your hand luggage, but delivery overseas is available.

✚ 168 G9 ✉ Plaça Commercial 5, 08003 ☎ 93 268 72 19 🕐 Tue–Sat 10.30–2, 5–8 🚇 Jaume I

ENTERTAINMENT AND NIGHTLIFE

L'ANTIC TEATRE

www.lanticteatre.com

This self-financed theatre is in a charmingly run-down 18th-century mansion near the Palau de la Música Catalana (▷ 144–147). It puts on a mixed bag of performances, from dance to documentary screenings, from music to mime. Given its 'alternative' status, quality is consistently high and there is a lovely terrace bar to chill out on after the show. Performances are mainly at weekends only. Check the door (or website) for details. Credit cards are not accepted.

✚ 168 G9 ✉ Carrer Verdaguer i Callís 12, 08003 ☎ 93 442 98 44 💶 From €5 🚇 Urquinaona

BAR MUDANZAS

A welcome oasis in the über-stylish Born neighbourhood, this is a traditional, old-fashioned café with a black-and-white tiled floor and wooden tables. It attracts an eclectic crowd of arty locals, fashionistas and a few stray tourists, enticed inside by the mellow atmosphere and friendly vibe.

⊞ 168 G10 ✉ Carrer Vidrieria 15, 08003 ☎ 93 319 11 37 ⏱ Daily 10am–2.30am Ⓜ Jaume I

BERIMBAU

This bar opened three decades ago and was originally a Brazilian dance hall. Today the colonial air remains, as does the samba and salsa music. It's a great place to begin an evening—sampling some delicious Brazilian cocktails made with fresh fruit juices. Credit cards are not accepted.

⊞ 168 G9 ✉ Passeig del Born 17, 08003 ☎ 93 319 53 78 ⏱ Daily 6pm–2.30am Ⓜ Jaume I

CATWALK

www.catwalk.net
You'll find the beautiful people at this hip place, all dressed in designer clothes. Upstairs the DJs play hip-hop, while downstairs house and techno create a more energetic feel. A number of different music nights are held throughout the week.

⊞ 169 J10 ✉ Carrer de Ramón Trias Fargas s/n, Marina Village, 08005 ☎ 93 224 07 40 ⏱ Thu–Sun midnight–6am ✋ €15 including a drink Ⓜ Ciutadella-Vila Olímpica

CENTRE CIVIC CONVENT DE SANT AGUSTÍ

www.bcn.cat/centrecivicsantagusti/castellano/index.html
This community centre offers a full programme of concerts, craft markets, workshops, and all kinds of other events. It also plays a central role in all the traditional local festivals from carnival to Three Kings (when Catalan children receive their Christmas presents). The bar, which is open to the public, has tables outside in the remnants of the old convent cloister.

⊞ 168 G9 ✉ Carrer del Comerç 36, 08003 ☎ 93 310 37 32 ⏱ Bar: Mon–Thu 10–10, Fri–Sat 11am–12am Ⓜ Arc de Triomf

ESPAI JOAN BROSSA

www.espaibrossa.com
The shows staged here include flamenco, contemporary ballet, French cabaret, magic, poetry and avant-garde productions, which may not be suitable for every audience.

⊞ 168 G9 ✉ Carrer d'Allada Vermell 13, 08003 ☎ 93 310 13 64 ✋ From €9 Ⓜ Arc de Triomf

EUSKAL ETXEA

The original, and by far the best, of the Basque tapas bars that have sprung up over the last few years, Euskal Etxea offers a delicious range of pintxos (small, bite-sized rations of food often on top of slices of bread) and good Basque wines, including an excellent Txacolí.

⊞ 168 G9 ✉ Placeta de Montcada 1–3, 08003 ☎ 93 310 21 85 ⏱ Daily 10am–12.30am Ⓜ Jaume I

GIMLET

This intimate, elegant bar is one of the finest coctelerias in the city. Smartly attired waiters expertly mix a wide range of cocktails, including the bar's namesake. The bar is popular with a theatrical crowd, and celebrities regularly drink here.

⊞ 168 G9 ✉ Carrer del Rec 24, 08003 ☎ 93 310 10 27 ⏱ Daily 10pm–3am Ⓜ Arc de Triomf

HIVERNACLE

Hivernacle is in an old conservatory in Parc de la Ciutadella. Coffee and refreshments are served amid exotic plants. Jazz and classical music concerts are held here during the summer.

⊞ 169 G9 ✉ Passeig de Picasso s/n, 08003 ☎ 93 295 40 17 ⏱ Mon–Sat 9am–12am, Sun 9–4 Ⓜ Arc de Triomf

IMAX

www.imaxportvell.com
One of the few IMAX cinemas that has three projection systems: IMAX, Omnimax and 3D. The screen is a spectacular 27m (90ft). You'll find it in the Maremagnum shopping complex at Port Vell.

⊞ 168 F11 ✉ Moll d'Espanya s/n, 08039 ☎ 93 225 11 11 ✋ €12.10 Ⓜ Drassanes

MIRAMELINDO

A wood-panelled, colonial-style, intimate space where weekday nights are relaxing. The cocktails should not be missed; try the Cuban mojitos (fresh mint, sugar, lime juice, rum and soda water) or caipirinhas (lime juice, sugar, brandy and ice) and then a coffee to help you regain a grasp on sobriety. Credit cards are not accepted.

⊞ 168 G9 ✉ Passeig del Born 15, 08003 ☎ 93 310 37 27 ⏱ Mon–Thu 8pm–2.30am, Fri–Sat 8pm–3.30am, Sun 7.30pm–2.30am Ⓜ Jaume I

OPIUM MAR

www.opiummar.com
One in a string of fashionable restaurant-bar-clubs that line the beachfront, Opium Mar takes its inspiration from the Orient. The interior is red, black and white, and low, cushioned benches allow guests to lounge slinkily while sipping on cocktails. Popular with the city's beautiful people, it turns into a nightclub on Thursday, Friday and Saturday nights. It also hosts concerts. Check the website for upcoming events.

⊞ 169 H11 ✉ Passeig Marítim de la Barceloneta 34, 08003 ☎ 93 414 63 62 ⏱ Daily 11am–late Ⓜ Ciutadella-Vila Olímpica

PALAU DE LA MÚSICA CATALANA

www.palaumusica.org
Attending a concert in this Modernista hall—the spiritual home of Catalan music—is an unforgettable experience, and the best way to appreciate the building. It was designed by Lluís Domènech i Montaner (1850–1923) and conceived for the Orfeó Català (▷ 144–147). Classical concerts dominate, but there is also some jazz and folk. There is a bar.

⊞ 168 G8 ✉ Carrer de Sant Francesc de Paula 2, 08003 ☎ 93 295 72 00 ✋ From €10 Ⓜ Urquinaona

SALA MONASTERIO

www.salamonasterio.com
In this small and welcoming venue, the well-mixed cocktails are

accompanied by live music. World music—from Argentine tango to Brazilian *forró*—features prominently, but anything goes. Admission is often free.

➕ 168 G10 ✉ Passeig Isabell II, 08003 ☎ 616 28 71 97 🕐 Mon–Thu, Sun 9.30pm–2.30am, Fri–Sat 9.30pm–3am 🖐 Free–€5 🚇 Barceloneta

SUBORN
www.suborn.net

Suborn is one of those places that never seem to fall out of favour, perhaps because it doesn't go overboard on style and attracts a regular crowd to meet, dance and shout over the electronic music. If it all gets a bit much, there is an outside terrace overlooking the Ciutadella Park where some innovative Mediterranean cuisine is served before the crowds roll in around midnight.

➕ 169 G10 ✉ Carrer de la Ribera 18, 08003 ☎ 93 310 11 10 🕐 Wed–Sat 8.30pm–3am 🚇 Barceloneta

YELMO CINEPLEX ICARIA
www.yelmocineplex.com

This multiplex has 15 screens, all showing subtitled original-language films. It's often busy, despite its considerable capacity.

➕ 169 J10 ✉ Carrer de Salvador Espriu 61, 08005 ☎ 93 221 75 85 🖐 €6–€7.50 🚇 Ciutadella-Villa Olímpica

SPORTS AND ACTIVITIES
BARCELONETA

Barcelona's large seafront consists of several beaches. Bordering the seafront in the Barceloneta area, this particular beach is a popular choice with families and couples. One of its main attractions is the good range of playing facilities for children, a rich selection of restaurants and bars, lounge chair rental and a range of water sports.

➕ 168 G10 🚇 Barceloneta

BICICLOT
www.biciclot.net
www.bikinginbarcelona.net

This bicycle club has quite a high profile in promoting cycling around

Barcelona and organizing cultural and art-inspired rides within the city. It also runs workshops throughout the region. You can rent bicycles here and find everything you'll need for your ride in the shop.

➕ 169 H10 ✉ Passeig Marítim de la Barceloneta 33, 08003 ✉ 93 221 97 78 🕐 Jun–end Sep daily 10–3, 4–8; Oct–end May Fri–Sun 10–3, 4–6 🖐 €18 per day, €5.50 per hour 🚇 Ciutadella-Vila Olímpica

LAS GOLONDRINAS
www.lasgolondrinas.com

One of the best ways to see the port is to take a boat ride. It's a 35-minute trip to the breakwater sea wall, and two hours to reach Port Olímpic. This is a good way to get a closer look at the old boats and yachts moored here. Credit cards are not accepted.

➕ 168 F10 ✉ Plaça del Portal de la Pau 1, 08001 ☎ 93 442 31 06 🕐 Apr–end Sep Mon–Fri 11–6, Sat–Sun 11.45–7; Oct–end Dec Mon–Fri 11–4, Sat–Sun 11.45–6; Jan–end Mar Mon–Fri 11–4, Sat–Sun 11.45–5 🖐 Adult €6.50–€13.50, child (4–10) €2.60–€5 🚇 Drassanes

SANT SEBASTIÀ

This beach is the first you reach, if you approach the sea from the old city, and is very busy in summer. Just about all members of the community use the beach, so you won't feel out of place or too much like a tourist. The section closest to the jetty is largely gay and nudist. It has showers, plus you can rent umbrellas and lounge chairs. In summertime there are several lively open-air bars. The beach is protected by a long breakwater, which culminates in Hotel Vela (▷ 138).

➕ 169 H11 🚇 Barceloneta

HEALTH AND BEAUTY
CENTRE DE TALASSOTERÀPIA
www.claror.cat

Located on the beachfront, this spa and sports centre has an astounding array of saltwater therapies from spa baths and saunas to strategically angled water jets. It doesn't have the glamour of a day spa; the aim is more therapeutic and clients

tend to be local and elderly. Mud and seaweed wraps as well as massage and facials are also on offer here, the first centre of its kind in Barcelona. Try to avoid mornings and lunchtimes, which are busy.

➕ 169 H11 ✉ Passeig Marítim de la Barceloneta 33–35, 08003 ☎ 93 224 04 40 🕐 Daily 7am–12am (until 10.30pm in Aug) 🖐 €15 weekdays, €17.80 weekends 🚇 Ciutadella-Vila Olímpica

FOR CHILDREN
L'AQUÀRIUM DE BARCELONA
▷ 136–137.

PARC DE LA CIUTADELLA

This is the largest green space in the city, with lots of room for the kids to run around in. They can take advantage of the play areas and boating lake, while parents can take a seat and watch (▷ 148).

➕ 169 H9 ✉ Passeig de Picasso 15, 08003 🕐 Daily 10–dusk 🖐 Free 🚇 Arc de Triomf

PARC ZOOLÒGIC
▷ 149.

Below A seahorse in Barcelona's aquarium

EATING

PRICES AND SYMBOLS

The prices given are the average for a two-course lunch (L) and a three-course dinner (D) for one person, without drinks. The wine price is for the least expensive bottle.

For a key to the symbols, ▷ 2.

7 PORTES

www.7portes.com

7 Portes was established in 1836 and has always served high-quality, traditional cuisine using fresh ingredients from the local market. Rice dishes are the main attraction, so don't miss the mixed fish and meat paella, or the *arròs negre* (rice cooked in squid ink). The stunning high-ceilinged dining room has a black-and-white marble floor and more than its fair share of mirrors. It is not possible to make a reservation, so plan to come early or be prepared to wait outside. Unlike most of the city's restaurants, 7 Portes serves meals all day.

✚ 168 G10 ✉ Passeig d'Isabel II 14, 08003 ☎ 93 319 30 33 🕐 Daily 1–1 ✋ L and D €40, Wine €10 🚇 Barceloneta

AGUA

www.grupotragaluz.com

Agua has the most popular terrace in the Vila Olímpica; when you are seated at your table, you can even get sand in your shoes. It is famous for its risottos and fish, and very popular with locals. Sunday lunchtime is busy, with people stopping for a beer and a bite to eat.

✚ 169 H10 ✉ Passeig Marítim de la Barceloneta 30, 08005 ☎ 93 225 12 72 🕐 Mon–Thu 1.30–4, 8.30–12, Fri–Sat 1.30–5, 8.30–1, Sun 1.30–5 ✋ L and D €35, Wine €15 🚇 Ciutadella-Vila Olímpic

AGULLERS

People flock to this pint-sized place, but there are only enough tables to seat 15 lucky people. The dishes are wholesome and the portions generous. Mercè Rosselló prepares excellent casserole, noodles and meat stew. This is not a place for leisurely sipping of coffee because, although nobody would actually show you the door, space is highly valued. Credit cards are not accepted.

✚ 168 G10 ✉ Carrer dels Agullers 8, 08003 ☎ 93 268 03 61 🕐 Mon–Fri 1–5.30, Sat 1–4 ✋ L €18, Wine €10 🚇 Jaume I

ALTA MAR

Alta Mar is one of the best-placed restaurants in the city, as it is perched up in the Sant Sebastian tower. It serves haute cuisine enhanced by the best-quality produce, but mostly leans towards fish dishes. The desserts are excellent: Try home-made mascarpone ice cream or sublime chocolate mousse. The huge restaurant is decorated like a luxurious yacht.

✚ 168 G11 ✉ Passeig Joan de Borbó 88, 08003 ☎ 93 221 00 07 🕐 Tue–Sat 1–3.30, 9–11.30, Mon 9pm–11.30pm ✋ L €70, D €90, Wine €20 🚇 Barceloneta

ANFITEATRO

You'll find a very creative and elaborate menu here, with squid, lamb, liver and onion tapas, rabbit stuffed with prawn, tortellini with cuttlefish and cod with shellfish. The restaurant is set in gardens and overlooks a central pool. It's a very romantic spot, particularly on summer evenings, when the gardens are candlelit.

✚ 169 J10 ✉ Avinguda del Litoral 37, Parque del Port Olímpic, 08005 ☎ 659 69 53 45 🕐 Mon–Sat 1.30–3.30, 8.30–12, Sun 1–4 ✋ L €25, D €50, Wine €20 ⬛ Section 🚇 Ciutadella-Vila Olímpica

Above *CDLC is the place to go for beachside snacks and meals with an Eastern flavour*

ANTIGA CASA CAN SOLÉ

Established in 1903, this tavern was frequented by harbour workers during their breaks. The news about its good food and reasonable prices spread quickly and, little by little, businessmen, cotton importers and even celebrities such as Joan Miró became regulars. It's just as popular today, with excellent rice dishes cooked in a variety of ways, such as in a casserole, in squid ink or served with lobster.

✚ 168 G10 ✉ Carrer de Sant Carles 4, 08003 ☎ 93 221 50 12 🕔 Tue–Sat 1.30–4, 8.30–11, Sun 1.30–4. Closed 2 weeks in Aug ✋ L €40, D €50, Wine €16 🚇 Barceloneta

AROLA

www.arola-arts.com

Chef Sergi Arola is the current star of Spanish haute cuisine. La Broche, his restaurant in Madrid, has two Michelin stars but his namesake eatery in Barcelona is a more casual affair. The pop-art decoration sets the tone for his creative cuisine, which puts as much emphasis on the presentation as it does the unusual mix of flavours. Try fresh clams with coriander (cilantro) sauce with a Caesar salad (a rarity in the city) or go for the lively *pica-pica* (tasting menu). Desserts include a heavenly vermouth-infused chocolate mousse. In summer, you can enjoy a platter of sophisticated tapas on sumptuous, cushioned sofas scattered on the terrace.

✚ 169 H10 ✉ Hotel Arts, Carrer de la Marina 19–21, 08005 ☎ 93 483 80 90 🕔 Wed 1.30–3.30, 8.30–11, Thu–Fri 1.30–3.30, 8.30–12, Sat 2–4, 8.30–12, Sun 8.30–11. Closed Jan ✋ L and D €60, Tasting menus €48 and €68, Wine €22 🚇 Ciutadella-Vila Olímpica

BAR JAI CA

A rowdy, friendly neighbourhood bar, Bar Jai Ca is tucked down a tiny back street in Barceloneta. The bar groans with all kinds of delicious morsels, from stuffed mussels with spicy tomato sauce to fried artichokes. Popular with locals, it's often packed full, particularly out on

the tiny pavement terrace, so get there early to ensure a seat.

✚ 168 G10 ✉ Carrer de Ginebra 13, 08003 ☎ 93 319 50 02 🕔 Daily from 7pm–late ✋ Tapas from €4, Wine €8 🚇 Barceloneta

LA BÁSCULA

www.labascula.net

A relaxed, arty café tucked away down a narrow street in the Born district, La Báscula occupies a high-ceilinged former warehouse, once used to store chocolate. Now, the walls are hung with colourful works of art, and chalkboards display the day's specials. Choose from tasty soups, pies, quiches and simple pasta dishes, and finish up with one of the tempting home-made desserts.

✚ 168 G9 ✉ Carrer dels Flassaders 30, 08003 ☎ 93 319 98 66 🕔 Tue–Sat 1–11.30 ✋ L and D €10 🚇 Jaume I

BESTIAL

www.bestialdeltragaluz.com

Bestial is right by the beach and in the shade of the Hotel Arts. The food served is primarily Italian, with a variety of risottos (with barbecued Norwegian lobster, wild asparagus or mushrooms), pastas (with basil, garlic and olive oil, or prawn and olives) and pizzas from the wood-fired oven. A huge glass facade faces an elegant, wood-decked terrace. There are DJ sets on summer nights.

✚ 169 H10 ✉ Carrer de Ramón Trias Fargas 30, 08005 ☎ 93 224 04 07 🕔 Mon–Thu 1–3.45, 8–11.30, Fri 1–3.45, 8–12.30, Sat–Sun 1–4.30, 8–12.30 ✋ L €17, D €40, Wine €17 🚇 Ciutadella-Vila Olímpica

BODEGA LA TINAJA

The wooden tables, soft candlelight, unusual wrought-iron lamps and decorative objects make this a good spot for a romantic meal. The menu includes rustic tapas, including platters of regional cheeses, Spanish hams and charcuterie.

✚ 168 G9 ✉ Carrer de l'Esparteria 9, 08003 ☎ 93 310 22 50 🕔 Tue–Sun 6–12 ✋ D €25, Wine €10 🚇 Jaume I

LA BOMBETA

This old fishermen's bar is perfect for those on a budget who still want to enjoy delicious, fresh seafood. You can either settle at a table or simply stand at the bar and dig into some of the generous tapas. Choose from steamed mussels, *esqueixada* (cold cod with vegetables) or fried squid, to name just a few. Even better, if you are having trouble adjusting to Spanish eating times, it's open all day. Credit cards are not accepted.

✚ 168 G10 ✉ Carrer de la Maquinista 3, 08003 ☎ 93 319 94 45 🕔 Thu–Tue 10am–midnight. Closed Sep and last 2 weeks of Feb ✋ L €10, D €15, Wine €9 🚇 Barceloneta

CAL PEP

www.calpep.com

There are mountains of the freshest seafood to be had in this tiny, much-loved tapas bar. Once seated at the bar itself, choose from sardines, prawns or whatever else is in season and watch as it is prepared before your eyes. Cal Pep is supposedly the humbler version of the owner's restaurant Passadis del Pep (in the same square), but most people prefer this option.

✚ 168 G10 ✉ Plaça de les Olles 8, 08003 ☎ 93 310 79 61 🕔 Mon 7.30pm–11.30pm, Tue–Sat 1.30–4, 8–11.30. Closed Aug ✋ L and D €50, Wine €15 🚇 Barceloneta

CAN MAJÓ

This restaurant, in the heart of La Barceloneta, serves excellent Mediterranean cuisine. Fresh fish and shellfish are used to enrich dishes such as lobster casserole, sautéed Norwegian lobster and baked hake. As it is right on the seafront, it's an idyllic place to dine out during the summer.

✚ 168 G11 ✉ Carrer del Almirall Aixada 23, 08003 ☎ 93 221 58 18 🕔 Tue–Sat 1–4, 8.30–11.30, Sun 1–4 ✋ L €30, D €40, Wine €10 🚇 Barceloneta

CAN RAMONET

Can Ramonet was established in 1763 and is arguably the oldest tavern in Barceloneta. The menu balances seafood, rice dishes and paellas, as well as black rice prepared with squid ink. If your appetite extends only to tapas, you can sit at one of the barrel-top tables. Should you prefer a full meal, the terrace is ideal. The beach is only a few steps away—perfect for an after-dinner stroll.

✚ 168 G10 ✉ Carrer de la Maquinista 17, 08003 ☎ 93 319 30 64 🕐 Daily 1–12 🍴 L and D €40, Wine €10 🚇 Barceloneta

LA CARASSA

La Carassa's typically bohemian interior lends an elegant dimension to the dining experience. The menu combines Catalan, French and even Swiss influences, reflected in the presence of delicious fondues on the menu. Try a chocolate fondue and dip pieces of apple, pear, strawberry, orange and banana into it.

✚ 168 G9 ✉ Carrer del Brosolí 1, 08003 ☎ 93 310 33 06 🕐 Mon–Sat 8.30pm–11pm. Closed Easter and 3 weeks in Aug 🍴 D €40, Wine €12 🚇 Jaume I

CARBALLEIRA

www.carballeira.com

A real insider's place, the wood-panelled, nautically themed Carballeira gets packed with locals who come for its superlative crab and lobster. Tanks in the doorway proffer several different species, from russet-hued king crab and pretty pink spider crab to spiny and slippery lobsters. Generally served simply boiled (with clarified butter, or alioli for those who want it), they'll do serious damage to your bank account, but it's worth it.

✚ 168 G10 ✉ Carrer de la Reina Cristina 3, Barceloneta, 08003 ☎ 93 310 38 86 🕐 Tue–Sun 1–4, 8–12. Closed Sun night, evenings on public holidays and Mon 🍴 L and D €65, Wine €15 🚇 Barceloneta

CARDAMÓN

www.cardamon.es

This looks like an old-fashioned Spanish tavern, with whitewashed walls, marble-topped tables and a wooden bar. It comes as some surprise, then, to discover that

the house speciality is curry—exceptionally good and authentically spicy curry, too. The Goa-style mussels are particularly good, prepared in a pungent ginger- and chilli-scented broth with a mighty kick. The thalis are served with accompaniments of excellent home-made chutneys.

✚ 168 G9 ✉ Carrer del Corders 31, 08003 ☎ 93 295 50 59 🕐 Tue–Sat 11–1, Sun 7–1 🍴 L €15, D €20, Wine €9 🚇 Jaume I

CASA CALVET

www.casacalvet.es

Gaudí's art nouveau Casa Calvet (▷ 139) was originally a textiles factory, but now the building is made up of flats on the upper levels with a ground-floor restaurant. Chef Miquel Alija's modern take on Mediterranean cuisine includes pea and squid soup, prawns cooked in rosemary oil and duck liver with Seville oranges. It also usually offers some vegetarian options.

✚ 168 G8 ✉ Carrer de Casp 48, 08010 ☎ 93 412 40 12 🕐 Mon–Sat 1–3.30, 8.30–11. Closed Aug 🍴 L €47, D €60, Wine €14 🚇 Urquinaona

CDLC

www.cdlcbarcelona.com

CDLC is a pleasant option for beachside dining. The eclectic menu includes Japanese sushi, sashimi and tempura, Chinese spring rolls and Indonesian satay, but they can also churn out decent salads, sandwiches and hamburgers at lunchtimes. The wonderful setting is the main draw: a beautiful wooden terrace overlooking the sea, shaded with pretty umbrellas and canopies.

✚ 169 H10 ✉ Passeig Marítim de la Barceloneta 32, 08005 ☎ 93 224 04 70 🕐 Daily 12pm–3am (restaurant until 1am) 🍴 Sandwiches from €10.50, main courses from €13.75, Wine €12 🚇 Ciutadella-Vila Olímpica

EL CHERIFF

This unassuming restaurant is much loved by Barceloneta locals. Some even claim the paellas are the best in the city, and certainly the

abundance of succulent seafood and cooked-to-perfection rice (not to mention the quirky carnation flower garnish) is hard to fault. Expect mussels lightly cooked in a marinara sauce, Denia prawns so fresh the meat literally falls out of the shells, and grilled razor clams simply dressed in olive oil and parsley. Weather permitting, reserve a table on the terrace. A real find.

✚ 168 G10 ✉ Carrer Ginebra 14, 08003 ☎ 93 319 69 84 🕐 Mon–Sat 1–4pm, 8–11. Closed October 🍴 L €30, D €40, Wine €15 🚇 Barceloneta

COMERÇ 24

www.projectes24.com

This is the most talked-about of Barcelona's wave of tapas bars run by chefs who aim to revolutionize Spain's bar food. Head chef Carles Abellán, who trained with renowned chef Ferran Adrià, serves up such exotic concoctions as truffle-filled eggs and asparagus with mandarin foam. This is a long way from your average slice of tortilla or bread rubbed with tomato, but you can wash the food down with a glass of old-fashioned wine.

✚ 169 G9 ✉ Carrer del Comerç 24, 08003 ☎ 93 319 21 02 🕐 Tue–Sat 1.30–3.30, 8.30–11. Closed last 3 weeks Aug 🍴 L and D €70, Tasting menu €62 and €84, Wine €27 🚇 Jaume I

LA COVA FUMADA

La Cova Fumada is a modest and noisy tavern with an open kitchen, boxes everywhere and marble tables shared by both harbour workers and business types. The food, however, is outstanding and the tapas, fish and meat in particular, are excellent. The menu, like the set-up, never changes. Although the restaurant has been open since the 1940s, there's no sign on the door. Find it close to the market, on the corner with Carrer de Sant Carles. Credit cards are not accepted.

✚ 168 G10 ✉ Carrer del Baluard 56, 08003 ☎ 93 221 40 61 🕐 Mon–Wed 9–3.30, Thu–Fri 9–3.30, 6–9, Sat 9–2. Closed Aug 🍴 L and D €15, Wine €8 🚇 Barceloneta

EMPERADOR

Right next to the Museu d'Història de Catalunya (▷ 140), Emperador's spacious terrace has a fabulous view over the harbour. Not surprisingly, eating outside is a popular choice during the summer months. Don't miss the cod with honey, a fantastic union of savoury and sweet. The cod croquettes and the octopus are also worth trying. The kitchen here is open all day.

🔢 168 G10 ✉ Palau de Mar, Plaça de Pau Vila 1, 08039 ☎ 93 221 02 20 🕐 Daily 12.30–11.30 🍴 L €40, D €45, Wine €12 🚇 Barceloneta

ENOTECA

The name suggests a wine bar and with more than 450 staggering varieties in its bodega the Enoteca is the city's most sophisticated watering hole. But with chef Jaime Pérez at the helm it is also a top culinary destination. You could try the foie gras with figs or let your senses be surprised by the combination of lamb chops and puréed chickpeas. The classy setting encompasses high-backed chairs and settees in wine shades and all the walls are lined with bottles you may peruse.

🔢 169 H10 ✉ Hotel Arts, Carrer de la Marina 19–21, 08005 ☎ 93 483 81 08 🕐 Mon, Tue 11.30–3.30, Mon–Sat 8pm–midnight 🍴 L and D €80, Tasting Menu €80, Wine €25 🚇 Ciutadella-Vila Olímpica

EL FORO

Succulent slabs of steak, pizzas, pastas, *butifarres* (Catalan sausages) and ribs *a la brasa* (barbecued) make up the menu of this split-level, wood-lined restaurant. Its popularity means you may have to wait, but judging by the queues outside most think it's worth it. A set menu is served on weekday lunchtimes, which includes steak and fries, plus wine and dessert for €10.

🔢 168 G9 ✉ Carrer de la Princesa 53, 08003 ☎ 93 310 10 20 🕐 Tue–Fri 9am–11pm, Sat 10am–12.30am, Sun 10am–11.30pm 🍴 L €10, D €30, Wine €10 🚇 Section 🚇 Arc de Triomf

KAIKU

Despite its beachfront location, it is easy to miss this unassuming restaurant, and yet it serves some of the freshest, most imaginative food in the city. Try the tantalizing sea anenome in tempura or ultra-fresh Galician clams to start, followed by the outstanding *arròs del xef*—a sublime paella-style dish with lightly smoked rice, prawns, mussels, chunky wild mushrooms and artichokes.

🔢 168 G11 ✉ Plaça de Mar 1, 08003 ☎ 93 221 90 82 🕐 Tue–Sun 1pm–4pm 🍴 L €30, Wine €10 🚇 Barceloneta

LITTLE ITALY

www.littleitaly.es

This restaurant is named after New York's Italian quarter and, although the chef is American, the food is not. The menu includes pasta, meat and fish dishes, and there's a comprehensive wine list. A number of informal, comfortable rooms make up the dining space, and there is live jazz on Monday, Tuesday and Wednesday nights, which starts at 9pm.

🔢 168 G9 ✉ Carrer del Rec 30, 08003 ☎ 93 319 79 73 🕐 Mon–Sat 1–4, 9–12.30 🍴 L fixed-price menu Mon–Wed €9.95, Thu–Sat €18–€24, D €30, Wine €12 🚇 Barceloneta

LLUÇANÈS

www.restaurantllucanes.com

This long-established restaurant moved in late 2007 from its former home in a small Catalan town to the spectacular Mercat de la Barceloneta (▷ 158). Owner-chef Àngel Pascual has already garnered accolades for his superb reinventions of classic Catalan and Mediterranean cuisine: the robust hare and lobster terrine reflects the traditional Catalan delight in fusing the flavours of *mar i muntanya* (sea and mountain).

🔢 168 G10 ✉ Plaça de la Font s/n, 08003 ☎ 93 224 25 25 🕐 Tue–Sat 1.30–3.30, 8.30–11.30, Sun 1.30–3.30 🍴 L and D €60; Menú Degustació €73; Menú Minimalista €102; Menú Temporada €43 (Tue–Fri lunch, Tue–Thu dinner), Wine €20 🚇 Barceloneta

EL MAGATZEM DEL PORT

The grounds of Palau de Mar are home to five restaurants, all serving similar cuisine, but the small Harbour Warehouse is known for its paellas and rice dishes. The restaurant presents a creative twist on traditional recipes and the chef seeks out all his ingredients at La Boquería market, ensuring his menu retains its quality and freshness.

🔢 168 G10 ✉ Palau de Mar, Plaça de Pau Vila 1, 08003 ☎ 93 221 06 31 🕐 Tue–Sat 1.30–4, 8.30–11.30, Sun 1.30–4 🍴 L and D €45, Wine €10 🚇 Barceloneta

MERENDERO DE LA MARI

www.merenderodelamari.com

This open-air restaurant is another based in the Palau de Mar. There's a wide selection of seafood and fish but the mussels, clams, snails and sea cucumber stew are particularly good. Panes of glass around the open kitchen allow customers to watch their food being prepared.

🔢 168 G10 ✉ Palau de Mar, Plaça de Pau Vila 1, 08003 ☎ 93 221 31 41 🕐 Daily 1–4, 8.30–11.30 🍴 L and D €40, Wine €17 🚇 Barceloneta

MONCHO'S CHIRINGUITO

www.monchos.com

One of the seven restaurants in Barcelona owned by the Moncho's chain, this branch became popular during the 1992 Olympics because of its location next to the beach. Locally the chain is known as the house of fish and paella, and there is a good selection of cuttlefish, octopus, prawns, cod, hake and more, mostly served fried. Salads are huge and always dressed with excellent olive oil.

🔢 169 H10 ✉ Platja Nova Icària 27, 08005 ☎ 93 221 14 01 🕐 Daily 12pm–2am 🍴 L €12, D €25, Wine €8 🚇 Ciutadella-Vila Olímpica

MOSQUITO

www.mosquitotapas.com

Part of the general jazzing up of the Sant Pere and La Ribera neighbourhoods, Mosquito is a laid-back bar serving decent wine and a solid range of pan-Asian tapas with plenty of vegetarian pizazz. Favourites include potato *chaat* (lentils and potatoes in a sweet and sour tamarind dressing) and aubergine (eggplant) and basil *gyoza* (dumplings). The latest in a number of innovations are homey Japanese midnight feasts on Fridays and Saturdays—perfect post-cinema or pre-clubbing.

✚ 168 G9 ✉ Carrer Carders 46, 08003 ☎ 93 268 75 69 🕑 Sun–Mon, Wed–Thu 7pm–12.30am, Fri 7.30pm–1.30am, Sat 7.30pm–2am 🖐 D €15, Wine €8 🚇 Arc de Triomf, Jaume I

MURIVECCHI

This family-run trattoria serves up some decent Italian fare at honest prices. There's a genuine wood-fired oven for pizza-lovers and the pasta dishes, such as tagliatelle with porcini mushrooms or a genuine carbonara, are also noteworthy. The desserts include a mean tiramisù. The only downside is the rather soulless interior, but compared with the other designer eateries in the immediate vicinity, Murivecchi makes for light relief.

✚ 169 G9 ✉ Carrer de la Princesa 59, 08003 ☎ 93 315 22 97 🕑 Daily 1–4, 8.30–12 🖐 L €12, D €30, Wine €11 🚇 Arc de Triomf

NOU CAN TIPA

This noisy bar on Barceloneta's main street is well loved among locals, serving steamed mussels, fresh fish and all manner of shellfish. Over and above the tapas, the bar is well known for its cod dishes. *Estar tip* in Catalan means to be full, so as the name indicates, portions are very generous. Booking is advisable.

✚ 168 G10 ✉ Passeig Joan de Borbó 6, 08003 ☎ 93 310 13 62 🕑 Tue–Sun 1–11.30 🖐 L €10, D €20, Wine €9 🚇 Barceloneta

ORIGEN 99,9%

www.origen99.com

An inviting little piece of Catalonia nestled in the multicultural Ribera area. Here you can buy or sample Catalan products carrying an official guarantee of quality. Each month the menu focuses on a particular area of Catalonia. Snacks are served all day; try tapas of your choice with a cava aperitif. For lunch, choose from *escudella i carn d'olla* (soup with meat), *fideuà* (fish noodles), toast with *escalivada* (roasted peppers, onions and eggplant), meatballs or cuttlefish. There are several branches, including one around the corner on Passeig del Born.

✚ 168 G9 ✉ Carrer de Vidreria 6–8, 08003 ☎ 93 310 75 31 🕑 Daily 12.30pm–1am 🖐 L and D €12, Wine €8 🚇 Barceloneta

PETRA

There's a Moroccan influence in this pretty restaurant, with walls of deep blue and multicoloured tiles. The innovative menu is eclectic, with a selection of salads, pasta dishes, main courses and desserts. Start with the refreshing mango and tofu salad, and follow with gnocchi with walnuts and gorgonzola or magret of duck.

✚ 168 G9 ✉ Carrer dels Sombrerers 13, 08003 ☎ 93 319 99 99 🕑 Tue–Sat 1.30–4, 9–11.30, Sun 1.30–4 🖐 L and D €20, Wine €9 🚇 Jaume I

EL REY DE LA GAMBA

www.elreydelagamba.com

This welcoming family restaurant serves a range of seafood, mostly grilled, such as lobster, fish and all types of *gambas* (shrimp): the restaurant's name means king prawns. There are also several rice dishes, but the restaurant is known for its black rice, made with squid ink. Plenty of room is available for larger groups, though booking is necessary. There is a good view over the harbour.

✚ 169 J10 ✉ Moll de Mestral 23–25, 08005 ☎ 93 221 00 12 🕑 Daily 11am–2am 🖐 L and D €40, Wine €9 🚉 Section 🚇 Ciutadella-Vila Olímpica

SALAMANCA

Silvestre and his staff meticulously take care of every detail to ensure that your meal is enjoyable. This restaurant serves outstanding seafood, such as prawns from Huelva, and oysters and clams, complemented by a broad list of wines and cavas. If you're not in the mood for fresh fish, try some of the many Iberian cold meats accompanied by tomato, garlic and olive oil-dressed bread. Eat al fresco on the terrace and enjoy the view. Unusually for Barcelona, they also offer a children's menu.

✚ 168 G11 ✉ Carrer de l'Almirall Cervera 34, 08003 ☎ 93 221 50 33 🕑 Daily 8am–1am 🖐 L €18, D €35, Wine €10 🚇 Barceloneta

SALERO

Creative cuisine based on Mediterranean and Asian influences. The relaxing, minimalist setting forms a striking contrast to the busy street outside. Franc, the chef and owner, prepares a delicious vegetable tempura, and the choice of salads is extensive—try one with nuts and honey. If you prefer meat, the teriyaki chicken or steak with mango are both good choices. The spectacular desserts include German cheese with hazelnuts and an impressive chocolate and orange concoction. Booking is essential.

✚ 168 G10 ✉ Carrer del Rec 60, 08003 ☎ 93 319 80 22 🕑 Mon–Fri 1.30–4, 8.30–1, Sat 9pm–2am, Sun 9pm–12am 🖐 L €15 (menu €12), Tasting menu €32, D €30, Wine €9 🚇 Barceloneta

EL TÚNEL DEL PORT

www.eltuneldelport.com

In another guise, El Túnel del Port has been around since 1923, but moved to the area when the Olympics were held. The cuisine is Mediterranean, and the seafood comes with all manner of vegetables. There are also *fideuàs* (like paella but with noodles instead of rice), grilled meat and traditional paella on the menu. The restaurant can seat up to 300 diners and the large dining rooms have terraces overlooking the sea.

✚ 169 J11 ✉ Moll de Gregal 12, 08005 ☎ 93 221 03 21 🕑 Tue–Sat 1–4, 9–12, Sun 1–4 🖐 L €25 (set menu €23.50), D €40 (set menu €32), Wine €10 🚇 Ciutadella-Vila Olímpica

PRICES AND SYMBOLS

Prices are the lowest and highest for a double room for one night. Breakfast is included unless noted otherwise. All the hotels listed accept credit cards unless otherwise stated. Note that rates vary widely throughout the year.

For a key to the symbols, ▷ 2.

BANYS ORIENTALS

www.hotelbanysorientals.com
This elegant, mid-range hotel with stylish accommodation and a soothing, Zen-like interior is one of the few in the Ribera area. The sleek, compact rooms are decked out in calm tones of white, beige and grape. The lack of amenities (there is no swimming pool or gym) may be a drawback for some, but judging by its popularity this is not a problem for most guests.
✚ 168 G9 ✉ Carrer de l'Argenteria 37, 08003 ☎ 93 268 84 60 💷 €105, excluding breakfast ⓘ 56 ⓢ ⓠ Jaume I

CHIC & BASIC

www.chicandbasic.com
A 19th-century town house in La Ribera has been transformed into this sleek budget hotel. It's a favourite with the young and hip, with a minimalistic feel—curtains made from strands of lights change colour at the touch of button. It is also home to the trendy White Bar restaurant. Some of the city's best shopping and sightseeing is just around the corner. They also run a great budget hostal in El Raval.
✚ 168 G9 ✉ Carrer de la Princesa 50, 08003 ☎ 93 295 46 52 💷 €96–€193, excluding breakfast ⓘ 31 ⓢ ⓠ Jaume I

GRAND HOTEL CENTRAL

www.grandhotelcentral.com
This large, elegant hotel sits on the edge of the fashionable El Born neighbourhood. The spacious, luxurious rooms are decorated in muted tones, and are equipped with state-of-the-art amenities. But the hotel's real draw is its stunning rooftop pool, which is larger than the tiny splash pools found in most other Barcelona hotels. From the water, or from the adjoining sun terrace, you can enjoy incomparable views across the rooftops.
✚ 168 G9 ✉ Via Laietana 30, 08003 ☎ 93 295 79 00 💷 €181–€290, excluding breakfast ⓘ 147 ⓢ ⌇ Outdoor 🎿 ⓠ Jaime I

HOTEL PULLMAN SKIPPER

www.pullman-barcelona-skipper.com
The enormous Pullman Skipper is a striking, ultra-modern, luxury hotel right on the seafront in Barceloneta. It has a long list of amenities, including two outdoor pools (one surrounded by gardens, the other with sea views), two excellent restaurants, four café-bars, a spa and wellness centre, and even a jogging circuit. The best rooms have terraces and splendid sea views, but all are immaculately furnished and well equipped.
✚ 169 J10 ✉ Avenida Litoral 10, 08005 ☎ 93 221 65 65 💷 €180–€340, excluding breakfast ⓘ 241 ⓢ ⌇ Outdoor 🎿 ⓠ Barceloneta

MARINA FOLCH

This small, basic, family-run hotel has everything you need for an inexpensive stay. It is within easy reach of Barceloneta, and there's a fabulous view of the old harbour from some rooms. Don't expect luxury, although one bonus is the reasonably priced restaurant (run by the same family) where you can tuck into good food. A few words of Catalan will be helpful and appreciated at this hotel.
✚ 168 G10 ✉ Carrer del Mar 16, 08003 ☎ 93 310 37 09 💷 €60–€70, excluding breakfast ⓘ 10 ⓢ ⓠ Barceloneta

PARK HOTEL

www.parkhotelbarcelona.com
Built in the 1950s, this hotel has been a recipient of the Ciutat de Barcelona prize for being the best refurbished hotel. The top four floors have wooden flooring and fittings, and are decorated in neutral tones with splashes of dark red in fabrics and wall coverings. The splendid original wraparound staircase and mosaic-tiled bar survive. All rooms have satellite TV, minibar, safety box and terrace.
✚ 168 G10 ✉ Avinguda del Marquès de l'Argentera 11, 08003 ☎ 93 319 60 00 💷 €79–€167, excluding breakfast ⓘ 91 ⓢ ⓠ Barceloneta

Above *There are hotels to suit all pockets in Port Vell and La Ribera*

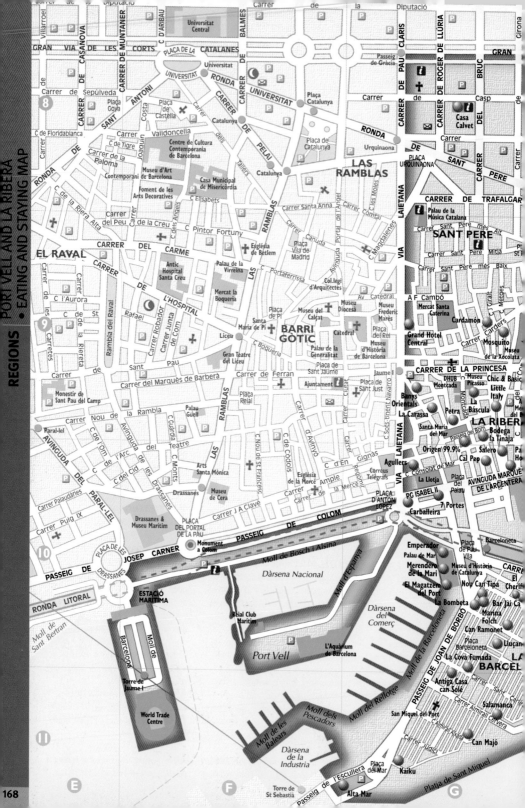

Villarroel

CARRER DE MUNTANER

C D'ARIBAU

BALMES

CLARIS

DE PAU

DE ROGER DE LLÚRIA

BRUC

Girona

Carrer de la Diputació

Universitat Central

PLAÇA DE LA CATALANES

GRAN VIA DE LES CORTS

GRAN

CARRER DE CASANOVA

CARRER

SANT ANTONI

Carrer de Sepúlveda

Universitat

RONDA

UNIVERSITAT

Plaça Catalunya

Passeig de Gràcia

CARRER DE

Casa Calvet

Carrer de Casp

Plaça Goya

Plaça de Castella

Catalunya

RONDA

DE

PELAI

Plaça de Catalunya

Carrer de Floridablanca

C de Tigre

Validoncella

Centre de Cultura Contemporània de Barcelona

Tallers

Urquinaona

PLAÇA URQUINAONA

CARRER

DE

SANT

PERE

CARRER DE TRAFALGAR

C de la Riera Alta

Carrer de la Paloma

Museu d'Art Contemporani de Barcelona

Casa Municipal de Misericordia

LAS RAMBLAS

Palau de la Música Catalana

RONDA

Carrer del Peu

Foment de les Arts Decoratives

C Elisabets

C de la Creu

C Pintor Fortuny

Carrer Santa Anna

LAIETANA

SANT PERE

Carrer Sant Pere més Alt

Carrer Sant Pere Mitjà

EL RAVAL

CARRER DEL CARME

LAS RAMBLAS

Església de Betlem

Carrer Canuda

Plaça Vila de Madrid

Carrer Sant Pere més Baix

Antic Hospital Santa Creu

Palau de la Virreina

CARRER

DE

L'HOSPITAL

Rafael

Mercat la Boqueria

Carrer Portaferrissa

Av Catedral

A F Cambó

Mercat Santa Caterina

Cardamón

Carrer del Rec

Mosquito

Carrer Junta de Com

Santa Maria de Pi

Plaça de Pi

Museu del Calçat

Museu Diocesà

Museu Frederic Marès

Grand Hotel Central

Museu de la Xocolata

Liceu

BARRI GÒTIC

Catedral

Museu del Rei

CARRER DE LA PRINCESA

Monestir de Sant Pau del Camp

Gran Teatre del Liceu

C Boqueria

Palau de la Generalitat

Museu d'Història de Barcelona

DHUB Montcada

Museu Picasso

Chic & Basic

Little Italy

Pau

Plaça de Sant Jaume

Jaume I

Banys Orientals

La Báscula

Petra

LA RIBERA

Carrer del Marquès de Barberà

Carrer de Ferran

Ajuntament

Plaça de Sant Just

La Carassa

Santa Maria del Mar

Bodega la Tinaja

Plaça Reial

Palau Güell

LAS RAMBLAS

Origen 99.9%

Cal Pep

Salero

Arts Santa Mònica

Drassanes

Aguilers

La Llotja

7 Portes

AVINGUDA MARQUÈS DE L'ARGENTERA

AVINGUDA DEL PARAL·LEL

Nou de la Rambla

Teatre

Espanya

Església de la Mercè

Correus Telègrafs

Museu de Cera

Carrer Ample

PG ISABEL II

Carballeira

Carrer Paludanes

Drassanes & Museu Marítim

PLAÇA DEL PORTAL DE LA PAU

Carrer J A Clavé

PLAÇA D'ANTONI LÓPEZ

Carrer Puig IX

PASSEIG DE COLOM

Emperador

Plaça de Pau Vila

Barceloneta

PLAÇA DE LES DRASSANES

JOSEP CARNER

Monument a Colom

Moll de Bosch i Alsina

Palau de Mar

Museu d'Història de Catalunya

Noy Can Tipá

El Cherif

ESTACIÓ MARÍTIMA

Moll d'Espanya

Dàrsena Nacional

Merendero de la Mari

Bar Jai Ca

RONDA LITORAL

Reial Club Marítim

Dàrsena del Comerç

El Magatzem del Port

Marina Folch

Can Ramonet

Moll de Sant Bertran

Moll de Barceloneta

L'Aquàrium de Barcelona

La Bombeta

PASSEIG DE JOAN DE BORBÓ

Plaça Barceloneta

Lluçanès

Torre de Jaume I

Moll de

Port Vell

Moll del Rellotge

La Cova Fumada

LA BARCEL

World Trade Centre

Antiga Casa can Solé

Salamanca

Moll dels Pescadors

San Miquel del Port

Carrer Almirall Cervera

Can Majó

Moll de les Balears

Dàrsena de la Industria

Plaça del Mar

Kaiku

Platja de Sant Miquel

Torre de St Sebastià

PASSEIG de l'Escullera

Alta Mar

E   F   G

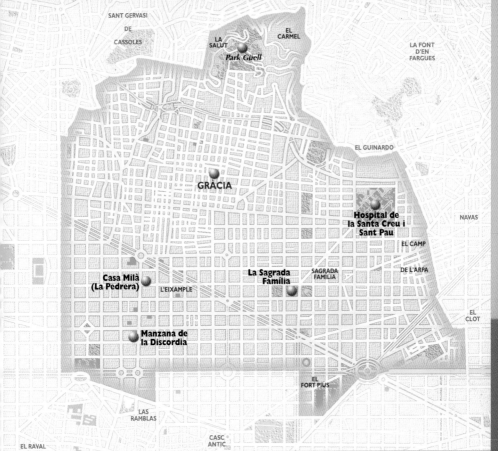

L'EIXAMPLE

By the start of the 19th century, Barcelona was burstling out of its medieval walls. These were finally demolished in the 1850s, and an elegant new neighbourhood, called L'Eixample (which means 'extension'), was laid out. It was constructed on an airy grid pattern, with wide boulevards and gardens. The wealthy commissioned the most fashionable architects of the age to construct their new mansions, many of which were built in the extravagant Modernista style. The greatest Modernista architect of all was Antoni Gaudí, whose extraordinary vision was entirely unique: his fairy-tale buildings resemble dragons, carnival masks or even swirls of ice cream. Some of his greatest works are found in L'Eixample, and include Casa Batlló; the Casa Milà (La Pedrera) apartment building; and the immense Temple Expiatori de la Sagrada Família, Gaudí's final—and still unfinished—work. This neighbourhood remains the most exclusive in central Barcelona, and is packed with luxurious hotels, glossy fashion boutiques and upmarket bars and restaurants.

Neighbouring Gràcia sits just west of L'Eixample but has a very different atmosphere. This was an independent town right up until 1897, with a working-class population notorious for their outspoken political views. It is still a *barri* popular with artists, writers and actors, and the narrow streets are lined with quirky shops, boho-chic bars, and the city's best art-house cinema can be found here. Although there are few major sights, it's a wonderful place for a stroll, thanks to its café-lined squares and relaxed atmosphere. On the edge of Gràcia is the whimsical Park Güell, a glorious, green expanse dotted with Gaudí's fairy-tale pavilions, which offers spellbinding views over the entire city.

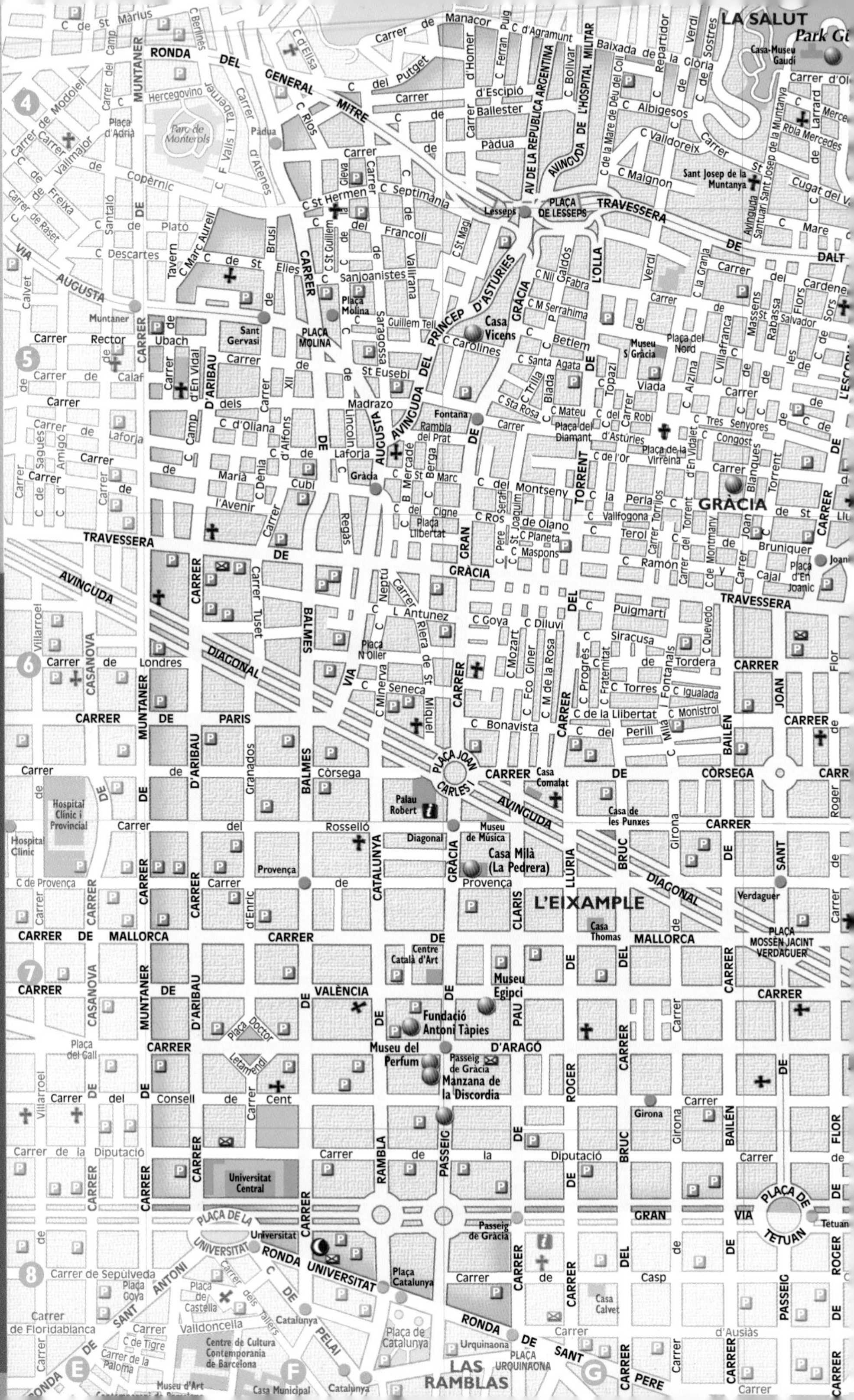

LA SALUT

Park Gü

Casa-Museu Gaudí

RONDA

GENERAL MITRE

Parc de Monterols

AVINGUDA DE L'HOSPITAL MILITAR

PLAÇA DE LESSEPS

TRAVESSERA

L'OLLA

DE

DALT

Casa Vicens

PLAÇA MOLINA

Museu S Gràcia

Plaça del Nord

GRÀCIA

Rambla del Prat

Plaça del Diamant

Casa de la Virreina

TORRENT

DE

GRÀCIA

Plaça Llibertat

PLAÇA JOAN CARLES I

Casa Comalat

TRAVESSERA

AVINGUDA

DIAGONAL

BALMES

PARIS

Hospital Clínic i Provincial

Hospital Clínic

CARRER DE MALLORCA

Palau Robert

Museu de Música

Casa Milà (La Pedrera)

Casa de les Punxes

PLAÇA MOSSÈN JACINT VERDAGUER

Verdaguer

L'EIXAMPLE

Casa Thomas

MALLORCA

BAILÈN

CÒRSEGA

DE

CARRER

Centre Català d'Art

Museu Egipci

VALÈNCIA

Fundació Antoni Tàpies

Museu del Perfum

D'ARAGÓ

Manzana de la Discòrdia

Passeig de Gràcia

Girona

Universitat Central

PLAÇA DE LA UNIVERSITAT

Universitat

Plaça Catalunya

PLAÇA DE TETUAN

RONDA UNIVERSITAT

GRAN VIA

Casa Calvet

PLAÇA DE CATALUNYA

LAS RAMBLAS

Centre de Cultura Contemporània de Barcelona

Casa Municipal

PLAÇA URQUINAONA

L'AUDITORI AND MUSEU DE LA MÚSICA

www.museumusica.bcn.cat

The Auditori was designed by Rafael Moneo and completed in 1999. Along with the Liceu opera house and the Palau de la Música Catalana, it is one of the city's top classical music venues and is famous for its outstanding acoustics. It was one of the first of the slew of new buildings constructed in the gentrification of the Glories district: others include the Teatre Nacional de Catalunya (1997) by Ricardo Bofill, and the conical Torre Agbar, designed by Jean Nouvel (2004). The Auditori is the official seat of the OBC (the Symphonic Orchestra of Barcelona and Catalunya), and hosts performances by the finest international orchestras and musicians. It also hosts several prestigious music festivals, including the Festival of Early Music and the World Music Festival. The Museu de la Música is located within the Auditori, and contains more than 500 instruments.

🛉 173 J8 ✉ Carrer Lepant 150, 08013 ☎ 93 256 36 50 🕓 Mon, Wed–Sat 10–6, Sun 10–8 🖐 Adult €4, child (under 16) free. Sun free after 3pm ⏰ Tours must be reserved in advance, tel 93 256 36 50. Musical audioguide available 🚇 Marina, Glories, Monumental 🚌 6, 7, 10, 56, 62, B21, B25 🚗

CASA MILÀ

▷ 176–177.

CASA VICENS

www.rutadelmodernisme.com

This bright and eccentric house was the first Modernista building to be constructed in the city. It was conceived as a holiday home for the tile manufacturer Manuel Vicens i Montaner, and his descendants still live here. It was one of Gaudí's first architectural projects and the year he signed the contract (1883) coincided with the beginning of La Sagrada Família (▷ 186–189).

Nearly all of the enigmatic facade is covered in tiles and the form of the building was inspired by the East. The result is an exotic impression of a series of desert pavilions complete with minaret-style turrets. This influence extended to the interior, particularly in the smoking room, with a giant lamp decorated with characters from the Koran and an ornate, sculptured ceiling. Casa Vicens is not open to the public, but photographs of the interior regularly appear in books about Gaudí.

🛉 172 G5 ✉ Carrer de les Carolines 18–24, 08006 🚇 Fontana 🚌 22, 24, 25, 27, 28, 31, 32 and all routes to Plaza Lesseps

FUNDACIÓ ANTONI TÀPIES

www.fundaciotapies.org

Antoni Tàpies is Catalonia's most prolific living artist. Born in 1923, he first trained as a lawyer but this direction soon changed and his work as a painter, draughtsman, printmaker and sculptor often defies definition. He is known for mixing two or more media and for challenging works that nearly always include the letter T. This recurring motif has been interpreted as having religious or sexual references, or perhaps it was used because it's the artist's initial. The Tàpies Foundation is in a former Modernista publishing house built by Lluís Domènech i Montaner (1850–1923) and was started in 1984 by the artist himself.

The foundation has always promoted art, and as well as housing an extensive collection of Tàpies's work, it also puts on regular shows from other contemporary artists. The library, which is open to the general public, houses an impressive collection of 20th-century art documents and a large section on Asian art. Be warned though, with its extreme designs, this foundation is for die-hard contemporary art fans only.

Cloud and Chair (1990), the sculpture by Tàpies that sits on the roof, was a symbolic gift to the city of Barcelona, and has become an integral part of L'Eixample's landscape.

🛉 172 F7 ✉ Carrer d'Aragó 255, 08007 ☎ 93 487 03 15 🕓 Tue–Sun

10–8 🖐 Adult €6, child (under 16) free 🚇 Passeig de Gràcia 🚌 7, 16, 17, 20, 22, 24, 28, 43 🚗 🚲

GRÀCIA

▷ 178.

HOSPITAL DE LA SANTA CREU I SANT PAU

▷ 179.

MANZANA DE LA DISCORDIA

▷ 180–182.

EL MONUMENTAL

This mock-Moorish bullring and museum is in L'Eixample, near to the Plaça de les Glories. It is one of two bullrings in Barcelona, the second being Las Arenas in the Plaça d'Espanya (▷ 76–77), which is being converted into a shopping and entertainment centre. Attendance at the bullring is poor as Catalans are not aficionados, and the future of El Monumental is uncertain. El Monumental was built in 1915 and is heady with Arabic influences, perhaps a homage to the spectacle itself, which has its roots in Andalucía. For details on bullfights ▷ 252.

🛉 173 J8 ✉ Gran Via de les Corts Catalanes 749, 08013 ☎ 93 245 58 03 🚇 Monumental 🚌 6, 56, 62, 75

Opposite *Moorish influences can be seen on the tiled exterior of Casa Vicens*
Below *The Auditori is famed for its acoustics*

CASA MILÀ

INFORMATION

www.lapedreraeducacio.org

⊕ 172 G7 ⊠ Passeig de Gràcia 92, 08027 ☎ 902 40 09 73 or 93 484 5900 ⊙ Mar–end Oct daily 9–8; Nov–end Feb daily 9–6.30 ✋ Adult €10, child (under 12) free ⊜ Diagonal ⊜ 7, 16, 17, 22, 24, 28 ⊏ Audiotours in Catalan, English, French, Spanish, Italian and German €3 ⊡ Excellent guidebooks available at both gift shops for €10–€15 ⊞ Two gift shops: one on the ground floor of the building with a fabulous collection of books and objects by local designers inspired by the Gaudían motif; the second in the apartment with books and faux Modernisme objects such as accessories and reproduction period toys

Above *Some of the curvaceous chimney stacks on the roof of La Pedrera*

INTRODUCTION

One of architect Antoni Gaudí's secular masterpieces, completed in 1912, Casa Milà (more commonly known as La Pedrera) has an eccentric, fantastical roof terrace with views over Barcelona. An introductory exhibition on Gaudí provides an insight into the architect's life and work.

Casa Milà was commissioned in 1906 by the businessman Pere Milà i Camps at a time when Passeig de Gràcia was the most fashionable address in town. Wealthy industrialists were attempting to outdo one another by building ever more fanciful Modernista houses, and Gaudí's brief was to surpass both the Casa Amatller and his own Casa Batlló (▷ 180–182) on the same street. Although it is now seen as perhaps the climax of Gaudí's creative genius, Casa Milà was ridiculed at the time and nicknamed La Pedrera (the quarry) because of its use of vast amounts of stone. This was Gaudí's last major secular commission—he spent the rest of his life working on the Sagrada Família.

The building stands like some giant, curving cliff face on the corner of Passeig de Gràcia and Carrer de Provença. With its wavy lines and undulating exterior, the building deliberately sets out to challenge the strict uniformity and grid plan of L'Eixample. Most of the eight floors still serve as private apartments, but other parts are administered as a cultural centre by the Fundació Caixa Catalunya, the cultural arm of a leading Catalan savings bank. Among the restoration projects the bank has financed is the recovery of the first-floor apartments where the Milà family lived. The partitions dividing some of the original rooms have been removed to reveal a fine Gaudí interior, with trademark organic curves and marine motifs, now used as an exhibition space, reached via a staircase from the entrance hall. The main entrance on Passeig de Gràcia leads to an inner courtyard, with a staircase to the first-floor art gallery.

To see the sixth-floor apartments, Espai Gaudí and the spectacular roof terrace, you need to buy a ticket from the booth on Carrer de Provença and take the side entrance into the building.

WHAT TO SEE

THE EXTERIOR

The creamy limestone exterior has been likened to everything from an abandoned stone quarry, hence its popular local nickname, La Pedrera, to the rippling waves of the sea. Gaudí was often inspired by marine life forms, and it is easy to imagine the twisting wrought-iron balustrades on the balconies, designed by Gaudí's collaborator Josep Maria Jujol (1879–1949), as a mass of seaweed. Perhaps the building's most remarkable feature is that it is said to contain not a single straight line or right angle in its construction. This is a supreme example of architecture turned into sculpture.

ESPAI GAUDÍ

The tour of the upper floors begins by taking the elevator to the attic, where the former laundry has been turned into an exhibition of Gaudí's life and work. This is an unexpectedly special space, its 270 brick arches lending it the feel of a Gothic cathedral. It is the best place in Barcelona to get an overview of Gaudí's architectural techniques, with scale drawings and models of his buildings as well as audiovisual displays. Of particular interest are the interior photographs of some of the Gaudí buildings that are not normally open to the public, including Casa Vicens (▷ 175).

THE APARTMENTS

Stairs lead down from the attic to Pis de la Pedrera, a pair of sixth-floor apartments which have been carefully restored to give a feel of early 20th-century Barcelona. A series of historical photographs is shown in the first, along with a display about the rapid technological changes that accompanied the Modernista architectural movement, such as the introduction of electricity and telephones, the opening of the metro, and the arrival of cinemas and department stores.

The second apartment, which is surprisingly spacious, is a reconstruction furnished in the style of a typical Modernista apartment, and gives an insight into the lives of the building's early inhabitants. A cabinet and bedroom suite by the Mallorcan furniture designer Gaspar Homar (1870–1953) are among the items on display, together with everyday objects, such as kitchen, bathroom and nursery equipment, which have been laid out in situ. From the apartment there are good views of the interior patio.

THE ROOF TERRACE

The high point of any visit is the remarkable roof terrace, with its chimneys and ventilation shafts in the shape of owls, warriors, helmeted centurions and others fashioned out of broken pottery, marble and glass. This must be one of the best examples anywhere in Barcelona of Gaudí's ability to take something functional and imbue it with a sense of fun. One of the chimneys is made up of broken champagne bottles, apparently left over after a house-warming party. Like the rest of the building, the rooftop is not flat but undulating, with a series of curves and stairways giving varying views over the interior patios and across the skyline, in which Gaudí's Sagrada Família (▷ 186–189) is dominant. In keeping with Gaudí's religious and nationalist leanings, the central chimney is based on the cross of St. George, the patron saint of Catalonia. Gaudí's original plans included a huge bronze figure of the Virgin Mary for the roof, but he was forced to revise his ideas following the Tragic Week of 1909 (▷ 35), when a number of churches were attacked in anarchist riots. Señor Milà feared religious imagery might attract a similar fate.

TIPS

» During August 30-minute classical music performances are held in the evening. The entrance fee is €8 to €15.

» For a view of the north side of the building, go next door to the furniture/design store Vinçon (▷ 198). The back terrace of the building affords the only glimpse of this exterior.

» Make time to visit the ground-floor gift shop (separate entrance) which, as well as having a superb range of gifts, is also part of the original structure.

Below *The roof terrace is one of Gaudí's most striking works*

GRÀCIA

INFORMATION
⊞ 172 G5 ℹ Plaça de Catalunya 17,
08002 ☎ 93 285 38 34 🕓 Daily 9–9
Ⓜ Diagonal or Fontana 🚌 16, 17, 22,
24, 25, 27, 28

One of the city's most picturesque suburbs, Gràcia was once an outlying village, annexed to the main city by the elegant Passeig de Gràcia. Yet this suburb still retains a strong sense of independence and many of the city's underground and alternative movements have their roots here. During the day, Gràcia's charm lies in strolling around its series of squares, including the Plaça del Sol, which is a relaxed place to have coffee. The majestic Plaça de la Virreina and the Plaça de Rius i Taulet with its stately watchtower are some of the oldest squares, but Gràcia also has new hard squares, made mostly from concrete, such as the Plaça John Lennon. Gràcia is not without a few Modernista buildings. Notable are the neo-Moorish Casa Vicens (▷ 175), an early work of Gaudí's, and the beautiful Casa Fuster by Domènech i Montaner, at the beginning of Gran de Gràcia, now a five-star hotel (▷ 204).

CULTURAL LIFE

The cultural life of the area is strong—the Verdi cinema complex shows films in their original language (▷ 199), and there are dozens of galleries, shops, bars and restaurants. The Carrer Verdi is a great place to shop for funky clothing. A visit to the annual Festa Major de Gràcia (▷ 255) will give you a sense of the pride that the locals have for their beloved *barri* (district). All year long, neighbourhood associations work on the elaborate decorations that are hung in the streets in mid-August. Each street chooses a different theme, from marine life to moonscapes, and competes for the prize of best-dressed street. The *barri* then becomes a giant stage for 10 days of no-holding-back fun.

Above *Ornate balconies decorate the buildings around Plaça del Sol*

HOSPITAL DE LA SANTA CREU I SANT PAU

A UNESCO World Heritage Site, this building challenges your notions of hospital design. The hospital is the largest work by Modernista architect Lluís Domènech i Montaner, who produced a beautiful, detail-rich building that was a working hospital until 2009. The complex covers 13.5ha (33 acres) and was conceived as a garden infirmary according to the wishes of its patron, the Paris-based banker Pau Gil i Serra. He had been impressed by the French trend of hospital villages. The complex consists of 48 mosaic-covered pavilions, serving the same purpose as wards in modern hospitals. All are highly ornate and are spread over various streets and leafy avenues. Heavy with symbolism, the hospital is almost a metaphor for the Modernista creed itself: Catalan nationalism, exuberant use of colour and an abundance of references to Mother Nature. There are many details, but watch out for the dainty, sculptured heads on the wooden doors of the individual pavilions and the elegant figures of Faith, Hope and Charity that flank the windows of the main building.

THE GARDENS

Domènech i Montaner was also a practical man: He built an enlightened series of underground walkways so that patients and staff were protected from bad weather when commuting from one pavilion to another. If you are not taking the guided tour, the hospital is not strictly open to the general public. However, nobody seems to mind if you take a discreet walk around the gardens and view the pavilions from the outside.

INFORMATION

www.santpau.es

✚ 173 J6 ✉ Carrer de Sant Antoni Maria Claret 167–171, 08025 ☎ 93 488 20 78 🕑 By guided tour (tel 93 317 76 52 to book visits) 11.15am (Catalan), 10.15am and 12.15pm (English), 1.15pm (Spanish). Group tours in Catalan, Spanish, English and French by prior arrangement 🖐 Adult €5, child (under 15) free; grounds free 🚇 Hospital Sant Pau 🚌 15, 19, 20, 35, 45, 47, 50, 51

Above *Detail of Domènech i Montaner's fabulous work on the roof*

INTRODUCTION

Three emblematic buildings stand side by side on the elegant Passeig de Gràcia, providing an outstanding insight into the Modernisme movement in the city. Built when Modernisme was in full swing, they are by the three undisputed masters of the movement. They are quite disparate in style and throw light on the consistently differing approaches of the architects. Only Casa Batlló and the ground floor of Casa Amatller are open to the public, but the exteriors are well worth a visit in their own right.

WHAT TO SEE

CASA BATLLÓ

This is the most famous of the trio, completed in 1906 for local textile baron, Josep Batlló i Casanovas, and designed by Gaudí. The rippling effect of the facade was achieved by covering the surface with pieces of broken ceramic (trencadís). The facade's depth of tone and movement are equal to that of an Impressionist painting and it glitters like a giant jewel. Casa Batlló is said to represent the legend of St. George, Catalonia's patron saint, and the dragon. The spectacular outline of the upper facade depicts the humped back of the dragon and the tiles represent its scales. The sinuous bones and tendons of the victims are seen in the framing of the windows, while the wrought-iron balconies are their skulls.

A tour of the interior gives you an insight into Gaudí's amazing design. Its richness is further revealed and the close-up view of the stained-glass windows in the living room is stunning, as is the terrace. On sunny days, the whole interior glows with natural light.

✉ Passeig de Gràcia 43, 08007 ☎ 93 216 03 66; advance ticket reservations 90 110 12 12 🕐 Mon–Sun 9–8 💶 Adult €11 (first-floor apartment or roof and patio), adult €16.50 (first-floor apartment, attic and roof), audioguide included in price, child (under 6) free 🛗

INFORMATION

www.rutadelmodernisme.com
www.casabatllo.cat

➕ 172 F7 ✉ Passeig de Gràcia 35, 41 and 43, 08007 🚇 Passeig de Gràcia 🚌 7, 16, 17, 22, 24, 28 🚍 Tours conducted by the Centre del Modernisme, in the main tourist office, by arrangement, taking in the exteriors of the Manzana, in Catalan, Spanish and English: adult €3, child €2 🛍 A well-stocked shop in Casa Batlló sells Gaudí- and Barcelona-related books and souvenirs. There is another gift shop, with a wide range of Amatller chocolates, in the lobby of the Casa Amatller

Above *Rich stained glass and detail on the extraordinary Casa Batlló*
Opposite *A wedding cake dome crowns Casa Lleó i Morera*

TIPS

» Casa Batlló is beautifully lit at night and its ceramic-clad facade glistens magically under the artificial light. Don't try to view the building's exterior at noon when it is very sunny as the reflected sunlight can be dazzling.

» Look for the Modernista maidens holding a camera and a lightbulb by sculptor Eusebi Arnau. They are among the few remaining features of the original Casa Lleó i Morera.

» The sculpture of St. George and the Dragon by the entrance of Casa Amatller serves as a neat contrast between the styles of Gaudí and Puig i Cadafalch.

Below *Window detail on Casa Lleó i Morera*
Below right *The inspiration for Casa Amatller was Dutch, Flemish and Gothic*

CASA AMATLLER

In contrast to Gaudí's nationalist overtones, the architect Josep Puig i Cadafalch (1876-1956) didn't shy away from northern European influences. This is very much in evidence at his Casa Amatller, the first building on the block. It was built in 1900, and Dutch and Flemish architectural influences can be seen, as well as a number of Gothic details. The facade is dotted with eccentric stone carvings of animals blowing glass and taking photographs, two of the architect's hobbies. These were executed by Eusebi Arnau, a decorative sculptor much in vogue at the time, who also used his talent on Casa Lleó i Morera next door. A massive restoration programme began in 2009, and it is hoped that the original Modernista private apartments will open to the public in 2013. Until then, guided visits to the lobby and Amatller's former photographic studio on the top floor offer an illuminating glimpse into the life of Barcelona's wealthy citizens at the turn of the 20th century.

✉ Passeig de Gràcia 41, 08007 ☎ 93 216 01 75 🕐 Lobby and shop: Mon–Sat 10–7, Sun 10–2 🎫 Guided tours Wed at 12pm, €10. Reservations tel 93 487 72 17

CASA LLEÓ I MORERA

The third of the Manzana's structures was adapted in 1905 from an existing building. Its style is what most people will relate to as the more typical international form of art nouveau, and not the Catalan version. Lluís Domènech i Montaner (1850–1923) was a politician and craftsman who lent a hand to every facet of his projects. He fully embraced the new materials of his field, which he then applied to building design, including this one. Although greatly modernized in 1943, the building still has a riot of detail: rounded corner balconies, female figures holding up innovations of the period, such as the lightbulb and telephone, and a wedding cake dome crowning the roof. To please the commissioner of the building, the local tycoon Albert Lleó i Morera, Domènech i Montaner included within the symbolism the recurring themes of the lion (*lleó*) and mulberry bush (*morera*). The upper floors of the building are now private offices and the ground floor houses a top leatherwear shop, which does not have much in the way of period detail. But some of the original furnishings can be seen at the Museu Nacional d'Art de Catalunya (▷ 72–75). ✉ Passeig de Gràcia 35, 08007

WHAT'S IN A NAME?

A play on words, as well as mythology, gives the Manzana de la Discordia its name. The title translates as both the 'block of discord' and the 'apple of discord' in Castilian. The latter term relates to the Greek goddess Eris who was known as Discordia to the Romans. She threw an apple onto Mount Olympus and declared it should be given 'to the fairest'. The resulting mayhem led to the Judgement of Paris and the Trojan War. This wordplay doesn't translate into Catalan, so you are likely to see it referred to as Illa de la Discòrdia, meaning 'block of discord', or Mansana de la Discòrdia, a Catalanized version of the Castilian name.

MUSEU EGIPCI

www.fundclos.com

In a well-lit building in the heart of L'Eixample, Barcelona's Egyptian museum provides a compact and accessible introduction to the art and artefacts of the pharaohs. The permanent collection starts with a reproduction of the Rosetta Stone, the tablet that helped provide the key to unlocking hieroglyphics. In the first room, various sarcophagi are laid out, including the delicate 'Lady of Kemet', a detailed relic named after the desert oasis where she was discovered. The mummified animals (including a baby crocodile) and vessels for the entrails of the deceased are bewitchingly macabre, and the sheer variety of personal effects reminds us of the ancient Egyptians' reverence for the afterlife. A fun way to see the collection is on a night tour (reservation required), when actors, dressed as Cleopatra or Ramses II, give a dramatized explanation of the exhibits. The signs in the museum are available in Spanish or Catalan only.

🚹 172 G7 ⊠ Carrer València 284, 08007 ☎ 93 488 01 88 🕐 Mon–Sat 10–8, Sun 10–2 💷 Adult €11, child (5–18) $8 🎧 Guided tours Sat 11am (Catalan), Sun 5pm (Spanish) included in admission price. Night tours: prices vary. Check website for details 🚇 Passeig de Gràcia

MUSEU DEL PERFUM

www.museodelperfume.com

Regia is one of the city's top perfumeries, and to its rear is the Museu del Perfum, with more than 5,000 examples of perfume bottles, flasks, distillers and all sorts of vessels from Grecian times to the present day. All the big French names are represented—Gallet, Lubin, Worth, D'Orsay—and there is also a section devoted to Eastern European perfumes, like the flaming-red bottles of Kremlin from the Soviet Union. Spain's own Myrurgia is given an entire section and the spectacular bottle by Salvador Dalí, Le Roi Soleil, has pride of place. More historic pieces are found in the Roman glass and Greek pottery sections and

there is also a showcase of highly decorated 19th-century bottles that were the height of fashion among the genteel set of their day. The museum also shows you how a brand's image can change over the decades, or how it stays the same—for example, the shape of the Chanel No. 5 perfume bottle has retained its classic lines since the 1930s.

🚹 172 F7 ⊠ Passeig de Gràcia 39, 08007 ☎ 93 216 01 21 🕐 Mon–Fri 10.30–1.30, 4.30–8, Sat 11–2 💷 Adult €5, child (under 12) free 🚇 Passeig de Gràcia 🚌 7, 16, 17, 22, 24, 28 🅿️

PARC DEL CLOT

www.bcn.cat/parcsijardins

The Parc del Clot is a good example of the urban renewal projects for which Barcelona is world renowned. In the suburb of Clot, the park draws on industry for its inspiration, in this case the national train company RENFE, the former occupants of the land. The park is laid out over three, shrub-covered levels, with the remains of the original walls of the 19th-century warehouse interwoven throughout. An ingenious touch is the series of stairs that act as acoustic barriers and as protection from flying tennis or basket balls, as most of the games areas are tucked away behind them. But perhaps more than any architectural merits, the Parc del Clot is an opportunity to experience *barri* life. It is always buzzing with parents and children, spontaneous soccer matches and people playing boules.

🚹 173 K8 ⊠ Carrer de Rosend Nobas s/n, 08018 (access: Carrer dels Escultors Claperós and Plaça de Valentí Almirall) and Plaça Joan Casanelles 🕐 24 hours 💷 Free 🚇 Clot 🚌 56, 62, 92

PARK GÜELL

▷ 184–185.

PASSEIG DE GRÀCIA

Two of Gaudí's most famous buildings and the city's most exclusive shops are to be found along the Passeig de Gràcia, the best-known road in Barcelona after Las Ramblas. Originally a dirt

Above Hieroglyphics on one of the exhibits on display in the accessible and absorbing Museu Egipci

road that connected the city to the nearby village of Gràcia, the Passeig de Gràcia became a popular strolling boulevard for the city's chattering classes, who enjoyed the open-air café on the corner of the Gran Via. At that time there were fields and stretches of country on either side, but as the Modernista movement got under way it became a showcase for the architects of the period. It is home to Gaudí's Casa Milà (▷ 176–177) and the Manzana de la Discordia (▷ 180–182). The dozens of city blocks surrounding the Passeig are collectively known as the Quadrat d'Or (Golden Square, ▷ 193) after the large number of Modernista apartments here, which is the highest concentration of architecture of this period anywhere in the world.

🚹 172 G7 🚇 Passeig de Gràcia or Diagonal

INFORMATION

www.bcn.cat/parcsijardins
www.rutadelmodernisme.com
www.casamuseugaudi.org

🕂 172 H4 ✉ Carrer d'Olot s/n, 08024
☎ Casa-Museu Gaudí: 93 219 38 11
🕐 Park: daily 10–dusk; Casa-Museu
Gaudí: summer daily 10–8; winter
daily 10–6 👋 Park: free; Casa-Museu
Gaudí: adult €5.50, child (under 10) free;
combined admission to Casa-Museu
Gaudí and Sagrada Família: adult €14
🚇 Lesseps 🚌 24, 25, 28, 31, 32, 74,
87 📖 Very pretty pictorial guidebook
available at the main gift shop, in Dutch,
German, Japanese, French, Italian,
Spanish, Catalan and English for €10
🍴 Terrace café overlooking the main
square 🛒 At the entrance, selling a
basic range of snacks 🎫 Shop at main
entrance and a smaller one in the Casa-
Museu Gaudí selling postcards, slides and
guidebooks ℹ For information on the
Park Güell project, walks around the park,
and descriptions of its flora and fauna,
visit the Centre d'Interpretació del Park
Güell, in the Gaudí-designed pavilion at
the Carrer d'Olot entrance. In the absence
of any guided or audiotours, this is a
valuable service for visitors ☎ 93 285 68
99 🕐 Daily 11–3 👋 Free

Above and opposite Mosaic details

INTRODUCTION

This playful, whimsical, fairy-tale park is laid out over 15ha (37 acres) on the
slopes of the unpromisingly named Mont Pelat (Bare Mountain).

Park Güell was commissioned in 1900 by Gaudí's patron, Count Eusebi
Güell. It was originally conceived as an English-style garden city (hence the
use of the English spelling of park), a residential estate surrounded by gardens,
which would provide a retreat for the wealthy. In the event, the project was not
a success. The plan was to build 60 houses, but only three appeared before
work was interrupted by the outbreak of World War I in 1914: One is now the
Casa-Museu Gaudí, one a school and the third is still a private residence. Güell
died in 1918, and four years later the unfinished estate was taken over by
the city of Barcelona as a municipal park. The count's loss was undoubtedly
Barcelona's gain as this has become one of the most attractive places in which
the people of Barcelona spend their spare time.

The best approach is via the main entrance on Carrer d'Olot, though this
does involve a steep walk up from the nearest bus stops on Carrer Mare de
Déu de la Salut. Alternatively, bus No. 24 drops you outside the side entrance
to the park on Carretera de Carmel. Although the main sights can be easily
seen in a visit of one to two hours, it is best to allow at least half a day. Take a
picnic and take your time exploring the network of paths, soaking up the sun
or sitting in the shade. The park tends to get very crowded in summer and
at weekends.

WHAT TO SEE

THE ENTRANCE

The entrance gate on Carrer d'Olot sets the tone for the entire park. Here is
a wrought-iron gate vaguely reminiscent of palm leaves, flanked by a pair of
gatehouses that come straight out of a children's fairy tale. In fact, they were
based on Antoni Gaudí's (1852–1926) designs and were inspired by the story of
Hansel and Gretel. The one on the right, topped by a mushroom, is the house
of the witch; on the left, surmounted by a double cross on the roof, is the
children's house. Both houses are almost totally covered in *trencadís* (▷ 185).
From here, a double stairway leads past a fountain adorned with the Catalan

shield towards a large salamander, also covered in *trencadís*. This well-loved creature has become an instantly recognizable symbol of the park and there is usually a queue to have your photograph taken alongside it. Behind the salamander is a covered bench in the form of an open mouth.

The staircase continues to the Sala Hipóstila (hypostyle, where a roof is supported by pillars). It was designed as a covered market place with kaleidoscopic patterns of glass and mosaic set into the ceiling in the shape of suns and moons.

THE SQUARE

Two further flights of steps on either side of the hall lead up to the focal point of the park, the main square surrounded by a serpentine bench. This wave-like, sinuous bench, attributed to Gaudí's assistant Josep Maria Jujol, is both a riot of colour and a giant jigsaw puzzle pieced together out of shards of broken ceramics. Its shape is thought to resemble a protective dragon watching over the park. With its palm trees and terrace café, this is undoubtedly the most social area of the park, and the ceramic bench is an attractive spot to soak up the afternoon sun and the sweeping views over the city. As with so much of Gaudí's work, the square combines fantasy with function. The surface of covered sand was designed to filter the rainwater into an underground reservoir through the columns of the market place below.

CASA-MUSEU GAUDÍ

The house in which Gaudí lived between 1906 and 1926, leaving just before his death, has been turned into a small museum. Designed by Gaudí's assistant Francesc Berenguer, this was the first home to be built on the site and it was used as a show home to attract prospective investors. Among the exhibits are furniture and mirrors from the Gaudí-designed houses of Casa Batlló (▷ 181), Casa Milà (▷ 176–177) and Palau Güell (▷ 108–109), along with Gaudí's wardrobe, bed and personal possessions.

THE WALKS

Park Güell contains more than 3km (2 miles) of woodland paths, together with viaducts and porticoes weaving their way through plantations of palm trees and Mediterranean pines. There are arches and slanting columns leaning into the hillside, giving the impression of a series of natural caves. In contrast to the bright gatehouses and ceramic bench, these effects were deliberately designed by Gaudí in monochrome stone, so that without looking carefully it is sometimes difficult to tell what is natural and what is man-made. For an energetic walk, take the path to the group of three crosses that marks the summit of the park.

TIPS

» Visit the information point at the main entrance, the original concierge's pavilion.

» After your visit, take a walk along the wall on Carrer d'Olot—it has a fabulous ceramic frieze with shields bearing the park's name.

» If there is a queue of people outside the Casa-Museu Gaudí, don't even attempt to go inside. The rooms are too small to get a good view of the contents if the place is crowded.

» Remember that the bus No. 24 is the only bus that drops you directly outside at the park's side entrance. The others, plus the nearest metro station, are about a 10- to 15-minute walk to the park. Access has been improved by the introduction of escalators in the surrounding steep streets, but the bus remains the easiest option.

TRENCADÍS

The method of piecing together broken pieces of pottery and glass to form an abstract mosaic is known in Catalan as *trencadís*, a technique thought to be the earliest example of collage. *Trencadís* can be found in many of Gaudí's works; it was here at Park Güell that the technique achieved its fullest expression. Nobody knows whether Gaudí discovered the technique by accident or if it was planned, but while working on Park Güell he became so obsessed with the idea that he ordered his workmen to scour local building sites in order to salvage any broken bottles, plates or tiles. There are also reports of bemused passers-by watching as workmen took delivery of brand-new tiles and smashed them up.

INTRODUCTION

Love it or loathe it, you cannot ignore the Temple Expiatori de la Sagrada Família (Expiatory, or Atonement, Temple of the Holy Family). Its towers and cranes are visible from all over Barcelona and it is the one must-see sight on every itinerary. Gaudí's extraordinary unfinished church is the symbol of Barcelona. It represents the culmination of Gaudí's eccentric genius, but still creates controversy with an ongoing building schedule using modern designs. The highest of the dramatic towers is 112m (367ft).

It is something of an irony that a building widely perceived as a triumph of Modernisme, with all its extravagance, should have been conceived as a way of atoning for the sins of the modern city. The original idea for the temple came from Josep Bocabella, a bookseller and conservative Catholic who had founded the Associació Josefina, an organization dedicated to St. Joseph. The first architect, Francesc de Paula del Villar, envisaged a conventional Gothic-style church, but when Gaudí took over the project at the age of 32 he was given free rein and his fantasies were let loose. Despite the playfulness of his architecture, Gaudí was a deeply religious man. In his later years, he devoted himself totally to the Sagrada Família, living like a recluse in a hut on the site, refusing to draw a salary, and begging passers-by and rich businessmen alike for money to allow work on the church to continue. In 1936, 10 years after Gaudí's death, his plans for the Sagrada Família were destroyed in an anarchist riot, so it is impossible to be certain what the finished building would have looked like. However, despite widespread opposition, work on the church resumed in 1952 and has gained momentum, fuelled by massive worldwide interest and financed by public subscription and the money from entrance fees. The current plan is to complete the temple by 2026 in time for the centenary of Gaudí's death, and masses will be held inside the church from the end of 2010. Controversial plans to build a tunnel beneath the site for the new high-speed AVE train have caused an outcry, with engineers fearing that the tunnel may damage, or even destroy, the building above. In 2009, the church was placed on the UNESCO World Heritage list of monuments in danger because of the fears for its safety during construction of the AVE tunnel.

Work on the church is progressing continually. Major work finished in 2004 on the cloisters, the Passion facade, the central apse and the chapel's vaults. More recently, stained glass has been inserted into the apse windows, and the central nave, which must support the weight of the central towers, is scheduled to be covered in 2010. Entry to the interior is at the Passion facade on Carrer de Sardenya. The whole area resembles a building site—the constant noise can act as a barrier to any notions of spirituality. Yet the sheer scale of the work will take your breath away. At first glance, the entire church looks like the work of a fevered imagination, but every detail of every spire, tower and column has its own precise religious symbolism, which is why the Sagrada Família has been called a catechism in stone.

The Sagrada Família's popularity means that it can get very crowded, so it is best to come early or late in the day.

WHAT TO SEE

PASSION FACADE

The figures on the Passion facade, the first sight that confronts you, are harsh and angular, evoking the pain and humiliation of Christ's crucifixion and death. The Catalan sculptor Josep M. Subirachs (born 1927), who completed these figures in 1990 and still has a workshop on the site, has come in for much criticism, but Gaudí (1852–1926) always intended that this should be a bleak

INFORMATION

www.sagradafamilia.org

✚ 173 H7 ✉ Carrer de Mallorca 401, 08013 ☎ 93 208 04 14 🕓 Apr–end Sep daily 9–8; Oct–end Mar daily 9–6, 25–26 Dec, 1 and 6 Jan 9–2 💷 Adult €12, child (10–17) €10, under 10 free; combined ticket for entry to the Sagrada Família and Casa-Museu Gaudí at Park Güell, valid for one month, €14; elevator €2.50. Tickets including guided tour adult €16, child (10–17) €12, under 10 free 🚇 Sagrada Família 🚌 19, 33, 34, 43, 44, 50, 51, 54 🎧 Audiotours €4 in English, French German, Italian, Spanish or Catalan. Guided tours daily May–end Oct 11am, 1pm, 3pm and 5pm; Nov–end Apr 11 and 1. Audioguides specifically for children (6–12) are available 📖 A large selection available in the two gift shops, ranging from €6 to €25 🍴 Food and snack machines only 🏛 Selling books about the church and Gaudí, plus the usual assortment of gift items with Sagrada Família imagery

Opposite *The Passion facade was completed in 1990*

TIPS

» Before you go in, take a walk around the exterior of the building and cross Carrer de la Marina to reach Plaça Gaudí, as the best views of the Nativity facade are from this small park.

» A five-minute walk up the Avinguda de Gaudí, towards the Hospital de Sant Pau, gives you a better view of the overall dimensions of the church.

» If you decide to use the audioguides, you will be asked to leave some identification (such as passport or driver's licence) as a deposit. If you don't have these on you, you may be asked for something of value instead, such as a credit card.

and barren counterpart to the joyful scenes of the Nativity facade. Six huge, leaning columns, like the trunks of uprooted trees, support a portico containing a series of sculptural groups depicting Christ's Passion and death, beginning with the Last Supper and ending with Christ on the Cross. The figures of Roman centurions are clearly influenced by Gaudí's chimneys on the roof of Casa Milà (La Pedrera, ▷ 176–177). Look for the *Kiss of Death*, a sculpture showing Jesus's betrayal by Judas, complete with a biblical reference in stone (Mark 14:45). The magic square next to it has rows, columns, diagonals and corners that all add up to 33. The significance of this, according to Subirachs, is that this was Christ's age at the time of his death. Subirachs was also responsible for the three sets of bronze doors on the Passion facade. The central doors are the largest and most imposing, entirely covered in sculpted phrases which appear in relief. One question in particular is highlighted, *Qué es la veritat?* (What is truth?), attributed to Pontius Pilate. More quotations, this time from Dante and from the Catalan poet Salvador Espriu, adorn the southern door, which depicts Jesus bearing the crown of thorns and being mocked by the crowds. The northern door shows Jesus praying in the garden of Gethsemane, as the apostles sleep.

NATIVITY FACADE

This is the sculptural high point of the church that was begun in 1891 and completed during Gaudí's lifetime in 1904. The stone carvings on the facade just drip with detail. The theme of the facade is the joy of creation at the birth of Jesus, and it deliberately faces east to receive the first rays of the rising sun. The focal point is the Nativity scene, and above the Holy Family are angels playing trumpets and singing to celebrate Christ's birth. Three doorways, dedicated to Faith, Hope and Charity, depict other biblical scenes, from the marriage of Mary and Joseph to the presentation of Jesus in the temple. At least 30 species of plants, native to both Catalonia and the Holy Land, have been identified on the facade, along with 36 different species of birds, echoing the theme that all creation worships Jesus. This theme reaches its climax in the Tree of Life, a ceramic green cypress tree swarming with doves, which sits atop the facade, nestling between the tall towers.

THE TOWERS

By the time Gaudí died, only one bell-tower had been completed, but there are now four towers above each of the Nativity and Passion facades. The final

Right *Two of the four towers above the Passion facade*
Below *Detail of the intricately sculpted Nativity facade*

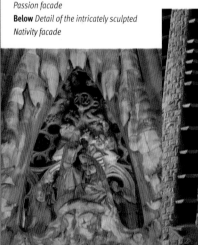

plans envisage a total of 18 towers, dedicated to the 12 apostles, the four evangelists (or Gospel writers), Christ and the Virgin Mary. The vast spires are clad in ceramic mosaics and have been likened to everything from wine bottles to cigars, as well as to the *castells* (human towers) that are a feature of Catalan festivals. Gaudí maintained that by looking at the towers, your gaze would be drawn to heaven, transmitting the words of the prayer *Sanctus Sanctus Sanctus, Hosanna in Excelsis* (Holy, Holy, Holy, Glory to God in the Highest), which is spelled out in broken ceramic tiles at the top. Spiral staircases give access to the towers, and there is also an elevator at each end of the building that will take you most of the way—a good option is to take the elevator up and then descend by the stairs (only for those with a head for heights). Climbing the towers gives close-up views of the spires and also allows you to look down over the central nave. Another good vantage point is the footbridge linking two towers above the doorway of the Nativity facade.

THE CRYPT

The crypt, designed in neo-Gothic style by the original architect Francesc del Villar, is reached by an entrance to the right of the Passion facade and now contains a modern museum (there is an elevator to the crypt). Among the items on display are some of Gaudí's scale models and drawings—though most were destroyed during the Civil War—along with sketches and casts for the Passion facade by Subirachs. Computer software illustrates Gaudí's ingenious and original techniques. You can look into the workshop where artists are preparing plaster casts for the Glory facade. One of the chapels, dedicated to Our Lady of Carmen, contains Gaudí's simple stone tomb, inscribed in Latin *Antonius Gaudí Cornet, Reusensis*, a reference to his home town of Reus.

A CHANGING CHURCH

It is envisaged that the nave will have five aisles, divided by a forest of pillars. Work is almost complete on four massive stone columns designed to support the central spire, which will be 170m (558ft) high and topped by a cross, making the Sagrada Família the tallest building in Barcelona. Around the spire will be four more towers, dedicated to the evangelists and topped with the symbols of an angel, an ox, an eagle and a lion. Standing in the nave, look left to see Gaudí's altar canopy and the neo-Gothic wall of the apse; to the right, work has begun on the Glory facade, which will eventually be the church's main entrance, together with four more towers. Straight ahead, across the transept, a doorway leads outside for a close-up look at the Nativity facade. The plans envisage that the entire church will one day be surrounded by an ambulatory, or external cloister. Despite the construction work, the completion of the church seems a long way off, but as Gaudí said: 'My client is in no hurry.'

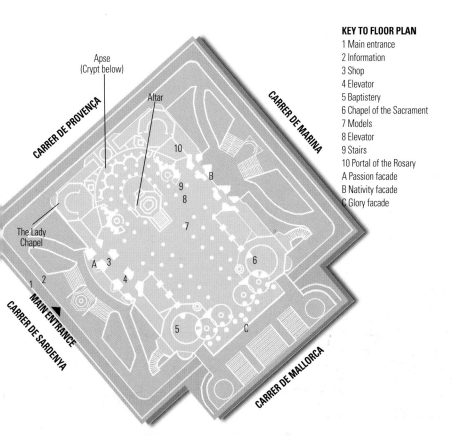

KEY TO FLOOR PLAN

1 Main entrance
2 Information
3 Shop
4 Elevator
5 Baptistery
6 Chapel of the Sacrament
7 Models
8 Elevator
9 Stairs
10 Portal of the Rosary
A Passion facade
B Nativity facade
C Glory facade

GRÀCIA

Small workshops and factories, a legacy of the area's strong industrial history, still dot Gràcia's narrow streets and lively squares, and the architectural heritage of Francesc Berenguer graces it with a few notable Modernista works.

THE WALK

Distance: 2.5km (1.5 miles)
Time: 1.5 hours
Start at: Gràcia FGC station
End at: Fontana metro station

HOW TO GET THERE

Train: Gràcia station is on a number of the suburban lines run by the FGC. They are linked with various metro stations, the main one being Catalunya.
Bus: 16, 17, 22, 24, 25, 27 and 28 will all take you to Gràcia.

★ Walk out of the FGC station, following the signs to the exit marked Plaça de l'Oreneta. Walk a few steps and turn left onto Carrer de l'Oreneta which soon reaches the Plaça de la Llibertat.

❶ The square is occupied by the first of two markets in Gràcia, Mercat de la Llibertat (1893), a wrought-iron affair designed by Fransesc Berenguer (1866–1914). In 2009 it emerged from an expensive refurbishment and the Modernista details gleam anew.

Walk down the right side of the square and exit along Carrer de la Riera de Sant Miguel. At the intersection with Carrer de Seneca turn left.

❷ You will find yourself in an open space in the middle of Gràcia's main street, Gran de Gràcia. Known as Jardins de Salvador Espriu, or more commonly the Jardinets (Little Gardens), they are the backdrop for various community activities throughout the year. Directly opposite is the area's best-known Modernista building, Casa Fuster (now a very plush hotel) designed by Lluís Domènech i Montaner (1850–1923). Directly behind, at No. 15, is Casa Francesc Cama Escurra, designed by Francesc Berenguer, with ornate stained-glass *glorietas* (oriels) jutting out onto the street.

With your back to the Jardinets, walk a few steps along Gran de Gràcia then turn right onto the narrow street, Carrer de Gràcia, which runs alongside Casa Fuster. The austere Santa Maria de Gràcia, originally a Carmelite convent, is on your left. Many of its stones were laid in 1835, although the building was expanded more than a century later, and it is the oldest church in the area. Continue walking to the end of Carrer de Gràcia, and when the road intersects with Carrer de Sant Pere Martir, take the road almost directly in front of you, Carrer de Domènec. Turn left onto Carrer de Mozart and keep walking straight ahead until you reach the Plaça de Rius i Taulet.

③ This is one of Gràcia's most appealing squares. With its fine clock tower and the quaint blue-and-white facade of Gràcia's early 20th-century town hall (also by Francesc Berenguer), it is an ideal place to stop for coffee and watch the comings and goings of life in the *barri*.

Walk through the square to Carrer del Penedès, the northern exit, then turn right and walk to the end of the street, until it meets Carrer de la Mare de Deu dels Desemparats.

④ The Mercat de l'Abaceria is to your left. It's a lot larger than the Mercat de la Llibertat, but what it lacks in architectural merit it makes up for as a hive of activity. It is also worth exploring the streets that fan out from it for basketware, ceramics and other local crafts.

Turn left onto Carrer de la Mare de Deu dels Desemparats and then left again onto the busy axis of Travessera de Gràcia. After a minute or so you will come to Carrer de Torrent de l'Olla; turn right, then take the first left onto Carrer Maspons.

Opposite *A cool, shady spot in sun-bathed Plaça del Sol*

Below *Casa Francesc Cama Escurra*

⑤ Here you will find the Plaça del Sol, a Gràcia institution. Restrained by day, it comes alive at night as a vibrant meeting and drinking place. As the name suggests, it is also a great place for a spot of sunbathing.

Exit the square in the opposite direction to which you entered—onto Carrer del Planeta. Turn right and walk until you meet Carrer de Torrent de l'Olla again. Turn left, then take the first right onto Carrer de Terol. This tiny street will bring you to Carrer de Verdi, Gràcia's fashionable hub. It is home to a number of fashion, book and art shops and Middle Eastern cafés, and to the cinemas of the same name that show the latest releases. Turn left to walk up Carrer de Verdi to Carrer d'Astúries. Turn right and walk to the next intersection.

⑥ The Plaça de la Virreina is Gràcia's most spacious square. It is dominated by the squat Església de Sant Joan with a chapel designed by Berenguer. The first service was held here in 1884, six years after the Plaça itself was completed. Retrace your steps along Carrer d'Astúries, cross over Carrer de

Verdi, and continue along this road. After a few minutes you will hit Gran de Gràcia and the Fontana metro station. Either end the walk here, or turn right along Gran de Gràcia and left onto Carrer de les Carolines to see an early work by Antoni Gaudí (1852–1926)—Casa Vicens (▷ 175) at No. 18.

WHEN TO GO
Any time, but take advantage of Gràcia's bars and restaurants at lunch or for a snack.

WHERE TO EAT
BAR CANIGÓ
An old-style, wood-lined bar frequented by students and locals. The giant-sized sandwiches are hearty enough to satisfy even the largest of lunchtime cravings.
✉ Carrer de Verdí 2 ☎ 93 213 30 49
🕐 Mon–Fri 4pm–2am, Sat 1pm–3am

PLACES TO VISIT
ESGLÉSIA DE SANT JOAN
✉ Plaça de la Virreina s/n ☎ 93 237 73 58 🕐 Mon–Sat 8.30–12.30

SANTA MARIA DE GRÀCIA
✉ Carrer de Sant Pere Màrtir 5 ☎ 93 218 75 72 🕐 Daily 10–1

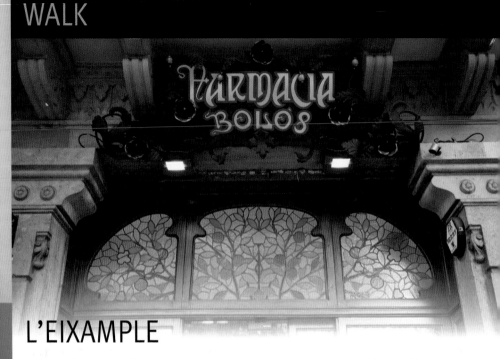

L'EIXAMPLE

L'Eixample (the Extension) was designed in 1859 as the city outgrew its medieval heart and became a canvas for Barcelona's budding Modernista movement. The result is an abundance of work from most of its key figures, all found within a short distance of each other.

THE WALK

Distance: 2.5km (1.5 miles)
Time: 1–1.5 hours
Start/end at: Manzana de la Discordia, Passeig de Gràcia

HOW TO GET THERE

Metro: Passeig de Gràcia station is on lines 3 and 4.
Bus: 7, 16, 17, 22, 24 or 28 will drop you nearby.

★ Start the walk at the intersection of Passeig de Gràcia and Carrer del Consell de Cent. The building on the corner is the Casa Lleó i Morera, the first of the trio of the Manzana de la Discordia (Block of Discord, ▷ 180–182). The other two on the block are Casa Amatller and Casa Batlló, a shimmering, sinuous building that takes its inspiration from the legend of St. George, Catalonia's patron saint, and his battle with the dragon. The Manzana should be on your left. Walk a few more steps north to Carrer d'Aragó, cross the road and turn left.

❶ The Fundació Antoni Tàpies (▷ 175) appears on your right, easily recognizable by the swirling wire cloud sculpture on the roof. The building itself was an old publishing house designed by Domènech i Montaner (1850–1923) in 1885. With a pronounced Arabic influence, it was considered a breakthrough work that ushered in the beginnings of the Modernista movement.

Continue along Carrer d'Aragó, with the Fundació on your right, to the next intersection, Rambla de Catalunya, and turn right. Walk up to the intersection with Carrer de València. Here you will find the Farmàcia Bolós (No. 77), a prime example of the dozens of functioning Modernista pharmacies around L'Eixample. Its florid wooden facade dates from 1902. Continue up Rambla de Catalunya and turn right onto Carrer del Rosselló. Walk until you reach the intersection with Carrer del Bruc.

❷ Casa de les Punxes (House of Spikes) was designed in 1906 by Josep Puig i Cadafalch (1867–1957), and is on your right. It is another key example of how Modernista architects hailed past eras and cultures in their work, in this case the Central European castles of the Middle Ages. A huge ceramic panel of St. George declares 'Holy Patron of Catalunya, give us back our freedom'.

Turn right onto Carrer del Bruc as far as the intersection of Carrer de Mallorca and then turn right again.

❸ Casa Tomas, on the right-hand side of the road, was designed by Lluís Domènech i Montaner. Although the house is one of his

Above *Casa Batlló's fantastic roof*
Above right *Pretty ceramics adorn the walls of Colmado Múrria*
Opposite *Elegant Farmàcia Bolós entrance*

best-known buildings, in fact the original design was substantially remodelled by a later architect, who added another three floors.

Continue walking along Carrer de Mallorca to Carrer de Roger de Llúria. Turn left and walk down to Carrer de Valencia. Here you are at the centre of the Quadrat d'Or (Golden Square), considered the most exclusive part of L'Eixample when the area started to take shape in the late 1800s. This particular intersection has three superb examples of Modernista apartment blocks. Walk a little farther down Carrer de Roger de Llúria to No. 85, on your right.

❹ Colmado Múrria is the best-conserved Modernista shop in the area. It originally supplied coffee, and the glass and ceramic exterior panels have elegant early 20th-century advertising. The best-known is the Anis de Monos girl, a languid maiden who was the symbol of a celebrated anise-based liquor that you can buy inside.

Walk down Carrer de Roger de Llúria to Carrer d'Aragó and turn right.

Continue for two blocks along Carrer d'Aragó and you will return to the starting point.

WHEN TO GO

Try to avoid early afternoon (2–4pm), as many main entrances to the Modernista apartment buildings are closed at this time. Outside these hours you may be allowed a peek at the detailed lobbies and lifts, depending on the amenability of the concierge.

WHERE TO EAT
LA BODEGUETA

L'Eixample has been taken over by franchise cafés. La Bodegueta is an exception, with its wood-lined tapas bar, barrelled wine, a great lunchtime menu and buzzing atmosphere. ✉ Rambla de Catalunya 100 ☎ 93 215 48 94 🕐 Mon–Sat 8am–2am, Sun 7pm–1am

PLACE TO VISIT
COLMADO MÚRRIA

▷ 195.

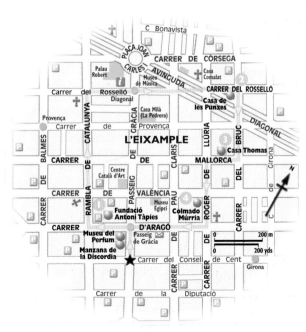

WHAT TO DO

SHOPPING

ADOLFO DOMÍNGUEZ
www.adolfodominguez.com
Adolfo Domínguez is one of Spain's top designers. His linen suits were responsible for a fundamental shift in Spanish men's fashion, but he designs womenswear and sportswear too. The target audience is chic urban professionals seeking something a little sophisticated. A cornerstone of his philosophy is that creases are aesthetic. The youth line, U, is bolder than the core collection and less expensive.
✚ 206 G8 ✉ Passeig de Gràcia 32, 08007 ☎ 93 487 41 70 ⓦ Mon–Sat 10–8.30 Ⓜ Passeig de Gràcia

AGATHA
www.agatha.fr
Agatha jewellery is known beyond Spain's borders and this store has a sizeable collection of pieces. It's best known for its cultured pearl necklaces, available in a range of tones and selectively designed for conservative clients. You'll also find gloves, handbags and sunglasses, as well as perfumes presented in beautiful bottles.
✚ 206 F6 ✉ Rambla de Catalunya 112, 08008 ☎ 93 415 59 98 ⓦ Mon–Fri 10.30–8.30 Ⓜ Diagonal

ALTAÏR
www.altair.es
Al-taïr is an Arabic word meaning the one that flies, and from the moment this bookshop opened in 1979 it has sourced reliable travel literature. The number of countries covered makes this the first and perhaps only stop if you are researching a trip. Altaïr's website is just as good, even helping you find somebody to travel with.

✚ 206 F8 ✉ Gran Vía de les Corts Catalanes 616, 08007 ☎ 93 342 71 71 ⓦ Mon–Sat 10–2, 4.30–8.30 Ⓜ Universitat

ANTONIO MIRÓ
www.antoniomiro.es
This shop is popular with the city's young professionals. Local designer Toni Miró is best known for his superbly tailored men's suits. Both his ladies' and men's collections are excellent value for money and the style is modern and simple.
✚ 206 F7 ✉ Carrer del Consell de Cent 349, 08007 ☎ 93 487 06 70 ⓦ Mon–Sat 10–2, 4.30–8.30 Ⓜ Passeig de Gràcia

ANTONIO PERNAS
Antonio Pernas, a Galician designer, is known for his understated, stylish jackets and suits. There's a great collection of modern and

Opposite Patisserie delights on sale in a traditional bakery

effortlessly sophisticated clothes and accessories, designed with the dynamic urban woman in mind.
🏠 206 G7 ✉ Carrer del Consell de Cent 314–316, 08007 ☎ 93 487 16 67 Ⓦ Mon–Sat 10.30–2, 5–8.30 Ⓜ Universitat

ARMAND BASI
www.armandbasi.com
This is the flagship store of this ultra-cool Spanish designer and is the only place in town that stocks his complete men's and women's collections. He began his career in the 1980s and his experience shows. Choose from soft leather jackets, timeless suits, classic knitwear, evening dress and a wide variety of accessories.
🏠 206 F7 ✉ Passeig de Gràcia 49, 08007 ☎ 93 215 14 21 Ⓦ Mon–Sat 10–8.30 Ⓜ Passeig de Gràcia

ART CLOTHING & VINTAGE
Don't miss this magical boutique in Gràcia. Local artist Mon Alós takes vintage clothes and customizes or remodels them into fabulous new creations. You'll also find some fine authentic vintage pieces by top designers.
🏠 206 F6 ✉ Carrer Doctor Rizal 22, 08012 ☎ 93 165 06 01 Ⓦ Tue–Fri 4.30pm–9pm, Sat 11–2, 5–9 Ⓜ FGC Gràcia

BOTIGA DEL TE I CAFÈS
This shop stocks more than 40 different teas, including Hawaii Flower and Pina Colada among other herbal and fruit infusions. Coffee is by no means ignored, with eight blends of organic coffee, including Puerto Rico Yauco Select. Botiga del Te i Cafès also sells accessories to aid in the preparation and serving of the perfect cup of either. Credit cards are not accepted.
🏠 206 F7 ✉ Plaça del Doctor Letamendi 30–33, 08007 ☎ 93 454 16 75 Ⓦ Mon–Sat 9–8.30 Ⓜ Passeig de Gràcia

LA BOUTIQUE DEL HOTEL
This shop is in the foyer of Axel, the city's upmarket 'gay hotel'. It stocks stylish menswear and accessories from the likes of John Richmond, Helmut Lang and Sonia Rykiel. It also stocks a good range of Levis Vintage and the new menswear range from cult French label Costume National.
🏠 206 F7 ✉ Carrer d'Aribau 33, 08011 ☎ 93 323 93 98 Ⓦ Mon–Sat 10.30–2.30, 4.30–8.30 Ⓜ Universitat

EL BULEVARD DELS ANTIQUARIS
www.bulevarddelsantiquaris.com
This boulevard, or shopping centre, on the Passeig de Gràcia has the largest selection of antiques in Barcelona. Just about everything you could want is here, from the unusual to the more usual large or small items of furniture, jewellery and china. A committee of experts oversees all the stores, giving items a guarantee of authenticity. In addition to the many antiques shops, there is a restoration service along with several good art galleries.
🏠 206 F7 ✉ Passeig de Gràcia 55–57, 08007 ☎ 93 215 44 99 Ⓦ Mon–Sat 10.30–2, 5–8.30 Ⓜ Passeig de Gràcia

BULEVARD ROSA
www.bulevardrosa.com
This shopping centre has two branches; the first was opened in Passeig de Gràcia and the second sprang up in Avinguda Diagonal. Both sites have a mixture of well-known label boutiques and outlets, as well as a handful of small local shops. It has a reputation for good-quality clothes and shoes.
🏠 206 F7 ✉ Passeig de Gràcia 55, 08007 ☎ 93 215 83 31 Ⓦ Mon–Sat 10.30–9 Ⓜ Passeig de Gràcia

CACAO SAMPAKA
www.cacaosampaka.com
This concept store takes the art of chocolate-making to a new level, with bars of chocolate and bon-bons infused with such exotic flavours as South American spices, flowers and herbs, and even truffle. One of their stylish boxes makes the perfect gift, and you can hand-pick what goes inside. There is also a café that serves up chocolate-laden delicacies, inviting sandwiches and the best cup of hot chocolate in Barcelona.
🏠 206 F7 ✉ Carrer del Consell de Cent 292, 08007 ☎ 93 272 08 33 Ⓦ Shop: Mon–Sat 9am–9.15pm, café: Mon–Sat 9–8.45 Ⓜ Passeig de Gràcia

CAMPER
www.camper.es
The Camper label, although conceived in Mallorca, has a high profile in Barcelona. You'll find comfortable, stylishly quirky shoes, made from high-quality leather. It is known around the world for its distinctive bowling shoe designs. The informal style of the shop reflects the concept of the label itself. There are several branches around town.
🏠 206 F7 ✉ Carrer de València 249, 08007 ☎ 93 215 63 90 Ⓦ Mon–Sat 10–9 Ⓜ Diagonal

CARLES GALINDO
This is an imaginative range of costume jewellery, fashioned using unconventional materials such as vinyl, plastic and nylon. The shop also sells black leather accessories with studs, well-worn leather belts, cashmere and vintage denim. These pieces combine to create a punk look embellished with artfully tarnished metals.
🏠 206 G5 ✉ Carrer de Verdi 56, 08012 ☎ 93 416 07 04 Ⓦ Mon–Sat 10–2, 4.30–9 Ⓜ Fontana

COLMADO MÚRRIA
This wonderful delicatessen is in an art nouveau building that features tiled art by the designer Ramón Casas (1866–1932). There is a wide range of fine products available at Colmado Múrria, which are sourced from all over the world. Try some of the finest Iberian cold meat or take home some delicious Norwegian salmon. As far as wines, cavas and spirits are concerned, the range is large and expertly selected.
🏠 206 G7 ✉ Carrer de Roger de Llúria 85, 08009 ☎ 93 215 57 89 Ⓦ Mon–Sat 10–1.30, 5–8 (also Fri 8–9.30) Ⓜ Passeig de Gràcia

CORIUMCASA

This shop sets out a clear identity in its style and stock: fine, elegant and seriously chic. The setting, in a Modernista building in L'Eixample, is countered by a modern approach to design, making use of materials like wood, velvet, linen and leather in the furniture and homewares it sells. The company will custom-make items of furniture if you wish. There is another branch at Passeig de Gràcia 106.

✚ 206 F7 ✉ Carrer de Provença 268, 08008 ☎ 93 272 12 24 🕐 Mon–Sat 10–2, 4.30–8.30 🚇 Diagonal

GASTÓN Y DANIELA

www.gastonydaniela.com

Tradition and quality have served Gastón y Daniela well in the face of mounting competition from companies using modern fabrics and techniques. The first branch opened in Bilbao 125 years ago, and throughout its lifetime the shop's clients have loved the great range of luxurious patterns and textiles available. Perfect for prints, fitted carpets, upholstery, mats and bedspreads.

✚ 206 G7 ✉ Carrer de Pau Claris 171, 08037 ☎ 93 215 32 17 🕐 Mon–Fri 10–2, 5–8, Sat 10.30–2 🚇 Diagonal

GEMMA PICHOT

Gemma Pichot's jewellery shop, which doubles as a studio, is in a former medal factory in the old Gràcia area. She has created an interesting setting, retaining the factory's original interior and furniture. The pieces on sale incorporate a lot of wood and glass, with designs inspired by nature. Credit cards are not accepted.

✚ 206 G5 ✉ Carrer d'Astúries 4, 08012 ☎ 93 237 59 23 🕐 Mon–Thu 10–2, 4–7, Fri 10–2. Closed Aug 🚇 Fontana

HIPÒTESIS

North of Plaça de Catalunya, this shop stocks all manner of jewellery by a number of different artists. There are pieces to suit all types of budget, and the collection is notable for its rich shades, interesting shapes and unusual textures. It's also a good place for hand-painted silk scarves and other garments.

✚ 206 F7 ✉ Rambla de Catalunya 105, 08008 ☎ 93 215 02 98 🕐 Tue–Fri 10–8.30, Mon, Sat 11.30–2, 5–8.30 🚇 Diagonal

JOAQUÍN BERAO

www.joaquinberao.com

Berao has designed jewellery for more than 30 years. His pieces are inspired by shells and sea creatures such as sea horses and starfish. His innovative work is well respected and is often exhibited at the Zurich Museum of Contemporary Art.

✚ 206 F7 ✉ Rambla de Catalunya 74, 08037 ☎ 93 215 00 91 🕐 Mon–Sat 10–2, 5–8.30 🚇 Diagonal

LAIE

www.laie.es

A bookshop with a magnificent stock of titles, Laie is also a venue for book presentations, exhibitions and literary discussion groups. Some of these events take place in the shop's café, where customers can sit, read, relax and, if they time it right, engage in academic debate.

✚ 206 G8 ✉ Carrer de Pau Claris 85, 08010 ☎ 93 318 17 39 🕐 Mon–Fri 10–9, Sat 10.30–9; Café Mon–Fri 9am–10.30pm, Sat 10am–10.30pm 🚇 Urquinaona

LA LLIBERTAT

Built at the end of the 19th century, this beautiful Modernista market in the Gràcia area has recently emerged from a major restoration programme, and its twirling wrought-iron details and pretty fountains gleam anew. It contains more than 40 stalls dedicated to fresh produce, including meat, fish, fruit and vegetables.

✚ 206 F6 ✉ Plaça de Llibertat 27, 08012 ☎ 93 217 09 95 🕐 Tue–Thu 8–3, 5–8, Fri 7am–8pm, Sat 7–3, Mon 8–3 🚇 Fontana

LOEWE

www.loewe.es

Loewe was started in 1846 and has always been the ultimate Spanish luxury fashion and accessory label. It sells top-quality leather goods, clothes and accessories, all classic and all stylish. Its international reputation is formed by the ladies' ready-to-wear collection, and is reflected by its flagship store, in a beautiful 19th-century mansion.

✚ 206 F7 ✉ Passeig de Gràcia 35, 08007 ☎ 93 216 04 00 🕐 Mon–Sat 10–8.30 🚇 Passeig de Gràcia

MANGO

www.mango.es

Selling innovative clothes at fair prices, Mango is one of Spain's internationally known stores. Since 1985 it has blossomed from five shops in its hometown of Barcelona to more than 900 worldwide. The designers prefer to use a basic palette mixed with the latest styles, ranging from casual to formal eveningwear and fun accessories.

✚ 206 F7 ✉ Passeig de Gràcia 65, 08007 ☎ 93 215 75 30 🕐 Mon–Sat 10–9 🚇 Passeig de Gràcia

MASSIMO DUTTI

www.massimodutti.com

Massimo Dutti has retail space in 30 different countries and has a complete range of lines, covering sophisticated fashion, urban chic and the sporty look. The basic, modern styles on the rails here are created using contemporary fabrics, but are good-quality and always remain practical and attractive.

✚ 206 F6 ✉ Vía Augusta 33, 08006 ☎ 93 217 73 06 🕐 Mon–Sat 10–9 🚇 Diagonal

MN JOIES

This tiny boutique in the Bulevard Rosa shopping centre is crammed with desirable objects. The jewellery is original and unusual, good quality and very reasonably priced, with ranges for both men and women.

✚ 206 F7 ✉ Botiga No. 84, Bulevard Rosa, Passeig de Gràcia 53, 08007 ☎ 93 216 02 40 🕐 Mon–Sat 10–3, 4.30–8 🚇 Passeig de Gràcia

OLI SAL

www.olisal.com

'Where gold is liquid' is the slogan of this aromatic shop, which is dedicated to olive oil in all its guises. Not only does it offer a wide range of high-quality olive oils, but it also has a range of soaps and bath foams made with olive oil. A variety of flavoured salt is also sold.

➕ 206 G6 ✉ Travessera de Gràcia 170, 08012 ☎ 93 415 06 24 🕐 Tue–Sat 10.30–2.30, 4.30–8.30, Mon 4.30–8.30 🚇 FGC Gràcia

ON LAND
www.on-land.com
On Land has an extensive collection of women's and men's clothing. Check out the house label or go for something by one of the featured new designers. Stylish seasonal outfits here include modern, angular tailoring from Catalans Josep Abril and Gabriel Torres, and the more romantic, feminine styles of womenswear designer Josep Font.

➕ 206 G7 ✉ Carrer de València 273, 08009 ☎ 93 310 02 11 🕐 Tue–Fri 11–2, 5–8.30, Sat 11–8.30, Mon 5–8.30 🚇 Passeig de Gràcia

Right *Catalan olive oil in a range of flavours*
Below *Elegant fashions by local designer Antonio Miró*

PILMA
www.pilma.com
Pilma sells modular furniture, upholstery, garden and terrace furniture, carpets, curtains, artwork, kitchen goods and accessories. The two buzzwords when it comes to design are simplicity and practicality, influencing the shapes and materials used. The shop itself is spacious, modern and airy.

➕ 206 F6 ✉ Avinguda Diagonal 403, 08008 ☎ 93 416 13 99 🕐 Mon–Sat 10–2, 4.30–8.30 🚇 Diagonal

QUILEZ
www.lafuente.es
One of the city's institutions at the heart of L'Eixample. Try the house blend of Colombian coffee Café Quilez, or a bottle of La Fuente cava. National and imported beers

number about 300 and there are selected wines from more than 100 different cellars. You should be able to find everything you need in food shopping too.

➕ 206 F7 ✉ Rambla de Catalunya 63, 08007 ☎ 93 215 23 56 🕐 Mon–Fri 9–2, 4.30–8.30, Sat 9–2 🚇 Passeig de Gràcia

RIERA
Established at the beginning of the 20th century, this is one of the city's best-known shops dealing in household accessories. Luxury and quality are the main themes, with an ample collection of glassware, cutlery and china. The Swedish Kosta-Boda glasswork is particularly attractive.

➕ 206 G7 ✉ Carrer d'Aragó 284, 08007 ☎ 93 215 14 13 🕐 Mon–Sat 10–8.15 🚇 Passeig de Gracia

SEÑOR

In a late 19th-century building, Señor has successfully combined traditional tailoring with the latest leather fashions for men. It stocks a number of prestigious international labels including Boss, Canali, Versace, Trussardi, Armani and Caramelo. A delivery service is available, either to your hotel or shipped back home.

🚇 206 G8 ✉ Passeig de Gràcia 26, 08007 ☎ 93 317 69 67 🕐 Mon–Sat 10–8.30 🚇 Passeig de Gràcia

VINÇON

www.vincon.com

Vinçon showcases modern European design in an enormous old palatial setting. The retail space here is vast, but the stock includes small items such as Filofaxes alongside stylish kitchenware. A must-see in Vinçon is one of Barcelona's most elaborate Modernista fireplaces. Vinçon is next door to one of Barcelona's most famous buildings, Casa Milà (La Pedrera, ▷ 176–177), and the two help trace the history of design in the city.

🚇 206 G7 ✉ Passeig de Gràcia 96, 08008 ☎ 93 215 60 50 🕐 Mon–Sat 10–8.30 🚇 Diagonal

ENTERTAINMENT AND NIGHTLIFE

ARENA

www.arenadisco.com

Barcelona has five Arena clubs and this is the longest established. House and techno fills the dance floor; the crowd is mixed and of all sexual orientations. It is not the place for a quiet night out. Credit cards are not accepted.

🚇 206 F8 ✉ Carrer de Balmes 32, 08007 ☎ 93 487 83 42 🕐 Mon–Sun midnight– 5.30am ✋ €6–€12 🚇 Universitat

EL BAR DEL MAJESTIC

Chic, discreet and peaceful, this café is in the grounds of the Majestic hotel (▷ 205). The clientele is mostly VIPs and young trendsetters. In the evenings, it's transformed into a piano bar. Sandwiches are also available.

🚇 206 G7 ✉ Passeig de Gràcia 68, 08008 ☎ 93 488 17 17 🕐 Daily 10am–2am 🚇 Passeig de Gràcia

BAR VELCRO

A relaxed, intimate lounge bar, Bar Velcro is a favourite with the boho-chic locals of Gràcia. Armchairs and low lighting make it a great place to unwind after an afternoon's sightseeing or shopping.

🚇 206 G6 ✉ Carrer Vallfogona 10, 08012 ☎ 610 75 47 42 (mobile) 🕐 Sun–Thu 8pm–1am, Fri, Sat 8pm–3am 🚇 Fontana

COLISEUM

www.grupbalana.com

This neo-baroque cinema was built in the 1920s with the intention of lending Barcelona a touch of the splendour of early US cinemas. It seats 1,689 people and has the latest cinematic technology, but doesn't show original-language films. Snacks are available.

🚇 206 F7 ✉ Gran Vía de les Cortes Catalanes 595, 08007 ☎ 902 42 42 43 ✋ €5.50–€7 🚇 Passeig de Gràcia

COMEDIA

Formerly a theatre, Comedia has been converted into a small multiplex cinema showing five movies at a time. It screens mostly international mainstream films, usually dubbed into Spanish. There are late performances at weekends and snacks are available.

🚇 206 F7 ✉ Passeig de Gràcia 13, 08007 ☎ 93 318 23 96 ✋ €5.50–€6.50 🚇 Passeig de Gràcia

DIETRICH

House music fills the dance floor here. One of the two large bars looks out onto a garden. There is also a stage, which is well-loved by the drag-queen regulars. It's a fun gay and lesbian venue where anything goes.

🚇 206 F7 ✉ Carrer del Consell de Cent 255, 08011 ☎ 93 451 77 07 🕐 Daily 10.30pm–3am ✋ Free 🚇 Universitat

LA FIRA

Fira means 'fairground', and this bar is so packed with items based on

this theme that it looks rather like a museum. It's popular with larger groups and a lively, boisterous place to spend your evening. Credit cards are not accepted.

🚇 206 F6 ✉ Carrer de Provença 171, 08036 ☎ 93 323 72 71 🕐 Tue–Sun 7pm–2.30am 🚇 Hospital Clinic

LES GENS QUE J'AIME

You'll find baroque surroundings here, with comfortable sofas on which to spend intimate, peaceful evenings. It's relaxed, comfortable and a little bohemian. You can even have your palm read. Credit cards are not accepted.

🚇 206 G7 ✉ Carrer de València 286, 08008 ☎ 93 215 68 79 🕐 Sun–Thu 6pm–2.30am, Fri–Sat 7pm–3am 🚇 Passeig de Gràcia

LIKA LOUNGE

Lika Lounge, which opened in 2007, is one of the few places in Barcelona where you can enjoy a really well mixed cocktail. It's also the only place in town with an ice bar. A sleek, glossy space, it attracts an equally sleek and glossy crowd. There are club nights on Wednesdays, Fridays and Saturdays.

🚇 206 F7 ✉ Passatge Domingo 3 (between Passeig de Gràcia and Rambla de Catalunya), 08007 ☎ 93 467 26 11 🕐 Mon–Sat 9pm–3am 🚇 Passeig de Gràcia

LUZ DE GAS

www.luzdegas.com

This old music hall is one the city's prime concert venues. Enjoy some great live music, ranging from blues to cover bands. Arrive early to avoid a long wait outside.

🚇 206 F6 ✉ Carrer de Muntaner 246, 08021 ☎ 93 209 77 11 ✋ From €15 🚇 Diagonal

MOND

The motto of this tiny bar is 'pop will make us free', and it has some very talented DJs. If you don't manage to get in before it fills up, there's always space to mingle outside on the Plaça del Sol. Credit cards are not accepted.

📍 206 G5 ✉ Plaça del Sol 29,
08012 ☎ 93 272 09 10 🕐 Sun–Thu
9pm–2.30am, Fri–Sat 9pm–3am 🚇 Fontana

OTTO ZUTZ
www.grupo-ottozutz.com
This is a popular spot in Gràcia and,
in keeping with that area, you will
need to dress smartly to get in. But
once inside you can choose to join
the dance floor, which mostly has
house music playing, or join the
beautiful people at the bar.
📍 206 F5 ✉ Carrer de Lincoln 15, 08006
☎ 93 238 07 22 🕐 Tue–Sat 11pm–6am
💵 €15 🚇 Fontana

TEATRENEU TEATRE
www.teatreneu.com
Gràcia is becoming a well-known
provider of lively entertainment
in the heart of the city. Theatres
such as Teatreneu, which puts on
contemporary plays, musicals and
dance, are springing up alongside
good restaurants and cafés.
📍 206 G8 ✉ Carrer de Terol 26–28,
08012 💵 From €5 🚇 Fontana

VERDI
www.cines-verdi.com
This was one of the first cinemas
in Barcelona to break the mould of
screening mainstream blockbusters.
It shows non-commercial, original-
language films, all subtitled in
Spanish. Snacks are available.
📍 206 G5 ✉ Carrer de Verdi 32,
08012 ☎ 93 238 78 00 💵 €5.75–€8.25
🚇 Fontana

VERDI PARK
www.cines-verdi.com
Due to the overwhelming success
of its first cinema, Verdi opened
a second multiplex nearby, which
also shows quality original-language
films. Snacks are available.
📍 206 G5 ✉ Carrer de Torrijos 49,
08012 ☎ 93 238 79 90 💵 €5.75–€8.25
🚇 Fontana

SPORTS AND ACTIVITIES
PISTA DE GEL
www.skatingclub.cat
This large, modern ice rink is very
central, making it easy to find

and useful for visitors. There is a
café-bar from where you can watch
skaters, and there are babysitters at
weekends and holidays so the young
ones can be looked after while
parents skate with older children.
📍 206 H7 ✉ Carrer de Roger de Flor 168,
08013 ☎ 93 245 28 00 🕐 Mon–Tue 10–
1.30, Wed–Fri 10–1.30, 5–8.30, Sat 10.30–2,
4.30–9, Sun 10.30–2, 4.30–8.30 (extended
hours during school holidays) 💵 Entrance
and skate rental: €12.90 🚇 Tetuán

HEALTH AND BEAUTY
AQUA URBAN SPA
www.aqua-urbanspa.com
The day spa craze has hit Barcelona
in a big way. Aqua Urban Spa
goes one step further by providing
specialized water-based treatments
for poor circulation, skin conditions
and cellulite, as well as a Turkish
steam bath, Roman bath, small
mineral water pools, spas and
pressure showers.
📍 206 G6 ✉ Carrer Gran de Gràcia
7, 08012 ☎ 93 238 41 60 🕐 Mon–Fri
9am–9.30pm, Sat 9.30–8.30 💵 75-min
treatment €51 🚇 Diagonal

FLOTARIUM
www.flotarium.com
Leave your cares behind you as you
step into one of the float tanks at
the Flotarium. The tanks are each

in a private room, with towels and
toiletries provided. Each session
lasts an hour.
📍 206 F6 ✉ Plaça Narcís Oller 3, 08006
☎ 93 217 36 37 🕐 10–10 💵 €35 per
session 🚇 FGC Gràcia

FOR CHILDREN
CASA MILÀ (LA PEDRERA)
▷ 176–177.

HAPPY PARC
www.happyparc.com
Children in need of letting off
some steam (and parents in
need of a break) love Happy Parc:
a giant warehouse filled with
squashy, rubbery, bouncy, rompy
contraptions. Tiny tots go to a
specially supervised, enclosed
area and monitors are on hand
throughout. Adults, meanwhile, can
enjoy a quiet coffee in the in-house
cafeteria or leave the building
altogether if their children are aged
over 6. There is another Happy Parc
at Comtes de Bel.loc 74–76.
📍 206 G8 ✉ Carrer de Pau Claris 97,
08004 ☎ 93 317 86 60 🕐 Sep–end Jul
Mon–Fri 5pm–9pm, Sat–Sun 11am–9pm,
Aug daily 5pm–9pm 💵 Hourly rate €4
🚇 Urquinaona

MUSEU EGIPCI
▷ 183.

Below *Museu Egipci has plenty of displays and activities that appeal to children*

PRICES AND SYMBOLS

The prices given are the average for a two-course lunch (L) and a three-course dinner (D) for one person, without drinks. The wine price is for the least expensive bottle.

For a key to the symbols, ▷ 2.

ALKIMIA

www.alkimia.cat

Awarded his first Michelin star in 2004, Jordi Vilà is known as the chef's chef. Vilà 'deconstructs' traditional recipes and is one of the forerunners of 'New Catalan Cuisine'. Thus *pa amb tomàquet* (bread rubbed with tomato pulp) will be liquefied and served in a shot glass, or grilled cuttlefish paired with duck 'meatballs'. Try the tasting menu of tapas-sized portions.
🕂 207 H6 ✉ Carrer de Indústria 79, 08025 ☎ 93 207 61 15 🕒 Mon–Fri 1.30–3.30, Mon–Sat 8pm–11pm. Closed Aug and Easter week 🖐 Lunch menu

€38, Tasting menu €58 and €74, Wine €20
🚇 Sagrada Família

BODEGA MANOLO

The excellent food that you find here makes up for the rather shabby appearance of this restaurant. Dishes include roasted aubergine (eggplant) with goat's cheese, grilled asparagus with anchovies and vinaigrette, pork liver with apples and several variations on cod. It has gained popularity among business people, who head up to Gràcia for lunch. Credit cards are not accepted.
🕂 207 H5 ✉ Carrer del Torrent de les Flors 101, 08024 ☎ 93 284 43 77 🕒 Tue–Wed 1–4, Thu–Sat 1–4, 9–11.30. Closed Aug 🖐 L €9, D €35, Wine €10
🚇 Joanic

BOTAFUMEIRO

www.botafumeiro.es

The first-class shellfish served here is a real attraction, even though this

restaurant has built its reputation on *arròs caldoso* (casseroled rice) and its house lamb. The service is faultless and there are some very good wines to accompany your meal. There's usually space at the bar, where you can sit on comfortable high stools. It is open late, so it's the ideal place to go for a post-cinema or concert bite to eat.
🕂 206 G6 ✉ Carrer Gran de Gràcia 81, 08012 ☎ 93 218 42 30 🕒 Daily 1.30–1 🖐 L €50, D €70, Wine €18 🚇 Section
🚇 Fontana

CATA 1.81

www.cata181.com

Cata means 'wine tasting' and this tiny bar offers a truly wonderful selection of wines: Unusually, many are also offered by the glass. The wines are accompanied by *platillos*—small dishes of tempting treats. Watermelon gazpacho is a summer favourite, but you could try rice with sea anemones and artichokes, or go for the mini hamburgers with a piquant mustard sauce. Don't miss out on the dessert selection: The chocolate coulant with a bitter orange filling is sublime.

✚ 206 F7 ✉ Carrer de València 181, 08011 ☎ 93 323 68 18 ◷ Mon–Fri 6pm–12am, Sat 6pm–1am ✦ Set menus €28–€34, Menu Bylopas €45 (includes wine), Tapas from €3 ◉ Passeig de Gràcia

CERVECERÍA CATALANA

A great choice for a superb, hassle-free meal. This tavern *(cervecería)* has the most spectacular tapas, ranging from Spanish omelettes to shrimp in garlic sauce, and sirloin canapés. Stop off here if you're shopping in the area; simply order a glass of wine and choose your tapas from the great display. Because of its popularity, it's also an ideal spot for people-watching.

✚ 206 F7 ✉ Carrer de Mallorca 236, 08008 ☎ 93 216 03 68 ◷ Daily 8am–1.30am ✦ L €15, D €15, Wine €8 ◉ Diagonal

CINC SENTITS

www.cincsentits.com.

Cinc Sentits means 'the five senses' and Canadian-bred chef Jordi Artal aims to please them all in his elegant, minimalist eatery. He strongly recommends the gourmet tasting menu with a choice of six enticing dishes. These can include a poached egg with onion confit, followed by pan-seared monkfish with romesco broth and finished with green apple sorbet. This is one of the city's newest Michelin starred winners; you should book well in advance.

✚ 206 F7 ✉ Carrer d'Aribau 58, 08011 ☎ 93 323 94 90 ◷ Tue–Sat 1.30–3.30, 8–11.30. Closed 8–31 Aug and Easter week ✦ L €49, D €69, Tasting Menu €64–€69, Wine €20 ◉ Passeig de Gràcia

DE TAPA MADRE

www.detapamadre.com

After breakfast has been served, an extensive selection of tapas

is available throughout the day: *morcilla mix* (black sausage), grilled meat, cold meats and fried fish are just some of the choices. For dessert, round off with the delicious *crema catalana*. Guests can sit on the terrace if the weather is good, or simply settle at the bar. Excellent Iberian produce is available to purchase, including oils and a variety of tinned goods.

✚ 206 G7 ✉ Carrer de Mallorca 301, 08037 ☎ 93 459 31 34 ◷ Daily 8am–12.30am ✦ L and D €30, Wine €12 ◉ Diagonal

DROLMA

Since it opened its doors in 1999, Drolma has earned its place as one of Spain's most renowned restaurants, reflected in its well-deserved Michelin star. Located inside the elegant Majestic hotel, the formal dining rooms are a fitting setting for chef Fermí Puig's haute cuisine. The exciting dishes may include tuna belly with a 'chantilly' of aromatic herbs, an impeccable spring vegetable risotto or pheasant cannelloni sprinkled with shards of black truffle. The oven-baked meats, such as goat or suckling pig, are legendary.

✚ 206 G7 ✉ Passeig de Gràcia 68, 08007 ☎ 93 496 77 10 ◷ Mon–Sat 1–3.30, 8.30–11. Closed Aug. Reservations essential ✦ L €94, D €135, Wine €25 ◉ Passeig de Gràcia

FLASH FLASH

Excellent hamburgers, salads and more than 70 kinds of tortilla are available in this uptown eatery where the 1970s interior and ambience attracts customers from all over the city. The murals on the walls were created by Leonardo Pómes, a famous local photographer of the period, and white leather sofas contrasting with red fittings complete the design. Tortillas come in all varieties and the bun-less hamburger is a treat.

✚ 206 F6 ✉ La Granada del Penedès 25, 08006 ☎ 93 237 09 90 ◷ Daily 1pm–1.30am ✦ L €15, D €25, Wine €10 ◉ Diagonal

IKASTOLA

Ikastola is made up of three very different spaces—a quiet bar, a small, comfortable restaurant and an interior terrace. A young crowd gathers in the evenings for simple dishes such as sandwiches or salad, and for excellent cocktails made with fresh juices. As an extra touch, there are chalkboards everywhere for the clientele to write or draw whatever they like. Credit cards are not accepted.

✚ 206 G6 ✉ Carrer de la Perla 22, 08012 ☎ 647 71 91 96 ◷ Mon–Thu 2–1, Fri–Sun 6pm–1am ✦ L and D €10, Wine €9 ◉ Fontana

L'ILLA DE GRÀCIA

www.illadegracia.com

Healthy food is served at reasonable prices in this simple setting. Some of the menu's main highlights are the garlic soup, stewed apples and the vegetable and potato pies. The food is nutritious and very generously portioned; one to remember if you ever want a quiet, inexpensive evening out.

✚ 206 G6 ✉ Carrer de Sant Domènec 19, 08012 ☎ 93 238 02 29 ◷ Tue–Fri 1–4, 9–12, Sat, Sun 2–4, 9–12. Closed 15–30 Aug ✦ L €10, D €15, Wine €8 ◉ ◉ Fontana

MESOPOTAMIA

This is a warm, peaceful and comfortable spot that was set up by Pius Hermés, a university professor of Semitic languages. A variety of meats, intensely seasoned with herbs and spices, are a staple of the menu as is the leg of lamb and aubergines (eggplant) marinated in yoghurt sauce. Oil lamps and exposed brick dominate the interior, and on weekends guests can request a *narguilé* or hookah (a water pipe for smoking tobacco), fruits and honey. There are two sittings every evening, so you will need to make reservations in advance. Credit cards are not accepted.

✚ 206 G5 ✉ Carrer de Verdi 65, 08012 ☎ 93 237 15 63 ◷ Tue–Sat 8.30pm–1am. Closed 23 Dec–8 Jan ✦ D €30, Wine €10 ◉ Fontana

MOO

Located inside the achingly fashionable Hotel Omm (▷ 205), the Moo restaurant is the second restaurant of the Roca brothers of the famed El Cellar de Can Roca near Girona. You can create your own tasting menu, choosing half-size portions of dishes such as chicken with olives and mango or foie with figs and a muscatel reduction. Be sure to leave room for their famous and phenomenal perfume-infused desserts.

✚ 206 G7 ✉ Carrer del Roselló 265, 08008 ☎ 93 445 40 00 🕔 Daily 1.30–3.30, 8.30–10.30 🍴 Lunch menu €45, D €80, Tasting menu (with wine pairing) €105, Wine €25 🚇 Diagonal

NOTI

The sleek, urban interior and the French/Mediterranean dishes have made this restaurant a hit with the city's media set. It takes a great deal of its styling influences from New York—the seating consists of plush velvet sofas and the waitstaff come clad in black. Risottos, steaks and fish dishes are the highlights, as is the highly polished interior that even extends to the restrooms.

✚ 206 G8 ✉ Carrer de Roger de Llúria 35, 08009 ☎ 93 342 66 73 🕔 Mon–Fri 1.30–4, 8.30–11.30, Sat 8.30–12 🍴 Set lunch menus €14–€24, dinner menu €36, Wine €20 🚇 Urquinaona

L'OLIVÉ

www.rte-olive.com
The dining room at this classic restaurant is spacious and elegant, with starched white linen table cloths and restrained, minimalist decoration. The Catalan cuisine is fresh and innovative, but remains based on tried-and-tested traditional recipes. The wide-ranging menu includes succulent rice dishes such as *rossejat* (a dense fish broth with tiny noodles), as well as seasonal favourites such as *calçots* (a type of onion, served chargrilled with a rich romesco sauce).

✚ 206 F7 ✉ Carrer de Balmes 47, 08007 ☎ 93 452 19 90 🕔 Mon–Sat 1–4, 8.30–12, Sun 1–4 🍴 L €20, D €35, Wine €14 🚇 Universitat

RÍO AZUL

www.elrioazul.com
Unlike most of the world's large, cosmopolitan cities, Barcelona is conspicuous by the fact it has hundreds of great Chinese restaurants but no Chinatown. Río Azul is on a busy thoroughfare but is easy enough to get to. It doesn't look like much from the outside, sporting the same luridly coloured, laminated menus as everywhere else, but rows of proper Peking duck hanging inside the glass partition to the kitchen are testament to greater things. Carved at the table, the succulent meat and delicious crispy skin is wrapped up in steaming pancakes with slivered spring onions (scallions) and cucumber. Complemented by lashings of hoisin sauce, this is one of the city's truely great Chinese treats.

✚ 206 F7 ✉ Carrer Balmes 92, 08008 ☎ 93 215 93 33 🕔 Mon–Sun 1–4, 8–12 🍴 L €10, D €30, Wine €10 🚇 Passeig de Gràcia or Diagonal

SALAMBÓ

Salambó mainly serves Catalan food but the menu also includes Hungarian dishes, such as *meleg* (beef or chicken with cheese). Pasta, stews, soups and burgers are also available. Although the restaurant cleverly maximizes its space, it still gets very busy, so booking in advance is recommended.

✚ 206 G5 ✉ Carrer de Torrijos 51, 08012 ☎ 93 218 69 66 🕔 Café: Wed–Mon 12pm–2am. Restaurant: Wed–Mon 1–4, 8.30–12.30 🍴 L €13, D €30, Wine €8 🚭 Section 🚇 Fontana

TÀBATA

www.restaurantetabata.com
It couldn't be simpler: Diners cook the food themselves, according to their own tastes. Order the raw meat, fish and vegetables, and a *taba*, a special Finnish stone, is delivered with the ingredients. When heated up, these stones keep their temperature for about three hours. Everything is served with salt and a range of specially prepared sauces. If this is too much effort, there are also salads and some pasta dishes. The restaurant is run by a foundation that helps people with disabilites find work. They also offer dinner with a flamenco performance on some nights.

✚ 206 G6 ✉ Carrer del Torrent de l'Olla 27, 08012 ☎ 93 237 84 96 🕔 Mon–Tue 1–4, Wed–Sat 1–4, 9–12 🍴 L €9.75, D €20, Wine €10 🚭 Section 🚇 Diagonal

EL TRAGALUZ

www.grupotragaluz.com
Beneath a huge glass ceiling, this restaurant is split over three floors: The à la carte menu is served on the first floor, while the ground-floor bar has a tapas menu. The food is essentially the same, but the portions vary in size—a great idea if you want to sample before committing to a sit-down meal. Try the salad with ginger or cod with roasted pepper and garlic.

✚ 206 F7 ✉ Passatge de la Concepció 5, 08007 ☎ 93 487 01 96 🕔 Tue–Sun 1.30–4, 8.30–12 🍴 L €25, D €40, Wine €19 🚇 Diagonal

Below *You will find tapas on offer in many eating establishments in L'Eixample*

PRICES AND SYMBOLS

Prices are the lowest and highest for a double room for one night. Breakfast is included unless noted otherwise. All the hotels listed accept credit cards unless otherwise stated. Note that rates vary widely throughout the year.

For a key to the symbols, ▷ 2.

ABALON

www.hotelabalon.com
The Medium hotel chain has six hotels in Barcelona. The Abalon is the closest of them to the Sagrada Família and Park Güell. It's a warm, family place helped by the complementary furnishings and interior design. Although a one-star hotel, it has parking and room service and all the rooms have a bath, satellite TV, radio and direct telephone line. There is also free WiFi internet access.

✚ 207 J6 ✉ Travessera de Gràcia 380–384, 08025 ☎ 93 450 04 60 🖐 €40–€105 ① 40 🅢 🅠 Hospital de Sant Pau

AC DIPLOMÀTIC

www.achoteldiplomatic.com
This four-star hotel is an excellent example of the city's love of contemporary design. All the rooms are minimally decorated with wooden panelling that contrasts with white linen or darker furnishings. There is a solarium, sauna, internet access, free minibar and parking.

✚ 206 G7 ✉ Carrer de Pau Claris 122, 08009 ☎ 93 272 38 10 🖐 €100–€350, excluding breakfast ① 211 (15 non-smoking) 🅢 🏊 Outdoor 🛇 🅠 Passeig de Gràcia

ACTUAL

www.hotelactual.com
This hotel is competitively priced and also claims an excellent spot, behind Casa Milà (La Pedrera), one of architect Antoni Gaudí's masterpieces. Small, modern and sleek, this is the place to stay if you want an intimate atmosphere in a sophisticated setting. All the rooms have a good range of facilities, such as cable TV, minibar and internet access.

✚ 206 G7 ✉ Carrer del Rosselló 238, 08008 ☎ 93 552 05 50 🖐 €115–€153, excluding breakfast ① 29 (12 non-smoking) 🅢 🅠 Diagonal

ALEXANDRA

www.hotel-alexandra.com
The Alexandra is in the heart of L'Eixample, so it's close to just about everything. All rooms have strong interiors, with reds, blues, blacks, wooden floors and panels, and are equipped with TV and minibar. The more expensive rooms have spa baths, and junior suites have a terrace. The hotel also has a restaurant, parking and free WiFi internet access.

✚ 206 F7 ✉ Carrer de Mallorca 251, 08008 ☎ 93 467 71 66 🖐 €175–€211, excluding breakfast ① 109 🅢 🅠 Diagonal

Above *The elegant bar of Casa Fuster hotel*

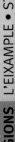

AMREY DIAGONAL

www.amrey-hotels.com

This was the first hotel to open in Poble Nou and it has set the standard with its impeccable service. It has become a local landmark in District 22@, the name given to the regeneration project of this industrial area, and is only steps away from the stores at Les Glòries, and from Bogatell beach. Rooms have been soundproofed and come equipped with individual climate control, internet connection, safety deposit box, minibar, telephone with voicemail and satellite TV. The café has daily fixed-price menus from €12 and à la carte dishes from the restaurant menu.

✚ Off map 207 K8 ✉ Avinguda Diagonal 161–163, 08018 ☎ 93 486 88 00 ✋ €234–€277, excluding breakfast ❶ 153 (45 non-smoking) ⬛ ⓐ Glòries

CASA FUSTER

www.hotelcasafuster.com

Inside an emblematic Modernista mansion and immaculately restored down to the last detail, this luxury hotel is the city's newest five-star. The belle époque rooms are replete with lush furnishings and touches such as hydro-jet baths and luxury toiletries. Many have balconies that look out onto the Passeig de Gràcia, Barcelona's top shopping avenue, and the hotel is within walking distance of major attractions such as the Sagrada Família and the Casa Milà. For sheer yesteryear elegance it cannot be surpassed.

✚ 206 G6 ✉ Passeig de Gràcia 132, 08008 ☎ 93 255 30 00 ✋ €342–€425, excluding breakfast ❶ 105 rooms (19 non-smoking) ⬛ ⬛ ⬛ ⓐ Diagonal

CONDADO

www.condadohotel.com

This comfortable hotel in L'Eixample is close to the shopping streets of Rambla de Catalunya and Passeig de Gràcia. The public areas, decorated in whites and blues, are refreshing after a hard day's shopping. The guest rooms were stylishly refurbished in cool cream and beige tones in 2006. Facilities include safety deposit boxes, satellite TV and minibar, and some have balconies.

✚ 206 F6 ✉ Carrer d'Aribau 201, 08021 ☎ 93 200 23 11 ✋ €150–€252, excluding breakfast ❶ 60 (30 non–smoking) ⬛ ⓐ Diagonal

CONDESTABLE

www.hotelcondestable.com

The Condestable is a sensible choice for visitors on a modest budget. The rooms are comfortable and well equipped. They all have a private bathroom. There is a café, a laundry service and parking.

✚ 206 F8 ✉ Ronda de la Universitat 1, 08007 ☎ 93 318 62 68 ✋ €50–€100, excluding breakfast ❶ 78 ⬛ ⓐ Universitat

CONTINENTAL PALACETE

www.hotelpalacete.com

Enjoy the excellent service at this refurbished 19th-century palace, where you can dine in sumptuous surroundings. Traditional elegance combines with modern practicality in the guest rooms, some of which overlook Rambla de Catalunya. Room and laundry service, bar, internet access, car rental, money exchange and a free 24-hour light buffet are available.

✚ 206 F8 ✉ Rambla de Catalunya 30, 08007 ☎ 93 301 25 70 ✋ €137–€222, excluding breakfast ❶ 19 ⬛ ⓐ Passeig de Gràcia

GALLERY

www.galleryhotel.com

This hotel belongs to the Design Hotel Association, an international organization for hotels that care about contemporary design. The modern, spacious rooms are neutral with strong accented tones in the soft furnishings. All are equipped with TV, fax, soundproofed windows and minibar. The restaurant serves first-rate Mediterranean food and haute cuisine. Business rooms are also available. There is no pool, but there is a terrace with lounge chairs.

✚ 206 F6 ✉ Carrer del Rosselló 249, 08008 ☎ 93 415 99 11 ✋ €90–€270, excluding breakfast ❶ 115 (22 non-smoking) ⬛ ⬛ ⓐ Diagonal

GRAN HOTEL HAVANA

www.silken-granhavana.com

This hotel was built in 1872 and although two modern elements were added—a glass canopy and a round clock—the traditional elegance of the original facade was preserved. The foyer, with its beautiful lamps and atrium, is particularly impressive. Rooms have cable TV, radio, minibar and Italian marble bathrooms. The restaurant serves excellent paella and Catalan cuisine, and there's a blues night on the first Thursday of the month. Parking is available and pets are welcome. Free WiFi internet access is available.

✚ 206 G8 ✉ Gran Vía de les Corts Catalanes 647, 08010 ☎ 93 341 70 00 ✋ €120–€230, excluding breakfast ❶ 145 (50 non-smoking) ⬛ ⬛ ⓐ Girona

GRANADOS 83

www.derbyhotels.es

This L'Eixample hotel, part of the prestigious Derby group, is in a pretty, quiet street. The rooms (some with private balconies) are luxurious, with African zebrawood and leather furnishings, and original Buddhist and Hindu works of art hang on the walls. There's a fashionable terrace bar next to the rooftop pool and a chic restaurant.

✚ 206 F7 ✉ Carrer d'Enric Granados 83, 08008 ☎ 93 492 96 70 ✋ €100–€215 ❶ 77 ⬛ ⬛ Outdoor ⓐ Passeig de Gràcia

GRANVIA

www.hotelgranvia.com

This hotel is right at the heart of town, just around the corner from Plaça de Catalunya, in a 19th-century palace. It has retained some elements of the palace's splendour, including furniture and works of art from that period, and the wide, sweeping staircase with its elegant banister. It has three meeting rooms, business facilities and a terrace garden. Room facilities include satellite TV and internet access. Parking is also available.

✚ 206 G8 ✉ Gran Vía de les Corts Catalanes 642, 08011 ☎ 93 318 19 00

€60–€140, excluding breakfast ☝ 53

🚇 Urquinaona

HOSTAL CENTRAL

www.hostalcentralbarcelona.com

This *hostal* in the L'Eixample is set in a well-preserved art nouveau house, next to Plaça de Tetuan. The rooms are basic but clean and centrally heated, and most have bathrooms (but no TV). There is a theme of light, pastel shades that runs throughout the interior. Staff are friendly and attentive. Smoking is not allowed.

✚ 206 H8 ✉ Carrer de la Diputació 346, 08013 ☎ 93 245 19 81 🖑 €60–€85 ☝ 20 🚇 Girona

HOSTAL OLIVA

www.hostaloliva.com

This well-kept *hostal* was built in 1931, and it's one of the few to be found along the expensive Passeig de Gràcia. The old-fashioned lift, marbled floors and mirrors create a wonderful art nouveau atmosphere. There are only 16 rooms, all of which have TVs. Some have bathrooms and a few overlook the beautiful

buildings nearby. It's a great place if you're on your own, as the area is very safe; the only downside is the noise from the wooden floorboards. Credit cards are not accepted.

✚ 206 G8 ✉ Passeig de Gràcia 32, 08007 ☎ 93 488 01 62 🖑 €66–€85, excluding breakfast ☝ 16 🚇 Catalunya

HOTEL OMM

www.hotelomm.es

Hotel Omm matches a striking facade with a luxury interior and public areas and a classy rooftop pool and terrace. The rooms have ample cupboard space, generous bathrooms, cool colour schemes of steel grey, cream and blue and an abundance of natural light. Amenities include DVD, flat-screen TV and internet access. On the ground floor, the hip cocktail bar is always buzzing and at the rear is the super-trendy restaurant Moo (▷ 202). The plush spa and wellness centre offers every conceivable health and beauty treatment in immaculate designer surroundings. For late-nighters there's the

upmarket basement nightclub. The bedrooms are all non-smoking, but there is a smoking area.

✚ 206 G6 ✉ Carrer del Rosselló 265, 08008 ☎ 93 445 40 00 🖑 €225–€315, excluding breakfast ☝ 59 (non-smoking) 📺 🚇 🏊 Outdoor 🚇 Diagonal

MAJESTIC

www.hotelmajestic.es

The Majestic dates from the early 20th century and it lives up to its name in every way. Run by the Soldevila Casals family for the past three generations, it's the epitome of quality service and hospitality. Every room has been carefully designed and has internet access and a PC connection. There's a fabulous restaurant, buffet and two bars, plus you can also enjoy a massage or use the health facilities, including sauna and steam room.

✚ 206 G7 ✉ Passeig de Gràcia 68, 08007 ☎ 93 488 17 17 🖑 €139–€499, excluding breakfast ☝ 301 (7 floors non-smoking) 🚇 🏊 Outdoor 📺 🚇 Passeig de Gràcia

Below *Five-star luxury with art nouveau style*

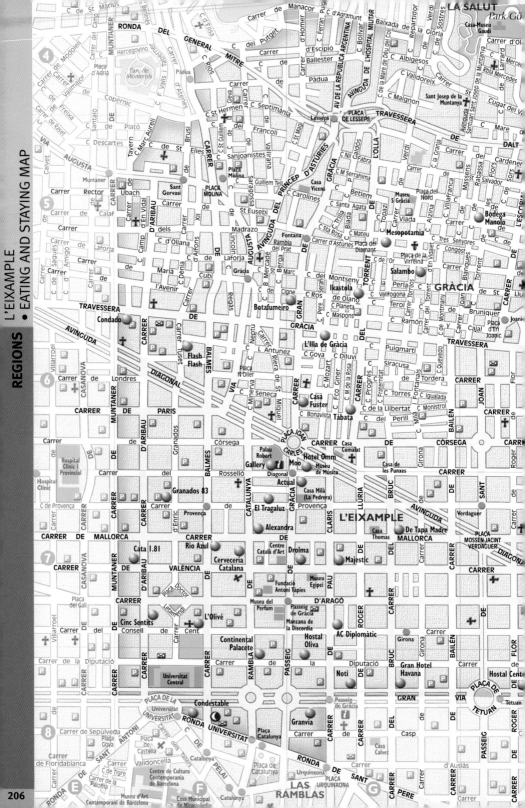

LA SALUT

Park Gü

Casa-Museu
Gaudí

GRÀCIA

L'EIXAMPLE

LAS
RAMBLAS

EXCURSIONS

A number of the city's most delightful attractions (▷ 218–219) are dotted around the edge of Barcelona. These include little-known delights like the labyrinth in Horta, which is surrounded by romantic baroque gardens with fountains and grottoes. Much better known is the amusement park—one of the oldest in Spain—which sits high on the hill of Tibidabo and enjoys incredible views over the entire city and out to sea.

Barcelona is perfectly placed for excursions, and public transport from the Catalan capital is generally very good. One of the most popular day trips from the city is to Montserrat, an immense monastery in a spectacular mountain setting reached by cable car or funicular railway, where the Black Madonna attracts thousands of pilgrims annually, and the magnificent mountain scenery entices walkers and birdwatchers. On the coast, the stylish seaside resort of Sitges has a pretty whitewashed old centre, a pink baroque church, and endless golden strands which are crammed in summer. Farther afield, there are more spectacular cliffs and beaches along the celebrated Costa Brava, where brash resorts alternate with perfectly preserved medieval villages and stunning bays. Inland, the ancient city of Girona has barely changed in centuries, and its cool stone alleys and passages are deeply atmospheric. The otherwise sleepy market town of Figueres is dominated by the eye-popping works of arch-Surrealist Salvador Dalí, gathered together in an astonishing museum topped with huge egg-shaped sculptures. Heading south of Barcelona, you can explore the wine country around Penedès, particularly beautiful in late summer, when the ripening vines snake across the hills. There are numerous *bodegas* to visit, offering guests the opportunity to try the wonderful range of local wines—reds, white and the champagne-like cavas.

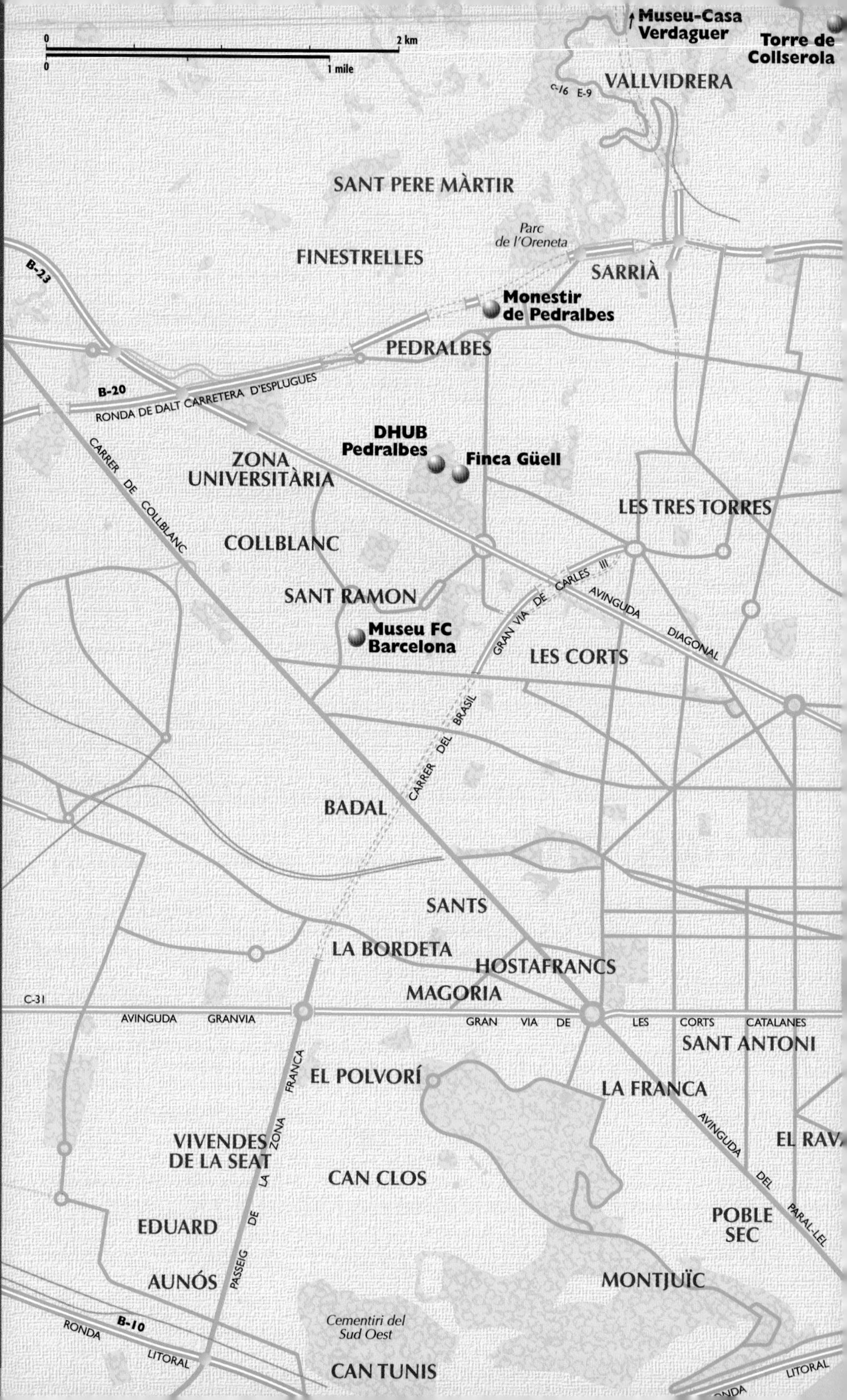

Museu-Casa
Verdaguer

Torre de
Collserola

VALLVIDRERA

C-16 E-9

SANT PERE MÀRTIR

Parc
de l'Oreneta

FINESTRELLES

SARRIÀ

B-23

Monestir
de Pedralbes

PEDRALBES

B-20

RONDA DE DALT CARRETERA D'ESPLUGUES

DHUB
Pedralbes

Finca Güell

CARRER DE COLLBLANC

ZONA
UNIVERSITÀRIA

LES TRES TORRES

COLLBLANC

SANT RAMON

Museu FC
Barcelona

GRAN VIA DE CARLES III

AVINGUDA

DIAGONAL

LES CORTS

CARRER DEL BRASIL

BADAL

SANTS

LA BORDETA

HOSTAFRANCS

MAGORIA

C-31

AVINGUDA   GRANVIA

GRAN   VIA   DE   LES   CORTS   CATALANES

SANT ANTONI

EL POLVORÍ

LA FRANCA

EL RAV

PASSEIG DE LA ZONA FRANCA

VIVENDES
DE LA SEAT

CAN CLOS

AVINGUDA   DEL   PARAL·LEL

POBLE
SEC

EDUARD

AUNÓS

MONTJUÏC

RONDA

B-10

LITORAL

Cementiri del
Sud Oest

CAN TUNIS

RONDA

LITORAL

2 km

1 mile

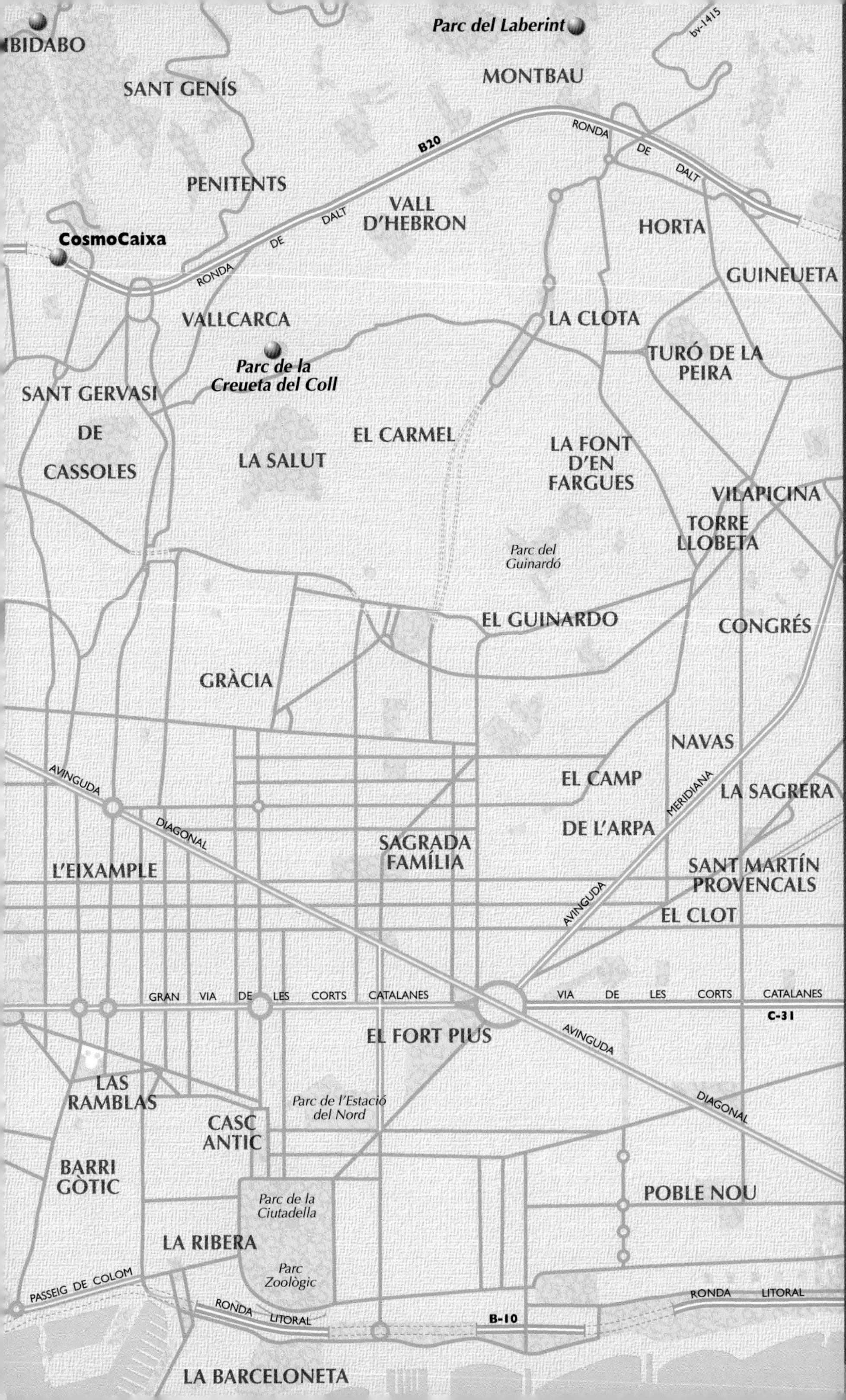

TIBIDABO

SANT GENÍS

MONTBAU

Parc del Laberint

bv-1415

B20

RONDA DE DALT

RONDA DE DALT

PENITENTS

VALL D'HEBRON

HORTA

CosmoCaixa

RONDA DE DALT

GUINEUETA

VALLCARCA

LA CLOTA

TURÓ DE LA PEIRA

Parc de la Creueta del Coll

SANT GERVASI

DE

CASSOLES

LA SALUT

EL CARMEL

LA FONT D'EN FARGUES

VILAPICINA

TORRE LLOBETA

Parc del Guinardó

EL GUINARDO

CONGRÉS

GRÀCIA

NAVAS

AVINGUDA

DIAGONAL

EL CAMP

DE L'ARPA

MERIDIANA

LA SAGRERA

L'EIXAMPLE

SAGRADA FAMÍLIA

AVINGUDA

SANT MARTÍN PROVENCALS

EL CLOT

GRAN VIA DE LES CORTS CATALANES

VIA DE LES CORTS CATALANES

C-31

EL FORT PIUS

AVINGUDA

DIAGONAL

LAS RAMBLAS

Parc de l'Estació del Nord

CASC ANTIC

BARRI GÒTIC

POBLE NOU

Parc de la Ciutadella

LA RIBERA

Parc Zoològic

PASSEIG DE COLOM

RONDA LITORAL

RONDA LITORAL

B-10

LA BARCELONETA

INTRODUCTION

This magnificent stretch of coastline was dubbed the Costa Brava (meaning 'wild coast') by a Catalan journalist in the early 20th century. Although no longer the rural idyll that it was back then, these rocky cliffs and turquoise bays, fishing ports and medieval villages remain extraordinarily enticing. The Costa Brava stretches for 200km (125 miles) from the tourist resort of Blanes all the way to the French border. The southern reaches of this coastline are most easily accessible from Barcelona, but it is the dramatic and unspoiled wilderness of the northern Costa Brava which has the most powerful pull.

WHAT TO SEE

THE MAIN RESORTS

Blanes and Lloret de Mar are the two biggest resorts on the southern Costa Brava, both popular with package tourists, and both blessed with spectacular sandy beaches. Neighbouring Tossa de Mar is a little more upmarket, with a charming old quarter on the clifftop. Sant Feliu de Guíxols has a sprinkling of Modernista mansions, while Platja d'Aro is a large, modern resort with long, family-friendly beaches. Palamós is one of the last towns to preserve a commercial fishing fleet and is famous for its plump, red prawns.

The next stretch of coast, from Palafrugell to L'Estartit, is utterly spellbinding, particularly around Calella and Llafranc: tiny coves, picturesque villages, cliffs swathed in Mediterranean pine, and a stunning cliff walk out to a lighthouse.

North of L'Estartit is L'Escala, a mellow resort popular with Catalan families, and beyond it stretches the wide Gulf of Roses. Extensive wetlands, the Parc Natural dels Aiguamolls de l'Empordà, are an important refuge for wild birds. Beyond them is the big resort of Roses, with more fine beaches. This is the gateway to the spectacular Cap de Creus (▷ 214), a starkly beautiful headland which culminates in the whitewashed fishing village of Cadaqués.

INLAND VILLAGES

Just inland from the Costa Brava are several immaculate villages, with carefully preserved historic centres. The most famous are the fortified villages of Pals and Begur, popular with wealthy second-homers from Girona and Barcelona. Peratallada is famous for its ceramics, and, around Easter in Verges,

INFORMATION

www.costabrava.org
Tourist Information
Blanes
www.visitblanes.net
🛈 Passeig Catalunya 2 ☎ 972 33 03 48
Cadaqués
www.visitcadaques.org
🛈 Carrer Cotxe 1 ☎ 972 25 83 15
Tossa de Mar
www.infotossa.com
🛈 Avinguda del Pelegrí 25, Edifici La Nau ☎ 972 34 01 08

HOW TO GET THERE

By train: Trains leave regularly from Sants and Plaça Catalunya for Blanes (1 hr 15 min), and from Sants and Passeig de Gràcia for Girona (1hr 18 min–1hr 44 min). Buses link Blanes and Girona with other towns along the Costa Brava.
By car: The C32 runs north along the coastline from Barcelona to Blanes. From here, a small, panoramic and very slow coast road, the GI682, runs north to Sant Feliu de Guíxols. For the northern reaches of the Costa Brava, it is usually faster to take the AP7-E15 motorway (toll).
By bus: Buses leave regularly from Estació del Nord for the Costa Brava. The main operator is Sarfa (www.sarfa.es).

Above *Rock formations at Cap de Creus*
Opposite *Picturesque Llafranc*

WHERE TO EAT
RESTAURANT CAP DE CREUS

This restaurant is spectacularly set on the easternmost tip of the Cap de Creus, reached via a narrow track from Portlligat. The menu features fresh fish and other Mediterrean fare, as well as excellent (if unexpected) Indian curries. Although it's usually open daily, call ahead to confirm. It's also a good spot for an evening drink.

✉ 17488 Cadaqués ☎ 97 219 90 05 🕐 Daily 10am–12am

RESTAURANT MARÍTIM

Superb seafood in a stylish setting makes this the best choice in Tossa de Mar. There's a pavement terrace with sea views, and the food combines classic Catalan recipes with plenty of contemporary flair. Go for the excellent *menú del degustació* (€40 per person).

✉ San Raimondo de Penyafort, Tossa de Mar ☎ 97 234 08 32 🕐 Daily 1–4, 8–11. Closed Nov–Feb

TIPS

» Although it is possible to reach the main towns and resorts by public transport, to find the quietest coves and beaches you will need your own car.
» Avoid August if possible: the entire Costa Brava is crammed with holidaymakers. June and September are the ideal months to visit.
» In winter, call in advance before making a special trip to a restaurant or museum. Many are closed during the winter, or operate erratic opening hours.

the townsmen still perform the Dance of the Dead just as they have since medieval times. In Ullastret, the vestiges of an ancient Iberian village have been discovered on the fringes of town.

EMPÚRIES

The ruins of ancient Empúries (tel 97 277 02 08; Jun–end Sep daily 10–8; Oct–end May daily 10–6; adult €3, child under 16 free) enjoy a beautiful setting on the shores of the Mediterranean. Founded in the sixth century BC, Empúries was the first and most important Greek colony on the Iberian peninsula. It was located on important trade routes and continued to thrive after the arrival of the Romans, who took the city in 218BC in the first step of their conqest of Hispania. Although many of the finest artefacts discovered here have been taken to Barcelona's archaeology museum (▷ 67), the superb Greek statue of Asclepius (Esculapi in Catalan), the finest in Spain, was recently returned here after major restoration.

CAP DE CREUS

The Pyrenees meet the sea at Cap de Creus, a craggy headland endowed with a savage beauty. There are few roads, and even fewer settlements, but this wild region has enchanted visitors from Picasso, who was seduced by the light, to Dalí, who built a home at Portlligat (tel 97 225 10 15; www.salvador-dali.org; 15 Jun–15 Sep daily 9.30–9; 9 Feb–14 Jun, 16 Sep–6 Jan Tue–Sun 10.30–6; adult €10, child 9–18 €8, under 9 free). The headland and the coastal waters are now a protected natural park, which offers excellent opportunities for hiking (including a section of the trans-Pyrenean walking path, the GR11), diving, snorkelling and sailing.

Right *The pretty fishing village of Cadaqués sits at the edge of Cap de Creus at the head of a bay*

COSMOCAIXA

After a major overhaul, the old Science Museum in Barcelona was reopened at the end of 2004, renamed CosmoCaixa—a multimedia extravaganza encompassing all the scientific disciplines. The museum is spread out over a massive 47,500sq m (500,000sq feet), with the exhibition spaces underground in a daring structure by local architects Esteve and Robert Terrades.

SALA DE LA MATÈRIA

A glass spiral walkway takes you down to the Sala de la Matèria—the museum's permanent collection. The fundamental laws of material, energy, waves and light, and the origins of the Earth and civilization are explained here, through 64 interactive models and games, both didactic and fun for young and old. All exhibits have explanations and instructions in English.

Some of the more spectacular exhibits are: an enormous Foucault's Pendulum, an extensive collection of fossils and artefacts, and plenty of bugs and insects behind glass. The museum has even managed to make rocks look appealing with an awesome 'Geology Wall'. Occupying an entire side of the massive hall, mighty examples of chalk, marble, volcanic and glacial rocks and stone are mounted from a dramatic height.

At the opposite end of the hall is the exotic 'Sunken Forest'—an Amazonian rainforest with more than 80 species of plant and tree and 50 species of animal life, allowing close encounters with the fish that dwell in the artificial pond and lizards, frogs, turtles and other Amazonian creatures living among the lush flora.

OTHER EXHIBITS

Under a futuristic dome, the Planetarium's child-friendly programme is divided into three parts: 'Genesis' (the history of the universe), 'Far-Off Galaxies' and 'The Blind Man with Stars in his Eyes' (or astronomy for kids).

Toca, Toca (or Touch, Touch!) is by far the most popular exhibit for the very young, inviting close (but supervised) contact with baby tortoises, lizards and even snakes in their natural habitat.

Click i Flash has been designed specially for children and conceived as their first introduction to the world of science. The Click section (for 3–6 year olds) allows them to contemplate light and perceptions of speed, force and balance, and the Flash section contains touchy-feely games and contraptions.

PLAZA DE LA CIENCIA

The exhibits continue outside the main building in the huge plaza. Take time to examine the Sun Dial, the 'Litofones' (musical rocks) and the 'Telescope of Sound'—two parabolic discs that allow two people to 'whisper' to each other from 40m (44 yards) away.

INFORMATION

www.cosmocaixa.com

✉ Carrer Teodor Roviralta 47–51, 08022 Barcelona ☎ 93 212 60 50 🕐 Tue–Sun 10–8 💶 Adult €3, child (under 8) free, child (8–16) €2, activities €1.50; planetarium and supervised activities, adult €2. Free first Sun of the month
🚇 FGC Avinguda del Tibidabo 🚌 17, 22, 58, 60, 73, 75 📷 Tue–Fri 11am and Sat, Sun 4pm. Cost: €2. No audiotours
🅿 In outside square 📚 Books and educational toys

TIPS

» Go in the afternoon to avoid school groups and ensure access to special exhibitions such as the Planetarium.
» You are only ensured entry to the permanent collection (Sala de la Matèria). Book for other exhibits, such as the Planetarium, Toca, Toca (animal nursery) and Click i Flash, on arrival, for an extra fee (generally €2).
» The hike up to the museum, as well as its sheer size, make for an exhausting day, so take breaks in the garden areas outside the museum.

Above *Foucault's Pendulum, one of the fascinating exhibits at CosmoCaixa*

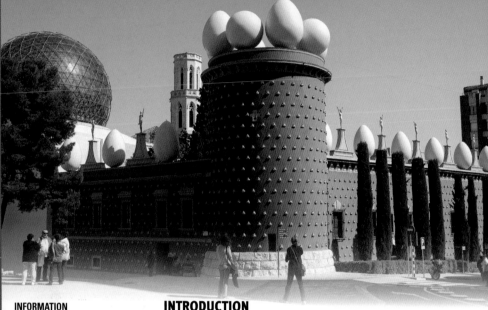

INFORMATION

www.figueres.cat

Tourist Information

🛈 Plaça del Sol s/n, 17600 Figueres

☎ 97 250 31 55

HOW TO GET THERE

By train: Trains leave regularly from Sants and the Passeig de Gràcia (1hr 39 min–2hr 23 min).

By car: Take the AP7/E15 motorway (toll) north from Barcelona for about 140km (87 miles): exit 4 for Figueres.

By bus: Regular buses leave from the Estació del Nord.

Above *Giant eggs line the roof edge of Dalí's Surrealist museum*

Opposite left *Museu del Joguet is a must for people who love toys*

Opposite right *One of the corner turrets of Castell de Sant Ferran*

INTRODUCTION

Salvador Dalí, the celebrated painter and arch-proponent of Surrealism, was born in Figueres in 1904 and maintained a strong connection with the city throughout his life. The Teatre-Museu Dalí remains the biggest reason for visiting Figueres, but, if you've got an hour or two to spare, there are a clutch of engaging smaller attractions. The bizarre museum dedicated to Dalí's works, topped with giant egg sculptures, dominates the small historic centre, where a tree-lined Rambla and a handful of small squares are scattered with terrace cafés. On the edge of the city is the gigantic, star-shaped fortress, the Castell de Sant Ferran.

WHAT TO SEE

TEATRE-MUSEU DALÍ

www.salvador-dali.org

In the early 1960s, Salvador Dalí purchased the ruins of the city's municipal theatre (badly bombed in the Civil War) in order to create a suitably surreal setting for a museum devoted to his works. The enormous theatre was completely rebuilt according to Dalí's wildly eccentric plans, and the building, which is crowned by a huge geodesic dome, is considered the largest Surreal object in the world. The museum contains a vast collection of Dalí's work spanning several decades, and has become one of the most popular attractions in Spain. Inside, there are surprises around every corner: whisk back a velvet curtain to reveal the skeleton of a fish, or climb a ladder to view a room morph into the features of Mae West. In the central patio, a diva warbles from the bonnet of a vintage Cadillac. Among the paintings, *Galarina* (1945), *Portrait of Pablo Picasso in the 21st Century* (1947), *Galatea of the Spheres* (1952) and *Christ of the Tramuntana* (1968) stand out. Dalí also donated a number of paintings from his eclectic private collection, with a wide variety of works by El Greco, Marcel Duchamp and Maria Fortuny among others.

The artist, who died in 1989, is buried in a plain crypt beneath the museum. One section of the museum (with a separate entrance and admission charge) contains a permanent exhibition of jewels designed by Dalí, which are displayed along with his paintings of them. There are 39 jewels on display, each unique, and all made with the finest metals and precious stones. They were made between 1941 and 1970, and finally acquired by the Salvador Dalí Foundation in 1999. Look for the breathtaking necklace, *The Tree of Life* (1949), an intricate swirl of gold studded with diamonds and sapphires.

✉ Plaça Gala Salvador-Dalí 5, Figueres ☎ 97 267 75 00 🕐 Jul–end Sep daily 9–8; Jun daily 9.30–6; Mar–end May, Oct Tue–Sun 9.30–6; Nov–end Feb Tue–Sun 10.30–6 ✋ Adult €11, child (9–16) €8, under 9 free 🖼

OTHER MUSEUMS

The Museu del Joguet (Carrer Sant Pere 1, tel 97 250 45 85; www.mjc.cat; Jun–end Sep Mon–Sat 10–7, Sun and public hols 11–6; Oct–end May Mon–Sat 10–6, Sun and public hols 11–2; €5) contains a huge collection of toys, with everything from century-old train sets to teddy bears and dolls. Many of the exhibits once belonged to celebrities such as the artists Salvador Dalí and Joan Miró, or the writers Federico García Lorca and Quim Monza. The Museu del Empordà (Rambla 2, tel 97 250 23 05; May–end Oct Tue–Sat 11–8, Sun 11–2; Nov–end Apr Tue–Sat 11–7, Sun 11–2; €2) offers an introduction to this region of northern Catalonia, with exhibits on the history, geology and geography of the area, plus a small collection of paintings. The paintings include works by outstanding Catalan artists such as Isidre Nonell, Joaquim Mir, Joaquim Sunyer, Pau Gargallo, Modest Cuixart and Antoni Tàpies. The archaeological collection is fascinating and contains finds from the numerous megalithic burial sites found in the Figueres region. The newest museum is the Museu Tècnica de l'Empordà (Carrer dels Fossos 2, tel 97 250 88 20; Tue–Fri 10–7, Sat 10–1, 4–7, Sun 11–2; €3), which displays antique cars and other mechanical devices.

CASTELL DE SANT FERRAN

This star-shaped fortress was begun in 1753, and is the largest historic monument in Catalunya. Spain had been forced to cede much of northern Catalonia to the French by the Treaty of the Pyrenees (1659) and this fortress was conceived (somewhat belatedly) in order to strengthen the new national border. The scale is staggering: the perimeter is more than 3km (2 miles) long, and the fortress could accommodate 6,000 troops and 500 horses.

✉ Pujada del Castell ☎ 97 250 60 94 🕐 Apr–end Sep daily 10.30–8; Oct–end Mar 10.30–3 ✋ Adult €3

TIPS

» Dalí fans may want to visit the three main Dalí-related sights, which have been dubbed the Dalí Triangle. This comprises the museum in Figueres, the castle Dalí, built for his muse Gala in Púbol; and the home they shared in Portlligat (▷ 214). See the website: www.salvador-dali.org for full details.

» The Teatre-Museu Dalí offers special night visits in August. Tickets include a glass of cava and film screenings on the interior patio.

WHERE TO EAT
MESÓN CASTELL

Tuck into the tapas at the bar or eat a full meal in the dining room at this traditional *asador* near the castle. It is well known for its roast meat and fish dishes, and the set menu on weekday lunchtimes is good value.

✉ Pujada del Castell, 17600 Figueres ☎ 97 251 01 04 🕐 Daily 12–11 ✋ L and D €30, Wine €10

EL CAFÉ DEL BARRI VELL

This sweet little café has a terrace on a small square in the old town. Changing exhibitions and live music give it an arty feel. The menu features light snacks and vegetarian options.

✉ Plaça Patates, 17600 Figueres ☎ 97 250 57 76 🕐 Jun–end Sep Tue–Sun 6pm–1am; Oct–end May Tue–Sun 12–12 ✋ L and D €10, Wine €8

DHUB PEDRALBES

www.museuceramica.bcn.es

www.museuartsdecoratives.bcn.es

The handsome Palau in the Parc de Pedralbes, landscaped gardens that once belonged to the Finca Güell next door, was built in 1924 as a residence for the royal family. Today it houses three museums; the Museu de Ceràmica, the Museu de les Arts Decoratives and the Museu Tèxtil i Indumentaria. The Ceramics Museum's collection stretches from the 11th century to the present day. Medieval, Arabic-influenced Mudéjar, plus other elaborate baroque and Renaissance pieces are among the highlights. One-off pieces from artists like Picasso and Miró take pride of place. The Decorative Arts Museum is smaller and falls short of covering Catalonia's important design heritage. The Modernisme glassware section is the highpoint of the collection of objects and furniture from the Middle Ages to the present day.

✉ Avinguda Diagonal 686, 08034 Barcelona ☎ 93 280 50 24 🕓 Tue–Sat 10–6, Sun 10–3 ✋ Adult €3.50, child (under 16) free; first Sun of every month free to all (entry is to both museums and Museu Tèxtil) 🚇 Palau Reial 🚌 7, 33, 63, 67, 68, 74, 75, 78 ♿

FIGUERES AND THE DALÍ MUSEUM

▷ 216–217.

FINCA GÜELL

www.rutadelmodernisme.com

The design of elements of the Finca Güell (Güell estate) was the first of many commissions Gaudí received from Eusebi Güell. Gaudí was put in charge of the gatehouses (pavellons), the coach house, a fountain and the main gate, the latter being the most dramatic element of the project. The hissing dragon jumps out at you from this spectacular example of wrought-iron design. The work was carried out by a local smith but the image is purely Gaudían, and dragons and lizards were to make regular appearances in his later work. This beast comes from the epic Catalan poem L'Atlàntida by Jacint Verdaguer

(see below) and is a reference to the voyage of Hercules and his battle with the dragon to enter the Garden of the Hesperides, a metaphor for the citrus gardens of the estate.

The mosaic-covered pavilions with their exotic turrets held the gatekeeper's lodge and the coach house. The latter is now the Reial Càtedra Gaudí, a place for study and research about the man and his work. Only the library is open to the public, but you get a good view of all the buildings from the gate, which is the highlight of the finca.

✉ Avinguda de Pedralbes 7, 08034 Barcelona ☎ 90 207 621, 93 317 76 52 🕓 Guided visits usually Fri–Mon 10.15 and 12.15 in English; 11.15 in Castilian Spanish and 1.15 in Catalan. Times can vary ✋ Adult €6, child (under 16) €2.50 🚇 Palau Reial 🚌 7, 63, 67, 68, 74, 75

GIRONA

▷ 220–221.

MONESTIR DE PEDRALBES

▷ 222–223.

MONTSERRAT

▷ 224–225.

MUSEU-CASA VERDAGUER

www.museuhistoria.bcn.es

This 18th-century house, in the middle of the Sierra de Collserola, was where Jacint Verdaguer (1845–1902) spent his last days. He was Catalonia's most famous poet and a key figure of the renaissance of Catalan culture known as the Renaixença. His last 24 days were spent here before his death on 10 June. Already a literary hero, Verdaguer's passing deeply moved the emerging Catalan nation and thousands attended his funeral. The exhibition shows the personal objects and some original writings of this man of letters, and the rooms have been preserved as they were before his death. Many of the explanations are only available in Catalan, so you would be wise to read up on the poet's life and heritage before you go, or take one of the special tours that explain

the contents of the house and surrounding countryside in relation to the writer's work.

✉ Vil.la Joana, Carretera de 'Església 104, 08017 Barcelona ☎ 93 204 78 05 🕓 Tue–Fri for groups by appointment only; Sat–Sun and public hols 10–2, no appointment needed ✋ Free 🚇 Baixador de Vallvidrera ♿ Free ♿

MUSEU FC BARCELONA

www.fcbarcelona.com

The city's soccer club is an obsession for many and its motto més que un club (more than a club) bears this out. Despite a seating capacity of nearly 100,000, tickets for important games are very hard to come by. The next best thing is to visit the museum, which offers tours of the empty stadium. The plush exhibition space has a three-part collection: El Museu Històric tells the history of the club through posters, photographs, trophies and other memorabilia; El Fons d'Art displays works by such artists as Dalí and Miró; and there is the world's largest collection of objects and curios from the 19th century to the present day all relating to the beautiful game. A new, second-floor space is dedicated to interactive exhibits. A treat for soccer fans is the tour of the chapel, the tunnel, the field and the press and club rooms. Architects Foster and Partners have been commissioned to remodel and enlarge the stadium. It is hoped that construction won't affect visitor access.

✉ Carrer d'Aristide Maillol, entrance 7 or 9, 08028 Barcelona ☎ 90 218 99 00 🕓 Apr–end Oct Mon–Sat 10–8, Sun 10–2.30; Nov–end Mar 10–6.30, Sun 10–2.30. Restricted hours on match days ✋ Museum and stadium: adult €17, child (under 13) €14. Museum only: adult €7.50, child (under 13) €6 🚇 Collblanc 🚌 15, 52, 53, 54, 56, 57, 75 ♿ Guided tours of the stadium during museum hours (last tour one hour before closing) ♿ ♿

PARC DE LA CREUETA DEL COLL

www.bcn.cat/parcsijardins

Perhaps only in Barcelona would you find an abandoned stone quarry turned into a park by the design team that rebuilt the waterfront for the 1992 Olympics. And perhaps only in this design-conscious city would it be complete with a swimming pool and a work by the country's most eminent sculptors. The shallow artificial lake, used as the pool, and the *Elogio del Agua*, a huge work of oxidized metal by Basque sculptor Eduardo Chillida (1924–2002), are typical of the sort of imaginative design Barcelona is renowned for in the creation of its public spaces. Summer is the best time to visit, when the local children are splashing around in the lake. At other times, try to go just before the sun sets, and enjoy the serenity of this truly unique oasis.

✉ Carrer de Castellterçol 24, 08023 Barcelona 🕐 Daily 10–dusk 🖐 Free 🚇 Penitents 🚌 25, 28, 87 ▣

PARC DEL LABERINT

www.bcn.cat/parcsijardins

The park is the oldest in the city and gets its name from the maze at its heart. Cultivated in the 18th century and fully restored 200 years later when it was acquired by the local council, it is laid out over three levels in 9ha (22 acres), with swooping terraces in the style of grand Italian gardens such as Rome's Villa Borghese. On the upper terrace there is an elegant pond that acts as the park's watering system and the lower terrace holds the small cypress labyrinth, the park's main attraction. The foliage itself is less formal, consisting mainly of natural pine forest, and the garden is replete with nooks and crannies, statues, Italianate balustrades and pagodas, making it one of the more private—and therefore romantic— parks in the city. Families have a great time here too, as children love the maze and there are a couple of play areas, allowing the adults the opportunity to sit back and breathe in the pine-scented air.

✉ Passeig dels Castanyers s/n, 08035 Barcelona 🕐 93 428 39 34 🕐 Daily 10–dusk 🖐 Adult €2, child (under 6) free; Wed and Sun free to all 🚇 Mundet 🚌 27, 60, 73, 76, 85

THE PENEDÈS REGION

▷ 226–227.

SITGES

▷ 228–229.

TARRAGONA

▷ 230–231.

TIBIDABO

www.tibidabo.es

Tibidabo is the highest point of the Collserola hills. At night, the church, the Sagrado Corazón, and the statue of Christ by Frederic Marès (1893–1991) are lit up. Most people, however, wind up its steep ascent for more earthly pleasures. The Parc d'Atraccions amusement park has spectacular views. Some of its rides and attractions date back to the early 20th century and one of the oldest is the charming L'Avio, a replica of the first plane that flew the Barcelona–Madrid route. More hair-raising fun is to be had from the Krüeger Hotel and the roller coaster. The journey to Tibidabo is part of the attraction—the 100-year-old Tramvia Blau (blue tram) rattles up from the train station to the beginning of the summit, and from there you make the rest of the trip in a funicular.

✉ Plaça del Tibidabo, 08035 Barcelona 🕐 93 211 79 42 🕐 Jul–end Aug Mon–Thu 12–10, Fri–Sun 12–11; Jun, Sep Mon–Fri 12–8, Sat–Sun 12–9; Mar–end May, Oct Sat–Sun 12–7; Nov–end Feb Sat–Sun 12–6 🖐 Adult €25, child under 120cm (47 inches) €9. Admission to Camí del Cel (which includes entry to a limited number of attractions): adult €11, child under 120cm (47 inches) €7 🚇 FGC to Peu de Funicular, then funicular; bus or FGC to Avenida Tibidabo, then Tramvia Blau, then funicular (only operates on opening days of fun park). The Tibibus runs from Plaça Catalunya directly to the Parc d'Atraccions (€2.60; the price is refunded with the purchase of admission tickets to the Parc d'Atraccions) 🚌 17, 60, 73, T2 🍴

TORRE DE COLLSEROLA

www.tibidabo.es

The British architect Sir Norman Foster has left his mark on Barcelona in the form of a telecommunications tower, which stands at 288m (945ft), on the Collserola hills, 488m (1600ft) above sea level. The main attraction of the tower *(torre)* lies in the *mirador*, the lookout point that has fantastic views of the city, Montserrat and, on a clear day, the Pyrenees. The space-age glass lift whisks you up to the top in less than two minutes, leaving you free to contemplate the 360-degree vista.

The Collserola National Park is a rambling 8,000ha (19,760 acres) of Mediterranean forest abundant in bird- and wildlife. Its easy walking and bicycle tracks make it a top Sunday destination for those looking for an alternative to the beach. The best way to take your bicycle up to Collserola is by train, hopping off at Baixador de Vallvidrera where there is an information office. Some of the picnic areas have barbecues to rent.

✉ Carretera de Vallvidrera al Tibidabo s/n, 08017 Barcelona 🕐 93 211 79 42 🕐 Wed–Sun 11–2, 3–dusk 🖐 Adult €5, child (7–14) €4, child (under 7) free 🚇 FGC to Peu de Funicular, then funicular de Vallvidrera, then No. 111 bus (in summer a little tram makes the link) ▣

Below *Torre de Collserola and Tibidabo*

INFORMATION

www.girona.cat/turisme

Tourist Information

ℹ Rambla de la Libertat 1, 17004

☎ 972 22 65 75 🕐 Mon–Fri 8–8, Sat 8–2, 4–8, Sun 9–2

HOW TO GET THERE

By train: Trains leave regularly from Sants and from Passeig de Gràcia, taking one hour.

By car: Take the A7 at Ronda Litoral, head north via A7 or the N-11.

By bus: Buses leave regularly from Estació del Nord.

Above *The cathedral stands amid ancient buildings on the banks of the Onyar River*

INTRODUCTION

Catalonia's second city has inherited a mix of styles from its many inhabitants. Often called a miniature Venice, it's a striking place to come and soak up history and culture, not to mention really fine dining with a riverside setting.

Girona is a prosperous city with a high standard of living. Its compact old quarter, with wonderful examples of Gothic and Romanesque churches and monasteries, the remains of a fascinating Jewish quarter and excellent local gastronomy make it a great place for a day trip or a long weekend. The original Roman walls that surround the city have remained remarkably intact given the regular sieges the town suffered over the centuries. As you wander around the top of the walls, views of the lush green countryside—nourished by a higher-than-average rainfall—are guaranteed, as are glimpses of the Onyar River, which runs through the city.

WHAT TO SEE

THE CATHEDRAL

The cathedral (Apr–end Oct Mon–Sat 10–8, Sun 10–2; Nov–end Mar Mon–Sat 10–7, Sun 10–2) stands on top of a hill that looks down over the winding streets of the old quarter, with a grand, 90-step stairway sweeping up to the entrance. The architecture is a mixture of styles, predominantly from the Gothic period with 18th-century touches. Its nave, an incredible feat of engineering, is the widest in Europe. The serene cloister is another highlight, where the capitals of its pillars depict biblical scenes and everyday life and legends. Pay the small entrance fee into the Chapter House, which contains the Museu Capitular and the cathedral's Treasury. By far the best item of this collection of religious objects is the breathtaking 12th-century *Tapestry of Creation*. It was probably originally double the size of the fragment on show. Its figures and icons represent chapters from the book of Genesis laid out in a circular design.

THE CALL

At the base of the cathedral lies the Call, the remains of the Jewish quarter. The Jewish community left an indelible mark on Girona's culture, from the end of the ninth century—when many emigrated here after the destruction of Jerusalem—to the late 1400s, when they were evicted from Spain by order of the Catholic King Ferdinand and Queen Isabella. Life for the Jewish people was hard and the area had turned into a ghetto by the beginning of the 15th century. In the heart of the quarter, the excellent Centre Bonastruc Ça Porta (Jul–end

Aug Mon–Sat 10–8, Sun 10–2; Sep–end Jun Mon 10–2, Tue–Sat 10–6, Sun 10–2) recreates what life was like for the Jewish people here through art exhibits, musical events, recitals and food tastings. The site was formerly a synagogue, and the complex also houses the Institute for Sephardic and Kabalistic Studies and the Catalan Museum of Jewish Culture. Don't miss the library as it has an important collection of medieval Jewish manuscripts.

Muslims also settled in Girona and the most vivid evidence of this is at the 12th-century Arabic Bathhouse (Banys Àrabs; Apr–end Sep Tue–Sat 10–7, Sun 10–2; Oct–end Mar Tue–Sun 10–2), a short walk from the Call. Found in one of the most atmospheric pockets of the old city, where vegetation seeps through the golden granite of the medieval buildings, the bathhouse is close to the Monastery of Sant Pere de Galligants and the church of Sant Nicolau, two fine examples of Romanesque architecture. The Museu d'Arqueologia (Jun–end Sep Tue–Sat 10.30–1.30, 4–7, Sun 10–2; Oct–end May Tue–Sat 10–2, 4–6, Sun 10–2) is in the monastery, with finds from the Palaeolithic to Visigothic periods discovered at digs in northern Catalonia. The cloister was once the old Jewish cemetery, as witnessed by the inscriptions in Hebrew.

MUSEUMS

Other museums include the Museu d'Història (Tue–Sat 10–2, 5–7, Sun 10–2) housed in an 18th-century Capuchin convent on Carrer de la Força, part of the old Roman city at an intersection with the Via Augusta. The area is dotted with antiques shops and workshops. The museum's collection has a mixture of exhibits from Catalonia's prehistoric times to the present day, and displays include Spain's first street lamps (which made their debut in Girona), tools, shields, dioramas and objects documenting life over the centuries.

The Museu d'Art (summer Tue–Sat 10–7, Sun 10–2; winter Tue–Sat 10–6, Sun 10–2) is also in the old quarter, in the beautifully restored Palau Episcopal. Most of the collection comes from the former Diocese Museum, including some 14th-century retables, baroque and Gothic tapestries, and items related to Catalonia's traditional dance, the *sardana*. A collection of paintings is on show from the renowned Olot School—19th-century landscape painters from the nearby town of the same name who were known for their use of light.

Lovers of more contemporary culture should visit the Museu del Cinema (Apr–end Sep Tue–Sun 10–8; Oct–end Mar Tue–Fri 10–6, Sat 10–8, Sun 11–3) near Plaça Independència. In 1994 the local council acquired one of the best cinematography collections in the world from local film-maker Tomàs Mallol (born 1923) and have created a hands-on experience. The exhibition takes you through ancient Chinese shadow puppetry to the arrival of commercial cinema through objects used in early film-making, footage and informative displays.

TIPS

» Leave the car behind—trains to Girona are fast and frequent from Barcelona.
» Stay for at least one meal as the restaurants in the old quarter are good on hearty local cuisine.
» To access the walls of the city, head for the Passeig Arqueològic, behind the Museu d'Arqueologia.

WHERE TO EAT
EL CELLER DE CAN ROCA

www.cellercanroca.com
Just outside the city centre is one of Spain's finest, multi-award-winning, restaurants. Reserve a table and be seduced by the Roca brothers and their avant-garde cuisine.
✉ Can Sunyer 48 ☎ 97 222 21 57
🕐 Tue–Sat 1–4, 9–11 🍴 L €70, D €100, Wine €20

BOIRA

Dine upstairs in the restaurant, with views over the river, or tuck into tapas out on the square at the bar below.
✉ Plaça Independència, 17001
☎ 97 222 29 33 🕐 Tue–Sun 1–4, 8–11 🍴 L €15, D €30, Wine €10

Below *Romanesque architecture is in evidence throughout Girona*

INFORMATION

✉ Baixada del Monestir 9, 08034
☎ 93 203 92 82 🕐 Apr–Sep Tue–Sat
10–5, Sun 10–8; Oct–Mar Tue–Sat
10–2, Sun 10–8 🖐 Adult €4, child
(under 16) free; admission allows free
entry to all seven sites run by MUHBA,
including Museu d'Història de Barcelona,
Casa-Museu Verdaguer, and Centre
d'Interpretació del Park Güell. Free first
Sun every month 🚇 Palau Reial 🚌 22,
63, 64, 75, 114 🚆 FGC Reina Elisenda,
then 10-minute walk 🎫 First Sun of the
month, in Spanish and Catalan, €2. No
audiotours ☕ Coffee, drink and snack
machines only

TIPS

» Look into the Gothic church next door,
used for prayer and song by the nuns,
before you leave. It is beautiful, to be
particularly enjoyed if you manage to find
the place near empty (closed 1–5).

» Large items, such as bags and
umbrellas, will need to be left at
reception to prevent damage to the
artworks.

Above *The tranquil three-tiered cloister
surrounds a herb garden*
Opposite *The 14th-century monastery
was home to the Order of St. Clare*

MONESTIR DE PEDRALBES

This well-preserved 14th-century stone monastery is a serene oasis in a busy
city. Barcelona's oldest surviving monastery is hidden away in the northern
district of Pedralbes, a wealthy suburb which still retains the feel of a country
town. It is one of the finest examples of Catalan Gothic architecture. The
collection of Old Masters that used to be housed here has now been moved to
the Museu Nacional d'Art de Catalunya (▷ 72–75), but an intriguing museum
of monastic life remains.

The monastery was founded in 1326 by Elisenda de Montcada, wife of
Jaume II of Aragón, for the nuns of the Order of St. Clare. Following the king's
death, Queen Elisenda retired to the convent and lived here until she died. A
small community of nuns still lives in the convent, but now resides in separate
modern quarters. The sounds of their vespers can often be heard filling the
street outside.

THE CLOISTER

The three-tiered Gothic cloister, with ornate well, herb garden and cypress,
palm and orange trees, exudes a sense of calm, helped by the gentle trickle of
the fountains. A few quiet moments here will give you a taste of the peaceful
life of the nuns. For the best views, stroll around the upper gallery, which
meanders its way around the building's exterior. Just off the cloisters are little
prayer cells, some of which contain original objects. The Pietat chamber has a
16th-century retable showing the Virgin Mary as a child.

CAPELLA DE SANT MIQUEL

The artistic highlight of the monastery is this magnificent chapel, which is
found off the cloister. It is vividly decorated with paintings by Ferrer Bassa,
a student of the Florentine painter Giotto, who is credited with introducing
the Italian-Gothic style to Catalonia. The murals, depicting scenes of Christ's
Passion on the upper level and the life of the Virgin Mary on the lower level,
were completed in 1346, two years before Bassa's death from the plague.

MONASTIC LIFE

A permanent exhibition depicts 14th-century monastic life through the original
infirmary, kitchen and refectory, where the Mother Superior would break
her vow of silence with Bible readings from the pulpit while the nuns ate in
silence around her. The chapter house includes the funeral urn of Sobirana de
Olzet, the first abbess. Descend into the basement, where a cell has intricate
dioramas of the life of Christ.

MONTSERRAT

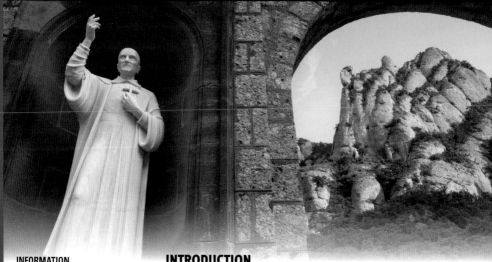

INFORMATION

www.abadiamontserrat.net

Tourist Information

ℹ️ Plaça de la Creu s/n ☎ 93 877 77 77

🕐 Daily 8.50–7.30

HOW TO GET THERE

By train: FGC train from the Plaça d'Espanya to Aeri de Montserrat, leaving every two hours, taking about one hour; then cable car or La Cremallera railway (check www.cremalleirademontserrat.com for times) to the monastery.

By car: Leave Barcelona by the B-20, take the A2 (exit Martorell), or the *autopista* Barcelona–Terrassa via the Valvidriera tunnels (exit Montserrat).

By bus: Julià Bus Company departs 9am from Plaça dels Països Catalans in Barcelona (beside Sants rail station), returns 6pm summer, 5pm winter.

Above *The peak of Montserrat viewed through an arch of the monastery*
Opposite left *The statue of La Moreneta, the Black Madonna, in the basilica*
Opposite right *The monastery nestles against the rocky mountain*

INTRODUCTION

Catalonia's spiritual heart, the immense monastery at Montserrat has a spectacularly rugged mountain setting, one of Spain's most impressive natural sights. Reports of miracles make it an intriguing place for visitors and pilgrims.

Montserrat's rocky peak rises to 1,236m (4,054ft) and its eerie formations can be seen for long distances. The main attraction is the Monastery of Montserrat and La Moreneta, the statue of the Black Madonna, inside the basilica. Every weekend thousands of pilgrims line up to pay their respects. The first mention of the complex dates back to the ninth century, but in 1811 it was attacked by the French during the Napoleonic Wars and its clergy were killed. Rebuilt in 1844, it became a symbol of Catalan defiance, particularly during General Franco's reign (1939–75) when a Sunday trip to Montserrat became akin to an expression of independence. Today the monastery is home to a community of more than 300 Benedictine monks.

Montserrat (literally meaning 'serrated mountain') is a fabulous place to walk around, with its lunar-like landscape, secretive chapels and hermits' caves, and some breathtaking views of the valley below.

WHAT TO SEE

LA MORENETA

Legend has it that the statue of the Madonna of Montserrat was actually carved by St. Luke and brought to Montserrat by St. Peter in AD50, but remained undiscovered in one of Montserrat's caves until the 12th century. Her name comes from her blackened face and body, and by touching her hand one is said to be touching the universe and showing the ultimate respect. She became the official patroness of Catalonia in 1881. After this, Montserrat became the most popular name for girls born all over Catalonia, along with the name of 150 churches in Italy and even an island in the Caribbean.

THE MONASTERY

Plaça de la Creu is the main entry point to the monstery, and is named after a huge cross *(creu)* with the phrase Who is God engraved on it in various languages. It was designed by Josep Subirachs (born 1927), the sculptor responsible for the Passion facade of La Sagrada Família (▷ 186–189). The square is surrounded by three buildings that are used as accommodation for the pilgrims. The Plaça de Santa Maria, the long esplanade designed by architect Josep Puig i Cadafalch (1867–1957), is the huge focal point that leads you to the threshold of the monastery. The facade's three upper arcades are decorated with reliefs of Christ and the Apostles and are built on polished mountain stone. The ruins of the Gothic cloisters (designed by Abbot Giuliano della Rovere, who later became Pope Julius II, 1443–1513) are to the left of the facade, but most were designed by Puig i Cadafalch in 1925.

The grandiose basilica was greatly damaged when Napoleon brought his army to Spain between 1808 and 1814, but it wasn't reconstructed until the end of the 19th century. As soon as you enter, your eyes are drawn upwards to the ceiling of the nave where the choir, the richly enamelled high altar and a small chapel with a silver throne are found. La Moreneta sits behind the altar in a glass case. Worshippers ascend a small staircase to touch her orb, which protrudes from the glass.

The nearby museum has a collection of gifts that have been brought to the Black Madonna by visiting pilgrims, including a couple of works by Picasso. Some of the other highlights of this diverse collection include important archaeological pieces from Mesopotamia and the Holy Land, an Egyptian mummy and liturgical objects connected with the monastery over the centuries. The collection of 13th- to 18th-century paintings includes works by El Greco and Caravaggio, and the French Impressionist section includes work by artists such as Monet, Sisley and Degas.

EXPLORING

If the commercialization gets too much, escape to the splendid mountain scenery surrounding the monastery. Commonly called a sea of stone, the unique, molten-wax-like peaks were formed by geological upheavals 10 million years ago and have been sculpted through erosion after the softer land that surrounded this mass sank down into the ground.

The tourist information office provides various walking maps, including the Camino de la Santa Cova (Route of the Holy Cave, where La Moreneta was found), along which you will see a couple of monuments by Puig i Cadafalch and Gaudí (1852–1926). There are 13 hermitages, all of which are signposted once you are at the top.

The mountain is also home to some fantastic bird and animal life—such as wild pigs and goats—and the rocky terrain is scattered with evergreen oak, pine and maple trees.

TIPS

» The Tot Montserrat card includes return train tickets from Barcelona, the Cremallera railway, both funicular trains (which take you up and down the mountain), entrance to the museum and audiovisual exhibition, and a self-service meal. It can be bought at any city FGC station for €32.50. The Trans Montserrat ticket offers the same package minus the meal and audiovisual exhibition for €19.50. For details of other tourist tickets, ask at the station.

» If you arrive before lunch, there is a service in the cathedral with La Escolania, the oldest boys' choir in Europe, at 1pm (12 on Sunday) or 7.10pm.

» Pack a picnic to enjoy among the pinkish peaks above the monastery.

» A train service for visitors with disabilities connects the parking area and the monastery.

PLACES TO VISIT
BASILICA

🕐 Mon–Fri 7.30–7.30, Sat–Sun 7.30am–8.30pm. Shrine of the Virgin: Jul–end Sep daily 8.30–10.30, 12–6.15, 7.30–8.30; Oct–end Jun 8.30–10.30, 12–6.15 ✋ Free

MUSEUM

🕐 Apr–end Sep Mon–Fri 9–5.45, Sat–Sun 9.30–6.30; Oct–end Mar daily 9–5.45 ✋ Adult €6.50, child (8–16) €3.50, child (under 8) free

AUDIOVISUAL EXHIBITION

🕐 Jul to mid-Sep daily 9–7.45; mid-Sep to Jun daily 9–5.45 ✋ Adult €2, child (8–16) €1, child (under 8) free

INFORMATION

www.ajvilafranca.es

Tourist Information

ℹ️ Carrer de la Cort 14, Vilafranca del Penedès, 508720 ☎ 93 818 12 54 🕐 Tue–Fri 9–1, 4–7, Sat 9–1, 5–8, Mon 4–7

HOW TO GET THERE

By train: From Sants, trains run to Vilafranca and Sant Sadurní d'Anoia, taking around 50 minutes, departing approximately every 30 minutes.

By car: Leave the city by the B-20 (at Ronda de Dalt or Ronda Litoral) or C-16 and to the A2 (exit 8 Terrassa) and then the A7 to reach Sant Sadurní d'Anoia, then stay on the A7 for Vilafranca.

Above *Caves Codorníu is a major producer of cava*

INTRODUCTION

Vineyards carpet the gently rolling valleys of the Penedès, Catalonia's wine region, which is also the production epicentre of cava, the Catalan version of champagne. With a handful of period *bodegas* (wineries) open to the public, superb local cuisine and the bustling capital Vilafranca, the Penedès region provides a welcome break from the city.

WHAT TO SEE

VILAFRANCA

This is the most logical starting point when exploring the region. Try to arrive on a Saturday morning and head straight to the main square, Plaça de la Vila. The Saturday open-air market is busy with vendors selling home-grown produce and shops in the old town doing a brisk trade.

To find out about the the region's wine-making history, head to the Vinseum (Museum de les Cultures del Vi de Catalunya, www.vinseum.cat; Tue–Sat 10–2, 4–7, Sun 10–2) on 12th-century Plaça Jaume I. The collection is housed in a former royal palace and is among the best in Europe. Its 11 halls show the history of the industry in the area through didactic dioramas and old production aids such as wine presses, with a wine-tasting in an 18th-century tavern at the end of the visit. The visit includes three galleries of paintings by local artists on wine-related themes and a substantial collection of Spanish and Catalan ceramics from the 15th century onwards. Also on Plaça Jaume I is the Basílica de Santa Maria (Jun–end Sep Tue–Sat 11–2, 5–9, Sun 11–2; Oct–end May Sat 11–2, 5–8, Sun 11–2), a 15th-century Gothic church with a 52m (170ft) bell tower that you can climb (summer only) for views of the town and the surrounding area.

The *castellers* (the human towers) of Vilafranca are generally considered to be the best in Catalonia. They normally perform outside the town hall, reaching incredible heights and wowing the crowd, but you are likely to see them only if your visit coincides with a local fiesta.

CODORNÍU
www.codorniu.es
You can learn all about cava production on a trip to the Codorníu *bodega*. Codorníu is a major manufacturer of the Catalan version of champagne and their winery is 10km (6 miles) from Vilafranca in Sant Sadurní d'Anoia, a pretty village where more than 85 per cent of cava is made.

This beautiful Modernista construction was designed by Josep Puig i Cadafalch (1867–1957), responsible for the Casa Amatller (▷ 182) and Casa de les Punxes (▷ 192) in Barcelona, at the end of the 19th century. Even the caves where the wine is left to age are elegant—and the most extensive of their kind in the world, with more than 25km (15 miles) of underground cellars. The complex is replete with art nouveau touches and details and there is a museum of interesting advertising posters from the past. Because the winery is too large to see on foot, a mini-train transports you around the complex, including the vast stocks of Chardonnay, Macabeo, Parellada and Xarel.lo grapes (the principal cava varieties), with wine-tasting to end your visit.
✉ Avinguda Jaume Codorníu s/n, 08770 Sant Sadurní d'Anoia ☎ 93 891 33 42 🕐 Mon–Fri 9–5, Sat–Sun 9–1, guided tours every hour, booking ahead required 💶 €4

FURTHER TOURS
Freixenet (tel 93 891 70 96, www.freixenet.es), another big-name cava producer, also gives tours of its headquarters (Mon–Thu 10–1, 3–4.30, Fri–Sun 10–1), next to the Sant Sadurní d'Anoia train station. Its facade is one of the area's landmarks.

Torres (tel 93 817 74 87, www.torres.es); Mon–Fri 9–5, Sat 9–6, Sun 9–1), one of Spain's largest wine-makers, includes a train ride through a virtual-reality tunnel where modern wine-making practices are explained.

VILLAGES AND TOWNS
Exploring the region's dozens of picturesque villages unearths pretty Gothic and Romanesque architecture. Gelida, a tiny, elevated village, has some Modernista chalets—dating from a time when it was a popular summer retreat—and the majestic Gothic church of Sant Pere del Castell. Olèrdola shows off a pair of Romanesque churches as well as an important archaeological site. The settlement, on the top of a craggy hill, was first an Iberian village, then later used by the Romans as a fort. There is a small archaeological museum (mid-Oct to end Mar Tue–Sun 10–2, 3–8; Apr to mid-Oct Tue–Fri 10–2, 3–6, Sat–Sun 10–4) next door to the site, belonging to the Museu d'Arqueologia de Catalunya and displaying finds from the area.

The old town of Sant Quintí de Mediona is a great place for a stroll, with fountains and grottoes and some of the prettiest countryside in the vicinity.

ACTIVITIES
The Penedès is perfect for lovers of outdoor sports. Cyclists fill the roads at the weekends, enjoying its gentle slopes and mild climate. Horseback-riding is another popular pastime and the tourist office can supply information on the area's *Hípicas* ranches, with horses that you can ride out on for the day.

Most *domingueros* (day-trippers) are mainly concerned with satisfying a more basic need. The area's gastronomy is well respected, helped of course by the fine local wines, which are readily available. Pull up to even the tiniest village on the weekend and the smell of *butifarres* (sausages) being cooked on an open coal fire will fill the air. Other local delicacies include wild pigeon and duck *(pato)*, and *calçots* (huge spring onions, or scallions) cooked on hot coals, which make a short appearance in February and March.

» If you possibly can, visit the region in late August or September. This is when the harvest *(vendemia)* is gathered in the Penedès, a magical time when vineyards are alive with grape-picking.

TIP

WHERE TO EAT
CAL BLAY VINTICINC
www.calblay.com
Catalan cooking is served here with a number of modern innovations and a good wine list.
✉ Josep Rovira 271, Sant Sadurní d'Anoia ☎ 93 891 00 32 🕐 Mon–Thu, Sun 1–3.30, Fri–Sat 1–3.30, 9–11.30 🍴 L €30, D €50, Wine €8

FONDA NEUS
www.casafonda.com
This restaurant was founded in 1929 and serves traditional dishes—*canelones* (cannelloni) is the most popular.
✉ Marc Mir 14, Sant Sadurní d'Anoia ☎ 93 891 03 65 🕐 Daily 1–4, 9–10. Closed 23 Jul–24 Aug 🍴 L €20, D €30, Wine €10

Below *The Codorníu family has been producing cava since 1551*

INFORMATION

www.sitgestur.cat

Tourist Information

🛈 Sínia Morera 1, 08870 Sitges ☎ 93 894 50 04 🕓 Jun–end Sep Mon–Sat 9–9; Oct–end May Mon–Fri 9–2, 4–6.30, Sat 10–1

HOW TO GET THERE

By train: Two or three trains every hour leave from Sants station and Passeig de Gràcia station, taking you along the coast in about 30–40 minutes.

By car: Take the C-246 from the Plaça d'Espanya southwest to Sitges or the AP7 through the Garraf Tunnels.

By bus: A regular bus service runs from Sants bus station, next to the main rail station.

Above *Palau Maricel, formerly a hospital, houses an eclectic art collection*

INTRODUCTION

The seaside town of Sitges has everything for a great day, and night, out—nine sandy beaches, excellent bars, restaurants and nightlife, a couple of very good museums and an abundance of Modernista architecture.

Set on a cliff face overlooking the sea, Sitges's topography is the reason its small historic quarter has remained so intact. Hannibal had to bypass it on his way to Rome and the town has managed to avoid attack because of its fortress-like characteristics. Fishing and wine-making have always been the local industries, now coupled with tourism. Sitges is also home to a large gay community.

The long promenade curves along the shoreline and is crowded with people even in winter. The water is generally only warm enough to swim in between June and October.

WHAT TO SEE

THE MUSEUMS

From the station, all streets lead down through the old town to the shore. Here your eyes will be drawn upwards to the majestic, whitewashed, 17th-century Church of Sant Bartomeu i Santa Tecla (Mass only, Mon–Fri 9am, 7.30pm, Sat 8pm, Sun 9am). Most of Sitges's historic buildings are clustered around it, as it stands tall and defiant on a cliff. The most important of these is Museu Cau Ferrat (Carrer Fonollar s/n, tel 93 894 03 64; Jun–end Sep Tue–Sun 10–2, 5–9; Oct–end May Tue–Sat 10–2, 3.30–6.30; adult €3, under 12s free), the former home of Modernista artist Santiago Rusinyol (1861–1931). Rusinyol and his cohorts were largely responsible for making Sitges fashionable by forming an artists' colony at his out-of-town hideaway in the 1890s.

Rusinyol was an avid collector of wrought ironwork, particularly the pieces of the Modernista period, which are the highlights of this collection, as are paintings of the period by the artist himself, his artistic soulmate Ramón Casas (1866–1932) and other contemporaries. The windows frame some splendid views of the sea and it is a fascinating glimpse into the mind of one of the key figures of the movement. The home itself is built in the *Indiano* style, the name given to the grand mansions of the returning merchants who had made their fortunes in the Americas. There are 88 examples of these in Sitges—a map of them is available at the tourist office.

Next door is the Palau Maricel, another elegant residence that is used for private functions. The Museu Maricel (open same times as Museu Cau Ferrat) has a small collection of Noucentista and Modernista art.

The Museu Romàntic (tel 93 894 29 69; open same times as Museu Cau Ferrat), the third in Sitges' trio of museums, is found in the heart of the old town. Also known as Casa Llopis, after the mansion's original owner, the collection is testimony to genteel, upper-class life at the end of the 18th century. Señor Llopis was another *Indiano* who returned from the New World a very rich man, as this wide-ranging exhibition of everyday objects and curios shows. The whole second floor is taken up with a doll collection that once belonged to the Catalan children's book writer and illustrator Lola Anglada.

OTHER SIGHTS

Admirers of contemporary architecture should take the 20-minute stroll down the Passeig Marítim to the Hotel Terramar. The huge, white, nautical-looking building is a Sitges landmark, and was the first of the grand hotels on this stretch of coast. The public areas were refitted in the 1970s, including the quirky, marine-themed foyer. The complex is surrounded by the Jardins del Terramar (summer Fri–Wed 10.30–8.30; winter Fri–Wed 10–5), which are a good place to cool off after the beach.

Sitges also stages a number of well-known festivals. It is the only place in Catalonia that takes Carnival in February seriously, with a week-long calendar of parties and parades, including a special Children's Day. The Sitges Festival International de Cinema in October draws top film-makers and is a showcase for new home-grown talent. One of the prettiest local customs takes place during the week of Corpus Christi in June when the streets of the old quarter are carpeted in flowers forming ornate patterns. The night of 23 June (St. Joan, or Midsummer's Eve) is one of the best times to be in Sitges, when there are beach bonfires and firework displays.

TIP
» If you take the train to Sitges, make sure you check the time of the last return train—those going back to Barcelona leave notoriously early.

WHERE TO EAT
EL FRESCO
You will find contemporary, fusion food on the menu at El Fresco, arguably the best restaurant in Sitges.
✉ Pau Barrabeitg 4 ☎ 93 894 06 00 🕓 May–end Sep Tue–Sun 8.30pm–midnight; Oct–end Apr Wed–Sun 8.30pm–midnight 🍽 D €40, Wine €15

Left *One of Sitges's picturesque white-washed streets*
Below *The baroque Sant Bartomeu i Santa Tecla church is the town's emblem*

INFORMATION

www.costadaurada.org
www.tarragonaturisme.cat

Tourist Information

ℹ️ Carrer Major 39, 43003 ☎ 977 25 07 95 🕐 Jul–end Sep Mon–Sat 9–9, Sun 10–3; Oct–end Jun Mon–Sat 10–2, 4–7, Sun 10–2

HOW TO GET THERE

By train: Express trains run every 15–45 minutes from Sants to Tarragona, taking about an hour.

By car: Take the N-340, or the motorway A2 and then the A7 via Vilafranca.

By bus: From outside metro station Maria Cristina, run by La Hispania (tel 977 75 41 47).

Above *The medieval cathedral cloister and garden*

INTRODUCTION

Greek writers called Tarragona Callipolis, the beautiful city, and it was founded in 218BC as a military camp by the Scipio brothers. It once outshone Barcelona, and remains open, airy and inviting, with some of the best Roman remains in Spain. The city's cultural legacy was recognized by UNESCO when Tarragona was named a World Heritage City in 2000. The Roman ruins bear witness to a time when it was a principal port in the Roman-dominated Mediterranean. To get your bearings on the city and its coastline, head for the Balcó del Mediterrani (Balcony of the Mediterranean), a clifftop lookout at the sea end of the main boulevard, the Rambla Nova. On the way there are some remarkably fine Modernista mansions and some of the most fashionable cafés.

From the lookout you can see Tarragona's most famous Roman relic, the stunning amphitheatre (Mar–end Sep Tue–Sat 9–9, Sun 9–3; Oct–end Feb Tue–Sat 9–5, Sun 10–3) built in the second century AD. It is the most vivid reminder that Roman Tarraco was once the capital of the province and a powerful seat in the Empire.

WHAT TO SEE

ROMAN REMAINS

Take a stroll around the Passeig Arqueològic (Apr–end Sep Tue–Sat 9–5, Sun 10–3; Oct–end Mar Tue–Sat 9–9, Sun 10–3; €3), on Avinguda Catalunya, a walkway that was built along part of the city walls. Measuring 6m (20ft) in width at some points, the massive inner walls were built by the Romans, while the outer walls were erected by the British during the War of Spanish Succession in the early 18th century. The three towers that form part of the walls—the Torre del Arquebisbe, the Torre del Cabiscol and Torre de Minerva—were built in the Middle Ages. Fountains, statues, gardens and other adornments complete the site.

The Pont del Diable (Devil's Bridge), the aqueduct on the outskirts of Tarragona towards the town of Valls (4km/2.5 miles), was built in the second century AD. Its 217m (712ft) length is still in perfect condition.

THE OLD CITY

This is where the main sights are concentrated. The highlight of medieval Tarragona is the cathedral (Jun to mid-Oct 10–7; mid-Oct to mid-Nov 10–5; mid-Nov to mid-Mar 10–2; mid-Mar to end May 10–6; combined entrance to cathedral and Museu Diocesà €3.80) in the Plaça de la Seu. It was begun in 1171, during the Romanesque period, but its architecture took on Gothic elements towards its completion in 1331. The mixture of styles is most evident upon entering, with the main door rich in Gothic sculptures and details while the two side doors are more sparse. Inside, the main altarpiece by 15th-century Catalan master Pere Joan (flourished 1418–55) illustrates the life and struggles of St. Tecla, Tarragona's patron saint. Other notable artworks consist of an elaborate chapel dedicated to St. Michael and retables from the 15th century. The Gothic cloister is beautiful, with perfect dimensions—look for the procession of mice. Off the cloister, you will find the Museu Diocesà (Jun to mid-Oct 10–7; mid-Oct to mid-Nov 10–5; mid-Nov to mid-Mar 10–2; mid-Mar to end May 10–6; combined entrance to cathedral and museum €3.80), with an extensive collection of religious relics, Renaissance paintings and tapestries.

The city's Archaeological Museum (Jun–end Sep Tue–Sat 10–8, Sun 10–2; Oct–end May Tue–Sat 10–1.30, 4–7, Sun 10–2; €2.40) was the first museum of its kind in Catalonia, with exhibits of everyday objects of old Tarraco. Mosaics are well represented, including the beautiful Medusa Head in Salon III. Next door, the restored *praetorium* (governor's residence) is where Emperor Augustus lived, and it is believed that Pontius Pilate was born here. It now houses the Museu de la Romanitat (Jun–end Sep Tue–Sat 9–9, Sun 9–3; Oct–end May Tue–Sat 9–7, Sun 9–3) displaying medieval and Roman finds, and lets you access the first-century Roman Circus through immense passageways.

The 15th-century Casa Castellarnau was home to one of the city's influential families until the 19th century, and in 1542 England's Charles I resided here during his stay in the city. Inside, its grand salons house the Museu d'Història (Jun–end Sep Tue–Sat 9–9, Sun 9–3; Oct–end May Tue–Sat 9–7, Sun 9–3; €3), an eclectic sum of three high-calibre private collections and single donations that have been acquired by the council. The highlight is the Molas Collection, a disparate series of archaeological and ethnographic exhibits from prehistory to the present. Spanish contemporary painting is on display too, dating from the beginning of General Franco's dictatorship (1939) to the 1960s, and includes a piece by Salvador Dalí (1904–89) donated by the artist himself and one of Joan Miró's (1893–1983) rare tapestries, which hangs in the entrance.

TIPS

» If it's hot, pack some swimwear as Tarragona has good beaches at Platja del Miracle and Platja del Cossis, as well as south of the city at Cambrils and Salou.
» Note that many monuments are closed on Mondays.

WHERE TO EAT

L'ANCORA

One of the best places in town to try fresh fish dishes near the port, L'Ancora is great value and is always packed with locals.

✉ Carrer Unio 8, 43001 ☎ 977 21 94 05 🕐 Mon–Sat 10–2.30, 5–9.30 🖐 L €15, D €30, Wine €8

LIZARRÁN

This is an ideal place to taste a variety of local and regional dishes. You have a choice of about 500 tapas—help yourself from the counter—plus breakfast and traditional casseroles for lunch and dinner. The list of wines is long.

✉ Plaza de la Font 16 ☎ 977 23 00 62 🕐 Daily 9am–1am 🖐 L €15, D €25, Wine €8

Below *The Passeig Arqueològic Roman aqueduct is to the north of the city*

There are lots of different ways to explore Barcelona and the towns and sights beyond. Take advantage of its coastal location with a boat trip or uncover a hidden history with a guided walk.

BESPOKE TOURS
BARCELONA GUIDE BUREAU
www.bgb.es
The BGB offer a range of walking or bus tours, including shopping tours. Interpreters can be provided. Prices are available on request.
✉ Via Laietana 54, 08003 ☎ 93 268 24 22

BICYCLE TOURS
UN COTXE MENYS
www.bicicletabarcelona.com
Cycle around the Barri Gòtic and the port area with a guide. Book in advance. Tours are also offered within Catalonia.
✉ Carrer de Esparteria 3, 08003 ☎ 93 268 21 05 (office Mon–Fri 10–2) 🕐 Jan–end Feb daily 11am; Mar–end Dec Mon, Wed, Fri 4.30pm, Tue, Thu, Sat 7.30pm 💶 €22 (including drink); bicycle rental: 1 hour €5, per day €15, per week €55

TERRA DIVERSIONS
Terra Diversions offer a wide range of bicycle tours, from a two-hour trip to the Collserola hills behind the city, to a week-long ride into the Pyrenees. They have itineraries to suit riders of all abilities, and they can also provide equipment and bicycle rental.
☎ 93 844 63 88 💶 From €38 (two-hour Collserola Tour)

BOAT TOURS
LAS GOLONDRINAS
▷ 161.

BUS TOURS
A range of these tours go around Barcelona and into Catalonia. The tourist office gives advice and provides an online booking service for a complete range of tours.

ALSA
www.alsa.es
✉ Alsatouring Travel Terminal (next to Estació de Sants) ☎ 93 244 98 34

Full-day tours
These tours whisk you through the city's biggest attractions. If a museum is closed, an alternative is provided. Check before you travel.
🕐 Daily, leaving 9.30am 💶 €98

Half-day tours
See some of the major sights on a three-hour tour. Different bus companies follow different itineraries, and morning and afternoon routes also differ. Check before you travel.
🕐 Daily 9.30am, 3.30pm 💶 Alsa: Adult €40, child €34, child (under 4) €20

BARCELONA TOURS
www.barcelonatours.es
These red buses, painted with famous Barcelona symbols, have two routes around the city; east and west. Get on and off as often as you like. Commentary is via headphones. Tickets can be bought on-board, or from travel agencies and at many hotels. (There's a 10 per cent discount for buying online.)
☎ 93 402 69 55 🕐 Daily 9–9, every 10–20 minutes (depends on season) 💶 One day: adult €17, child €10. Two days: adult €21, child €13

BUS TURÍSTIC
▷ 46.

JULIÀ TOURS
www.juliatours.es
✉ Ronda de la Universitat 5 ☎ 93 317 64 54 💶 Adult €43.20, child (under 7) free

CAR TOURS
GO CAR
www.gocartours.es
These tiny, yellow 'cars' are small and zippy—ideal for negotiating the city traffic. Each has a GPS system, and a commentary to ensure you don't miss a thing.
☎ 93 269 17 92 💶 From €35 for 1 hr

GUIDED WALKS
ASSOCIACIÓ CALL DE BARCELONA
www.calldebarcelona.org
This group promotes the history of the Jewish community within the city and there is a short tour of the old synagogue.
✉ Carrer de Marlet 5, 08006 ☎ 93 317 07 90 🕐 By arrangment 💶 €2

TURISME DE BARCELONA
www.barcelonaturisme.com
The tourist office has guided walks around the city. Book in advance.
✉ Plaça de Catalunya, 08002 ☎ Reserve tours in advance by calling 93 285 38 32, or buy online at the city's tourist website

Barri Gòtic
🕐 Mon–Sun 10am in English 💶 Adult €12.50, child (4–12) €5

Gourmet
🕐 Fri–Sat 11am in English 💶 Adult €19, child €7, includes two tastings

Modernisme
🕐 Fri–Sat 4pm in English 💶 Adult €12.50, child (4–12) €5, child (under 4) free

Picasso
🕐 Tue–Sun 10.30am in English 💶 Adult €19, child (4–12) €7, includes admission to Picasso Museum

HELICOPTER TOURS
HELIPISTAS
www.barcelonahelicopters.com
Take in the whole of the city on a helicopter ride. Flights last five to ten minutes. They also offer flights farther afield, including Montserrat or the Costa Brava.
☎ 902 19 40 73 🕐 Daily 9–7 💶 €45–€80 per person

PRACTICALITIES

Practicalities gives you all the important practical information you will need during your visit from money matters to emergency phone numbers.

BARCELONA

TEMPERATURE

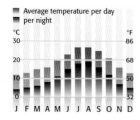

■ Average temperature per day
■ per night

RAINFALL

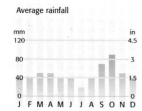

Average rainfall

WEATHER

CLIMATE

Barcelona has a temperate, Mediterranean climate with cool winters and warm summers. Temperatures are rarely extreme, and the weather is usually bright and sunny (the city enjoys an average of seven hours of sunshine a day). However, downpours are not uncommon, particularly in September, October and February which are the rainiest months, so pack an umbrella. The high humidity can make July and August uncomfortably warm, and visitors from northern climes might consider choosing a hotel room with air-conditioning during the hottest summer months.

WHEN TO GO

The city has become a year-round destination, and it doesn't really have a peak season. Your choice will most likely depend on what sort of weather you want.

» Spring, especially March and April, is an unpredictable season. It can be cloudy and rainy or bright and sunny, depending on your luck.

» The best months to visit the city are May, June and September, when the weather is warm and pleasant and you will find lots of events taking place.

» The real heat of summer takes hold during late July and August. It can be very hot and humid, leading to the occasional thunderstorm, and local residents often escape the city at this time. During the height of summer, many restaurants, shops and museums close or reduce their opening hours.

» September and October are officially the city's wettest months, but October in particular still benefits from bright sunny days.

» Between November and Christmas is a lovely time to visit the city, with seasonal markets and religious pageantry.

» The winter, December through to the end of February, is cool rather than very cold, but it has been known to snow.

» Other times that you might want to consider avoiding are national holidays (▷ 244) when many of the major attractions are closed, although national celebrations and fiestas are on show.

» Check whether Barcelona is holding one of its huge trade fairs at the time of your visit. If so, reserve accommodation well ahead as many of the hotels get booked up by business travellers.

WEATHER REPORTS

» For information on the current weather forecast, check the website of your local news network station, such as the BBC (www.bbc.co.uk) or CNN (www.CNN.com).

» There are several dedicated weather websites including:
www.weather.com
www.idealspain.com
www.wunderground.com
www.meteocat.com

WHAT TO TAKE

» If you forget to take anything, you will be able to buy it in Barcelona, unless it is a very specialized item.

» The clothing you pack will depend on the time of year you visit, but you should bring a range of clothes for different weather conditions, even if you are visiting in summer. Bring an umbrella, a raincoat, comfortable walking shoes and at least one warm top for the evenings.

» You should also bring suitable clothing for visiting churches, although the rules about length of skirt, casualness of shoes or bare arms are quite relaxed.

» Barcelona is an incredibly laid-back city and this is reflected in the residents' dress sense. Locals are stylish but in a bohemian, quirky and original, rather than a traditional, way. There are very few occasions on which a jacket and tie will be required.

TIME ZONES

Barcelona is on CET (Central European Time), one hour ahead of GMT (Greenwich Mean Time).

City	Time difference	Time at 12 noon in Barcelona
Amsterdam	0	noon
Berlin	0	noon
Brussels	0	noon
Chicago	-7	5am
Dublin	-1	11am
Johannesburg*	+1	1pm
London	-1	11am
Montréal	-6	6am
New York	-6	6am
Perth*	+7	7pm
Rome	0	noon
San Francisco	-9	3am
Sydney*	+9	9pm
Tokyo*	+8	8pm

Summer Time begins on the last Sunday in March and ends on the last Sunday in October. For starred countries, which do not have daylight saving, take off one hour during Summer Time.

» If you are on any prescribed medication, bring enough with you for the period of your visit.

» If you are going to take tablets out of their original packaging to reduce the amount you need to carry, or have a serious illness, you might consider getting a letter from your doctor stating your medical condition and what medication you are on. This will help you if you are stopped by customs or if you need to get emergency treatment while you are away.

» Take photocopies of important documents, such as passport and travel insurance. Keep a separate note of the serial numbers, as well as the numbers of traveller's cheques in case of loss or theft.

» Make sure you have addresses and telephone numbers of emergency contacts, and who to call if you need to cancel your credit cards.

DOCUMENTS
PASSPORTS AND VISAS

» All visitors must carry a valid passport, or in the case of EU nationals, a national ID card may be used. You are required by law to keep one of these documents on you at all times. You need to produce some form of photo ID when making a credit card purchase.

» EU visitors do not require a visa for entry. Visitors from the US, Canada, Japan, Australia and New Zealand require a visa for stays exceeding 90 days.

» Always check with the consulate about visa requirements and entry regulations as they are liable to change, often at short notice. Visit www.tourspain.es, www.gospain.org, www.fco.gov.uk or www.travel.state.gov. For addresses of consulates and embassies, ▷ 241.

» Always keep a separate note of your passport number and a photocopy of the page that carries your details.

TRAVEL INSURANCE

» Make sure you have adequate travel insurance including medical coverage, repatriation, baggage and money loss. Also, if your insurer has a 24-hour helpline then remember to bring the number with you.

» If you rely on your credit card insurance, check exactly what is covered.

» Report losses or theft to the police and obtain a signed statement (una denuncia) from a police station (comisaría), which you will need to make an insurance claim.

CUSTOMS

The import of wildlife souvenirs and other products from rare and endangered species may be either illegal or require a special permit. Before you make a purchase you should check current customs regulations. See the panel below for more details.

CUSTOMS

GOODS YOU BUY IN THE EU

These are in line with other EU countries. There is no limit on the amount of foreign currency or euros that you can bring into Spain (although carrying cash or bank transfers of over €300,000 can be questioned by the authorities). Tax-paid goods for personal use (such as video cameras) can be brought in from other EU countries without customs charges being incurred. Guidance levels for tax-paid goods bought in the EU are as follows:

» 800 cigarettes; or	» 10 litres of spirits
» 400 small cigars; or	» 90 litres of wine (of which only 60 litres
» 200 cigars; or	can be sparkling wine)
» 1kg of smoking tobacco	» 20 litres of fortified wine (such as
» 110 litres of beer	port or sherry)

VISITING SPAIN FROM OUTSIDE THE EU

You are entitled to the allowances shown below only if you travel with the goods and do not plan to sell them. Travellers over 18 can take in:

» 200 cigarettes; or	» 2 litres of still table wine
» 100 small cigars; or	» 2 litres of sparkling wine, fortified wine
» 50 cigars; or	or other liqueurs
» 250g of smoking tobacco	» 50g of perfume
» 1 litre of spirits or strong liqueurs	» 250cc/ml of eau de toilette

SPANISH EMBASSIES ABROAD

COUNTRY	ADDRESS	TELEPHONE/WEBSITE
Australia and New Zealand	15 Arkana Street, Yarralumla, ACT 2600, Canberra	02 6273 3555, www.maec.es
Canada	74 Stanley Avenue, Ottawa, Ontario K1M 1P4	613/747-2252, www.maec.es
The Netherlands	Lange Voorhout 50, 2514 EG The Hague	70/302 4999, www.maec.es
Republic of Ireland	17a Merlyn Park, Ballsbridge, Dublin 4	01 269 1640, www.maec.es
UK	39 Chesham Place, London SW1X 8SB	020 7235 5555, www.maec.es
	Visa information	0906 550 8970
	Suite 1a, Brook House, 70 Spring Gardens, Manchester, M2 2BQ	0161 236 1262
	63 North Castle Street, Edinburgh EH2 3LJ	0131 220 1843
USA	150 East 58th Street, New York, NY 10155	212/355-4080, www.maec.es
	5055 Wilshire Blvd., Suite 960, Los Angeles, CA 90036	213/938-0158

MONEY

Spain is one of 16 European countries that have adopted the euro as their currency. Euro notes and coins replaced the former currency, the peseta, in 2002.

BEFORE YOU GO

» It is advisable to use a combination of cash, traveller's cheques and credit cards, rather than relying on any one means of payment during your trip.

» Check with your credit card company that you can withdraw cash from ATMs. You should also check what fee will be charged for this, and what number you should call if your card is stolen (▷ right).

» Traveller's cheques are a relatively safe way of carrying money as you are insured if they are stolen. Remember to keep a note of their numbers separate from the traveller's cheques themselves.

EXCHANGE RATES

The exchange rate per euro for visitors from the UK, US and Canada is subject to daily fluctuation. Good websites for checking rates are www.oanda.com and www.xe.com.

CREDIT CARDS

Most restaurants, hotels and shops accept credit cards, but some may have a minimum charge. You are required to show a form of photo ID with most credit card purchases. Smaller hotels, *pensions* and *hostales*, as well as some shops and cafés will still require cash. Ticket machines at metro stations also accept credit cards. Note that chip-and-pin technology is still being introduced to Spain, and can sometimes cause problems when paying for goods.

ATMS

These are widespread throughout the city, known as *telebanco*, and have instructions in a choice of languages, including French, Italian and German. If your card has the Maestro or Cirrus facilities (look for the red, white and blue logos) you will be able to pay for goods and services as well as withdraw cash.

BANKS

There is no shortage of banks, which tend to be open Monday to Friday 8.30–2, Saturday 8.30–1, but close Saturdays in summer. Some also open on one afternoon a week, usually Thursday. Most have a foreign exchange desk *(cambio* or *canvi)*. Remember to bring your passport if you want to change traveller's cheques.

CHANGING MONEY

You can change money at bureaux de change, which are dotted around the city and open until very late. The exchange rate won't be good, but commission is generally not charged. You can also change money at some branches of El Corte Inglés department store, including at the Plaça de Catalunya branch.

Ask for the *servei de cambi* (Catalan) or *servicio de cambio* (Spanish).

LOST/STOLEN CREDIT CARDS
Ring one of the following contact numbers in case of loss or theft:
American Express cards
902 37 56 37
American Express traveller's cheques
900 81 00 29
Diners Club
902 40 11 12
MasterCard
900 97 12 31
Visa
900 99 11 24

WIRING MONEY

In an emergency you can have money wired from home, but this can be very expensive and time-consuming. You can send and receive money via agents such as Western Union (www.westernunion.com) or MoneyGram (www.moneygram.com).

DISCOUNTS

» Seniors can get reductions on some museum entry charges on production of an identity document.
» An International Student Identity Card (ISIC; www.isic.org) may help obtain free or reduced entry to museums and attractions as well as other discounts.
» Other discount passes are available (▷ 43 and 244).

TAXES

» Sales tax, at 7 per cent and known as IVA, is added to everything, including all services such as hotel accommodation and meals in restaurants. This is non-refundable. For all other goods and services 16 per cent is added.
» Visitors from non-EU countries are entitled to a reimbursement of the 16 per cent tax paid on purchases to the value of more than €90.15, which needs to be spent in the same store and on the same day.
» The store must provide a properly completed invoice itemizing all goods, the price paid for them, and the tax charged, as well as full address details of both the vendor and purchaser.
» The goods and the invoice(s) should be taken to the booth provided at Spanish customs on your departure from the EU, prior to checking in your baggage.
» Alternatively, tax can also be reclaimed through Global Refund Tax Free Shopping, a service offered by major retailers worldwide; visit www.globalrefund.com.

TIPPING

» Tipping is still a relatively new culture in Spain and locals usually only tip small amounts. High sums of money will not be expected.
» There will be no service charge added to your bill when you are in the city, so you should be prepared to leave a tip (see table, right).

TIPPING

Tipping is usually expected for services. As a general guide, the following applies:

Restaurants	5–10 per cent*
Bar service	change*
Cafés	5 per cent*
Tour guides	optional
Taxis	3–5 per cent, more if carried luggage
Chambermaids	€1–€2
Porters	€1–€2
Toilet attendants	€1

*Or more if you are particularly impressed with the level of service

SOME EVERYDAY ITEMS AND HOW MUCH THEY COST

Takeout sandwich	€2.50–€3.50
Bottle of mineral water (from a shop, half a litre)	€0.40–€1
Cup of coffee (from a café, espresso)	€1–€1.85
Beer (half a litre)	€3.50–€4
Glass of house wine	€2–€4
Spanish national newspaper	€1–€1.20
International newspaper	€3–€5
Litre of petrol (98 unleaded)	€1.20
(diesel)	€0.97
Metro ticket (single)	€1.40

FOREIGN BANKS

NAME	ADDRESS	TELEPHONE
Citibank	Plaça de Catalunya 1	902 24 12 00
ABN AMRO	Avinguda Diagonal 662	93 205 10 93
HSBC	Avinguda Diagonal 605	93 322 22 23
Barclays	Passeig de Gràcia 45	93 481 20 00
Deutsche Bank	Plaça de Catalunya 19	93 318 47 00
Lloyds TSB	Rambla de Catalunya 123	93 236 33 00
The Bank of Tokyo/Mitsubishi	Avinguda Diagonal 605	93 494 74 50
The Chase Manhattan Bank	Josep Irla i Bosch 5–7	93 203 03 12
Banca Nazionale del Lavoro	Avinguda Diagonal 468	93 238 77 00

Left *Several pharmacies in and around the city have striking Modernista facades*

HEALTH

Spain's national health service works alongside the private sector, and its hospitals are generally of a high standard.

BEFORE YOU GO

» No inoculations are required, but it is a good idea to check when you last had a tetanus shot and, if it was more than 10 years ago, have a booster before you travel.

» Spain has a standard agreement with other EU countries entitling EU citizens to a certain amount of free or reduced-cost health care, including hospital treatment. You'll need a European Health Insurance Card (EHIC; formerly the E111 form).

» If you will need treatment for a pre-existing condition while you are away, such as injections, you should apply to your department of health for an E112. You should only apply if it's necessary and not on a just-in-case basis.

» All visitors are strongly advised to take out full health insurance, despite having an EHIC. For non-EU visitors full health insurance is an essential requirement.

» US visitors are likely to find that their existing health policy stays effective when they travel abroad, but it is wise to check this before leaving home.

» If you think you will need to renew a prescription, ask your doctor to provide you with the chemical name of the drug before you travel, as it may be marketed under another name in Spain.

IF YOU NEED TREATMENT

» You will need to confirm that the doctor you visit works within the Spanish state health service in order to use your EHIC. Make it clear to the doctor that you want to be treated under this system.

» In some clinics there are separate surgery times for private patients and those treated under the health service. Make sure you are being treated at the appropriate surgery.

» If you are treated as a private patient, or go to a private health clinic, you will not be entitled to your money back.

EMERGENCY TREATMENT

The telephone number 061 is for the ambulance service. The number 112 is for help throughout Europe.

FINDING A DOCTOR

» A doctor *(metge)* can be found by asking at the local pharmacy *(farmàcia)*, at your hotel's reception desk, by calling the city information line on 010 or by looking in the phone book *(Pàgines Grogues)*.

» If you need to see an English-speaking doctor, contact the Centre Mèdic Assistencial de Catalonia, Carrer de Provença 281, tel 93 215 37 93. This is a private clinic and charges apply.

PHARMACIES

» Pharmacies *(farmàcia)* usually have a flashing green cross outside

USEFUL NUMBERS	
Emergencies (across EU)	112
Ambulance	061
Information Line	010
Police (Mossos d'Esquadra)	088

OPTICIANS			
OPTICIAN	ADDRESS	TELEPHONE	OPENING HOURS
Arense	Ronda Sant Pere 16	93 301 82 90	Mon–Sat 10–9
Cottet	Carrer de Muntaner 277	93 209 95 55	Mon 10–1, 4.30–8, Tue–Fri 9.30–1.30, 4.30–8, Sat 10–1.30
Cottet	Rambla de Catalunya 105	93 488 35 22	Mon–Sat 10–8.30
Grand Optical	El Triangle, Plaça de Catalunya 4	93 304 16 40	Mon–Sat 10–10

HEALTHY FLYING

» Visitors to Spain from as far as the US, Australia or New Zealand may be concerned about the effect of long-haul flights on their health. The most widely publicized concern is deep vein thrombosis, or DVT. Misleadingly called 'economy class syndrome', DVT is the forming of a blood clot in the body's deep veins, particularly in the legs. The clot can move around the bloodstream and could be fatal.

» Those most at risk include the elderly, pregnant women and those using the contraceptive pill, smokers and the overweight. If you are at increased risk of DVT see your doctor before departing. Flying increases the likelihood of DVT because passengers are often seated in a cramped position for long periods of time and may become dehydrated.

TO MINIMIZE RISK:

Drink water (not alcohol)

Don't stay immobile for hours at a time

Stretch and exercise your legs periodically

Do wear elastic flight socks, which support veins and reduce the chances of a clot forming

EXERCISES

1 Ankle rotations	2 Calf stretches	3 Knee lifts
Lift feet off the floor. Draw a circle with the toes, moving one foot clockwise and the other counterclockwise	Start with heel on the floor and point foot upward as high as you can. Then lift heels high keeping balls of feet on the floor	Lift leg with knee bent while contracting your thigh muscle. Then straighten leg pressing foot flat to the floor

Other health hazards for flyers are airborne diseases and bugs spread by the plane's air-conditioning system. These are largely unavoidable but if you have a serious medical condition seek advice from a doctor before flying.

and are found across the city. A pharmacy displays a red or green cross when it is open at night.

» Staff will normally be able to provide excellent over-the-counter advice, often in English. For minor ailments it is usually worth consulting a pharmacist before trying to find a doctor, because the quality of this advice will often be sufficient.

» Many drugs that can only be obtained on prescription in other countries are available without one in Spain, so again, check at a pharmacy.

» There is always at least one pharmacy open 24 hours a day. Check in a pharmacy window for details. Farmàcia Alvarez, Passeig de Gràcia 26 and Farmàcia Clapés, La Rambla 98 are open 24 hours.

DENTAL TREATMENT

» Dental treatment is expensive in Spain, so try to have a dental check-up before leaving home.

» Check your medical insurance before you go to see if it covers emergency dental treatment. There is no reciprocal arrangement using an EHIC.

» A walk-in clinic can be found at Institut Odontològic de Barcelona, Carrer de Calàbria 251, tel 93 439 45 00.

OPTICIANS

» It is a good idea to pack a spare pair of glasses or contact lenses in case you lose or break what you usually wear.

» Opticians can be found in the phone book under Òptics, or ask at the nearest pharmacy.

WATER

It is generally safe to drink the tap water (unless it is marked no potable), although it may have a strong taste of chlorine. Mineral water (aigua mìneral) is widely available and not expensive. It is sold carbonated (con gas/amb gas) or still (sin gas/sense gas).

SUNSHINE

» The city can get very hot and sunny, and not just in summer. Always protect against sunburn and dehydration by dressing suitably in loose clothing, covering your head, applying high-factor sunscreen (particularly important for children and fair-skinned people) and drinking about 2 litres (4 pints) of water a day in really hot weather.

» During the hottest part of the day you will see few locals out and about on the streets. The most sensible thing is to go local and have a siesta, or at least stay in the shade between 1pm and 4pm if your itinerary allows it.

COMPLEMENTARY MEDICAL TREATMENT

» Alternative medicine, such as homeopathy and reflexology, is becoming increasingly popular. It is not offered as part of the health service and has no legislation covering it. You should therefore be very careful in your choice of practitioner.

» You can find a list of homeopathic doctors at the Col-legi Oficial de Metges de Barcelona, tel 93 567 88 88, www.comb.cat.

» CENAC (naturopathy, homeopathy, acupuncture; Rambla de Catalunya 7, tel 93 412 64 10, www.cenac.info)

» Bienestar Barcelona (Ronda Sant Père 40, Pral 1a, tel 93 302 18 35) is an American-run chiropractic centre, which also teaches breathing and relaxation techniques.

HOSPITALS WITH EMERGENCY DEPARTMENTS (URGÈNCIES)

HOSPITAL	ADDRESS	TELEPHONE
Hospital de Barcelona	Avinguda Diagonal 660	93 254 24 00
Hospital Clínic i Provincial	Carrer de Villaroel 170	93 227 54 00
Hospital del Mar	Passeig Marítim Barceloneta 25–29	93 248 30 00
Hospital de la Santa Creu i Sant Pau	Sant Antoni Maria Claret 167	93 291 94 84

BASICS

ELECTRICITY
» The power supply is 220 volts.
» Plugs have two round pins. It is a good idea to bring an adaptor.
» Visitors from North America should bring a transformer for appliances operating on 110/120 volts.

LOCAL WAYS
» The continental kiss (one kiss on each cheek) is used among friends only. Always offer to shake hands when you meet people, even if it's not for the first time.
» Follow the custom of having a siesta at lunchtime or be prepared to have a long lunch. The siesta isn't as widespread as it once was, but a number of shops and some museums close until 4 or 5pm.
» Late lunches push evening meal times to past 9pm; it may be difficult to get dinner before this time.
» You should show respect and dress accordingly when visiting the cathedral and other religious places. Most, if not all, are still active places of worship. Never take photographs when a service is taking place.
» Residents will warm to you if you try a few words of Spanish, but will love you all the more if you use Catalan, with words such as si us plau (please) and gràcies (thank you).
» Don't refer to Catalan as a dialect.
» Most hotel, museum and tourist office staff speak at least a few words of a number of languages, and many speak one or two languages very well, so you should be able to get your message across. Don't be surprised if they want to try out their language skills on you.

MEASUREMENTS
Spain uses the metric system. Distances are measured in metres and kilometres, fuel is sold by the litre and food is weighed in grams and kilograms.

PLACES OF WORSHIP
Worshippers of any religion should be able to find the appropriate church, temple or synagogue, but Catholics obviously get the biggest choice, with services at the cathedral and other churches listed in Sights (▷ 54–207).

Anglican
✉ St. George's Church, Carrer de Horaci 38 ☎ 93 417 88 67; www.st-georges-church.com

Jewish
✉ Sinagoga de Barcelona, Carrer d'Avenir 24 ☎ 93 200 61 48; www.cibonline.org

Muslim
✉ Centre Islàmic, Avinguda Meridiana 326 ☎ 93 351 49 01

Protestant/Evangelist
✉ Església Protestant Barcelona Centre, Carrer Tallers 26 ☎ 93 318 97 98; www.esglesiatallers.org

Roman Catholic
✉ Parròquia María Reina, Carretera d'Esplugues 103 ☎ 93 203 55 39 ⊕ Mass in English 10.30am on Sunday only

SMOKING
» The airport, train stations, metro and buses are non-smoking. You will be fined if you are caught. Increasingly smoking is also banned in public buildings.
» Smoking is not allowed in art galleries, museums, theatres and cinemas.
» Larger cafés and restaurants are required by law to provide a non-smoking area. Smaller establishments are either entirely smoking or non-smoking, with almost 95 per cent remaining smoking. All establishments must post a sign stating whether they are smoking or non-smoking at the entrance.

TOILETS
» Public toilets are rare and are often not pleasant. In large department stores, museums, galleries and places of interest, standards are likely to be much higher, with baby-changing facilities also available.
» You can also use the facilities in cafés, bars and restaurants, but as these are usually for customers only, it is polite to buy something before doing so.
» Words to keep a look out for are aseos or servicios in Castilian or lavabos in Catalan.

VISITING WITH CHILDREN
» Children are welcome just about anywhere in the city. They are routinely taken out with the family at night and are allowed to stay up late.
» Children's menus are not widely available, but most restaurants will provide you with a smaller portion, if you ask.
» For something a bit different, and for tired feet, use the cable-car rides around Montjuïc (▷ 64–66) and the tour buses (▷ 232).
» Some of the squares in the city, such as the Plaça de Sant Miguel behind the Ajuntament (City Hall), have small, fenced-off playgrounds. They are free and open to everyone. There are several in the fantastic Parc de la Ciutadella (▷ 148).
» Metro Line 2 has lifts at every station. The TMB information offices (▷ 43) provide maps showing stops with lift access to the platforms.
» Public transport is free for children under four years old.
» The tourist office has a list of child-minding services. Or ask at your hotel reception. For English-speaking babysitters, try Tender Loving Canguros (tel 647 605 989; www.tlcanguros.com). Prices start at €8 per hour, plus a €15 agency fee.

CONVERSION CHART

FROM	TO	MULTIPLY BY
Inches	Centimetres	2.54
Centimetres	Inches	0.3937
Feet	Metres	0.3048
Metres	Feet	3.2810
Yards	Metres	0.9144
Metres	Yards	1.0940
Miles	Kilometres	1.6090
Kilometres	Miles	0.6214
Acres	Hectares	0.4047
Hectares	Acres	2.4710
Gallons	Litres	4.5460
Litres	Gallons	0.2200
Ounces	Grams	28.35
Grams	Ounces	0.0353
Pounds	Grams	453.6
Grams	Pounds	0.0022
Pounds	Kilograms	0.4536
Kilograms	Pounds	2.205
Tons	Tonnes	1.0160
Tonnes	Tons	0.9842

FINDING HELP

PERSONAL SAFETY

Barcelona is much like any other Western city when it comes to crime. You should be safe against personal attack, but petty crime, especially pick-pocketing, is fairly common. Visitors who are not on their guard are main targets, so take some sensible precautions:

» Never carry more cash than you think you will need.

» Wear bags slung diagonally across your chest rather than hanging from a shoulder or in a rucksack-type bag. If you use a bag around your waist, don't assume that it's safe, as thieves know that you will be keeping valuables in it. Back pockets are also prone to pickpockets.

» Keep belongings close by in crowded areas and on the metro.

» Be aware of ploys to distract your attention by thieves working in pairs. The most common ploys include being told that you have dropped your keys, or that a bird has messed your coat. Ignore gypsies proffering flowers, or young women bearing clipboards and asking you to sign 'a petition'.

» Stick to brightly lit, main thoroughfares at night.

» Never leave belongings on view in a parked car.

» Keep any valuables in the hotel safe.

» Las Ramblas is becoming one of the areas to be most on your guard for pickpockets, as well as hustlers who separate you from your money using ploys like card tricks or asking which cup the ball is under.

WOMEN VISITORS

You should not feel uneasy about visiting Barcelona. You are unlikely to receive any unwanted attention of the clichéd Spanish-waiter kind, and if you use the guidelines above, your trip should be a safe one.

POLICE

There are three different types of police force in Spain. Each force deals with different aspects of public order.

» *Guardia Urbana*, whose main responsibility is urban traffic, are the local police. They are identifiable by their blue uniforms and the white-checked bands on their vehicles.

» *Policía Nacional*, who wear navy blue uniforms and berets, deal with law and order and national security.

» *Guardia Civil*, who are responsible for border posts, policing country areas, highways and the coast, wear olive green.

» Catalonia has its own police force, the *Mossos d'Esquadra*, who wear red and black hats.

» If you need help, contact the *Mossos d'Esquadra* at your nearest police station *(comisaría)*. In the Ciutat Vella (Barri Gòtic, El Raval and La Ribera) go to Carrer Nou de la Rambla 76–78 and in L'Eixample go to Gran Via 456. There is usually someone who can speak English.

» Take the time to report thefts to the police, especially if you intend to make a claim for the loss. You will need a police report to pass on to your insurance company.

LOSS OF PASSPORT

» Always keep a separate note of your passport number and take a photocopy of the page that carries your details, in case of loss or theft.

» You can also scan the most important pages of your passport and email them to yourself at an email account which you can access anywhere, such as www.hotmail.com or www.googlemail.com.

» If you lose your passport or it is stolen, report it to the police and then contact your nearest embassy or consulate for assistance.

LOST PROPERTY

» If you lose an item around the city, visit the Servei de Troballes at the Ajuntament, Carrer de Cuitat 9, tel 010.

» If you lose something on public transport, you can contact one of the TMB offices (▷ 43) to see if it's been handed in. It will then be sent to the Plaça de la Universitat branch for collection.

» If an item of lost property is not claimed from the TMB offices within seven days, it goes to the city's lost-and-found (Servei de Troballes) offices in the Ajuntament, off the Plaça de Sant Jaume, in Carrer de Cuitat (see above).

LANGUAGE ASSISTANCE

There are many businesses providing translation services in Barcelona. These include Context European Translation Services (Carrer de Pau Claris 149; tel 932 157 540; www.context-bcn.com) and International House Translation (Carrer de Trafalgar 14, tel 93 268 86 10, www.ih-translation.com). The tourist office can provide you with a full list.

EMBASSIES AND CONSULATES

COUNTRY	ADDRESS	TELEPHONE	WEBSITE
Australia	Plaça Gal.la Placídia 1–3	93 490 90 13	www.embaustralia.es
Canada	Plaça de Catalunya 9, 1st floor	93 412 72 36	www.canadainternational.gc.ca
France	Ronda de la Universitat 22	93 270 30 00	www.consulfrance-barcelone.org
Germany	Passeig de Gràcia 111	93 292 10 00	www.barcelona.diplo.de
Ireland	Gran Via Carles III 94	93 491 50 21	—
Italy	Carrer de Mallorca 270	93 467 73 05	www.consbarcelona.esteri.it
UK	Avinguda Diagonal 477	93 366 62 00	www.ukinspain.com
USA	Passeig de Reina Elisenda 23	93 280 22 27	www.embusa.es

ESSENTIAL INFORMATION

PRACTICALITIES

COMMUNICATION

TELEPHONES

National numbers: All telephone numbers in Spain have a nine-digit number, which includes the area code—all area codes start with a 9. You must include the area code even when making a local call. Some provinces have two-digit codes; others have three digits. In Barcelona it is 93. The state telephone company is Telefónica.

International calls: To call Spain from the US, prefix the area code and number with 011 34; from the UK prefix with 00 34. To call the US from Spain prefix the area code and number with 00 1; to call the UK, dial 00 44, then drop the first 0 from the area code. See the table below for more country codes.

CALL CHARGES

» Cheap national calls can be made between 8pm and 8am during the week and throughout the weekends.
» Using the telephone in your hotel room is bound to be more expensive than using a payphone out on the street, whatever time you call.
» A small additional charge is made for connecting to some countries, which varies from €0.15 to €0.20.

PUBLIC TELEPHONES

» Public phone boxes are blue or silver and you won't have to go far to find one. Look for the *teléfon* signs.

INTERNATIONAL DIALLING CODES

Australia	00 61
Belgium	00 32
Canada	00 1
France	00 33
Germany	00 49
Greece	00 30
Ireland	00 353
Italy	00 39
Netherlands	00 31
New Zealand	00 64
Spain	00 34
Sweden	00 46
UK	00 44
USA	00 1

» They operate with both coins and phone cards (*tarjeta telefonica* or *credifone*), available from news-stands, post offices and tobacconists, and have instructions printed in English. Phones will accept 1 and 2 euro coins as well as 5, 10, 20 and 50 cents or phone cards of €6, €12 and €30. Note that *cabinas* (phone booths) do not give change, so can be an expensive way to call. There is a list of free numbers to dial inside the *cabina* for operator assistance, call charges etc.
» The international operator number is 1008 for Europe, 1005 for the rest of the world. For national directory enquiries, ring 11818.
» There are dozens of phone rooms (*locutori*) across the city, where you pay the attendant at the end of your call. These can be the cheapest way to make calls to countries outside Europe and the US, such as Australia or Asian countries, and also for national, European and US calls. *Locutorios* (and some convenience stores) also sell telephone call cards which provide you with as much as four hours of phone time (to another fixed phone) anywhere in the world for as little as €6. The most comfortable way to use these is from your hotel room. You dial a local number, punch in a pin number and dial the number. Connections can sometimes be erratic but the savings are well worth it.

MOBILE PHONES

» Check with your phone company before leaving home that you can use your phone abroad and what the call charges will be.
» You will be charged for picking up calls when you are not in your home country.
» If your mobile phone SIM card is removable, it makes sense to replace it with a Spanish card on

PHONE ROOMS (LOCUTORIOS)

STREET	TELEPHONE	OPENING HOURS
Carrer de Sant Pau 32–38	93 318 40 58	Daily 10am–midnight
Carrer de Canvis Vells 11	—	Daily 10am–midnight
Plaça de Catalunya (in RENFE rail station below the Plaça)	—	Daily 9–9
Avinguda de Roma 79–81	—	Daily 10am–11pm

USING A COIN-OPERATED PHONE

1 Lift the receiver and listen for the dialling tone.

2 Insert the required coin or coins. The coin drops as soon as you insert it.

3 Dial or press the number.

4 If you want to cancel the call before it is answered, or if the call does not connect, press the coin release lever or hang up and take the coins from the coin return.

5 The call is answered.

AREA CODES WITHIN SPAIN	
Madrid	91
Barcelona	93
Seville	95
Bilbao, Vizcaya	94
Valencia	96
Santander	942
Navarra	948
Granada	958

arrival. You will then be able to use the Spanish mobile system at local rates.

» You can rent mobile phones in Barcelona from Rent a Phone, Carrer de Numància 212, tel 93 280 21 31.

ADDRESSES IN SPAIN

» The abbreviation s/n stands for *sin número* and signifies a building that has no street number. This is mostly used by businesses, shops and museums.

» The abbreviation o, as in 1o, stands for *primer pis* (first floor) and signifies the floor of a building in an address.

» The letter a, as in 1a, stands for *primer porta* (first door) and signifies the number of an apartment.

SENDING AND RECEIVING POST

» Stamps (*sellos* in Castilian; *segells* in Catalan) are available from tobacconists (*estancs*), where you will see a brown and yellow symbol. Some hotels also sell them and have a post box you can use.

» Post boxes are bright yellow.

» The postal service is not fast. Letters and postcards to other EU countries will take up to a week to arrive and up to two weeks to the United States.

» Use the address Lista de Correos, 08070 Barcelona, Spain, if you want to be able to collect mail while on holiday. You will need to take your passport with you to collect it.

» Say something is *urgente* if you want to send it express.

» Use the Postal Exprés system if you want to send a parcel within Spain. It guarantees next-day delivery to main cities or within 48 hours to the rest of the country.

» The current rates for sending a letter weighing up to 20g are: within Spain €0.30, within Europe €0.64, to the rest of the world €0.78.

POST OFFICES

» The city's main post office (*correos*) is at Plaça d'Antoni López, at the bottom of the Via Laietana, open Mon–Sat 8.30am–9.30pm, Sun 9–2, www.correos.es.

» There are lots of branches around the city (see table below). Opening times for these branches are generally Mon–Sat 8.30am–8.30pm. The website (also in English) lists all opening hours.

INTERNET ACCESS

» This is common in hotels across the city and there is a huge range of internet and cyber cafés (see table below). Internet access is also available at some libraries. The city now offers free WiFi in public spaces throughout the city. See www.bcn. cat/barcelonawifi (also in English) for a list of locations.

» The international coffee shop chain, Starbucks, has free WiFi.

» Set up an email account with a provider such as Hotmail (www.hotmail.com) or Yahoo! (www.yahoo.com). Do this before you leave home and you will be able to send and receive emails while you are away.

Above Post boxes in the main post office at Plaça d'Antoni López

POST OFFICE BRANCHES
Avinguda Pedralbes 22
Carrer d'Aragó 282
Carrer de Balmes 76
Carrer de València 231
Gran de Gràcia 118
Plaça Bonsuccés s/n
Plaça Urquinaona 6
El Prat Airport, Terminal B
Ronda de la Universitat 23

INTERNET CAFES
Barnet
Barra de Faro 3 (just opposite Picasso Museum)
Café Idea Internet
Plaça Comercial 5
Inetcorner
Carrer Sardenya 306
www.inetcorner.net
Travel Bar
Carrer Boqueria 27
www.travelbar.com

TICKETS AND OPENING TIMES

OPENING TIMES

The traditional shutdown at lunchtime and over the weekend is less observed in this city than it is in more rural areas of Spain. However, there are still times when places are shut when you might not expect them to be. The heat of summer means that many places will reduce their opening times or close altogether during August.

BANKS

These are open Monday to Friday 8.30–2, Saturday 8.30–1, but close Saturdays in summer. It is unusual for banks to be open in the afternoon, although savings banks, such as LaCaixa, are open all day Thursday.

MUSEUMS

There is a lot of variation in the opening times for museums and other attractions, so check before you go. Generally, places are closed on Mondays or Tuesdays. It's also likely that small museums will close for lunch.

RESTAURANTS

Lunch is served from around 1.30pm–4pm, with dinner served from 9pm. Some restaurants will open earlier in the evening to cater for visitors who haven't yet adjusted to Mediterranean time.

SHOPS

Most shops close at 1.30pm–2pm and do not reopen until 4pm–5pm. They are open much later into the evening, often until around 9pm. You will find a number of smaller places close on Saturday afternoons and Sundays. The larger stores don't observe these times, opening instead throughout the day and on Saturdays.

Nearly all shops close on Sundays, except on the two Sundays before Christmas. The Maremagnum shopping centre (▷ 159) is open every day of the year. (Shops also close in August.)

PASSES

» If you want to immerse yourself in the city's art, buy the Articket pass, which gives free admission to six art galleries: the Museu Nacional d'Art de Catalunya (MNAC), the Fundació Joan Miró, the Fundació Antoni Tàpies, the Centre de Cultura Contemporània de Barcelona (CCCB), the Centre Cultural Caixa Catalunya at Casa Milà (La Pedrera) and the Museu d'Art Contemporani de Barcelona (MACBA). The pass can be bought from the museums' ticket offices or the tourist office at Plaça de Catalunya. It is valid for six months and costs €20.

» The Ruta del Modernisme is an itinerary that guides you to 115 Modernista works ranging from palatial residences to humble shops. The Centre del Modernisme (tel 902 07 66 21; www.rutadelmodernisme. com; Mon–Sat 10–7, Sun 10–2) at Plaça de Catalunya 17 sells a detailed guidebook (€12) that includes a book of discount vouchers for the major sights.

» When you buy either the Barcelona Card (▷ 43) or a Bus Turístic ticket (▷ 46) you will also get discounted entry to a whole host of places.

DISCOUNTS

» Seniors can get reductions on some museum entry charges on production of an identity document.

» An International Student Identity Card (ISIC; www.isic.org) may help obtain free or reduced entry to many museums and attractions as well as other discounts at stores.

» Many museums and attractions have lower admission charges for children, and those under five often get in free.

» The local council has recently introduced an initiative in which many city-run museums offer free admission on Sunday afternoons. The institutions which currently participate in this scheme are: Museu Picasso, Museu d'Història de Barcelona, Museu de Ciències Naturals (including the Jardí Botànic), Museu Barbier-Mueller d'Art Precolombí, Museu Frederic

NATIONAL HOLIDAYS
1 January
New Year's Day*
6 January
Epiphany*
March/April
Good Friday and Easter weekend*
1 May
Labour Day
May/June
Monday after Pentecost (Whit Monday)
24 June
St. John's Day*
15 August
Feast of the Assumption
11 September
National Day of Catalonia*
25 September
Feast of La Mercè*
12 October
National Day of Spain*
1 November
All Saints' Day*
6 December
Constitution Day
8 December
Feast of the Immaculate Conception
25 December
Christmas Day*
26 December
St. Stephen's Day*
*Denotes a holiday that is most respected and observed.

Marès, the Centre de la Imatge de la Virreina and Centre de Cultura Contemporània de Barcelona.

NATIONAL HOLIDAYS

» If you are in the city on a national holiday (see above) and want to visit a particular sight, phone ahead to check if it's open.

» If a national holiday falls on a Thursday or Friday, it's possible that celebrations will extend over the weekend, particularly if it's one of the more important days.

» The National Day of Spain on 12 October is not widely celebrated in Barcelona, but is marked with a day off.

» Many smaller shops and businesses close on the day or days following a national holiday.

TOURIST OFFICES

Tourist offices are identified by the use of the letter i and have a number of diamonds over the top of it. They don't have their own telephone numbers, as one central number serves all of them.

» The largest of the city's tourist offices is at Plaça de Catalunya. Here you will find the biggest selection of services: information on places of interest, transport and culture, a booking service for last-minute accommodation, an excellent gift shop and a branch of Caixa de Catalunya, which will change money for you and allow you to buy tickets from its Tel-Entrada system (▷ 250–251).

» Plaça de Sant Jaume has information, an accommodation booking service and a branch of Caixa de Catalunya; Estació de Sants has information and a branch of Caixa de Catalunya; and the airport has visitor information and an accommodation booking service.

» An army of people in red jackets take to the city streets in summer (Jun–end Sep), ready to assist visitors. They are known as *Casaques Vermelles* (red jackets) and work in pairs.

TOURIST OFFICES

Plaça de Catalunya
www.barcelonaturisme.com
☎ National calls: tel 807 117 222 (€0.40 per minute), international calls: tel +34 93 368 97 30
🕐 Daily 9–9

Plaça de Sant Jaume
✉ Inside the Town Hall, Carrer Ciutat 2
🕐 Mon–Fri 9–8, Sat 10–8, Sun and holidays 10–2

Estació de Sants, Plaça dels Països Catalans
🕐 Jul–end Aug daily 8–8; Sep–end Jun Mon–Fri 8–8, Sat–Sun and holidays 8–2

Airport terminals A and B
🕐 Daily 9–9

SPANISH TOURIST OFFICES ABROAD

CANADA
✉ 34th Floor, 2 Bloor Street West, Toronto, Ontario M4W 3E2 ☎ 416/961-3131 www.spain.info/ca/tourspain

GERMANY
✉ Myliusstrasse 14, 60325 Frankfurt-am-Main ☎ 69 72 50 33 (also in Berlin, Dusseldorf, Munich); www.spain.info/de/tourspain

UK AND REPUBLIC OF IRELAND
✉ 2nd Floor, 79 New Cavendish Street London, W1W 6XB ☎ 020 317 2010/ 0870 850 6599, www.tourspain.co.uk

USA
Los Angeles: ✉ 8383 Wilshire Boulevard, Suite 960, Beverly Hills, CA 90211
☎ 323/658-7195
New York: ✉ 666 Fifth Avenue, 35th Floor, New York 10103 ☎ 212/265-8822 www.spain.info

CATALAN TOURIST BOARDS OPEN TO THE PUBLIC
UK
✉ 3rd Floor, 17 Fleet Street, London EC4Y 1AA
☎ 020 7583 8855

USEFUL WEBSITES

www.barcelonaturisme.cat
This is the official tourist site and it covers a vast range of topics and has lots of helpful information. Its biggest drawback is that you have to dig around for the information, which is hidden under some very broad headings (in Castilian, Catalan, English and French).

www.bcn.cat
Run by the city council, this site is aimed at local residents. However, it does have a good section on tourism with information on opening times of major sights, plus practical information, such as the location of the nearest hospital (in Castilian, Catalan and English).

www.catalunyaturisme.com
Run by the Catalan government, this website gives comprehensive information on Catalonia—everything from the beaches to museums. It has links to the cultural website www.turismedecatalunya.com, with information on the region's culture and traditions.

www.fodors.com
A comprehensive travel-planning site that lets you research prices and book air tickets, aimed at the American market (in English).

www.renfe.es
The official site of the national railway company has information on arriving by train, and for trips out into Catalonia and beyond (▷ 51 and 208–231; in Castilian and English).

www.theaa.com
If you are planning to drive to the city or rent a car when you are there, visit this site for up-to-date travel advice (in English).

www.tmb.net
This is the very useful website of Barcelona's local transport company, with route options and advice on fares (in Castilian, Catalan and English).

MEDIA, BOOKS AND FILMS

TELEVISION

Television is loved in Spain and in bars you will often find a TV set showing a news or sports channel. There are many channels, but the ones that you are likely to come across are listed below.

» The two national state-run channels are TVE1, which shows films, reality TV and a lot of sports, and TVE2, with documentaries, interviews and European films.

» TV3 is a Catalan station with a wide-ranging schedule entirely in Catalan: a good place to practise your language skills.

» Canal 33 is another Catalan station that shows films and documentaries.

» Most hotels have satellite, cable or digital television that will allow you to view international channels such as BBC World, CNN and Sky.

RADIO

Most stations in Barcelona are on the FM frequency and the majority of these tend to be music based.

» The state-run public radio company is Radio Nacional de España (RNE), which has a current affairs station (RNE 1, 738AM), a classical music station (Radio Clásica, 99FM), a pop music station (Radio 3, 98.7FM) and a sports and entertainment station (RNE 5, 576AM).

» You can listen to the BBC World Service on 12095, 9410 and 6195 short wave, depending on the time of day.

NEWSPAPERS AND MAGAZINES

Newspaper readership in Spain is not as high as in other European countries, with TV and radio regarded as more entertaining purveyors of information. However, there is still a wide choice of publications available.

» Spain's most popular national newspapers are *El País* and *El Mundo*, both of which have very informative events listings, particularly in the weekend editions.

» The biggest-selling newspaper in the city is Barcelona's own *La Vanguardia*. Its excellent listings supplement *Que Fem* is published on Fridays.

» Popular English-language newspapers and magazines are on sale at stands along Las Ramblas and at newsagents in Gràcia.

» US publications such as the *International Herald Tribune, USA Today* and the *Wall Street Journal* are also readily available. They tend to appear in the afternoon of the day of publication, or the next day.

» An English-language version of *El País* is available inside *The Herald Tribune*, from Monday to Saturday.

» The magazine market is dominated by TV weeklies and celebrity gossip glossies, with the queen of them all, *¡Hola!*, continuing to thrive.

NEWSPAPERS	
ABC	A national, conservative daily
Catalonia Today	English-language monthly with local and some international news
El Mundo	A national, centre-right daily
El País	A national daily with a Catalonian edition that leans to the left
El Periódico de Catalunya	A centre-left daily, published in Catalan and Spanish
La Razón	A right-wing national daily
La Vanguardia	A Catalan daily that is more conservative with excellent listings sections

BOOKS

» *Homage to Catalonia* (Penguin Modern Classics) is George Orwell's bittersweet memoir of his experiences as a member of the International Brigade during the Spanish Civil War and is a moving account of a time in Barcelona's history that was inspirational to the young writer.

» *Gaudí: a Biography* (HarperCollins, 2002) by Gijs van Hensbergen is the most complete critical biography of the great architect.

» The first volume of John Richardson's definitive *A Life of Picasso* (Pimlico, 1997) is a fascinating account of the artist's early life in the city. This story of Picasso's formative years spent with the great Catalan artists of the age is a vivid account of turn-of-the-20th-century Barcelona, an artistic hothouse that moved to a distinctly bohemian beat.

» *Barcelona* (Harvill, 2001) by Robert Hughes provides an overview of Catalan art and the Catalan character, and attempts to get closer to the reasons why this corner of the Iberian peninsula has always stood out for its distinctive traditions and attention to detail. The book wasn't well received among many Catalans, who objected to an outsider's perspective of their beloved city, but remains to this day the most complete account of Barcelona available in English.

» It is hard to find English translations of the many Catalan writers who chronicle life in their home town, one exception being Eduardo Mendoza, who has written a number of novels set in the city. *City of Marvels* (Harvill, 1988) is his account of the difficulties of life in turn-of-the-20th-century Barcelona.

» Another is *The Soldiers of Salamis* (*Soldados de Salamina*) by the Catalan writer Javier Cercas. It was published in May 2003 by Bloomsbury and was one of Spain's most impressive best-sellers for three years. The novel tells the story of the last days of the Spanish Civil War in Catalonia and the retreat of the republican army to the Pyrenees.

» *Homage to Barcelona* (Picador, 2002) by Colm Toibin is an informative, visitor- abroad account of the history of Barcelona and life in the Catalan capital today.

» Ildefonso Falcones's novel *La Catedral del Mar* (*The Cathedral of the Sea*; 2006), based around the construction of the cathedral of Santa Maria del Mar, was a huge hit.

» *The Shadow of the Wind* (Weidenfeld & Nicolson, 2005) by Carlos Ruiz Zafón is a haunting story set in Barcelona after the Civil War.

MAPS

There is a street map at the back of this guide (▷ 270–285) and a metro map in the inside back cover. All the tourist offices have free street maps if you want to pick up something else while you are in the city. Free metro and pocket bus maps are available from stations and the TBM offices (▷ 43). There is an excellent interactive city map on the website www.bcn.cat/guia.

FILMS

Barcelona has great locations for directors looking to give their films historical detail or to use as a spectacular backdrop to tell their stories.

» Pedro Almodóvar won an Oscar for his direction of *All About My Mother* (1999), which he considered a tribute to Barcelona, a city he has always admired for its sense of freedom. The film captures Barcelona's essence in its rather melodramatic portrayal of a place filled with a collection of larger-than-life characters.

» Catalonia's best-known director is probably Bigas Luna, whose films are always controversial in their treatment of quintessentially Spanish obsessions. His film *La Teta y La Luna* (1994), which was shot in and around Barcelona, is the story of a young boy who falls in love with a breast.

» Veteran director Carlos Saura's *Marathon* (1993), the official film of the 1992 Olympic Games, is a beautifully shot record of one of the proudest moments in Barcelona's more recent history.

» Ken Loach's *Land and Freedom* (1994), loosely based on Orwell's book, charts the adventures of a young English communist in Spain during the Spanish Civil War.

» *Gaudí Afternoon* (2001) is the American director Susan Seidelman's film, based on a novel of the same name by Barbara Wilson. It uses Gaudí's buildings as a backdrop to this comedy.

» French Director Cédric Klapisch's *L' Auberge Espagnole* (2004) tells the story of a group of international Erasmus students living in a run-down apartment in El Raval. The film was an international hit, as much for its depiction of the city's laid-back lifestyle as for its backdrop of the old city.

» *Vicky Cristina Barcelona* (2008) was a huge hit for Woody Allen, and starred Penélope Cruz, Scarlett Johansson and Javier Bardem, with Barcelona as a glorious backdrop.

SHOPPING

Spain offers good value for money, even if it's not as cheap as it used to be, and Barcelona is the country's top shopping destination. The city's retail make-up has changed dramatically over the past decade, with more and more stores selling imported and regional goods, which is a reflection of the city's budding multiculturalism. But there are still plenty of home-grown products to hunt down.

While it may be tempting to head to the malls and department stores, nothing compares with the experience of seeking out small, local establishments. Catalonia was once known as a nation of shopkeepers and this is how most residents still shop: small outlets with personal service. Nobody seems to mind waiting for just the right cut of ham off the bone or a perfectly matching button. This sort of one-to-one contact is part of the experience for the visitor and all it takes is confidence in your communication skills.

FOOD
One of the best choices, either for yourself or as a gift, is food. Catalonia's cured pork travels and keeps extremely well. *Botifarras* (rich pork sausages), *fuet* (a type of salami) and other varieties are produced throughout the region but are particularly good from the city of Vic. Other good buys include local cheeses: there are several specialist shops and market stalls which offer a fine selection of Catalan artisanal cheeses, including the creamy *mató* which is usually served with honey as a dessert. Olives are also popular gifts and are readily available at most markets. You can usually try the different varieties before making your selection. Have your selections vacuum-packed *(envasar al buit)* and once sealed they will keep for months. Most visitors reach for a Rioja, but wine from the Catalan regions of Penedès (the home of cava—a sparkling wine) and Priorat are gaining a good reputation among viniculturalists. Some of the larger stores (such as El Corte Inglés, ▷ 121) can arrange to have larger purchases shipped home. If you are planning to take your food item home with you, check customs regulations.

LEATHER
Spanish leatherwear is world famous and a bargain compared to Italian price tags. Shoes—many of them made on the Balearic island of Mallorca—are fabulous, both in terms of design and quality, particularly the Camper brand, which is available everywhere. Leather coats and jackets are sold along Las Ramblas and while the selling technique may be a bit aggressive, a luxurious leather jacket at a bargain price is worth it.

DESIGN
Barcelona shines in the field of fashion and design. Young designers display their wares in tiny shops in La Ribera district, in the streets

around the MACBA (▷ 68–69) in El Raval and in Gràcia. Museum shops are also good places to pick up trendy objets d'art and no true design junkie should miss out on Vinçon: the emporium that has launched many local designers (▷ 198). Vinçon is the best known of several fantastic interior design shops to be found in the elegant L'Eixample neighbourhood.

CRAFTS

Many objects can be picked up for a couple of euros. Basic beige and yellow ceramics from Catalonia's Costa Brava are inexpensive and plentiful, especially the everyday, fired terracotta *cassoles* (dishes) that you will probably spot on your tapas bar visits. The *porró*, a classic Catalan drinking jar with a long spout, is easy to find, but not so easy to drink from unless you've had years of practice. Although you won't see many people using them in Barcelona, they are still popular in country bars and restaurants: the adept ensure an arc of wine lands squarely in the mouth even when held at arm's length. Reproduction Modernista tiles are a stunning asset to bathrooms and kitchens. The

espardenya (*alpargatara* in Spanish), the Catalan espadrille (rope sandal), usually has two-toned ribbons that wrap around the ankle, making stylish summer shoes. *Espardenyes* are traditionally worn when dancing the stately Catalan round dance, the *sardana*. Most of these items can be picked up in souvenir shops, but they are likely to be mass-produced, so try and seek them out in *barri* stores and markets.

SHOPPING AREAS

The narrow lanes of the Barri Gòtic (Gothic Quarter) are packed with small, specialist shops: antiques rub shoulders with quirky fashion shops along the Carrer dels Banys Nous, and chocolatatiers and art galleries can be found along Carrer Petritxol. The Carrer Portaferrissa and the Avinguda del Portal de l'Àngel are lined with all the main high-street chains, from H&M to Zara. Carrer d'Avinyó has more offbeat fashion, and the delightful Plaça del Pi has regular markets selling everything from paintings to local honey.

The gritty but hip Raval district is best for second-hand stores and vintage boutiques, offbeat fashion by young designers, art galleries

(especially around Carrer del Doctor Dou) and vinyl record stores.

La Ribera is the best area to come to find unique and original fashions from up-and-coming designers. Its narrow streets are a delight to wander around, and you'll find scores of enticing boutiques selling upmarket fashion and accessories. The area is also well known for its contemporary design shops, selling ultra-modern furnishings and decorative objects. Traditionally, the area around the Basílica de Santa Maria del Mar sold jewellery, particularly the Carrer de l'Argenteria (Silversmith Street), and there are still some fine contemporary jewellery shops in this neighbourhood. It's also a great place to come for gourmet foodstuffs, with chic new delis, wine shops and old-fashioned specialists selling everything from freshly roast coffee to dried fruits.

The Passeig de Gràcia is the main shopping street of L'Eixample, with branches of all the major chain stores. At the lower end of the street, you will find Spanish mid-range staples such as Zara and Mango, while all the major international fashion names—Chanel, Gucci, Loewe among them—are found at the upper end, close to the intersection with Avinguda Diagonal. La Diagonal is also a major fashion centre, with more high-end fashion chains and stylish interior design shops.

With Barcelona's wide choice of performances, you can hear every type of music, watch cutting-edge modern dance, opera or classical ballet, go to the theatre, or take in an art-house film at the cinema.

There's some of Spain's best nightlife in Barcelona, where club culture is taken seriously and top DJs make regular appearances. The scene evolves constantly, with bars and clubs often opening, closing and changing management, and the city's resident DJs skipping from one venue to another.

Make a point of collecting flyers when you arrive and pick up free listings magazines, such as *Barcelona Metropolitan* and *Time Out Barcelona* (in Catalan). Things get going late, so set out to hit the bar scene at around 11pm or later and be prepared to wait in line before partying at the clubs until 5am or 6am. Weekends are particularly frenetic, when locals, weekenders from all over Europe and huge numbers of UK bachelor parties come face to face at popular night-time venues. Entry to bars and cafés is usually free, but expect to pay to get into the clubs. Keep hold of your entrance ticket, though—it usually includes a complimentary drink.

CINEMAS
Barcelona has plenty of venues, from single-screens to multi-complexes. Some show movies in the original language with Spanish subtitles.
» First showings are usually 4pm–4.30pm, and the most popular is at 10pm–10.30pm.
» Many cinemas have a reduced-price day, the *día del espectador*, usually on Monday or Wednesday.
» Cinema listings are in the *Guía del Ocio*, *Time Out Barcelona* (in Catalan), and the newspapers.
» Smoking is not permitted in the city's cinemas.

CLASSICAL MUSIC, DANCE AND OPERA
The star venues are L'Auditori (▷ 175), home to the city's symphony orchestra, the OBC, and the Palau de la Música Catalana (▷ 144–147, 160). The city's churches have occasional concerts. The tourist office will be able to provide information.

Barcelona is Spain's most vibrant city for contemporary dance, particularly by groups such as the Gelabert-Azzopardi Companyia de Dansa and Metros, who appear during festivals. You can catch visiting ballet companies at the Liceu, as well as flamenco companies. The city has its own *tablaos*, places where you can see flamenco, such as Poble Espanyol (▷ 77).

» The season runs from September to the end of June.
» Buy tickets from the box offices, by phone or via Servi-Caixa or Caixa Catalunya (see below).
» Get information in the monthly *Informatiu Musical* from tourist offices, *Guía del Ocio* and the daily press.
» Smoking is not permitted in the auditoria of these venues.

CONTEMPORARY LIVE MUSIC
Rock, jazz, *rumba catalana* and Catalan music thrive alongside the vibrant DJ-based scene, and the city is famous for its live music and summer festivals. Latin, Cuban and the sounds of Africa also have strong followings.
» Listings magazines include the *Guía del Ocio* (in Spanish, with a small English section); *Time Out Barcelona* (Catalan); *Barcelona Metropolitan* (a free English magazine available in bars and cafés); and the excellent weekly pull-out *Que Fem?* (with *La Vanguardia* newspaper on Fridays); all available at news-stands, bars and shops.
» Friday's edition of *El País* carries the excellent *Tentaciones* magazine.
» Note that many smaller music venues close in August, but outdoor concerts are often held during the summer.
» Tickets are usually purchased at the door.

THEATRE
Catalan theatre, with its blend of music, dance and spectacular production, seamlessly crosses the language barrier, making theatre far more accessible than elsewhere in Spain. Look for companies such as Els Comedients, whose shows are based on mime, folklore, circus and music; La Cubana, popular for its mix of glitz and audience participation; and the mainstream Lliure. Els Comedients and La Cubana have no fixed base, but Lliure, the city's most prestigious company, is based at Teatre Lliure (Carrer de Montseny 47).
» The main season runs from September to the end of June.
» Performances start between 9pm and 10.30pm. Some theatres have 6pm–7pm performances on Wednesday, Saturday and Sunday; most theatres close on Monday.
» Buy tickets at box offices (some are cash only).
» The magazines *Guía del Ocio*, *Time Out Barcelona*, *Barcelona Metropolitan* and *Que Fem?* have listings.

TICKETING IN BARCELONA
Services run by two savings banks, known as Servi-Caixa (La Caixa, tel 902 33 22 11; www.serviticket.com) and Tel-Entrada (Caixa Catalunya, tel 902 10 12 12; www.telentrada.com), allow you to book tickets on the internet, over the counter in some

branches, by telephone, or via the ticket machines in bigger branches.

NIGHTLIFE

The summer scene is different from the rest of the year. Some outdoor clubs only operate from June to the end of September and there's the bonus that others, normally weekend-only venues, will be pulling in the huge crowds. This is when Barcelona's waterfront setting comes into its own, with beach bars spilling out onto the sand.

Don't miss the final part of nights out in the city: breakfast at one of Barcelona's all-night bars where you can finish the evening with fresh pastries and chocolate, or boost your energy for more clubbing.

WHAT'S WHERE

» Maremagnum and the Port Olímpic for salsa, mainstream rock and house clubs.
» Plaça Reial and the Barri Gòtic for pop, rock, funk and soul.
» El Raval for old-established bars and clubs.

» La Ribera for designer bars and clubs.
» Montjuïc for non-stop all-night clubbing.
» L'Eixample and Gràcia for trendy clubs, salsa, samba and tango.
» Zona Alta (including Sarrià, Puxtet, Sant Gervasi and Tibidabo) for serious poseurs and those who have money to spend.

GAY AND LESBIAN

Barcelona's gay and lesbian scene is among the best in Europe, with hundreds of establishments supplying everything from gym access to restaurants and accommodation, as well as some of the best party nights. Nightlife brings many types of people together, so you'll have a great time even at places that are not strictly gay—el ambiente (the atmosphere) is all. Head for L'Eixample, known as the 'Gayxample' with the largest concentration of gay venues in the city, to start your explorations.

Remember that Barcelona is close to Sitges (▷ 228–229), a short

journey down the coast, which is also known for its gay nightlife.
» The group Coordinadora Gai-Lesbiana is your best source of information for what's happening in and around the city. This umbrella organization works with the Ajuntament (town hall) on all issues of concern to the gay community in Barcelona, and should be your first stop. You can drop by during the evening (Mon–Sat 9–2, 5–8) to pick up literature and information. You can find Coordinadora Gai-Lesbiana at Carrer Violant d'Hongria 156, 08014 (tel 93 298 00 29) or visit the website: www.cogailes.org.
» There are two publications that you should look out for: the *Gay Barcelona* map, which is updated annually, and the *Nois* magazine, which is comprehensive in its coverage and accurate in the information supplied; for more details visit the website: www.revistanois.com. You'll find both of these useful publications at the shop Sestienda on the Carrer de Rauric 11, Barri Gòtic (tel 93 318 86 76).

and the minimum age to attend a bullfight is 14.

Bridging the gap between watching and doing is Barcelona's Marathon, established in 1977 and attracting huge crowds of runners and spectators alike. If you want to take part, visit the website at www.barcelonamarato.es. You can register online or download an application form to register by post.

GETTING INVOLVED

For exercise gentler than the marathon, consider using one of the many *poliesportius* (sports halls) run by the town hall. These range from basic to superbly equipped gyms with pools; they welcome visitors and charges are low.

Hot weather may make cooling off a priority, which is not a problem when there are more than 25 municipally run, inexpensive pools and a choice of beaches on the edge of the city. Head farther out and you'll find golf, riding and watersports. Above all, remember that Barcelona is blessed with some lovely green spaces, where you can stroll, jog or simply relax. Tibidabo and Montjuïc are biggest, but don't neglect Park Güell, Pedralbes or Parc de Joan Miró.

For more information on the city's sporting facilities contact: Servei d'Informació Esportiva, Avinguda de l'Estadi 30–40, Montjuïc (tel 93 402 30 00).

ON THE BEACH

During the summer, beach culture reigns. You can visit a major museum in the morning and splash around in the sea after lunch. Barceloneta beach (▷ 138) is the most central and also the hangout of the city's surfers and windsurfers. Out-of-town beaches tend to be cleaner and quieter, and have good public transport links. The Macanet-Massanes train (from Plaça de Catalunya RENFE station every half hour) skirts the immediate northern coast, and all stops are near the beach. Family-friendly Castelldefells, with its endless sandy beaches, is a short train ride to the south.

SPORTS AND ACTIVITIES

You will find plenty of options for sports all over the city, whether you want to experience the buzz of a live match, or work off some of those delicious Catalan meals. As a general rule, tickets for the major venues are available via the Servi-Caixa or Tel-Entrada booking services (▷ 250–251).

SOCCER

Barcelona has some superb facilities in the shape of the Olympic complex on Montjuïc, which are regularly used for soccer and American football, as well as for international sporting events. Soccer is top of the list for locals, and many visitors too. The city's main clubs are FC Barcelona and RCD Espanyol. The season runs from September to the middle of June and most league matches take place on Saturday and Sunday evenings. You shouldn't have much trouble getting hold of a ticket for a RCD Espanyol game, but Barça, which has more season ticket holders than there are seats in the stadium, is another matter. However, some 4,000 tickets go up for sale a week before matches, so phone the club (▷ 218) to find out the time, and line up at the ticket office on the Travessera de les Corts at least an hour before the box office opens. You'll find up-to-the-minute information for both clubs by visiting www.fcbarcelona.com and www.rcdespanyol.com.

OTHER SPORTS

After soccer, basketball is Spain's best-loved spectator sport, and Barcelona has two major teams competing in the league, FC Barcelona (run and financed by the soccer team) and Club Juventut Badalona. Their season runs from September to the end of May and matches are played mainly on Saturday and Sunday evenings.

If tennis is your thing, Barcelona's Reial Club de Tenis hosts an important 10-day tournament in April as part of the ATP circuit. Find out more at www.rctb1899.es.

Unlike other areas of Spain, support for bullfighting in Catalonia has never been particularly strong, and the Catalan government dislikes it. However, the season runs from April to the end of September,

FOR CHILDREN

Barcelona has lots going on for children. The city itself, with its quirky Modernista buildings, picturesque cobbled streets and bustling waterfront, has a high entertainment factor, and there's a good choice of museums, parks and attractions. If your children need to let off steam, head for the parks, hills or beaches, or consider a day out at one of the nearby coastal resorts. Within the city, children's attractions are focused around Montjuïc, Tibidabo and the Port Vell. Even getting there will be fun by way of the trams, funiculars, cable cars and *golondrinas*, the harbour boats. If you want to throw in a bit of education, children enjoy watching the craft demonstrations at the Poble Espanyol, while the hands-on exhibits in museums such as the CosmoCaixa and the Museu de l'Història de Catalunya are big draws.

IN THE CITY

In July and August, many museums stage fun activities for kids as part of the Estiu als Museus (Summer in the Museums). Find out more at tourist information offices and La Virreina (▷ 104).

The Ajuntament puts on regular children's entertainment, including concerts, puppet shows and magic shows, mainly held in local civic halls. La Virreina can fill you in on these.

If your children prefer their entertainment outdoors, Barcelona has beautiful, sandy beaches and green parks, not forgetting the zoo and aquarium.

PORT AVENTURA

Port Aventura is one of Europe's biggest and best parks. It's an hour and 15 minutes by train from Barcelona, with its own railway station, making it an easy option if your children have had their fill of the city's cultural charms. The main park is divided into five zones: Mediterranean, Polynesia, the Far West, Mexico and China, and all five zones have a selection of themed rides and entertainment, with plenty for small children as well as teenagers and adults. The admission price gives you unlimited rides; a supplement gets you admission to

the adjoining Costa Caribe water park. The park has plenty of food outlets and buggy rental.

Port Aventura is at Salou (tel 977 90 90 77; ticket information 902 20 20 41; RENFE train information 902 24 02 02; www.portaventura.es). Admission is from €44 for adults, and from €35 for children aged 4–10 years. To reach Port Aventura by car take the A7 (La Jonquera to Valencia) and turn off at exit 35.

Above *The Font Màgica (Magic Fountain) with its spectacular water and light displays set to music is a great hit with children in Plaça d'Espanya*

FESTIVALS AND EVENTS

Barcelona's cultural department runs a comprehensive information office with details of cultural events and festivals. It also sells tickets and has an excellent bookshop: Centre d'Informacío de la Virreina, Palau de la Virreina, La Rambla 99 (tel 93 301 77 75, Mon–Fri 10–2, 4–8). The 010 city information phone line has details of festivals, as does the cultural section at www.bcn.es.

There are a number of elements that have become part of Barcelona's festivals, and you will see some or all of them at the major events, especially in the *barris* (districts).

» *Castells* are human towers, formed by up to nine levels of people balancing on the shoulders of the level below. It is a superb illustration of balance and communal collaboration.

» *Gegants* and *capsgrossos*: *Gegants* (giants) are huge papier-mâché and wooden figures, often representing historical and folkloric characters. They are accompanied by the *capsgrossos* (bigheads), capering characters wearing huge mask heads.

» *Correfoc* means fire-running, when a parade of dragons runs through the streets spitting fire and showering onlookers with sparks from the firecrackers they carry, all accompanied by a compelling drumbeat.

JANUARY
CAVALCADA DELS REIS
This is the procession of the three kings through the city, celebrating the Epiphany. They throw sweets for the children, who receive their Christmas presents on this day.
✉ Moll de la Fusta to Plaça de Sant Jaume ✪ 6 Jan ⊞ Drassanes for Moll de la Fusta

FEBRUARY
CARNESTOLTES
This 10-day pre-Lent carnival takes place all over the city, with processions, dancing, street markets and concerts, culminating in the Enterrament de la Sardina (Burial of the Sardine) on Montjuïc to mark the Lenten fasting to come.

MARCH
SANT MEDIR DE GRÀCIA
A procession of traditionally dressed men, mounted on horses, wends its stately way to the hermitage of Sant Medir for a bean feast: something residents of Catalonia are known for. Sweets are traditionally given away during the parade and the evening ends in fireworks.
✉ Collserola ✪ 3 Mar

MARCH–APRIL
SETMANA SANTA
A number of religious processions held on Palm Sunday and throughout the week leading up to Easter Sunday. Churches around Barcelona participate, but the principal processions take place in Barri Gòtic.
✪ Week before Easter

APRIL
SANT JORDI
St. George's Day honours Catalonia's patron saint. Traditionally, men give women a rose and receive a book in exchange. As a consequence, book- and rose-sellers will be out and about in the city.
✪ 23 Apr

FERIA DE ABRIL
There is a large Andalusian population in Barcelona, and they started this 10-day festival, celebrating all things Andalusian, with flamenco and food.
✉ Diagonal-Mar 🚇 Besòs-Mar

FESTIVAL DE MÚSICA ANTIGA
Indoor and outdoor concerts are performed by ensembles from all over Europe.
✉ Barri Gòtic 🚇 Jaume I

MAY
TALLERS OBERTS
www.tallersoberts.net
Tallers Oberts (Open Workshops) lets you experience the work of local artists and artisans in their own workplace. Pick up a map from the tourist office or download one from the website, and take a peek at a potter at his wheel, jewellers and other craftspeople. Many of their wares are on sale.

FESTA DE LA DIVERSITAT
This three-day festival is part of a wider one across Spain. It aims to bring together Barcelona's ethnically diverse population, with concerts, stands and food from different parts of the community.
✉ Moll de la Fusta 🚇 Drassanes

FESTIVAL DE FLAMENCO DE LA CUITAT VELLA
www.tallerdemusics.com
This is a great chance to catch some world-class flamenco. Most concerts take place at the CCCB (▷ 59) and in some of the smaller bars and clubs around the old city. Performances cover dance, song and *nuevo flamenco*, a fusion of flamenco with jazz and rock.
🕐 Late May

JUNE
SÓNAR
www.sonar.es
Barcelona's three-day cutting-edge electronic music festival includes exhibitions, concerts and chilled-out dance venues.
🕐 Mid-Jun

SANT JOAN
The night before the feast of St. Joan is La Nit del Foc (night of fire), with spectacular firecracker displays, processions and dancing all over the city.
🕐 23 Jun

JUNE–JULY
BARCELONA FESTIVAL GREC
www.barcelonafestival.org
Barcelona's main performing arts festival gets it name from the Teatre Grec (▷ 77), the faux Greek amphitheatre on Montjuïc. This is where a large number of the theatre, music and dance performances take place.

AUGUST
FESTA MAJOR DE GRÀCIA
A huge district festival, taking place over 10 days, with vibrantly decorated streets, entertainment and feasting (▷ 178). Here you will see *gegants*, *castells* and *correfoc*.
✉ Gràcia

SEPTEMBER
DIADA DE CATALUNYA
This is the region's national day, which actually commemorates the day the city was taken by Philip V in 1714 (▷ 31). It is a serious day by comparison to other festivals, and you are likely to see political demonstrations.
🕐 11 Sep

FESTES DE LA MERCÈ
Held in the name of Our Lady of Mercy, this week-long celebration marks the end of summer with music, procession, *gegants*, *castells*, *correfoc*, concerts, firecrackers, dancing and music. It is one of the best festivals in the city.
🕐 Around 24 Sep

MOSTRA DE VINS I CAVES DE CATALUNYA
www.mostradevinsicaves.com
This fair coincides with La Mercè festival (see above) and gives you the chance to sample Catalonia's wines and cavas. Join the queue to buy tasting tickets, which include

a tasting glass. Local cheeses and other goods are also sold.
✉ Maremagnum 🕐 Late Sep
🚇 Drassanes

FESTA MAJOR DE LA BARCELONETA
Gràcia's *festa major* may get most of the glory, but the fishing enclave of Barceloneta also knows how to put on a good show and for many it is a more authentic expression of neighbourhood pride. Activities include *habanera* (sea-shanty) concerts by the port and all-night dancing in the streets. Watch in amazement how tiny shops selling light switches transform themselves into mojito bars for the occasion.
🕐 Late Sep–early Oct

OCTOBER–DECEMBER
FESTIVAL INTERNATIONAL DE JAZZ DE BARCELONA
One of the key festivals in this jazz-loving city, attracting a wide range of national and international names.
✉ Palau de la Música 🚇 Urquinaona

NOVEMBER
TOTS SANTS
All Saints' Day is the day when people traditionally visit the graves of their loved ones—and eat *castanyas* (sweet chestnuts) and *panellets* (small sweet cakes) from food stands.
🕐 1 Nov

DECEMBER
FIRA DE SANTA LLÚCIA
A Christmas market selling all you could need to celebrate the Christian festive season, including trees, decorations and gifts. There are traditional nativity figures and a life-size nativity in Plaça de Sant Jaume.
✉ Plaça de la Seu 🕐 1–23 Dec
🚇 Jaume I

CAP D'ANY
New Year's Eve is celebrated with parties and public celebrations—eat 12 grapes while midnight chimes to ensure enough good luck to last for the year ahead.
🕐 31 Dec

Eating out in this city is a real pleasure, with the emphasis firmly on seasonal and fresh produce, and a huge range of restaurants, snack bars, tapas bars, cafés and *granjas* feeding residents and visitors throughout the day and night. Spain has no true national cuisine, apart from paella (saffron-flavoured rice, chicken and seafood), tortilla (omelette) and gazpacho (tomato- and pepper-based chilled soup), as cooking is firmly regional.

Barcelona, however, has embraced mainstream Europe more wholeheartedly than anywhere else on the peninsula, and the city's cosmopolitan air shines through in its restaurants. Regional Catalan dishes and ingredients are to the fore, but there is a good range of places serving food from other parts of Spain and from other countries—something not readily available in many other Spanish cities. But if you are dying for a fast-food burger, you will find that too.

BREAKFAST
The first meal of the day *(desayuno,* or *esmorzar* in Catalan) is usually eaten by city residents between 9am and 10am, often after they've started work. In hotels, breakfast may be included in the room price, but if not, head for a bar or café. The quintessential breakfast is chocolate with churros *(xocolata amb xurros)*, a thick sweet chocolate served with strips of deep-fried dough, which you dip in the chocolate. Otherwise choose a croissant, doughnut or roll with ham or cheese.

LUNCH
The main meal *(almuerzo,* or *dinar* in Catalan) is served between 2pm and 4pm, and is traditionally the most important meal of the day. In Barcelona most restaurants serve a *menú del dia,* a fixed-price menu with a choice of a starter, main course, dessert, bread and a drink. It's excellent value and a good way to sample some of the city's more expensive restaurants.

DINNER
Cena (sopar in Catalan) starts any time after 9pm, and continues until midnight, though traveller-oriented restaurants open as early as 8pm. It's traditionally a lighter meal than lunch, such as salads, soups and egg dishes.

VEGETARIAN FOOD
There are few exclusively vegetarian restaurants in Barcelona, but an increasing number of places serve good vegetable dishes. You may need to be on your guard, however, as some of the more traditional places may use meat stock, ham or pork fat, and still think they're serving meat-free dishes.

CHILDREN
Children's menus are non-existent, but they'll be welcome at all establishments, except the most expensive restaurants. If your children want smaller or plain meals, tapas are a good choice, with options such as bread or tortilla.

RESERVATIONS
Booking is advised in mid- to upper price range restaurants, particularly for groups of four or more and at the weekends. For less formal places, such as tapas bars, you can walk

in and secure a table, even if you have to wait at the bar for a space to become available. However, if there is an establishment that you really want to visit, check out whether booking is necessary.

MONEY

Locals usually tip only small sums. For visitors, a small tip at any bar or restaurant and 10 per cent of the bill is usual. More expensive restaurants will add a 7 per cent tax to the bill. The menu will state if this is the case. All major credit cards are accepted (although American Express and Diners Club cards are rarely accepted), except in smaller places; these are indicated in the listings.

SMOKING

Smoking is usually permitted. If this is not the case, or a non-smoking section is available, this is stated within the listings.

A QUICK GUIDE TO CATALAN CUISINE

TASTES

Catalan cooking is related to Spanish and French cuisine, but is highly individual and uses combinations of textures and tastes to give it an extra twist. Signature elements that distinguish Catalan dishes include:

» **Sofregit**, onion and tomatoes gently sautéed in olive oil.
» **Allioli**, garlic and olive oil mayonnaise served with meat and seafood.
» **Samfaina**, an onion, garlic, peppers and aubergine (eggplant) mix served with grilled meat and fish.
» **Picada**, a sauce made with garlic, bread, chillies, nuts and parsley used to enrich and thicken stews and casseroles.
» **A la brasa**, meat, fish or sausage grilled over an open charcoal fire.

GRANJAS

These are very much part of the city refreshment scene and were originally outlets for fresh dairy products. They still concentrate on dairy-based goodies, and are great places to come for coffee, milkshakes (*batidos*) and thick hot chocolate topped with a mountain of whipped cream (*suizos*). They're also strong on cakes and pastries, and make good stops for weary sightseers in need of a sugar boost, but you won't be guaranteed a beer in many of them.

HORCHATERIAS

Another alternative is the *horchateria* (*orxateria* in Catalan), which sell the wonderfully refreshing drink *horchata*, made from crushed tiger nuts. This curdles once it's made, so it has to be drunk on the spot while it's fresh.

When ordering in both *horchaterias* and *granjas* follow the general rule: pay as you leave. You can attract attention by a polite *oiga* (hear me), which should bring you the waiter. Tipping is discretionary here, but most people round up the bill to the nearest euro.

TAPAS

Tapas, snacks once traditionally served free with a drink, are Spain's great contribution to the European culinary scene, and you'll find a good range of tapas bars in Barcelona. Tapas range from a few olives or almonds to tortilla, chunks of meat and fish, cured ham, shellfish, anchovies, salads, meat croquettes and wonderful vegetable dishes laced with garlic and chilli. They can be either hot or cold, but don't just see them as a snack or pre-dinner eat. Make a few selections and have them as your evening meal. If you are still hungry, you just order more.

TAPAS ETIQUETTE

When you enter a tapas bar, the food will be laid out on the counter for you to choose from (useful if your Spanish isn't great, as you can point at what you like the look of), listed on a chalkboard behind the bar or, in some of the more expensive bars, on menus. If you want more than a mouthful or two, ask for a *ración*, a larger serving. Don't worry about keeping account of how many different dishes you order, as the bartender will normally keep track of what you've had.

FAST FOOD

International burger chains can be found in Barcelona. Two nationwide chains, Pans & Co and Bocatta, serve *bocadillos* (sandwiches) and other snacks and have branches throughout the city. Don't be confused, though, as a sandwich in Barcelona is akin to a toasted sandwich, made using sliced white bread. The Catalan version is an *entrepan*, made with a French baguette or rolls.

ALCOHOLIC DRINKS

Beer is one of the most popular choices and comes in bottles or on draught; ask for a *canya* or *canya doble* for a larger glass. Estrella, Voll-Damm and Black-Damm are the Catalonian specials and imported beers are widely available. However, wine is probably still first choice. House wines are more than acceptable, which is useful as good wines tend to be expensive. The sparkling wine cava makes a good aperitif. Spirits are inexpensive and served in hefty measures. Long drinks such as *gin-tonic*, *vodka-tónica* and *cuba-libre* (rum and cola) are popular.

SOFT DRINKS

Locals normally drink bottled water in restaurants; ask for *aigua amb gas* (sparkling) or *sense gas* (still). The full range of international soft drinks is everywhere. Fresh fruit juice (*suc*) and *granitzat* (slush) are also widely available.

Coffee is served in bars, cafés and *granjas*. It's normally served as good, strong black espresso (*café sol/solo*). If you want milk, ask for a *café tallat/cortado*, a small cup with a drop of milk, or *café amb llet/café con leche*, made with lots of hot milk. Tea is hard to find; try an *infusion*, such as *manzanilla* (camomile) instead.

Launching yourself into the city's vibrant restaurant culture can be a daunting experience if you don't speak Castilian, let alone Catalan, and working out what's on the menu something of a challenge. But don't be put off, as a few key words will help and the menu reader below will familiarize you with individual foods and dishes that you are likely to come across. Each is given in Catalan, followed by the Castilian in brackets, although some dishes are regional and are therefore not translated.

PLATS (PLATOS) COURSES
els entrants (los entrantes) appetizers
el primer (el primero) first course
el segon (el segundo) main course
postres (postre) dessert

CARN (CARNE) MEAT
ànec (pato) duck
anyell (cordero) lamb
bistec (bistec) steak
botifarra negra (butifarra negra) blood sausage
carn (carne) beef
conill (conejo) rabbit
fetge (hígado) liver
gall dindi (pavo) turkey
llengua (lengua) tongue
perdiu (perdiz) partridge
pernil dolç (jamón cocido) cooked ham
pernil (jamón serrano) cured ham
peus (pies) trotters
pollastre (pollo) chicken
porc (cerdo) pork
salsitxa (salchicha) sausage
vedella (ternera) veal
xoriço (chorizo) spicy sausage

PEIX (PESCADO) FISH
anxoves (anchoas) anchovies
bacallà (bacalao) salted cod
llenguado (lenguado) sole
lluç (merluza) hake
llobarro (lubina) sea bass
moll (salmonete) red mullet
rap (rape) monkfish
salmó (salmón) salmon
truita (trucha) trout
tonyina (atún) tuna

MARISC (MARISCOS) SEAFOOD
anguila (anguila) eel
calamars (calamares) squid
cranc (cangrejo) crab
gambes (gambas) prawns (shrimps)
llagosta (langosta) lobster
musclos (mejillones) mussels
ostres (ostras) oysters
pop (pulpo) octopus

VEDURES (VERDURAS) VEGETABLES
albergínia (berenjena) aubergine (eggplant)
bròquil (brécol) broccoli
carabassó (calabacín) courgette (zucchini)
ceba (cebolla) onion
cogombre (pepino) cucumber
col (berza) cabbage
enciam (lechuga) lettuce
espàrrecs (espárragos) asparagus
faves (habas) broad beans
mongetes tendres (judías verdes) green beans
pastanagues (zanahorias) carrots
patates (patatas) potatoes
pebrots (pimientos) peppers
pèsols (guisantes) peas
xampinyons (champiñones) mushrooms

MÈTODE DE CUINA (MÉTODO DE COCINA) COOKING METHODS
a la brasa (a la brasa) flame-grilled (broiled)

a la planxa (a la plancha) grilled
al forn (al horno) baked, roasted
cru (crudo) raw
escumat (poché) poached
farcit (relleno) stuffed
fregit (frito) fried
rostit (asado) roast

ESPECIALITATS (ESPECIALIDADES) SPECIALS

allioli (alioli) a kind of mayonnaise with garlic but without egg
amanida mixta (ensalada mixta) salad that can include a wide range of vegetables
amanida russa (ensalada rusa) Russian or little salad made of potato, peas, carrots and mayonnaise
arròs (arroz) rice dishes, some cooked with fish, others with vegetables, meat or sausages
bacallà a la biscaïna (bacalao a la vizcaína) salted cod in a sauce of piquant peppers and sweet chillies
canelons similar to cannelloni, but stuffed with tuna or spinach as well as meat and covered in white, rather than tomato, sauce
escalivada a dish of peppers, aubergine (eggplant) and courgette (zucchini)
escudella meat and vegetable stew
fideuà paella made with fine noodles
gaspatxo (gazpacho) chilled soup made from puréed bread and garlic, raw peppers, tomatoes and cucumber
mandonguilles amb salsa (albóndigas en salsa) meatballs in sauce, usually tomato
pa amb tomàquet (pan con tomate) bread rubbed with tomato, sprinkled with salt and drizzled with olive oil
paella the most famous of the *arròs*, but saffron is used less than in the traditional Valencian dish
patates braves (patatas bravas) potatoes in a spicy tomato sauce
tortilla española Spanish omelette made with potatoes
tortilla francesa plain omelette
xurros (churros) strips of fried dough covered in sugar

POSTRES (POSTRE) CAKES AND DESSERTS

amb nata (con nata) with cream
bunyols (buñuelos) warm, sugared, deep-fried doughnuts, sometimes cream-filled
cassoleta de fruites (la tartaleta de frutas) fruit tart
crema catalana a creamy sweet custard, served cold with a crackling layer of caramelized sugar on top
flam (flan) crème caramel
gelat (helado) ice cream
pastís (pastel) cake
pastís de formatge (la tarta de queso) cheesecake
pastís de xocolata (el pastel de chocolate) chocolate cake
pijama (pijama) ice cream with fruit and syrup
postres de músic (postre de músico) dessert of dried fruit and nuts

FRUITA (FRUTA) FRUIT

albercoc (albaricoque) apricot
cirera (cereza) cherry
gerd (frambuesa) raspberry
llimona (limón) lemon
maduixa (fresa) strawberry
meló (melón) melon
taronja (naranja) orange
pera (pera) pear
pinya (piña) pineapple
plàtan (plátano) banana

poma (manzana) apple
préssec (melocotón) peach
raïm (uva) grape

BEGUDES (BEBIDAS) DRINKS

aigua amb gas (agua con gas) sparkling water
aigua sense gas (agua sin gas) still water
cafè (café) coffee
cervesa (cerveza) beer
gel (hielo) ice
llet (leche) milk
suc de taronja (zumo de naranja) orange juice
te (té) tea
vi blanc (vino blanco) white wine
vi negre (vino tinto) red wine

ENTREMESOS (ENTREMESES) SIDE DISHES

amanida (ensalada) salad
formatge (queso) cheese
mantega (mantequilla) butter
ou (huevo) egg
pa (pan) bread
patates fregides (patatas fritas) French fries
sopa (sopa) soup

CONDIMENTS (ADREZO DE MESA) CONDIMENTS

pebre (pimienta) pepper
sal (sal) salt
sucre (azúcar) sugar

RESTAURANTS BY CUISINE

Barcelona has restaurants specializing in dishes from different regions, so visitors to the city can sample the cooking of the entire country of Spain. There are also fine-dining establishments and a variety of international cuisines on offer. Fast food, in the form of tapas, is some of the best in Europe, but if you yearn for a burger, a taste of home or a sandwich, you'll find it here too.

AREAS AT A GLANCE
» Barceloneta, **Port Vell** and **Port Olímpic**: Known for their fish and seafood.
» Barri Gòtic: Strong on good value traditional Catalan restaurants and tapas, with some Spanish regional food.
» L'Eixample and **Zona Alta**: Expect high prices, with food and service to match.
» Gràcia: More traditional Catalan eateries, and some international and regional food.
» El Raval and **Poble Sec**: Plenty of Catalan choice.

» La Ribera: The hot spot for the newest trends, with designer restaurants frequently opening.

The restaurants are listed alphabetically in the Eating section of each region.
Here they are listed by cuisine.

CATALAN
Agut	Barri Gòtic
Antiga Casa Can Solé	Barceloneta
Ca l'Isidre	El Raval
Café de l'Acadèmia	Barri Gòtic
Café de l'Òpera	Las Ramblas
Can Culleretes	Barri Gòtic
Casa Calvet	L'Eixample
Casa Leopoldo	El Raval
Cervecería Catalana	L'Eixample
Julivert Meu	El Raval
Kaiku	Barceloneta
L'Olivé	L'Eixample
Origen 99,9%	La Ribera
Orxateria Sirvent	L'Eixample
Pitarra	Barri Gòtic
Els Quatre Gats	Barri Gòtic

ITALIAN
Bestial	Port Olímpic
Buenas Migas	Las Ramblas
Little Italy	La Ribera
Il Mercante di Venezia	Barri Gòtic
Murivecchi	La Ribera

JAPANESE
Hello Sushi	El Raval
Shunka	Barri Gòtic

MEDITERRANEAN
El Magatzem del Port	Port Vell
Merendero de la Mari	Port Vell
Pla	Barri Gòtic
Sukur	Las Ramblas
La Tomaquera	Poble Sec
Taxidermista	Barri Gòtic

NOUVELLE CUISINE
Alkimia	L'Eixample
Alta Mar	Barceloneta
Anfiteatro	Port Olímpic
Arola	Port Olímpic
Biblioteca	El Raval
Cinc Sentits	L'Eixample
Drolma	L'Eixample
Limbo	Barri Gòtic
Lluçanès	Barceloneta
Moo	L'Eixample
El Tragaluz	L'Eixample

ORIENTAL

Río Azul — Gràcia

REGIONAL SPANISH

Agua — Port Olímpic
Ikastola — Gràcia
Mesón David — El Raval
Rías de Galicia — Poble Sec

SEAFOOD

Carballeira — Barceloneta
Emperador — Port Vell
El Rey de la Gamba — Port Olímpic
Moncho's Chiringuito — Port Olímpic
Salamanca — Barceloneta
El Túnel del Port — Port Olímpic

SPANISH

7 Portes — Port Vell
Agullers — La Ribera
Bodega Manolo — Gràcia
Botafumeiro — Gràcia
Can Majó — Barceloneta
Can Ramonet — Barceloneta
El Cheriff — Barceloneta
La Cova Fumada — Barceloneta
Nou Can Tipa — Barceloneta
Quo Vadis — El Raval

SWISS

La Carassa — La Ribera

TAPAS BARS

Bar Jai Ca — Barceloneta
Bodega La Tinaja — Barri Gòtic
La Bombeta — Barceloneta
Brisa del Mar — Barri Gòtic
Cal Pep — La Ribera
Cata 1.81 — L'Eixample
Comerç 24 — La Ribera
De Tapa Madre — L'Eixample
Ginger — Barri Gòtic
Inopia — L'Eixample
Quim — Las Ramblas
Quimet, Quimet — Poble Sec
Taller de Tapas — Las Ramblas
Vinatería del Call — Barri Gòtic

VEGETARIAN

La Báscula — Vegetarian
Biocenter — El Raval
L'Illa de Gràcia — Gràcia
Organic — El Raval
Salambó — Gràcia

INTERNATIONAL

Ànima — El Raval

Arc Café — Barri Gòtic
Bar Ra — Las Ramblas
Cardamón — Barri Gòtic
CDLC — Port Olímpic
Enoteca — Port Olímpic
Flash Flash — Gràcia
El Foro — La Ribera
Fragile — El Raval
Living — Barri Gòtic
Mama Café — El Raval
Maur — L'Eixample
Mesopotamia — Gràcia
Noti — L'Eixample
Petra — Barri Gòtic
Pla dels Àngels — Barri Gòtic
Polenta — Barri Gòtic
Rita Blue — El Raval
El Salón — Barri Gòtic
Salero — Barceloneta
San Telmo — Poble Sec
Silenus — El Raval
Tàbata — Gràcia
Tapioles 53 — Poble Sec
Venus Delicatessen — Barri Gòtic
Zoo — Barri Gòtic

There are hotels all over Barcelona and, thanks to the excellent public transport system, most are no more than 20 minutes or so from the heart of town. This is a real bonus, given the huge demand for hotel rooms in recent years, due to the city's growth in popularity. Whether you aim for the ultimate luxury of the top-end hotels or just want somewhere clean and simple to sleep, you'll find it.

There are times when hotel rooms are hard to come by, particularly in the summer and during the major trade fairs, which run at intervals all year. All accommodation in Catalonia is officially regulated by the Generalitat, the regional government, and is broken down into two categories.

HOTELS

These are denoted by (H) and rated on a scale of one to five stars. All rooms must have a private bathroom to qualify as a hotel and the number of stars is determined by the amenities provided. You can expect five-star hotels to be truly luxurious, with superb facilities and a high level of service. Four-star hotels will be almost as good and the accommodation first-class, while a three-star hotel will cost appreciably less. Rooms in these hotels will all have TV and air conditioning, but the public areas will be less imposing. Hotels with one- or two-star ratings are relatively inexpensive, will be clean and comfortable, and rooms will often have private bathrooms

in two-star places. Simpler hotels rarely have restaurants or provide breakfast.

Many hotels in Barcelona are built around an inner courtyard. Rooms overlooking this will be quiet but may be gloomy. Ask for an outside room if you want light or a view and don't mind street noise.

The attitude towards smoking in Barcelona has changed dramatically in recent years, and now many hotels are completely smoke free. Others offer non-smoking rooms.

HOSTALS

Hostals (HS) sometimes classify themselves as *fondes*, *pensions* or *residències*, are rated on a scale of one to three stars and are normally less expensive than hotels. Many will have a number of rooms with bathrooms. *Hostals* tend to be family-run, very few of them have restaurants and many do not serve breakfast. A three-star *hostal* is generally on a par with a two-star hotel, but star ratings should not be taken as an automatic guide to facilities or cost.

SELF-CATERING ACCOMMODATION

Barcelona has hundreds of self-catering holiday apartments available for short-term rent. Prices can start as low as €60 per day. Unless you are in Barcelona already, the best place to book them is online. Reputable agencies include www.oh-barcelona.com and www.friendlyrentals.com. Be wary as this industry is still largely unregulated. Ask to see digital images of the property, check out the location from an independent source such as www.tmb.net or the online map www.bcn.cat/guia and ask about extra costs such as cleaning.

FINDING A ROOM

If you haven't booked in advance, the tourist offices in the Plaça de Catalunya and the Plaça de Sant Jaume have hotel booking desks where you will usually be able to find something. They charge a deposit against the cost of the room. Once at the hotel, it's perfectly acceptable to ask to see the room before you make up your mind.

PRICING

Room rates vary according to the season, sometimes by as much as 20 per cent. Other times when prices will soar are during national holidays or festival periods. The quietest time for hotels is January, February and August (when most Spanish businesses close for the annual holiday). Hotels will often quote their most expensive prices—ask if they have anything less expensive. All room costs are liable to 7 per cent tax on top of the basic price. This is annotated separately on bills, but may not have been included in the original quote. If you want the total price for your stay, ask when you make the reservation. The best deals are almost always available online.

TIPS ON STAYING IN BARCELONA

» Check-out is normally noon, although at some *hostals* it may be 11am so check.

» Hotels will often store your luggage until the end of the day if you have an afternoon or evening flight.

» Hotels are often willing to put an extra bed in a room for a small charge, which is ideal for families with children.

» If you want to use the hotel parking area, if available, expect to pay extra and book a space when you reserve the room.

» Few Barcelona hotels have weekend or short-term discount rates, but it's still worth asking when you book.

» If you have problems with charging, ask to see the *llibre de reclamacions*, the complaints book, which all establishments are legally required to keep and have inspected by tourist and hotel officials. Such a request generally produces an instant result.

ONLINE BOOKING

www.madeinspain.net
www.priceline.com
www.all-hotels.com
www.hotelconnect.co.uk
www.barcelonahotels.es
www.hotelsbarcelona.org
www.interhotel.com/spain/es

HOTELS BY AREA

Details of hotels are given in each region. Here they are listed by area:

Barceloneta
Hotel Pullman Skipper
Marina Folch

Barri Gòtic
1898
Catalonia Albioni
Colón
Continental
Cortés
De l'Arc
Duquesa de Cardona
Hostal Ítaca
Hostal Nilo
Hotel Neri
Husa Oriente
Le Méridien Barcelona
Pensión Segre
Regencia Colón
Silken Ramblas

L'Eixample
AC Diplomàtic
Actual
Alexandra
Amrey Diagonal
Casa Fuster
Condado
Condestable
Continental Palacete
Gallery
Gran Hotel Havana

Granados 83
Granvia
Hilton Barcelona
Hostal Central
Hostal Goya
Hostal Oliva
Hotel Jazz
Hotel Omm
Majestic

Gràcia
Abalon

El Raval
Barceló Raval
Casa Camper
Catalonia Ducs de Bergara
Center Ramblas
Gat Raval
Gaudí
Hosteria Grau
Hotel Ciutat Vella
Lleó
Market Hotel
Peninsular

La Ribera
Banys Orientals
Chic & Basic
Grand Hotel Central
Park Hotel

Sants
Catalonia Roma
Torre Catalunya

Barcelona's first hotels were built in Las Ramblas, El Raval and Barri Gòtic, and it's still the area with the widest choice of less expensive accommodation. Prices may be steep for what you get, but it's a good location, though it can be noisy, and street crime may be a problem. Barcelona's other main hotel area is L'Eixample, with a wide range of places to stay, and a good choice of mid-range hotels and *hostals*.

Catalan pronunciation differs considerably from Castilian (Spanish). It is more closed and less staccato than Castilian, but is likewise nearly always phonetic, with a few rules. When a word ends in a vowel, an n or an s, the stress is usually on the penultimate syllable; otherwise, it falls on the last syllable. If a word has an accent, this is where the stress falls. Both languages are summarized below.

CATALAN

au	**ow** as in wow
c	**ss** or **k** (never **th**)
ç	**ss**
eu	**ay-oo**
g	**g** or **j** (never **h**)
gu	(sometimes) **w**
h	silent
j	**j** (never **h**)
ig	**ch** at the end of a word: **vaig** sounds like batch
ll	**lli** as in million
l.l	**ll** as in silly
ny	as in canyon
r/rr	heavily rolled
s	**z** or **ss**
tg/tj	**dge** as in lodge
tx	**ch** as in cheque
v	**b** (**vi**, wine, sounds like 'bee')
x	**sh** as in shake

SPANISH

a	as in pat
ai, ay	as **i** in side
e	as in set
au	as **ou** in out
i	as **e** in be
ei, ey	as **ey** in they
o	as in hot
oi, oy	as **oy** in boy
u	as in flute

CONSONANTS AS IN ENGLISH EXCEPT:

c	before i and e as **th**
ch	as **ch** in church
d	at the end of a word becomes **th**
g	before i or e becomes **ch** as in loch
h	is silent
j	as **ch** in loch
ll	as **lli** in million
ñ	as **ny** in canyon

qu	is hard like a **k**
r	usually rolled
v	is a **b**
z	is a **th**, but **s** in parts of Andalucía

The translations are given first in Catalan, then in Spanish.

USEFUL WORDS

yes/no
sí/no .... *sí/no*

please
si us plau .... *por favor*

thank you
gràcies .... *gracias*

there
allà .... *allí*

where
on... *dónde*

here
aquí ....*aquí*

when
quan ....*cuándo*

why
per què .... *por qué*

how
com... *cómo*

who
qui..*quién*

I'm sorry
Em sap greu .... *Lo siento*

excuse me
perdoni................................ *perdone*

large
gran.. *grande*

small
petit .... *pequeño*

good
bo.. *bueno*

bad
dolent...*malo*

open
obert .... *abierto*

closed
tancat.................................... *cerrado*

MONEY

Is there a bank/bureau de change nearby?
Hi ha un banc/una oficina de canvi a prop?
¿Hay un banco/una oficina de cambio cerca?

Can I cash this here?
Puc cobrar això aquí?
¿Puedo cobrar esto aquí?

I'd like to change sterling/dollars into euros
Vull canviar lliures/dòlars a euros
Quiero cambiar libras/dólares a euros

Can I use my credit card to withdraw cash?
Puc fer servir la targeta de crèdit per a treure diners?
¿Puedo usar la tarjeta de crédito para sacar dinero?

What is the exchange rate?
Com està el canvi?
¿Cómo está el cambio?

COLOURS

black
negre .... *negro*

blue
blau .... *azul*

brown
marró .... *marrón*

green
verd.. *verde*

grey
gris... *gris*

red
vermell...................................... *rojo*

white
blanc .... *blanco*

yellow
groc.. *amarillo*

SHOPPING

When does the shop open/close?
A quina hora obre/tanca la botiga?
¿A qué hora abre/cierra la tienda?

Could you help me, please?
Que em pot atendre, si us plau?
¿Me atiende, por favor?

How much is this?
Quant costa això?
¿Cuánto cuesta esto?

I'm looking for...
Busco...
Busco...

I'm just looking
Només miro
Sólo estoy mirando

I'd like...
Voldria...
Quisiera...

I'll take this
M'enduc això
Me llevo esto

Do you have anything smaller/larger
Té alguna cosa més petita/gran?
¿Tiene algo más pequeño/grande?

Please can I have a receipt?
Em dóna un rebut, si us plau?
¿Me da un recibo, por favor?

Do you accept credit cards?
Accepten targetes de crèdit?
¿Aceptan tarjetas de crédito?

bakery
el forn .... *la panadería*

bookshop
la llibreria............................. *la librería*

butcher's shop
la carnisseria...................*la carnicería*

fishmonger's
la peixateria...................*la pescadería*

jewellers
la joieria............................... *la joyería*

pharmacy
la farmàcia .... *la farmacia*

market
el mercat.........................*el mercado*

shoeshop
la sabateria.......................*la zapatería*

supermarket
el supermercat ...... *el supermercado*

HOTELS

Do you have a room?
Té una habitació?
¿Tiene una habitación?

I have a reservation for...nights
Tinc una reserva per a...nits
Tengo una reserva para... noches

How much per night?
Quant es per nit?
¿Cuánto por noche?

May I see the room?
Que puc veure l'habitació?
¿Puedo ver la habitación?

Single room
Habitació individual
Habitación individual

Twin room
Habitació doble amb dos llits
Habitación doble con dos camas

Double room
Habitació doble amb llit de matrmoni
Habitación doble con cama de matrimonio

With bath/shower/toilet
Amb banyera/dutxa/vàter
Con bañera/ducha/váter

Is the room air-conditioned/heated?
Té aire condicionat/calefacció l'habitacío?
¿Tiene aire acondicionado/calefacción la habitación?

The room is too hot/cold
Fa massa calor/fred a l'habitació
Hace demasiado calor/frío en la habitación

no smoking
prohibit fumar
se prohibe fumar

I'll take this room
Em quedo l'habitació
Me quedo con la habitación

Is there an elevator in the hotel?
Hi ha ascensor a l'hotel?
¿Hay ascensor en el hotel?

Is breakfast/lunch/dinner included in the price?
S'inclou l'esmorzar/el dinar/el sopar en el preu?
¿Está el desayuno/la comida/la cena incluido/-a en el precio?

When is breakfast served?
A quina hora se serveix l'esmorzar?
¿A qué hora se sirve el desayuno?

I am leaving this morning
Me'n vaig aquest matí
Me voy esta mañana

Can I pay my bill, please?
El compte, si us plau
La cuenta, por favor

Will you look after my luggage until I leave?
Em pot guardar l'equipatge fins que me'n vagi?
¿Me puede guardar el equipaje hasta que me vaya?

Could you please order a taxi for me?
Em demana un taxi, si us plau?
¿Me pide un taxi, por favor?

swimming pool
la piscina
la piscina

RESTAURANTS
See also the menu reader,
▷ 258–259.

What time does the restaurant open?
A quina hora obre el restaurant?
¿A qué hora abre el restaurante?

I'd like to reserve a table for... people at...
Voldria reservar una taula per a... persones per a les...
Quiero reservar una mesa para... personas a las...

We'd like to wait for a table
Ens volem esperar fins que hi hagi una taula
Queremos esperar a que haya una mesa

A table for..., please
Una taula per a..., si us plau
Una mesa para..., por favor

Could we sit here?
Que podem seure aquí?
¿Nos podemos sentar aquí?

Is this table free?
Està lliure aquesta taula?
¿Está libre esta mesa?

Could we see the menu/wine list?
Podem veure la carta/carta de vins?
¿Podemos ver la carta/carta de vinos?

What do you recommend?
Què ens recomana?
¿Qué nos recomienda?

Is there a dish of the day?
Té un plat del dia?
¿Tienen plato del día?

How much is this dish?
Què costa aquest plat?
¿Cuánto cuesta este plato?

I am a vegetarian
Sóc vegetarià
Soy vegetariano/a

The food is cold
El menjar és fred
La comida está fría

The food was excellent
El menjar ha estat excel.lent
La comida ha sido excelente

I ordered...
He demanat...
Yo pedí...

This is not what I ordered
Això no és el que jo he demanat
Esto no es lo que yo he pedido

Can I have the bill, please?
Em duu el compte, si us plau?
¿Me trae la cuenta, por favor?

Is service included?
Que hi ha inclòs el servei?
¿Está incluido el servicio?

The bill is not right
El compte no està bé
La cuenta no está bien

waiter/waitress
el cambrer/la cambrera
el camarero/la camarera

GETTING AROUND
Where is the information desk?
On hi ha el taulell d'informació?
¿Dónde está el mostrador de información?

Where is the train/bus station?
On hi ha l'estació de trens/autobusos?
¿Dónde está la estación de trenes/autobuses?

Where is the timetable?
On hi ha l'horari?
¿Dónde está el horario?

Does this train/bus go to...?
Va aquest tren/autobús a...?
¿Va este tren/autobús a...?

Does this train/bus stop at...?
S'atura aquest tren/autobús a...?
¿Para este tren/autobús en...?

Do I have to get off here?
He de baixar aquí?
¿Me tengo que bajar aquí?

Do you have a subway/bus map?
Té un mapa del metro/dels autobusos?
¿Tiene un mapa del metro/de los autobuses?

Can I have a single/return ticket to...
Em dóna un bitllet senzill/d'anada i tornada a...?
¿Me da un billete sencillo/de ida y vuelta para...?

How much is a ticket?
Quant costa un bitllet?
¿Cuánto vale un billete?

Is this the way to...?
Aquest és el camí per a anar a...?
¿Es éste el camino para ir a...?

Where can I find a taxi?
On puc trobar un taxi?
¿Dónde puedo encontrar un taxi?

Please take me to...
A..., si us plau
A..., por favor

I'd like to get out here, please
Parí aquí, si us plau
Pare aquí, por favor

Go straight on
Continuï tot recte
Siga recto

Turn left
Tombi a l'esquerra
Gire a la izquierda

Turn right
Tombi a la dreta
Gire a la derecha

Cross over
Passi a l'altre costat
Cruce al otro lado

ferry
el transbordador
el ferry

smoking/non-smoking
fumadors/no fumadors
fumadores/no fumadores

Train/bus station
L'estació de trens/autobusos
La estación de trenes/autobuses

CONVERSATION
What is the time?
Quina hora és?
¿Qué hora es?

I don't speak Catalan/Spanish
No parlo català/espanyol
No hablo catalán/español

Do you speak English?
Parla anglès?
¿Habla inglés?

I don't understand
No ho entenc
No lo entiendo

Please repeat that
Si us plau, repeteixi això
Por favor, repita eso

Please speak more slowly
Si us plau, parli més a poc a poc
Por favor, hable más despacio

What does this mean?
Què significa això?
¿Qué significa esto?

Excuse me, I think I'm lost
Perdoni, em sembla que m'he
perdut
Perdone, creo que me he perdido

Write that down for me, please
M'ho pot escriure, si us plau?
¿Me lo puede escribir?

My name is...
Em dic...
Me llamo...

What's your name?
Com es diu?
¿Cómo se llama?

Hello, pleased to meet you
Hola, molt de gust
Hola, encantado/a

I'm from...
Sóc de...
Soy de...

**This is my wife/daughter/
husband/son**
Aquesta és la meva dona/filla/Aquest
és el meu marit/fill
Esta es mi mujer/hija/marido/hijo

This is my friend
Aquest és el meu amic
Este es mi amigo

I live in...
Visc a...
Vivo en...

Good morning/afternoon
Bon dia/Bona tarda
Buenos días/Buenas tardes

Good evening/night
Bona nit
Buenas noches

Goodbye
Adéu-siau
Adiós

See you later
Fins després
Hasta luego

I don't know
No ho sé
No lo sé

You're welcome
De res
De nada

How are you?
Com estàs?
¿Cómo estás?

May I/Can I?
Puc?
¿Puedo?

That's all right
D'acord
Está bien

TIMES/DAYS/MONTHS/HOLIDAYS

morning		
el matí		*la mañana*
afternoon		
la tarda		*la tarde*
evening		
el vespre		*la tarde*
day		
el dia		*el día*
night		
la nit		*la noche*
today		
avui		*hoy*
yesterday		
ahir		*ayer*
tomorrow		
demà		*mañana*
now		
ara		*ahora*
later		
més tard		*más tarde*
spring		
primavera		*primavera*
summer		
estiu		*verano*
autumn		
tardor		*otoño*
winter		
hivern		*invierno*
Monday		
dilluns		*lunes*
Tuesday		
dimarts		*martes*
Wednesday		
dimecres		*miércoles*
Thursday		
dijous		*jueves*
Friday		
divendres		*viernes*
Saturday		
dissabte		*sábado*
Sunday		
diumenge		*domingo*
week		
la setmana		*la semana*
month		
el mes		*el mes*
year		
l'any		*el año*

January
gener .... enero
February
febrer .... febrero
March
març.. marzo
April
abril.. abril
May
maig... mayo
June
juny .... junio
July
juliol .... julio
August
agost.. agosto
September
setembre .... septiembre
October
octubre .... octubre
November
novembre .... noviembre
December
desembre .... diciembre
Easter
Pàsqua .... Semana Santa
Christmas
Nadal.................................... Navidad
pilgrimage
romeria .... romería
holiday (vacation)
vacances.......................... vacaciones

TOURIST INFORMATION
Where is the tourist information office, please?
On hi ha l'oficinal
d'informació, si us plau?
¿Dónde está la oficina de
información, por favor?

Do you have a city map?
Té un plànol de la ciutat?
¿Tiene un plano de la ciudad?

Can you give me some information about...?
Té cap informació sobre...?
¿Tiene alguna información sobre...?

I am interested in...
M'interessen...
Me interesan...

What time does it open/close?
A quina hora obre/tanca?
¿A qué hora abre/cierra?

Are there organized excursions?
Hi ha excursions organitzades?
¿Tiene alguna excursión organizada?

Are there boat trips?
Hi ha excursions amb vaixell?
¿Hay paseos en barco?

Are there guided tours?
Hi ha visites amb guia?
¿Hay visitas con guía?

Where do they go?
On van?
¿Dónde van?

Is there an English-speaking guide?
Hi ha cap guia que parli anglès?
¿Hay algún guía que hable inglés?

Is photography allowed?
S'hi poden fer fotos?
¿Se pueden hacer fotos?

What is the admission price?
Quant costa l'entrada?
¿Cuánto cuesta la entrada?

Where is the museum?
On hi ha el museu?
¿Dónde está el museo?

Can we make reservations here?
Podem fer-ne les reserves aquí?
¿Podemos hacer las reservas aquí?

Could you reserve tickets for me?
Em pot reservar les entrades?
¿Me puede reservar las entradas?

Could I book...tickets for the... performance?
Podria reservar...entrades per a la
funció de...?
¿Podría reservar...entradas para la
función de...?

Is there a discount for senior citizens/students?
Fan descompte per a la tercera edat/
els estudiants?
¿Hacen descuento para la tercera
edad/los estudiantes?

What time does the show start?
A quina hora comença la funció?
¿A qué hora empieza la función?

ILLNESS AND EMERGENCIES
I don't feel well
No em trobo bé
No me encuentro bien

Could you call a doctor?
Pot cridar un metge?
¿Puede llamar a un médico?

I feel nauseous
Estic marejat/Tinc ganes de vomitar
Tengo ganas de vomitar

I have a headache
Em fa mal el cap
Me duele la cabeza

I am allergic to...
Sóc al.lèrgic a...
Soy alérgico/a...

I am on medication
Estic amb medicació
Estoy con medicación

How many tablets a day should I take?
Quantes pastilles m'he de prendre
al dia?
¿Cuántas pastillas tengo que tomar
al día?

I need to see a doctor/dentist
Necessito un metge/dentista
Necesito un médico/dentista

I have a bad toothache
Tinc un mal de queixals horrible
Tengo un dolor de muelas horrible

Can you recommend a dentist?
Que em pot recomanar un dentista?
¿Me puede recomendar un
dentista?

Where is the hospital?
On hi ha l'hospital?
¿Dónde esta el hospital?

Call the fire brigade/police/ ambulance
Truqui als bombers/la policia/una
ambulància
Llame a los bomberos/la policía/una
ambulancia

I have had an accident
He tingut un accident
He tenido un accidente

I have been robbed
M'han robat
Me han robado

I have lost my passport/wallet/ purse/handbag
He perdut el passaport/la cartera/el moneder/la bossa
He perdido el pasaporte/la cartera/el monedero/el bolso

Is there a lost property office?
Que hi ha una oficina d'objectes perduts?
¿Hay una oficina de objetos perdidos?

Where is the police station?
On hi ha la comissaria?
¿Dónde está la comisaría?

Help!
Auxili
Socorro

Stop, thief!
Al lladre
Al ladrón

NUMBERS
1	u (un, una)/*uno*
2	dos/*dos*
3	tres/*tres*
4	quatre/*cuatro*
5	cinc/*cinco*
6	sis/*seis*
7	set/s*iete*
8	vuit/*ocho*
9	nou/*nueve*
10	deu/*diez*
11	onze/*once*
12	dotze/*doce*
13	tretze/*trece*
14	catorze/*catorce*
15	quinze/*quince*
16	setze/*dieciséis*
17	disset/*diecisiete*
18	divuit/*dieciocho*
19	dinou/*diecinueve*
20	vint/*veinte*
21	vint-i-u/*veintiuno*
30	trenta/*treinta*
40	quaranta/*cuarenta*

50	cinquanta/*cincuenta*
60	seixanta/*sesenta*
70	setanta/*setenta*
80	vuitanta/*ochenta*
90	noranta/*noventa*
100	cent/*cien*
200	dos-cents/*doscientos*
1,000	mil/*mil*
million	milió/*millón*

IN THE TOWN
bridge
el pont............................... *el puente*

castle
el castell.............................*el castillo*

cathedral
la catedral .... *la catedral*

church
l'església.............................*la iglesia*

gallery
la galeria d'art .... *la galería de arte*

toilets
els lavabos .... *los aseos*

monument
el monument ....*el monumento*

museum
el museu............................*el museo*

palace
el palau ....*el palacio*

old town
la ciutat vella............... *la ciudad vieja*

park
el parc ....*el parque*

river
el riu.....................................*el río*

town
la ciutat .... *la ciudad*

town hall
l'ajuntament.............*el ayuntamiento*

corner
la cantonada..................... *la esquina*

entrance
entrada................................ *entrada*

exit
sortida..................................... *salida*

intersection
l'encreuament .... *el cruce*

traffic lights
el semàfor..................... *el semáforo*

no parking
prohibit aparcar ......*prohibido aparcar*

pedestrian zone
zona per a vianants ..... *zona peatonal*

Can you direct me to...?
Com es va a...? ... *¿Cómo se va a...?*

POST AND TELEPHONES
Where is the nearest post office/ mail box?
On hi ha l'oficina de correus més pròxima/la bústia més pròxima?
¿Dónde está la oficina de correos más cercana/el buzón más cercano?

What is the postage to...?
Quant costa enviar-ho a...?
¿Cuánto vale mandarlo a...?

I'd like to send this by air mail
Vull enviar això correu per aeri
Quiero mandar esto por correo aéreo

Where can I buy a phone card?
On puc comprar una targeta telefònica?
¿Dónde puedo comprar una tarjeta de teléfono?

I'd like to speak to...
Voldria parlar amb...?
¿Me puede poner con...?

Who is this speaking, please?
Amb qui parlo, si us plau?
¿Con quién hablo, por favor?

Have there been any calls for me?
Que hi ha hagut cap telefonada per a mi?
¿Ha habido alguna llamada para mí?

Please ask him/her to call back
Li pot dir que em telefoni
Le puede decir que me llame

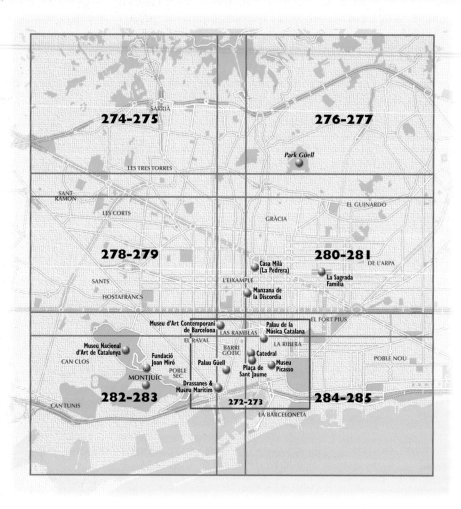

SARRIÀ

274-275

276-277

Park Güell

LES TRES TORRES

SANT RAMON

LES CORTS

EL GUINARDO

GRÀCIA

278-279

Casa Milà
(La Pedrera)

280-281

DE L'ARPA

SANTS

L'EIXAMPLE

La Sagrada
Família

HOSTAFRANCS

Manzana de
la Discordia

Museu d'Art Contemporani
de Barcelona

EL FORT PIUS

Palau de la
Música Catalana

LAS RAMBLAS

Museu Nacional
d'Art de Catalunya

EL RAVAL

LA RIBERA

POBLE NOU

BARRI
GÒTIC

Catedral

CAN CLOS

Fundació
Joan Miró

Palau Güell

Museu
Picasso

MONTJUÏC

POBLE
SEC

Plaça de
Sant Jaume

282-283

Drassanes &
Museu Marítim

284-285

CAN TUNIS

272-273

LA BARCELONETA

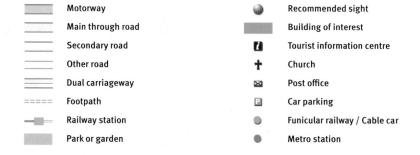

272-273

0	250 m
0	250 yds

274-285

0	500 m
0	500 yds

	Motorway			Recommended sight
	Main through road			Building of interest
	Secondary road		**i**	Tourist information centre
	Other road		**✝**	Church
	Dual carriageway		**✉**	Post office
=====	Footpath		**P**	Car parking
	Railway station			Funicular railway / Cable car
	Park or garden			Metro station

MAPS

Map references for the sights refer to the individual locator maps within the regional chapters. For example, La Sagrada Família has the reference ✚ 173 H7, indicating the page on which La Sagrada Família is found (173) and the grid square in which La Sagrada Família sits (H7).

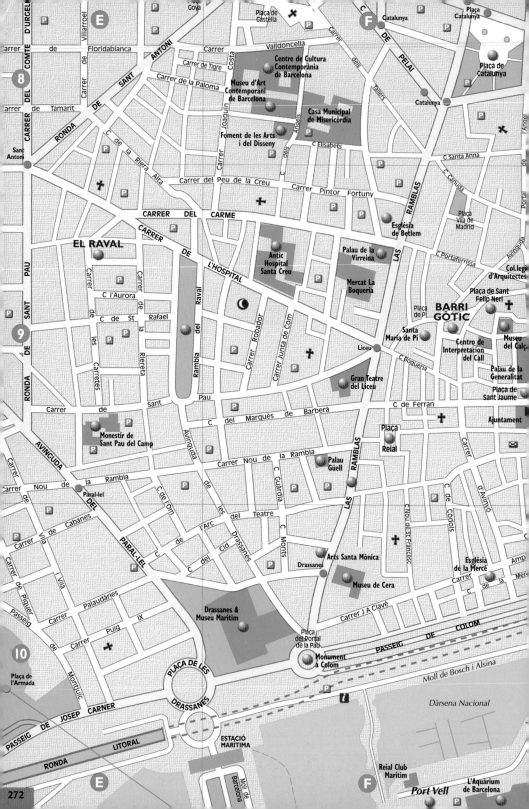

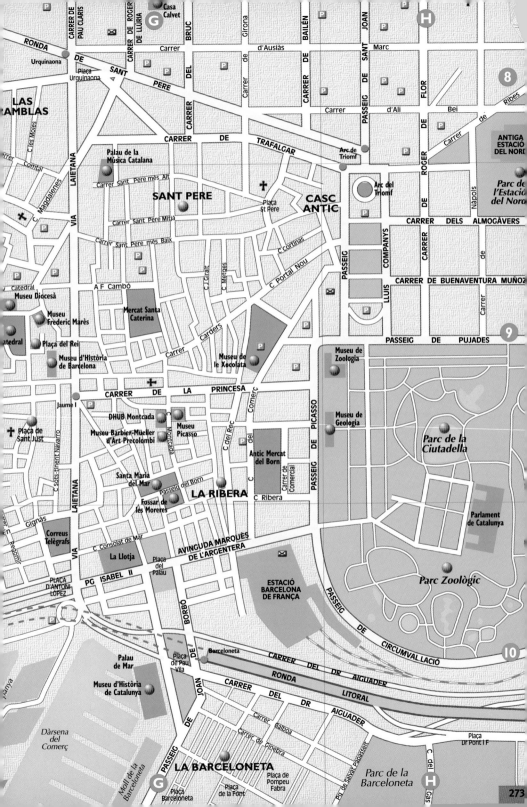

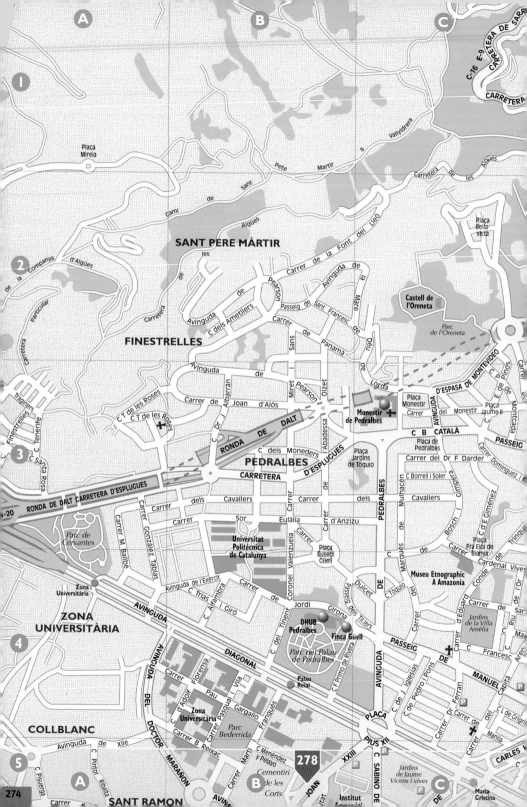

A

I

Plaça
Mireia

2

de la Companya

d'Algües

particular

Carretera

Carretera

Traginers

Finestrelles

Tenerife

C Santa Rosa

3

Pearson

Carrer de la Font del Lleó

Avinguda   de

SANT PERE MÀRTIR

les

de

sant

de

Cami

Algües

Pete   Martir

Pete

Vallvidrera

a

Carretera   de   les   Algües

Plaça
Bellavista

Castell de
l'Oreneta

Parc
de l'Oreneta

Plaça
Bellavista

FINESTRELLES

Avinguda

C dels Ametllers

Passeig de Sant Francesc

Avinguda   de

Mare

Carrer

de

Panama

Deu

de

Lorda

D'ESPASA DE MONTEVIDEO

C de Prïnós

E de de

Montcada

Carrer   de

Joan   d'Alòs

Dr J Alparrán

C T de les Roses

C T de les Roses

Miret

Sans

Olzet

Pearson

RONDA   DE   DALT

l'Abadessa

Monestir
de Pedralbes

Plaça
Monestir

Carrer

del   Monestir

Plaça
Jaume II

AVINGUDA

PASSEIG

Moncada

C B CATALÀ

Carrer del Dr F Darder

Carrer Dominguez I

PEDRALBES

C dels Moneders

D'ESPLUGUES

Plaça
Jardins
de Toquio

Plaça
Pedralbes

CARRETERA

RONDA DE DALT CARRETERA D'ESPLUGUES

=-20

Parc de
Cervantes

Zona
Universitària

Carrer   González Tablas

Carrer M. Ballbé

Carrer

Carrer

dels

Cavallers

Sor

Eulalia

Carrer

Valenzuela

Coronel

Carrer

Universitat
Politècnica
de Catalunya

Carrer   dels

d'Anzizu

Plaça
Eusebi
Güell

Avinguda de l'Exèrcit

C Trias

Alfambra

i Giró

Carrer

C del Tinent

Jordi
Girona

Passeig   dels   Tillers

Dulcet

Cavallers

PEDRALBES

C Mulhacén

de

Marquès

C Borreli i Soler

Cavallers

Bosch   i   Gimpera

C d'E Giménez

Plaça
Fra Eloi de
Bianya

Carrer

C Toquio

Conde

Cardenal Vives

Museu Etnographic
A Amazonia

Tringu

DE

C de'l   or

Riu

de

Sar

ZONA
UNIVERSITÀRIA

AVINGUDA   DEL

DIAGONAL

DHUB
Pedralbes

Finca Güell

Parc del Palau
de Pedralbes

Palau
Reial

PASSEIG

DE

MANUEL

Capita

Jardins
de la Villa
Amèlia

Carrer

d'Eduard

Francesc

4

Carrer

Florensa

Carrer

Vila

Franquesa

Gargallo

Pau

d'Adolf

DOCTOR   MARAÑON

Carrer   B Reixac

Zona
Universitària

Parc
Bederrida

Carrer   Martí

C Menéndez
y Pelayo

Pasqual

278

PLAÇA

PIUS XII

C de J. Iglesias

C de Pedro Pons

JOAN

XXIII

C   SABINO DE

Carrer   Dr. Ferran

P

Carrer   de

Jardins
de Jaume
Vicens i vives

Carrer   de

Manila

CARLES

P

Maria
Cristina

COLLBLANC

Avinguda   de   Xile

C Pisuerga

C Pintor   Ribalta

Carrer

5

A

SANT RAMON

AVIN

B

Cementiri
de les
Corts

Institut

C

DE

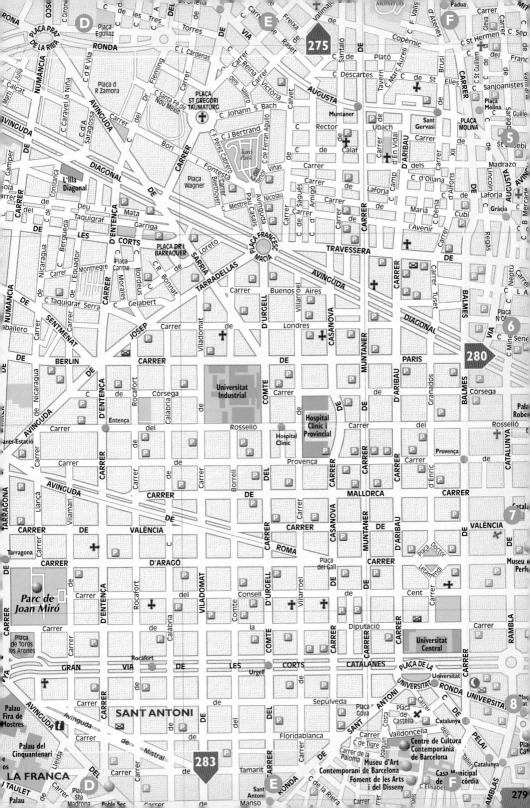

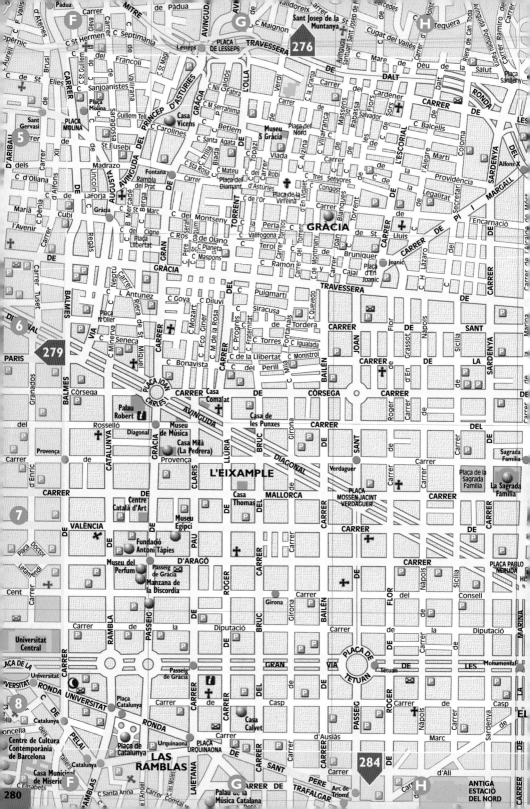

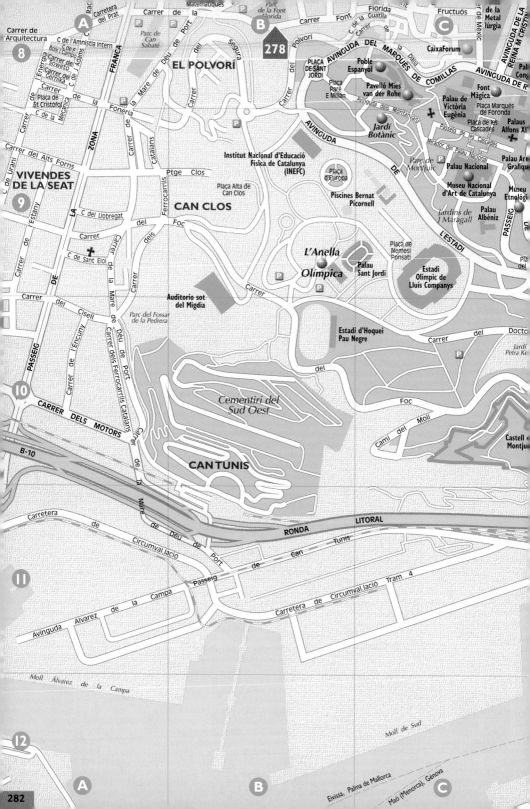

Carretera del Prat

Carrer de la Mare de Déu del Port

Carrer de l'Arquitectura

Parc de Can Sabaté

EL POLVORÍ

Carrer de l'Amnistia intern

C de l'Amnistia intern

C de la
Energía
Boix i Campo
Carrer de Soweto
Carrer de Cernika

Plaça de
St Cristòfol

C de la Medicina

ZONA FRANCA

Carrer de la Foneria

Carrer del Alts Forns

VIVENDES DE LA SEAT

C de Urani

Carrer de l'Estany

C del Llobregat

Carrer de Sant Eloi

Carrer de la Mare de Déu de Port

Ferrocarrils Catalans

Ptge Clos

Plaça Alta de Can Clos

CAN CLOS

Carrer del Foc

Carrer dels Ferrocarrils Catalans

PASSEIG DE LA

Carrer de l'Encuny

Carrer del Cisell

10

CARRER DELS MOTORS

B-10

Carretera de Circumval·lació

CAN TUNIS

Parc del Fossar de la Pedrera

Cementiri del Sud Oest

Carrer

Auditorio sot del Migdia

Carrer de la Mare de Déu de Port

11

Carretera de Circumval·lació

Passeig de Can Tunis

RONDA LITORAL

Avinguda Álvarez de la Campa

Carretera de Circumval·lació Tram 4

Moll Álvarez de la Campa

12

Moll de Sud

Carrer de la Font Florida

Parc de la Font Florida

Carrer Font

Florida

C de la Guatla

Carrer de la Dàlia

Fructuós

de Mèxic

de la Metal·lúrgia

AVINGUDA DE LA REINA MA CRISTINA

278

PLAÇA DE SANT JORDI

Plaça Paré E Millàn

Poble Espanyol

Pavelló Mies van der Rohe

AVINGUDA DEL MARQUES DE COMILLAS

CaixaForum

AVINGUDA DE R

Font Màgica

Pal Comp

Avinguda dels Montanyans

Jardí Botànic

Plaça d'Europa

Piscines Bernat Picornell

AVINGUDA DE

Parc de Montjuïc

Palau de Victòria Eugènia

Plaça Marqués de Foronda

Plaça de les Cascades

Passeig de les Cascades

Mirador del Palau Nacional

Palaus Alfons XI

Palau Nacional

Museu Nacional d'Art de Catalunya

Palau Art Grafiqu

Museu Etnològic

Jardins de l Maragall

Palau Albéniz

L'ESTADI

L'Anella Olímpica

Plaça de Nemesi Ponsati

Palau Sant Jordi

Estadi Olímpic de Lluís Companys

Estadi d'Hoquei Pau Negre

Carrer del

Docto

Jardí Petra Ke

Camí del Moli

Carrer del Foc

Castell Montjuï

Pla del

Maó (Menorca), Gènova

Eivissa, Palma de Mallorca

8

9

Institut Nacional d'Educació Física de Catalunya (INEFC)

D **E** **F**

AVINGUDA

Carrer Carrer de Sepúlveda Plaça SANT ANTONI Plaça de Cata
ira de Avingud Goya Costa Carrer UNIVERSITAT
ostres **D** SANT ANTONI de **E** Plaça **F** PELAI Plaç
Carrer P Mistral Carrer de Castella Catalunya **8** la
Palau del de 279 Floridablanca Validonceila Centre de Cultura Cat
Cinquentenari Carrer C de Tigre Contemporània Catalunya
de P Carrer de la Joaquin de Barcelona
Tamarit Paloma Museu d'Art Talbers C Santa An
LA FRANCA Carrer P Sant Contemporani de Barcelona Casa Municipal C Canuda
TAULET Plaça Antoni Foment de les Arts de Misericòrdia Plaça
Palau Municipal Sta Madrona Poble Sec Manso i del Disseny C Elisabets Vila del
d'Esports Ricart Carrer Carrer del Peu de la Creu Cels Àngels Madrid
Teatre Mercat de l'Oliura Parlament EL RAVAL C de la Riera Pintor Fortuny Església
de les Flors Carrer de Alta Palau de la de Betlem
Inst del C. del Marquès CARRER CARRER DEL Virreina
Teatre de Campo Sagrado C l'Aurora DE CARME Mercat La Museu de
Santa C del St L'HOSPITAL Boqueria Calça
RONA Madrona Carrer Rafael Plaça
Museu d'Arqueologia Margarit Aldana Antic Hospital Maria de Pí de Pí BAR
de Catalunya Tapioles Santa Creu Rambla Liceu GÒTIC **9**
Teatre Grec Cabanyes DE Palau Güell Gran Teatre Plaça
Fundació POBLE salva Carrer del Liceu Sant Jau
Joan Miró SEC Roser Monestir de C de Ferran
Plaça del Sant Pau del Camp Palau Plaça Ajuntan
Neptu Carrer Nou de la Rambla Güell Reial
MONTJUÏC AVINGUDA C de Lafont C de l'Om Teatre RAMBLAS Arts Església
Avinguda de de Cabanes C del Cid Santa Mònica de la Merc
Miramar Passeig Villa Drassanes Museu Monument
MONTJUÏC Montjuïc de Cera a Colom
Jardins MIRAMAR de Miramar Montjuïc C l'Vila Drassanes & PLAÇA **10**
Mossèn Cinto Plaça Museu Marítim DEL PORTAL Dàrsena Nacior
Verdaguer Carles Ibañez PLAÇA DE LES DE LA PAU
Plaça Mirador DRASSANES
ran Capita Plaça de la ESTACIÓ **284**
Sardana Plaça de MARÍTIMA
Avinguda del Castell l'Armada PASSEIG DE JOSEP CARNER Reial Club Port Vell
Telefèric Jardins del Marítim
Castell de Carretera Josep Costa LITORAL Barcelona Torre de
Montjuïc i Llobera Jaume I **11**
RONDA Moll de Torre de
Moll de Sant Bertran World Trade St Sebastià
Dàrsena de Centre
Sant Bertran Moll de
Moll de la Costa Catalunya
Dàrsena del Moll de Moll
Morrot Ponent Occidental Moll Nou
Moll del Pont Mòbil Moll Oriental
Contradic Moll de Llevant
Moll Adossat **12**
Passeig de l'Escullera
D **E** **F**

ACKNOWLEDGEMENTS

The Automobile Association would like to thank the following photographers, companies and picture libraries for their assistance in the preparation of this book.

Abbreviations for the picture credits are as follows: (t) top; (b) bottom; (l) left; (r) right; (AA) AA World Travel Library.

2 AA/M Bonnet;
3t AA/M Bonnet;
3c AA/M Bonnet;
3b AA/M Bonnet;
4 AA/S Day;
5 AA/M Bonnet;
6 AA/M Bonnet;
7 AA/M Bonnet;
8 AA/M Bonnet;
9l AA/M Bonnet;
9r AA/M Bonnet;
10 AA/M Bonnet;
11 AA/M Bonnet;
12 AA/M Bonnet;
13l AA/M Bonnet;
13r AA/M Bonnet;
14 AA/M Bonnet;
15l AA/M Jourdan;
15r AA/M Bonnet;
16 Graham Salter/Photolibrary.com;
17l Imagebroker/Alamy;
17r CuboImages srl/Alamy;
18 Andrew Watson/Photolibrary.com;
19l AA/M Bonnet;
19r AA/M Bonnet;
20 AA/M Bonnet;
21t AA/M Bonnet;
21b AA/M Bonnet;
22 AA/M Bonnet;
23l AA/M Bonnet;
23r AA/M Bonnet;
24 AA/M Bonnet;
25 AA/M Bonnet;
26 Bob Masters/Alamy;
27t Mary Evans Picture Library;
27b Arxiu de la Paeria, Lleida, Catalunya, Spain/Index/The Bridgeman Art Library;
28 AA/M Jourdan;
29l Biblioteca Universidad, Barcelona, Spain/Index/The Bridgeman Art Library;
29r AA/N Setchfield;
30 Palacio del Senado, Madrid, Spain/Index/The Bridgeman Art Library;
31l AA/M Bonnet;
31r AA/M Bonnet;
32 AA/M Bonnet;
33l AA/M Bonnet;

33r AA/M Bonnet;
34 AA/M Bonnet;
35l AA/M Bonnet;
35r Illustrated London News;
36 Miguel Angel Yuste/Photolibrary. com;
37l AA/M Bonnet;
37r AA/M Bonnet;
38 AA/M Bonnet;
39 AA/M Bonnet;
40 Barbara Boensch/Photolibrary. com;
42 AA/M Bonnet;
46 AA/M Bonnet;
48 AA/S Day;
49 AA/M Bonnet;
51 Jon Mikel Duralde/Alamy;
52 AA/M Bonnet;
53 AA/M Bonnet;
54 AA/M Bonnet;
58 Antoni Traver/Photolibrary.com;
60 AA/M Bonnet;
61 AA/C Ashton;
62 AA/M Bonnet © Succession Miró/ ADAGP, Paris and DACS, London 2010;
63 AA/M Bonnet © Succession Miró/ ADAGP, Paris and DACS, London 2010;
64 AA/S Day;
65 AA/M Jourdan;
66 Xavier Subias/Photolibrary.com;
67 Ingolf Pompe 52/Alamy;
68 AA/M Bonnet;
69l AA/M Bonnet;
69r AA/M Bonnet;
70 AA/M Bonnet;
71l AA/M Bonnet;
71r AA/M Bonnet;
72 AA/M Bonnet;
73 AA/M Bonnet;
74l AA/M Bonnet;
74r AA/M Bonnet;
75t AA/M Bonnet;
75b AA/M Jourdan;
76 AA/M Bonnet;
78 AA/S Day;
79 AA/M Bonnet;
80 Xavier Subias/Photolibrary.com;
82 AA/M Bonnet;

85 AA/S McBride;
87 AA/M Bonnet;
88 AA/M Bonnet;
92 AA/M Bonnet;
96 AA/M Bonnet;
97 AA/M Bonnet;
98 AA/M Jourdan;
100 AA/M Bonnet;
101 AA/M Jourdan;
102l AA/M Chaplow;
102r AA/M Chaplow;
103 AA/M Bonnet;
104 Josep Curto/Photolibrary.com;
105 AA/M Bonnet;
106 AA/P Wilson;
107 AA/M Bonnet;
108 Bora/Alamy;
109 Images & Stories/Alamy;
110 Gregory Wrona/Alamy;
111l AA/M Bonnet;
111r AA/M Bonnet;
112 Tono Labra/Photolibrary.com;
113 AA/M Bonnet;
114 AA/M Bonnet;
115l AA/M Bonnet;
115r AA/M Bonnet;
116 AA/M Bonnet;
118 AA/M Bonnet;
120 AA/M Bonnet;
123 AA/M Bonnet;
125 AA/M Bonnet;
128 AA/M Bonnet;
132 AA/M Bonnet;
136 AA/M Bonnet;
137 AA/M Bonnet;
138 AA/M Bonnet;
139 AA/M Bonnet;
140 AA/M Bonnet;
141 Elan Fleisher/Photolibrary.com;
142 AA/M Bonnet painting belongs to the Museu Picasso de Barcelona © Succession Picasso/DACS, London 2010;
143 AA/M Bonnet;
144 AA/M Bonnet;
146 AA/M Bonnet;
147l AA/M Bonnet;
147r AA/M Bonnet;
148 AA/M Bonnet;
149 AA/M Bonnet;

150 AA/M Bonnet;
151 AA/M Bonnet;
152 AA/M Bonnet;
153 IMGBarcelona/Alamy;
154 AA/M Jourdan;
155 AA/M Chaplow;
156 AA/M Bonnet;
157 AA/M Chaplow;
158 Lonely Planet Images/Alamy;
161 AA/M Bonnet;
162 AA/M Bonnet;
167 AA/K Blackwell;
170 AA/M Bonnet;
174 AA/M Bonnet;
175 Travelpix/Alamy;
176 AA/M Bonnet Courtesy of the Caixa Catalunya;
177 AA/M Bonnet Courtesy of the Caixa Catalunya;
178 AA/S Day;
179 Look Die Bildagentur der Fotografen GmbH/Alamy;
180 AA/M Bonnet;
181 AA/M Bonnet;
182l AA/M Bonnet;
182r AA/C Ashton;
183 AA/M Bonnet;
184 AA/M Bonnet;
185 AA/M Bonnet;
186 AA/M Bonnet;
188l AA/M Bonnet;
189r AA/M Bonnet;
190 AA/M Bonnet;
191 AA/M Bonnet;
192 AA/M Bonnet;
193l AA/M Bonnet;
193r AA/S McBride;
194 AA/S McBride;
197l AA/S McBride;
197r AA/S McBride;
199 ;
200 AA/M Bonnet;
202 Photodisc;
203 AA/M Bonnet;
205 AA/M Bonnet;
208 J LL Banús/Photolibrary.com;
212 Xavier Florensa/Photolibrary. com;
213 AA/M Chaplow;
214 AA/M Bonnet;
215 AA/M Bonnet;
216 AA/M Bonnet;
217l AA/M Bonnet;
217r AA/M Bonnet;

219 AA/S Day;
220 Maurizio Borgese/Photolibrary. com;
221 Luis Castaneda/Photolibrary. com;
222 AA/M Bonnet;
223 AA/M Bonnet;
224 AA/M Bonnet;
225l AA/S Watkins;
225r AA/M Bonnet;
226 AA/M Bonnet;
227 AA/M Bonnet;
228 AA/M Bonnet;
229l AA/M Bonnet;
229r AA/M Bonnet;
230 AA/P Enticknap;
231 Howard Sayer/Alamy;
233 AA/M Bonnet;
236 AA/C Sawyer;
237 AA/M Bonnet;
238 AA/M Bonnet;
242 AA/M Bonnet;
243 AA/M Bonnet;
246 AA/M Bonnet;
247 Bertrand Collet/Alamy;
248 AA/M Bonnet;
249l AA/M Bonnet;
249r AA/M Bonnet;
251 AA/M Bonnet;
252 AA/M Bonnet;
253 AA/M Bonnet;
254 AA/M Jourdan;
256 AA/M Bonnet;
258 AA/S McBride;
259 AA/M Bonnet;
260 AA/M Bonnet;
261 AA/M Bonnet;
262 AA/M Chaplow;
271 Juergen Henkelmann Photography/Alamy

Every effort has been made to trace the copyright holders, and we apologise in advance for any accidental errors. We would be happy to apply any corrections in the following edition of this publication.

CREDITS

Managing editor
Sheila Hawkins

Project editor
Lodestone Publishing Ltd

Design
Low Sky Design Ltd

Picture research
Lesley Grayson

Image retouching and repro
Jackie Street

Mapping
Maps produced by the Mapping Services Department of
AA Publishing

Main contributors
Sarah Andrews, David Campi, Paula Canal,
Mary-Ann Gallagher, Tony Kelly, Sally Roy,
Damien Simonis, Suzanne Wales,
The Content Works

Updater
Mary-Ann Gallagher

Indexer
Marie Lorimer

Production
Lorraine Taylor

Published by AA Publishing, a trading name of AA Media Limited, whose registered office is
Fanum House, Basing View, Basingstoke, RG21 4EA. Registered number 06112600.
A CIP catalogue record for this book is available from the British Library.

ISBN 978-0-7495-6755-2

KeyGuide is a registered trademark in Australia and is used under license.
Colour separation by AA Digital Department
Printed and bound by Leo Paper Products, China

We believe the contents of this book are correct at the time of printing. However, some details, particularly prices, opening times and
telephone numbers do change. We do not accept responsibility for any consequences arising from the use of this book.
This does not affect your statutory rights. We would be grateful if readers would advise us of any inaccuracies they may encounter, or any
suggestions they might like to make to improve the book. There is a form provided at the back of the book for this purpose, or you can email us
at travelguides@theaa.com

A04201
Maps in this title produced from mapping © MAIRDUMONT/Falk Verlag 2011
Weather Chart statistics supplied by Weatherbase © Copyright 2003 Canty and Associates, LLC
Transport map © Communicarta Ltd, UK

Find out more about AA Publishing and the wide range of travel publications and services the AA provides by visiting our website at
theAA.com/shop

READER RESPONSE

Thank you for buying this KeyGuide. Your comments and opinions are very important to us, so please help us to improve our travel guides by taking a few minutes to complete this questionnaire.

You do not need a stamp (unless posted outside the UK). If you do not want to cut this page from your guide, then photocopy it or write your answers on a plain sheet of paper.

Send to: **KeyGuide Editor, AA World Travel Guides**
FREEPOST SCE 4598, Basingstoke RG21 4GY

Find out more about AA Publishing and the wide range of travel publications the AA provides by visiting our website at theAA.com/shop

ABOUT THIS GUIDE

Which KeyGuide did you buy? ....

Where did you buy it? ....

When? ....month .... year

Why did you choose this AA KeyGuide?
☐ Price ☐ AA Publication
☐ Used this series before; BARCELONA
☐ Cover ☐ Other (please state)

Please let us know how helpful the following features of the guide were to you by circling the appropriate category: very helpful (VH), helpful (H) or little help (LH)

	VH	H	LH
Size	VH	H	LH
Layout	VH	H	LH
Photos	VH	H	LH
Excursions	VH	H	LH
Entertainment	VH	H	LH
Hotels	VH	H	LH
Maps	VH	H	LH
Practical info	VH	H	LH
Restaurants	VH	H	LH
Shopping	VH	H	LH
Walks	VH	H	LH
Sights	VH	H	LH
Transport info	VH	H	LH

What was your favourite sight, attraction or feature listed in the guide?

Page................. Please give your reason ....
....

Which features in the guide could be changed or improved? Or are there any other comments you would like to make?

....

ABOUT YOU

Name (Mr/Mrs/Ms)..

Address ....

....

....

Postcode.. Daytime tel nos..

Email...
Please only give us your mobile phone number/email if you wish to hear from us about other products and services from the AA and partners by text or mms.

Which age group are you in?
Under 25 ☐   25–34 ☐   35–44 ☐   45–54 ☐   55+ ☐

How many trips do you make a year?
Less than1 ☐   1 ☐   2 ☐   3 or more ☐

ABOUT YOUR TRIP

Are you an AA member?   Yes ☐ No ☐

When did you book?............. month................. year

When did you travel?.............month................. year

Reason for your trip?   Business ☐   Leisure ☐

How many nights did you stay? ....

How did you travel?   Individual ☐   Couple ☐   Family ☐   Group ☐

Did you buy any other travel guides for your trip? ....

If yes, which ones?...

Thank you for taking the time to complete this questionnaire. Please send it to us as soon as possible, and remember, you do not need a stamp (unless posted outside the UK).
AA Travel Insurance call 0800 072 4168 or visit www.theaa.com

Titles in the KeyGuide series:
Australia, Barcelona, Britain, Brittany, Canada, China, Costa Rica, Croatia, Florence and Tuscany, France, Germany, Ireland, Italy, London, Mallorca, Mexico, New York, New Zealand, Normandy, Paris, Portugal, Prague, Provence and the Côte d'Azur, Rome, Scotland, South Africa, Spain, Thailand, Venice, Vietnam, Western European Cities.
Published in July 2009: Berlin

AA Travel Insurance call 0800 072 4168 or visit www.theaa.com